# VICTORY
# COOKBOOK

The material in this book has previously been published under the titles:
**We'll Eat Again** (Hamlyn, Octopus Publishing Group 1985)
**The Victory Cookbook** (Hamlyn, Octopus Publishing Group 1995)
**Post-War Kitchen** (Hamlyn, Octopus Publishing Group 1998)

This collection first published in 2002 by Chancellor Press,
an imprint of Bounty Books
Reprinted in 2003 (twice), 2004, 2005 (three times), 2006, 2007, 2008,
2009 (twice), 2010 and 2011

This edition published in 2014 by Chancellor Press,
an imprint of Bounty Books,
a division of Octopus Publishing Group Ltd,
Endeavour House, 189 Shaftesbury Avenue,
London WC2H 8JY
www.octopusbooks.co.uk

An Hachette UK Company
www.hachette.co.uk

ISBN: 978-0-753726-86-0

A CIP catalogue record for this book is available from the British Library.

Printed in China

# VICTORY
# COOKBOOK
## NOSTALGIC FOOD AND FACTS 1940-1954

CHANCELLOR PRESS

# FOREWORD

People of all ages express a desire to learn more about the way in which the British people coped during the Second World War. Films and television programmes have shown the devastation caused by enemy action in many parts of Britain and the gallantry of our forces in the various theatres of war. This book pictures home life in Britain, with the foods and meals that we had during, and after, the war.

If you compare the food of those years with the range of ingredients of today, and our interest in dishes from around the world, it may seem that we had an impossible life-style. Yes, food was severely rationed from 1940 to 1954, and the population had to manage without many ingredients they had taken for granted in pre-war days but they managed. The fact that adults kept fit and children grew strong and healthy must prove that the British at home won their battle, just as the forces overseas were victorious. In fact our diet during rationing years was very much in keeping with the advice on healthy eating given today.

Rationing of many foods was introduced gradually from January 1940. The list of rationed foods and quantities allowed are given in this book, so you can picture how alarming it was when we first faced these small portions. Meat rationing was a special problem, both for the authorities and for us, for we had always enjoyed generous amounts of our high quality joints, chops and steaks.

The Ministry of Food controlled food supplies and, under Lord Woolton, Minister of Food, gathered together the finest nutritionists to plan the nation's needs. Information for the public came from the Food Facts shown in newspapers and on cinema screens, and there were recipe leaflets and broadcasts on BBC radio. As you read the book you will see that the Food Facts are informative but often they are amusing as well; keeping cheerful was an essential role for the people at home. We were the Kitchen Front and we had to fight our battle with as much energy as the forces overseas fought theirs.

The Ministry Food Advice Division employed dieticians and many home economists, to help people throughout the country. Our role, for I was one of the food advisers, was to conduct cookery demonstrations and talks to show what interesting things could be made with the rationed and unrationed foods available.

Many dishes included potatoes and carrots (you will meet Potato Pete and Dr. Carrot in the book). Do try these wartime dishes for yourself, I am sure you will be pleasantly surprised at their good flavour. Chefs of today have asked me 'Are you not surprised, Marguerite, how imaginative our food has become?' I answer, 'Yes I enjoy today's dishes but I have met imaginative food before. If the women and men had not been clever with cooking the sparse selection of foods during rationing, we could not have been a healthy nation.'

1945 was wonderful! In May we celebrated victory in Europe (VE Day) and in August victory over Japan (VJ Day), and how Britain celebrated! There were street and other parties galore. Today many people enquire 'Did you get special rations for these?' Indeed we did not, the celebratory meals had to come from foods we had available. By 1945, though, we had become experts at 'making a little go a long way'. The victory dishes in this book show both home cooking and some dishes from the countries of our allies.

We did not expect rationing to end in 1945 but neither did we imagine it would go on until 1954. The years immediately after the war brought bread then potato rationing — two foods that had never been short before. In 1952 our very much admired King George VI died and his beautiful daughter Elizabeth became our Queen. By that date tea and preserves had come off ration, so we could spread our breakfast toast with marmalade and cheer ourselves with many cups of tea. In 1953, the year of the Coronation, other foods were de-rationed so we made special dishes in honour of the occasion with fresh eggs, cream, chocolate and extra sugar. Finally in 1954 all fats and meat became plentiful. The dishes in the post-war section of the book show how we began to change our cooking and also enjoy using some of the latest kitchen appliances that were coming on the market.

Please do cook the dishes you find throughout the book and you will not only discover just why we kept healthy for 14 long years, but also why we are grateful that rationing is no longer here.

*Marguerite Patten*

# *We'll* EAT AGAIN

# Introduction

'You want to get through your work and difficulties with the same spirits you expect of the Forces in action . . . . Well, thanks to government planning, the foods that will feed you and your family to the pitch of fighting fitness are right at your hand. They have been deliberately chosen to that purpose. To release ships and seamen on the fighting fronts, you, on the 'Kitchen Front', have the job of using these foods to the greatest advantage. Here is how to do it:

FIRST: *Your rations and allowances*. These are the *foundation* of your fighting diet. Take your full share of them always.

NEXT: *Vegetables*. These provide many of the vitamins so essential for good health and buoyant vitality.

THIRD: *Unrefined or whole-grain foods* – flour, oats, etc. These also supply valuable health factors, and, of course, add bulk to build up satisfying meals.

Spread your rations and allowances so that you get part of each of them *every* day, making sure that each member of your family gets his proper share.'

The words quoted above were from early material published by the Ministry of Food. These summarize the way we approached feeding our families during the war years and indeed for some time after the war ended.

When war was declared I was a Home Economist in the electrical industry and was used to giving cookery demonstrations that were based on delicious and lavish recipes; obviously these demonstrations were no longer possible. Instead we turned our attention to giving suggestions on the best ways to keep the family well fed. I co-operated with the local authority in Lincoln and in the evenings travelled around the villages to demonstrate to local groups. The Ministry of Food started publishing Food Facts in 1940 and I used their hints together with some of my own economical recipes.

I well remember visiting one local hall. The only appliance available was an elderly oil cooker. The caretaker cleaned this and the demonstration started. The cooker produced fumes and smoke like a London peasouper fog and the audience and I spent the session gasping for breath with tears raining down our cheeks. Fortunately in other places the equipment was rather more efficient.

In 1942 I went to the Ministry of Food as one of their Home Economists; I was based at Cambridge. My very first demonstration there took place in the market square. My colleagues and I erected our stall and demonstrated to the shoppers in the open market. We were in competition with the stallholders selling fruit, vegetables and other commodities, so we speedily learned to 'shout up'.

The Food Advice Division of the Ministry of Food gave demonstrations in our own centres, in markets and in the canteens of factories. We visited the outpatients departments in hospitals and welfare clinics to talk to patients, mothers-to-be and mothers of babies. We set up counters in large shops and demonstrated there with the help of small portable cookers. Many Home Economists drove small mobile vans and touring caravans, which were parked in convenient spots and the demonstration began as soon as passers-by gathered round. Our campaign was to find people, wherever they might be, and make them aware of the importance of keeping their families well fed on the rations available. Looking back I feel we were horribly bracing and we never sympathised with people over food problems if they grumbled. Most people, though, never complained and appreciated that we were trying to be helpful.

# INTRODUCTION

Perhaps this is a good place to recall the rations. These varied slightly from month to month as foods became slightly more or less plentiful. I have inserted metric measures – unknown in Britain at that time – so that younger people reading this book can appreciate the small amounts.

This is the ration for an adult *per week*:

| | |
|---|---|
| **Bacon and ham** | 4 oz (100 g) |
| **Meat** | to the value of 1s. 2d. (6p today). Sausages were not rationed but difficult to obtain; offal was originally unrationed but sometimes formed part of the meat ration. |
| **Butter** | 2 oz (50 g) |
| **Cheese** | 2 oz (50 g) sometimes it rose to 4 oz (100 g) and even up to 8 oz (225 g) |
| **Margarine** | 4 oz (100 g) |
| **Cooking fat** | 4 oz (100 g) often dropping to 2 oz (50 g) |
| **Milk** | 3 pints (1800 ml) sometimes dropping to 2 pints (1200 ml). Household (skimmed, dried) milk was available, I think this was 1 packet each 4 weeks. |
| **Sugar** | 8 oz (225 g) |
| **Preserves** | 1 lb (450 g) every 2 months |
| **Tea** | 2 oz (50 g) |
| **Eggs** | 1 shell egg a week if available but at times dropping to 1 every two weeks. Dried eggs—1 packet each 4 weeks. |
| **Sweets** | 12 oz (350 g) each 4 weeks. |

In addition, there was a monthly points system. As an example of how these could be spent, the 16 points allowed you to buy one can of fish or meat or 2 lb (900 g) of dried fruit or 8 lb (3.6 kg) of split peas.

Babies and younger children, expectant and nursing mothers, had concentrated orange juice and cod liver oil from Welfare Clinics together with priority milk. This milk was also available to invalids.

During 1942 I was loaned to the scientific division of the Ministry of Food to go to various school canteens to assess the food value and vitamin content of school dinners. School meals were started during the war years to make quite certain that school children had the best possible main meal (remember most mothers were working long hours for the war effort).

The area in which I worked covered all East Anglia, and I was responsible for a second Food Advice Centre in Ipswich. As much of this was a rural area where large amounts of fruit were grown, I had a number of sessions in charge of 'Fruit Preservation Centres' in schools or other large kitchens where groups of ladies would gather to make preserves from local grown fruit and specially supplied sugar. The recipes were set by the Ministry of Food to ensure that the completed preserves could be stored and sold as part of the rations. The sessions were not entirely peaceful, for most ladies were experienced housewives, with their own very definite ideas on how jams should be made; some wanted to use their own recipes and addressed me firmly. 'Young woman, I was making jam before you were born'—quite right— but my job was to ensure that every completed pot of jam contained 60% sugar and was carefully sealed to ensure it really would keep well under all conditions, so I had to stand firm.

My work in East Anglia terminated when I left just before my daughter was born. I returned to the Ministry of Food—but this time in the London area—when she was several months old. I was fortunate enough to find a good nannie to care for the baby during the day. The work in London was similar to that in East Anglia but concentrated more on the big canteens, on factories, on hospitals and on public demonstrations.

At the end of 1943 I took over the Ministry of Food Advice Bureau at Harrods. This meant the end of travelling and the start of concentrated daily demonstrations.

I had two demonstrations each day from Monday to Friday and one on Saturday morning so that I was continually trying to find new ideas. The Ministry of Food leaflets were an invaluable guidance and many of the members of my audience a wonderful inspiration. Some people came from abroad and generously contributed ideas based on their own countries cuisine. A percentage of the people had never cooked before—they had relied on professional cooks. Imagine learning to cook at that particular time; in fact these people generally became inventive and clever cooks.

I was one of the contributors to the Kitchen Front early morning broadcasts on the B.B.C. and was able to pass on my favourite recipes to a wider audience.

Many of the ingredients available, such as dried egg and wartime (National) flour, were a challenge to any cook, but it was surprising how we learned to cope with these and produce edible dishes. As you follow the recipes you will find frequent mention of cups

(use a $\frac{1}{2}$ pint (300 ml) measure or breakfast cup). The teacup given in some recipes means a generous $\frac{1}{4}$ pint (150 ml) measure. The amounts of salt and pepper given are rather generous by todays standards so add these more sparingly.

Virtually every cook in Britain behaved like a zealous squirrel—we bottled and/or dried fresh fruits; we salted beans; we prepared economical chutneys and pickles; we made the very best use of every available ingredient. The chapter that begins on page 92 gives some of the most popular recipes.

As you read through this book you will find a wide variety of dishes, many of which are very much in keeping with the advice given by nutritionalists nowadays. We ate lots of vegetables and home-produced fruits but little fat, sugar or meat. Our menus may have been monotonous, but both adults and children were incredibly healthy and we all felt that we were playing a vital role towards the ultimate victory when we could all happily look forward to eating much more varied and exciting dishes once again.

# IMPORTANT FACTS

The phraseology used in the book is that given in the original recipes and may need a little explaining, for example we always talked about 'tinned' and not 'canned' foods.

## Dried eggs

This refers to the dried egg powder available on rations books. This was pure egg with all the moisture removed. To reconstitute dried egg blend 1 LEVEL tablespoon dried egg powder with 2 tablespoons water (this is the equivalent of a fresh egg). If people were generous with the amount of dried egg powder they were inclined to have a somewhat unpleasant taste. In some recipes the egg powder could be used dry from the tin.

## Measures

The term GILL is used in some recipes, this was very popular until after the second world war when it was no longer used as it seemed to cause confusion.

1 gill equals $\frac{1}{4}$ pint in recipes

A dessertspoon measure was frequently used, this is equivalent to a good $\frac{1}{2}$ tablespoon.

## Household milk

This was the skimmed milk powder available on rations books. It was blended with water to make the equivalent of fresh milk. Put 1 pint of lukewarm water into a container. Measure 4 level tablespoons of the milk powder and sprinkle it—a little at a time—on top of the water while beating briskly with an egg whisk, fork or wooden spoon.

## Oven temperatures

In some recipes the oven settings may appear high by today's standards. This is because most of the recipes contained relatively little fat and speedy baking could be recommended.

The equivalent descriptions and modern settings are given below. The term very moderate used to be given; nowadays many people do not use these words.

**A very cool oven:** often called very slow or very low is 90–120°C, 200–250°F, Gas Mark 0–$\frac{1}{2}$

**A cool oven:** often called slow or low is 140–150°C, 275–300°F, Gas Mark 1–2

**A very moderate oven:** nowadays generally called moderate is 160°C, 325°F, Gas Mark 3

**A moderate oven:** is 180°C, 350°F, Gas Mark 4

**A moderately hot oven:** is 190–200°C, 375–400°F, Gas Mark 5–6

**A hot oven:** is 220°C, 425°F, Gas Mark 7

**A very hot oven:** is 230–240°C, 450–475°F, Gas Mark 8–9

# Soups

A flask of soup was very comforting on a cold winter night when firewatching or on Home Guard Duty, or even to take down to the shelter. The more substantial ones made nourishing lunches or suppers. We learnt to make delicious stocks from vegetable trimmings and a few bacon rinds and to thicken soups with oatmeal or to pack them with root vegetables or beans for a filling meal.

When you come home tired and cold after a long day's work, there's nothing so cheering for you as soup. Thick soup is nourishing, a meal in itself. Soup is very easy to digest, an important point when you are

> **War-work and Home-work**

tired. And, if you keep a soup-pot handy on the stove, soup is as easy to make as A B C. Look after your soup-pot and then make one of these delicious soups for the evening.

# BORTSCH

*Cooking time:* 2 hours 5 minutes    *Quantity:* 4 helpings

1 oz dripping or margarine
1 large raw beetroot, peeled and grated
2 potatoes, peeled and chopped or grated
1 carrot, peeled and chopped or grated
1 onion, peeled and chopped and grated

12 oz cabbage, chopped or grated
2 tomatoes, chopped
2 bay leaves
water or stock (see method)
salt and pepper
pinch mixed herbs
chopped parsley

METHOD: Melt the dripping or margarine in a pan and fry the beetroot for about 5 minutes. Put all the vegetables and bay leaves into a saucepan, together with the beetroot. Completely cover with water or stock and bring to the boil. Remove any scum, put on the lid and simmer slowly for 2 hours. Add seasoning and pinch of mixed herbs. Serve garnished with parsley.

# Forward the Soup Pot

If you can use stock for the basis of your soups they will be all the better for it, more nourishing, more tasty. The *soup-pot* need not use up hours of fuel. Put your root vegetables (all except turnips), bacon rinds, etc., in a large pot with plenty of water. Cook slowly for $\frac{1}{2}$ hour. Boil vigorously for a minute or two then put straight into the hay box or into the oven when the baking is done to use up the last of the heat. The soup-pot should be brought to the boil every day. Green vegetables and outside leaves may be added to the stock if it is to be used at once. Don't disturb the fat on top of the stock for this preserves the flavour, but remove before use. When you want to make a soup you just take some of this stock, add what flavourings or vegetables you fancy as in the recipes on these pages and in a very short time your soup will be ready.

I used to think one didn't oughter
Make a soup from vegetable water.
But this, my dear – this IS a snorter!

# VEGETABLE SOUP

METHOD: Fry 2 oz rolled oats or oatmeal in 1 oz margarine. Blend with a little of 2 pints of water, then add the rest of the water and bring to boil. Add 3 potatoes, 4 carrots, $\frac{1}{2}$ small swede, 1 leek if you have it, sliced or cut into cubes. Cook for 1 hour. Just before serving add pepper and salt and some chopped parsley. The quantities given are sufficient for 4 helpings.

# QUICK VEGETABLE SOUP

*Cooking time:* 30 minutes     *Quantity:* 4 helpings

½ oz dripping
12 oz mixed vegetables, diced
1½ pints water or stock

salt and pepper
chopped parsley

METHOD: Melt the dripping in a saucepan, add the vegetables and cook gently in the fat for a good 5 minutes. Add the liquid and simmer slowly for 25 minutes. Season the soup, then rub through a sieve to make a purée. Reheat and serve sprinkled with chopped parsley.

# QUICK SOUP

*Cooking time:* 30 minutes     *Quantity:* 6 helpings

4 breakfast cups stock or
    water
1 lb mixed vegetables
1–1½ teaspoons salt
2 tablespoons wheatmeal
    flour

1 tablespoon household milk
chopped parsley or
    watercress or sliced
    cabbage

METHOD: Put 3 breakfastcups of stock or water on to boil, then wash and grate or shred the vegetables. Add salt and vegetables to stock and cook till tender, season. Blend flour and household milk with 1 breakfast cup of water and pour on to the soup, stir and cook for 3–5 minutes. Serve with parsley, watercress or cabbage.

## QUESTIONS YOU ASK

**Can you give me a new soup recipe?**
Here's a delicious one: *Golden Barley Soup.* Grate or mince 2 lb. of carrots, put with 1 small teacup of barley into 1 quart of water and simmer for 2½ hours. Roll a piece of margarine the size of a walnut in 1 tablespoonful of flour and stir it into the soup. Cook fast for 8 minutes, season. Serves 4 or 5 helpings.

# CREAM OF PARSNIP SOUP

*Cooking time:* 25–30 minutes     *Quantity:* 6 helpings

3 pints stock or water
1–1½ lb parsnips
½ leek
3 teaspoons salt
pepper

2 oz flour
¼ pint household milk
2 tablespoons chopped
    parsley

METHOD: Put stock or water on to boil while shredding the parsnips and leek. When boiling add shredded parsnips and leek. Boil for 20 minutes, season, add blended flour and milk and simmer for 3–5 minutes, stirring all the time. Serve with parsley.

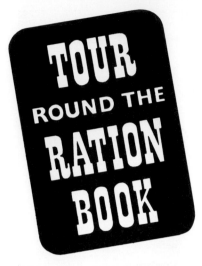

This year's Ration Book is a much simpler affair than last year's three books, and you should get familiar with it from the start. So here we take you on a conducted tour, with stops at the principal objects of interest! Cut this out and read it with the Ration Book in front of you. Then you will see how simple it has all been made.

**THE CHILD'S BOOK**
R.B.2. will be used in exactly the same way except that the tea coupons will be marked when oranges are bought, and will not be cut out.

**YOUR OLD RATION BOOKS** should be kept until the end of August. They may still be needed – for instance for July preserves, or your first tin of dried eggs. If they contain special authorisations keep them until these are used up. Do not transfer them to your new book.

**THE FRONT COVER.** Check the entries with your identity card. If there is any difference report it to the Food Office.

**PAGE 2** You should by now have filled in the details at X. See that they agree with those on the front cover. Fill in Y if under 18. Leave Z alone.

**PAGE 5** is the first of the coupon pages. See how they are now all divided (Points as well) into four-weekly periods numbered 1 to 13. This will help you to "keep your place" and make shopping easier. You have re-registered by now of course, so the counterfoils have been cut out by the shops. You need not fill in the spaces marked B unless you deposit whole pages with your retailer.

**PAGE 9** now combines in one the coupons for butter, margarine and cooking fats.

**PAGE 11** will be used for the ordinary and the special ration of cheese.

**PAGE 13** will record your purchase of eggs. Remember that you won't get them every week. Poultry keepers will get no shell eggs.

**PAGE 15** combines sugar and preserves. The squares marked Q, R, S will not be used at present.

**PAGE 17** Tea coupons will be cut out by the retailer, four at a time.

**PAGES 25 TO 34** are Points Coupon pages. They are just the same as those in the old pink book but the four-week periods are referred to by number instead of date.

**PAGE 25** MUST CONTAIN THE NAMES AND ADDRESSES OF YOUR RETAILERS. It is illegal to use the Ration Book if these are not filled in. The column on the left is for noting the deposit of whole pages.

**PAGE 39** Fill in if you deposit any rows of Points Coupons, also fill in the bottom line if you deposit your tea coupon page. Note this specially because it is new.

**BACK COVER** (page 40) has two panels. Panel 1 (at the top) will be used for soap, which may still be bought at any time during the four-weekly period. Panel 2 will not be used yet.

# OATMEAL SOUP

*Cooking time:* 1 hour    *Quantity:* 4 helpings

1 oz margarine
2 medium onions, grated or finely diced
2 tablespoons medium oatmeal

1 pint cold water
salt and pepper
½ pint milk
3 medium carrots, grated

"I'll put pep in your step." says Potato Pete

METHOD: Heat the margarine in a pan, add the onions and cook for 5 minutes. Blend the oatmeal with the cold water, tip into the pan and stir as the mixture comes to the boil; season lightly. Simmer steadily for 30 minutes, stirring frequently, then add the milk and carrots and cook for a further 15 minutes.

# CHEESE SOUP

*Cooking time:* 25 minutes    *Quantity:* 4 helpings

2 tablespoons chopped onion or leek, if possible
1½ oz margarine
2 cups household milk
2 cups water

2 tablespoons flour
1 cup grated cheese
salt and pepper
2 tablespoons chopped parsley

METHOD: Add onion and margarine to milk and water, bring to the boil, cook for 15 minutes, stirring all the time. (Remember household milk catches more easily than ordinary milk, so stirring is important.) Blend flour with a little milk, stir in and cook for a few minutes to thicken. Add cheese and seasoning. Stir until the cheese is melted, but do not boil again. Add parsley and serve very hot.

# POTATO AND WATERCRESS SOUP

*Cooking time:* 40 minutes    *Quantity:* 4 helpings

1 lb potatoes
1 pint vegetable stock
1 teaspoon margarine

1 pint household milk
pepper and salt
2 bunches watercress

FOOD IS A MUNITION OF WAR — DON'T WASTE IT

METHOD: Wash and peel potatoes and chop in small pieces. Cook potatoes in stock till soft, mash against side of pan with wooden spoon, add margarine, milk and seasoning. Reheat and just before serving add chopped watercress.

### MINESTRONE SOUP

**Cooking time:** 2 hours **In-gredients:** 3 oz haricot beans, 1½ pints water, 2 oz quick cooking macaroni, salt and pepper, 1 oz dripping or oil, 1 onion, peeled and finely grated, 1 stick celery, chopped, ½ table-spoon chopped parsley, 8 oz tomatoes, fresh or bottled or tinned, chopped, 8 oz cabbage, chopped, 1 pint water, grated cheese. **Quantity:** 4 helpings

Soak the beans for 24 hours in the 1½ pints of water. Cook slowly for 1½ hours or until soft then strain. Cook the macaroni for 7 minutes in a saucepan of boiling salted water then strain. Heat the dripping or oil, fry the onion, celery and parsley for 5 minutes. Add the tomatoes, cabbage and 1 pint water and bring to the boil. Put in the beans, macaroni and seasoning to taste. Simmer for 20 minutes. Serve sprinkled with grated cheese. This soup is very thick but a little extra liquid could be used for a thinner soup.

# MOCK OYSTER SOUP

*Cooking time:* 1 hour 10 minutes    *Quantity:* 4 helpings

1–1½ lb fish trimmings
1 teaspoon salt
1 pint water, plus extra water
1 blade mace
6 white peppercorns
1 clove
2 teaspoons mixed herbs

1 small onion or leek, sliced
8 oz artichokes, peeled and sliced
½ teaspoon pepper
2 tablespoons flour
¼ pint milk
chopped parsley

METHOD: Wash the fish and cook in the salted water with the mace, peppercorns, clove and mixed herbs in a muslin bag, and onion or leek for 30 minutes. Strain off the stock and make up to 1 pint with water. Cook the artichokes in the stock for 30 minutes. Add the pepper and sieve. Blend the flour with the milk, add to the soup and stir until it boils. Cook gently for a further 5 minutes. Sprinkle with chopped parsley before serving.

★     ★     ★

# HOLLANDAISE SOUP

*Cooking time:* 10 minutes    *Quantity:* 4 helpings

1 oz margarine
1 oz flour
¾ pint white stock or water with few drops flavouring, e.g. beef extract
¼ pint milk
1 reconstituted dried egg or 1 shell egg

salt and pepper
3 tablespoons cream from top of milk or unsweetened evaporated milk
1 tablespoon peas
1 tablespoon diced cucumber or gherkin

METHOD: Melt the margarine in a pan, stir in the flour. Cook for 3 minutes, remove the pan from the heat and gradually stir in the stock, or water and flavouring, and milk. Bring to the boil and cook until thickened. Add the egg and seasoning to taste. Cook *very slowly* for a further 3 minutes. Add the cream or milk. Garnish with peas and diced cucumber or gherkin.

# FISH SOUP

*Cooking time:* 20 minutes.    *Quantity:* 4 helpings

1 oz margarine
2 oz flour
2 pints fish stock (see under method)
¼ pint milk

salt and pepper
1 tablespoon chopped parsley
1 reconstituted dried egg or 1 fresh egg
watercress

METHOD: Melt the margarine in a pan, stir in the flour and cook for several minutes, stirring well. Remove from the heat and gradually add the fish stock. Boil steadily until the soup thickens, then add the milk, seasoning and parsley. Whisk in the egg. Stir over a gentle heat, do not allow the soup to boil, for a further 5 minutes. Serve garnished with watercress.

**To Make Fish Stock**
Fish trimmings are invaluable to make an interesting stock. The fish bones, fish heads and skins should be used.

Put the fish trimmings into a pan with water to cover, add a peeled onion, a little chopped celery, a pinch of mixed herbs and seasoning. Cook slowly for 30 minutes, no longer. Strain.

## A CHRISTMAS GIFT

Everyone, grown-up or child, who has to take packed lunches, craves for a good *hot* lunch now and then, and therefore would welcome the gift of a portable hay-box. Soup, stew, sausage and mash, shepherd's pie, or any other favourite dish keeps *really* hot in this box, for several hours. You can make the portable hay-box from a spare gas-mask carrier. It's very simple. Full directions will be sent if you write to the Ministry of Food.

# SCOTCH BROTH

*Cooking time:* 2½–3 hours    *Quantity:* 4 helpings

1 oz pearl barley
8 oz stewing beef, diced
2 pints water
3 oz onions or leeks, sliced
8 oz carrots, diced

1 lb swede, peeled and diced
salt and pepper
2 oz cabbage, sliced
1 tablespoon chopped parsley

METHOD: Put the barley into cold water, bring to the boil then strain.

Put the barley, beef and 2 pints water in a pan; bring to the boil and skim. Simmer for 1 hour then add the prepared onions or leeks, carrots and swede with the seasoning. Cook for 1½ to 2 hours. Add the cabbage 15 minutes before serving. Skim any surplus fat off the soup. Remove the meat with a perforated spoon. Place the chopped parsley in a soup tureen, pour in the broth. The meat is served as a separate course.

# Pea Pod Soup

Wash the pods thoroughly and place in a deep saucepan. Add 2 sprigs of mint, 1 large potato, and chives, onion or spring onion (if available), a good pinch of salt and pepper, and cover with boiling water. Cook with the lid on until tender. Rub the vegetables and the pods through sieve, then return to the saucepan. Blend a little flour (1 oz to each pint) with cold water, add some of the hot soup to it. Return all to the saucepan and stir until boiling and the soup is creamy. Serve very hot.

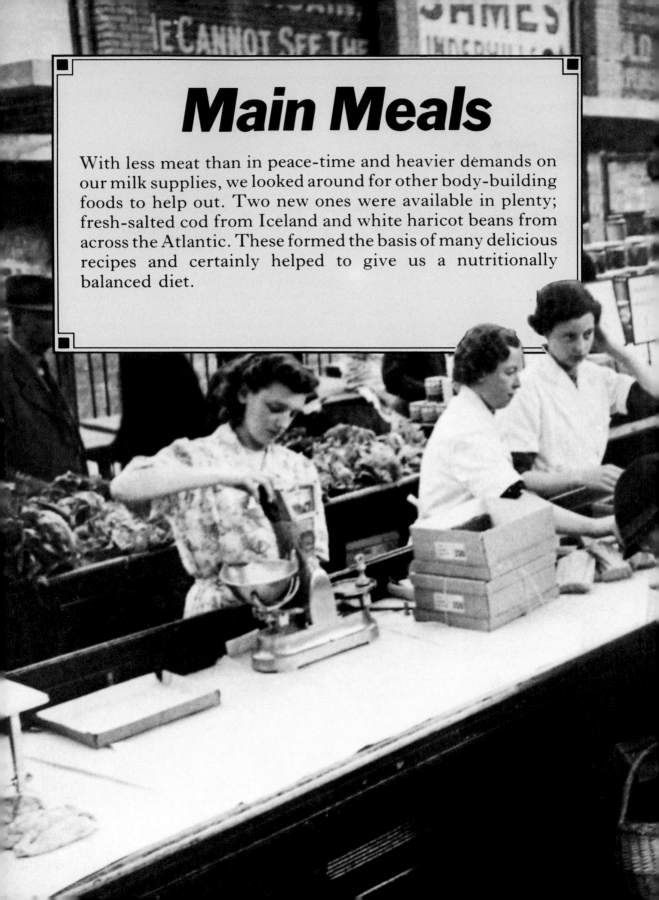

# Main Meals

With less meat than in peace-time and heavier demands on our milk supplies, we looked around for other body-building foods to help out. Two new ones were available in plenty; fresh-salted cod from Iceland and white haricot beans from across the Atlantic. These formed the basis of many delicious recipes and certainly helped to give us a nutritionally balanced diet.

More good news on the Kitchen Front—extra fish is now coming into the country; regular supplies of a new type of fish—Fresh-Salted Cod. It's almost free from bones, it's easy to cook, and there's no waste. Above all—it's cheap: the maximum retail price is 9d. per lb.

Fresh-Salted Cod requires soaking in water for 48 hours before cooking. Your fishmonger will do this and when you buy it, it will be ready to cook.

## TO THE FISHMONGER

Your customers will like the Fresh-Salted Cod but a lot depends on the care taken in de-salting. Soak in cold water, with the skin uppermost for 24 to 48 hours; if there is much fish in relation to water, change the water—probably more than once. Always add bicarbonate of soda to the water; one heaped teaspoon to 1 gallon. Never de-salt more than required for the day's sales and explain to your customers that Fresh-Salted Cod must be treated as fresh fish and cooked the day it is bought.

FOOD FACTS

## BAKED FISH CAKES

*Cooking time:* 20 minutes    *Quantity:* 4 helpings

4 oz cooked fresh-salted cod
1 lb mashed potatoes
2 large well-mashed carrots
1 teaspoon mixed sweet
  herbs

1 dessertspoon Worcester
  sauce
1 rasher of bacon cooked and
  chopped, if liked
browned breadcrumbs

METHOD: Mix ingredients thoroughly, form into small round cakes and roll each in fine, well-baked breadcrumbs. Put the cakes on greased baking tin and bake for 20 minutes in a moderate oven. This is a particularly good way of making fish cakes as no fat is required.

## FISH PIE (1)

*Cooking time:* 30 minutes    *Quantity:* 4 helpings

1 pint white or parsley sauce
¾ lb cooked fresh-salted cod
1 lb sliced cooked carrots or
  swedes

1 lb sliced cooked potatoes
chopped parsley
pepper
browned breadcrumbs

METHOD: Put a layer of sauce at the bottom of a dish, arrange in alternate layers the fish and vegetables and sauce, finishing with potatoes. Sprinkle the parsley and seasoning between the layers. Cover the top with crisped breadcrumbs (much improved if tossed in bacon fat). Put the dish into a moderate oven to get thoroughly hot.

## FISH PIE (2)

Follow the directions for the Fish Pie on this page but add 2 sliced cooking apples to the other ingredients.

# STEAMED FISH ROLL

*Cooking time:* 1½ hours    *Quantity:* 4 helpings

PASTRY
8 oz self-raising flour or plain flour with 1 teaspoon baking powder
2 oz suet, chopped
2 oz raw potato, grated
water to bind
FILLING
4 oz fresh-salted cod, cut into small pieces

6 oz vegetables (cauliflower, grated raw or cooked mashed carrots or parsnips or swedes or cooked peas)
1 tablespoon brown gravy or sauce
1 teaspoon vinegar
pepper

METHOD: Make a dough with the flour, or flour and baking powder, suet and raw potato and enough water to make a stiff dough. Roll out, spread with the fish and vegetables moistened with gravy or sauce and the vinegar. Dust with pepper, roll up. Wrap the roll in greased paper and steam for 1½ hours. Serve with gravy or sauce.

# SUET CRUST PASTRY

You save suet by using grated potato, as in the recipe above for Steamed Fish Roll.

Our Sailors don't mind risking their lives to feed you—and your family—but they do mind if you help the U-boats by wasting food.

# CURRIED COD

*Cooking time:* 10 minutes    *Quantity:* for 4 people

1 tablespoon dripping
1 tomato or 2 or 3 spring onions if possible
1 tablespoon gravy powder
1 dessertspoon curry powder
about 1 pint vegetable boilings or water

1 tablespoon chutney or stewed apple
1 dessertspoon sugar
OTHER INGREDIENTS
1 lb fresh-salted cod, either boiled or baked
1 lb sliced cooked carrots

METHOD: Melt the dripping, fry the tomato or onions cut small, stir in the gravy powder and curry powder. When it is well bound, gradually add boiling liquid to form a thick sauce. Stir in the chutney or apple and sugar. Add the fish and the carrots cut in small pieces and simmer for 5 to 10 minutes. Serve with plenty of plain boiled potatoes.

# FISH ENVELOPE

*Cooking time:* 20–30 minutes     *Quantity:* 4 helpings

MASHED POTATO PASTRY
8 tablespoons national flour
4 tablespoons mashed potato
2 oz fat
FILLING
12 tablespoons cooked mixed
  vegetables, mashed

salt and pepper
4 oz cooked or tinned fish,
  well drained
½ teacup thick white sauce

METHOD: Blend the flour and potato together, soften the fat slightly and blend in with the potato mixture. It is rarely necessary to add any water to bind. Roll out thinly and divide in two. Spread one piece with the cooked vegetables mashed and seasoned. Cream the fish with the white sauce and spread on the other piece of pastry. Put together and bake in a hot oven for 20–30 minutes. Eat hot or cold.

# FISH IN SAVOURY CUSTARD

*Cooking time:* 45 minutes     *Quantity:* 4 helpings

4 small fillets of fish or 2 fish
  cutlets
1 egg or 1 reconstituted egg
½ pint milk

salt and pepper
1 teaspoon chopped parsley
small pinch mixed herbs

METHOD: Arrange the fillets or cutlets in a greased dish. If possible, roll these. Beat the egg, pour on the milk. If using dried egg, the milk should be poured on boiling. Add seasoning, parsley and herbs. Pour over the fish and bake in a very moderate oven for approximately 45 minutes. It is advisable, as with all baked custards, to stand the dish in another containing cold water.

Night and day men of the Royal Navy cheerfully risk their lives to guard your food. They don't mind danger but waste gives them the creeps!

# COD CASSEROLE

METHOD: Skin 1½ lb fresh-salted cod, bring to boil, simmer 15 to 20 minutes, flake and remove any bones. Parboil and slice thinly 1 lb parsnips. Slice one small cabbage crossways. Arrange in layers in a pie dish or stewing jar, sprinkling each layer with a little chopped parsley, leek when possible, and small pieces of margarine. Blend a dessertspoon of cornflour with 1 pint of water, pour in. Cover with lid or paper, bake in moderate oven 40 minutes.

# FISH CHARLOTTE

*Cooking time:* ¾ to 1 hour    *Quantity:* 4 helpings

8 oz bread (equals 6 slices)
a little fish paste
¾ lb fish
4 tablespoons chopped
   parsley

1½ teaspoons lemon substitute
salt and pepper

METHOD: Spread the slices of bread on both sides with the paste. Cut one of the slices to fit the bottom of the basin. Remove crusts. Line the rest of the basin with slices of bread, cut in strips. Chop up the crusts into small dice. Cover the fish with boiling water and leave for 1 to 2 minutes. Take out, remove the skin and bones and flake into smallish pieces. Add parsley, lemon substitute, and salt and pepper to taste. Put a layer of fish into the basin, cover with the diced crusts and pack in alternative layers, until the basin is filled, finishing with a layer of diced crusts. Press down well, cover with an upturned saucer and steam for ¾ to 1 hour. Serve hot with a green vegetable or cold with a salad.

# BAKED FISH WITH MASHED TURNIPS

*Cooking time:* 45 minutes    *Quantity:* 4 or 5 helpings

1 large fillet fresh-salted cod
pepper
2 oz margarine
2 lb turnips, peeled and diced
salt

2 tablespoons flour
1 pint turnip water and milk
3 tablespoons capers or
   mustard

METHOD: Put the fish in a baking tin or fireproof dish, season well with pepper and put the margarine, cut in small pieces on top. Cover with a paper and bake for 30 minutes in a slow oven.

Cook the turnips in salted water until tender. Drain thoroughly and mash with pepper. Keep very hot.

Make the sauce by pouring off as much fat as possible from the fish into a saucepan. Stir in the flour and blend well over a very low heat. Gradually stir in the pint of turnip water and milk, cook until smooth and creamy. Add the capers or mustard to taste.

Make a bed of the mashed turnips, dish the fish on it and pour over the sauce.

## BROWN FISH STEW WITH BEANS

**Cooking time:** 25 minutes **Ingredients:** 1 oz dripping or cooking fat, 1 lb white fish, diced, 8 oz onions, sliced, 2 tomatoes, sliced, 1 tablespoon flour, 1–2 teaspoons gravy browning, $\frac{1}{2}$ pint fish stock or water, 1 teaspoon Worcester sauce (optional), salt and pepper, 8 oz cooked or canned haricot beans. **Quantity:** 4 helpings

Heat the dripping or fat in a large saucepan. Add the fish and heat until golden brown then carefully remove from the pan. Put in the onions and tomatoes, cook for a few minutes, then stir in the flour and gravy browning. Blend in the fish stock or water and Worcester sauce, if using this, and a little seasoning. Bring to the boil, stir until slightly thickened, then return the fish to the pan. Heat for a few minutes, add the beans and continue heating for 3–4 minutes.

## USEFUL FUEL-SAVERS

Warm foods are not the only 'warming foods'—you don't need a hot meal every day.

*Never heat the oven for one cake or pudding, plan a baking day.*

Try to arrange with neighbours to share ovens. One day one neighbour could cook two or three joints; another day, someone's milk pudding might be tucked into a not quite full oven, or a cake baked while a casserole is slowly cooking. While you are doing this, you are not just helping each other. You are helping the Miners who work to provide our fuel.

# FISH BAKE

*Cooking time:* 30 minutes    *Quantity:* 4 helpings

1 lb potatoes, grated
salt and pepper
2 large onions, grated
2 tablespoons chopped parsley

$1\frac{1}{2}$ lb fish, cooked and flaked—cod, haddock, hake or mackerel
$\frac{1}{4}$ pint milk

METHOD: Grease a shallow casserole well. Put a layer of grated potato on the bottom, season well, add a sprinkling of the onion and parsley, then a layer of fish; continue filling the casserole like this ending with potato. Pour over the milk. Cover with a piece of greased paper, then put on the lid. Bake in the centre of a moderately hot oven for a good 30 minutes. This may be served hot or cold.

# DEVILLED HERRINGS

*Cooking time:* 15 minutes    *Quantity:* 4 helpings

4 medium sized herrings
$\frac{1}{2}$ oz margarine
1 teaspoon made mustard
1 teaspoon vinegar
1 teaspoon Worcester sauce

pinch salt
1 tablespoon sugar
$\frac{1}{4}$ pint water
1 onion, grated
$\frac{1}{2}$ teaspoon pickling spice

METHOD: Split the herrings and take out the backbones. Cream the margarine, add the mustard, vinegar, Worcester sauce, salt and sugar. Spread this paste on the herrings. Roll tightly. Put into a saucepan with the water, onion and pickling spice. Simmer gently for a good 10 minutes. Serve hot or cold.

Mackerel may be cooked in the same way, but they will take slightly longer.

# FISH FLAN

*Cooking time:* 35 minutes    *Quantity:* 4 helpings

pastry made with 6 oz flour,
  etc, see pages 52 and 53
2 tablespoons chopped onion
½ oz dripping
3 tablespoons flour
1 teaspoon paprika

½ pint milk and water
1 teaspoon salt
1 tablespoon vinegar
1 lb white fish, steamed and
  flaked
chopped parsley

METHOD: Line an 8 inch sandwich tin or flan ring with the pastry and bake blind in a moderately hot oven for 20 minutes. Fry the onion in the dripping for 5 minutes without browning, stir in the flour and paprika and cook for 1 minute. Add the liquid and bring to the boil, stirring all the time, and boil gently for 5 minutes. Add the salt, vinegar and fish; heat through and turn into the hot flan case. Garnish with chopped parsley.

# HERRING PLATE PIE

*Cooking time:* 25–30 minutes    *Quantity:* 4 helpings

1½ oz cooking fat or
  margarine
6 oz plain flour
½ teaspoon salt
2 tablespoons finely grated
  raw potato
water to mix, if necessary
4 tablespoons grated raw
  potato

6 tablespoons chopped celery
8 tablespoons chopped leek
½ tablespoon vinegar
¼ teaspoon grated nutmeg
1 teaspoon salt
pinch of pepper
½ tin herrings (12 oz size)

METHOD: Rub the fat or margarine into the flour and salt. Add the finely grated potato and mix to a stiff dough with water. Roll out half the pastry and line an 8 inch ovenproof pie plate or tin. Place half the grated potato, celery and leek on the pastry and sprinkle with the vinegar, nutmeg and seasoning. Cut the herrings in half lengthways, place on the mixture and add the remainder of the potato, celery and leek. Roll out the remaining pastry and cover the pie. Make an inch slit on the top. Bake in a hot oven for 25–30 minutes.

## PILCHARD LAYER LOAF

*This is something new and very nice.*
**Cooking time:** 30 minutes, plus time to make sauce **Ingredients:** 1 small national wheatmeal loaf, 1 5-oz tin pilchard (4 points), ¾ pint thick white sauce, see page 69, 1 teaspoon mustard, 2 tablespoons vinegar, salt and pepper.
**Quantity:** 4 helpings

Cut off the crusts (using them later for toast or rusks) and slice the loaf lengthwise into four. Spread each slice with pilchards mashed with a little sauce and seasoning. If the pilchards are not packed in tomato sauce you may care to add a little piquant sauce to this mixture. Dip the layers in water to moisten, then place one on top of the other to re-form a loaf. All this can be done in advance. When required, place the pilchard loaf in a fireproof dish and pour over the sauce, mixed with the mustard, vinegar and seasoning. Bake in a moderate oven for about 30 minutes. Serve with green vegetable.

This is the question of the week: *Did you get your National Wholemeal Bread?* More and more bakers are baking it now, but if you can't get it locally write to the Ministry of Food, London, giving the name and address of your baker.

## DINNER FOR A KING

Bakehouse Mutton makes a good, satisfying, heartening mid-day meal. Here is how to make it for 4 or 5 people.

Scrub 2½ lb potatoes and cut into thick slices. Put in a baking tin and season with salt and pepper. Pour over a teacup of water. Roll up 2 breasts of lamb (boned), lay them on top of the potatoes, cover with margarine papers and bake in a moderate oven for 1½ hours. Remove the paper and brown the meat for about 20 minutes before serving.

# ARTICHOKES IN CHEESE BATTER

*Cooking time:* 30 minutes    *Quantity:* 4 helpings

1 lb artichokes
salt and pepper
4 oz plain flour
1 tablespoon dried egg

¼ pint milk or milk and water
2–3 oz cheese, grated
1 teaspoon baking powder
little fat for frying

METHOD: Scrub the artichokes and boil in salted water until tender. Peel and cut in thick slices. Mix the flour, seasoning and egg, add enough of the milk, or milk and water, to make a thick batter, beat well; add the remaining liquid. Lastly add the cheese and baking powder. Heat the fat in a frying pan, dip the artichoke slices in the batter and fry in the hot fat until golden brown.

Alternatively the artichokes may be mixed with the batter and baked in the oven in the same way as a Yorkshire pudding, see page 100.

# BACON TURNOVERS (1)

*Cooking time:* 30 minutes    *Quantity:* 4 helpings

PASTRY
12 oz self-raising flour or
    plain flour with 3
    teaspoons baking powder
pinch salt
3 oz cooking fat or bacon fat,
    see method
water

FILLING
4 oz fat bacon rashers
2 cooked leeks, finely
    chopped
8 oz cooked potatoes, diced
1–2 tablespoons chopped
    parsley

METHOD: Sift the flour and salt, rub in the cooking fat. You could use the fat that runs from the bacon if it is allowed to become cold, see page 37, instead of the cooking fat. Bind with water. Grill and chop the bacon rashers, cool then mix with the leeks, potatoes and parsley. Roll out the pastry and cut into 4 large rounds. Put the bacon mixture in the centre of each round; moisten the edges of the pastry with water. Fold over to make a turnover shape and seal firmly. Bake in the middle of a hot oven for 25 minutes until crisp and brown. Serve hot or cold.

There is another recipe on page 37.

## BEAN MEDLEY

**Cooking time:** 1½ hours **Ingredients:** ¾ lb haricot beans (soaked overnight), 1½ pints water, salt and pepper, 1 tablespoon treacle, 1½ lb mixed vegetables (carrots, parsnips, leeks etc), diced, 2 oz grilled chopped bacon, chopped parsley. **Quantity:** 4 helpings

Soak the beans overnight and put them into a pan with water, pepper and treacle. Partly boil. Add salt and diced vegetables and cook until tender and the water absorbed. Dish up, cover with the bacon and sprinkle with chopped parsley. Serve with bread and butter and watercress.

# SAVOURY CHARLOTTE

*Cooking time:* about 1 hour    *Quantity:* 4–5 helpings

2 lb mixed vegetables
salt and pepper
2 rashers streaky bacon
1 small wheatmeal loaf

1 tablespoon wheatmeal flour
3 tablespoons chopped
  parsley

METHOD: Prepare and slice the vegetables and cook until tender in just enough water to cover, seasoning with salt and pepper. Cut off the bacon rinds and cook with the vegetables. Grill the rashers. Cut slices of bread about ¼ in thick to fit the top and bottom of a cake tin (don't use the crusts). Then cut the rest of the bread into fingers about 1 in wide and ½ in thick and the same height as your cake tin. Dip all the bread into the fat from the grilled bacon. Cover the bottom of the tin with the slice of bread and press the fingers neatly round the side, fitting them closely together.

When the vegetables are cooked, drain them (saving the liquid of course) and mash thoroughly with a fork. Make a ½ pint of parsley sauce by thickening the vegetable liquid with the flour and adding 2 tablespoons of the parsley and add it to the mash. Stir in the bacon, chopped small, and pour the mixture into the cake tin. Fit the lid of bread on top. Cover with a margarine paper. Bake in a moderate oven for about 30 minutes when the charlotte should turn out firm and crisp. Sprinkle with parsley and serve with parsley sauce or brown gravy.

## CANADIAN BAKE

**Cooking time:** 2 hours
Soak 1½ lb small white haricots for 24 hours then simmer till quite soft (about 1½ hours). Mash well and mix with 1 lb mashed potatoes and ¼ lb chopped boiled American bacon. Flavour with a dessertspoon of sage, teaspoon of sugar and some pepper. If too stiff, add a little bean water. Sprinkle sides and bottom of a greased pie-dish with breadcrumbs. Press the mixture well in, cover with a greased paper and bake in a moderate oven for about 30 minutes. Serve with cabbage and gravy. **Quantity:** 6 helpings

# CHINESE CAKE

*Cooking time:* 2½ hours    *Quantity:* 4 helpings

1½ lb haricot beans
salt and pepper
1 lb firm mashed potatoes
4 oz fat boiled bacon

2 teaspoons dried sage
1 teaspoon sugar
crisp breadcrumbs

METHOD: Soak the haricot beans for 24 hours, then simmer them for 1½ hours in enough salted water to keep them covered. Mash beans thoroughly, mix with potato, chopped bacon, sage, pepper and sugar. If the paste seems stiff, add a little bean water.

Grease a cake tin, sprinkle the sides and bottom with the breadcrumbs, press the mixture into the tin, cover with a greased paper and bake in a moderate oven for 1 hour. Serve with cabbage or Brussels sprouts and brown gravy.

# Give them Beans

Look ahead to next winter, and plant beans now. Haricots are the best kind. You'll be glad to have a store of them. They are fine food, and a clever cook can work wonders with them.

# FOOD
## FACTS

**OATMEAL DOWN IN PRICE! Thanks to the Government subsidy, loose oatmeal and rolled oats (oat flakes) cost today only 3½d per lb. or less.**

THERE are *3* good reasons why you should eat plenty of oatmeal. First, for fitness; oatmeal gives you energy, helps to protect you from illness, and makes strong bones and healthy blood. Secondly, it is home-produced. Thirdly, it is economical; you can add it to almost every kind of dish to make it go further and increase its food value. Here you will find a few suggestions.

### *Oatmeal Flour*

Mix your week's supply of flour with a quarter of the bulk of oatmeal; this will add to its flavour and make it more wholesome. You will not need quite so much fat with it either. *Remember, though, oatmeal contains fat and will keep only a few weeks.*

### *Oatmeal for soups and stews*

Thicken your soups and stews with oatmeal. It will give them a delicious flavour and greatly increase their nourishment.

### *Oatmeal Mince*

Mince 1 lb skirt of beef. Toast ¼ lb coarse oatmeal in the oven until it is crisp and nutty. Add it to the beef with salt and pepper and a grated carrot, and mix well. Moisten with water or stock. Cook in a covered casserole in a low oven for 2½–3 hours.

### *OATMEAL STUFFING*

This is particularly useful for making meat, fish or poultry go further.

Boil 3 oz coarse oatmeal in 1½ teacups water for 30 minutes. Mix well with 2 oz breadcrumbs, salt and pepper, 1 teaspoon mixed sweet herbs, 1 teaspoon chopped parsley, 1 grated onion (if you can get it) and a pinch of mace if liked. Bind with a little melted dripping if necessary.

## OATMEAL SAUSAGES

*Cooking time:* 30 minutes    *Quantity:* 4 helpings

2 tablespoons chopped onion
  or leek
½ oz cooking fat or dripping
4 oz oatmeal
½ pint water

2 teaspoons salt
¼ teaspoon pepper
2 oz chopped meat or sausage
  or bacon
browned breadcrumbs

METHOD: Fry the onion or leek in the fat or dripping until lightly browned. Work in the oatmeal, add the water gradually and bring to the boil, stirring all the time. Cook for 10–15 minutes, stirring frequently. Add the seasoning and chopped meat or sausage or bacon, mix well and spread on a plate to cool. Divide into 8 portions and roll into sausage shapes. (These may be prepared the previous day). Coat with browned crumbs and either fry in a little hot fat or grill.

## HUNT PIE

**Cooking time:** 35 minutes
**Ingredients:** ¾ to 1 pint of water (in which lentils soaked), 2 oz chopped leek, ¾ lb chopped root vegetables and cabbage, 4 oz lentils (soaked overnight), 2 oz minced meat, ½ teaspoon meat or vegetable extract, salt and pepper. **Pastry:** 2 oz oatmeal, 2 oz flour, 1 level teaspoon baking powder, water to mix, salt, 1 dessertspoon chopped mint and parsley. **Quantity:** 4 helpings

Bring water to boil, add leek, vegetables, lentils, meat extract, seasoning. Put on pan lid, cook for 10 to 15 minutes, stir to prevent sticking. Make pastry, press into a round, place on top of the meat, vegetables etc. Replace lid. Cook for a further 15–20 minutes. Lift pastry with a slice, slide meat, etc, into a dish, put pastry on top, sprinkle with chopped parsley and mint. Serve with mashed potatoes and watercress.

## PIGS IN CLOVER

For this wholesome and economical dish you will need 6 medium, well-scrubbed potatoes, 6 skinned sausages and some cabbage. With an apple corer, remove a centre core lengthways from each potato and stuff the cavity with sausage meat. Bake the potatoes in the usual way and serve on a bed of lightly chopped, cooked cabbage.

# A meaty subject...

### She needs as much meat as he does!

### Do heavy workers need more meat?

No. Daily wear and tear on the tissues is not materially affected by the kind of work done.

## STEAK AND VEGETABLE RAGOÛT

*Cooking time:* 2¼ hours   *Quantity:* 4 helpings

1 lb root vegetables in season
a little fat
1 lb stewing steak in one piece

1 breakfastcup of previously soaked dried peas or beans
salt and pepper
water

METHOD: Prepare and fry the vegetables in a little fat. Fry the meat on both sides lightly. Cut some of the meat into small pieces, leaving a good shaped piece of the meat 'solid'. Place all in a saucepan with the peas or beans, seasoning and water. Simmer gently for about 2 hours. Take out the large piece of meat and serve the rest as a stew. Part of the main piece of meat can be sliced and warmed up with hot gravy for other meals.

## QUESTIONS YOU ASK

'For only 12 points you can get a lovely big tin of American pork sausagemeat' says Mrs Merry, 'But what's the best way to use it?'

There's lots of ways to use it, but here's one of our favourites and the beautiful clean pork fat in the tin is wonderful for making pastry.

# FILLETS OF PORK

METHOD Flake ½ lb pork sausagemeat (with the outside fat removed), then mix in ½ lb mashed potatoes and one cupful of crisp breadcrumbs. Season well with pepper and salt adding a pinch of sage if liked. Then bind with a thick sauce made from the meat juices taken from the can, and made up to 1 teacup measure with vegetable stock and 1 tablespoon flour plus a little of the pork fat from the tin.

Divide into nine or ten sections, shape into finger rolls, coat in more crumbs, and fry or bake till heated through and crisp-coated, with a light greasing of pork fat for the frying pan or baking tin.

These are delicious by themselves, or served with Leek Sauce.

## MINCE SLICES

*Cooking time:* 5 to 7 minutes    *Quantity:* 4 helpings

8 oz mince (any cooked
   meat)
4 oz cooked mashed potatoes

4 oz stale breadcrumbs
salt and pepper
fat, optional

METHOD: Mix well together the mince, mashed potatoes, breadcrumbs and salt and pepper. Turn out on floured board and roll into an oblong ¼ inch thick. Cut into slices and fry in a small quantity of hot fat, or grill for 5 to 7 minutes. Serve with leek sauce, mashed potatoes and a green vegetable.

## SAVOURY MEAT ROLL

*Cooking time:* 2 hours    *Quantity:* 4 helpings

4 oz stale bread
¾ lb sausage meat
5 oz pinto beans, cooked and
   mashed
pepper and salt

1 teaspoon made mustard
1 teaspoon thyme
gravy browning
browned breadcrumbs

METHOD: Soak the stale bread in water until soft. Squeeze out the water and mash the bread with the sausage meat, the mashed beans, pepper, salt, made mustard and thyme. Add gravy browning until the mixture is a rich brown. Press very firmly into a greased 2 lb stone jam jar or tin, and steam for 2 hours. Roll in browned breadcrumbs and serve hot with brown gravy, or cold with a raw cabbage heart salad and boiled potatoes.

### *LEEK SAUCE*

**Cooking time:** 25 minutes
**Ingredients:** ½ pint milk and water, half a leek chopped, salt and pepper, 1 oz flour, pinch of herbs. **Quantity:** 4 helpings

Put some of the milk, or milk and water, leek and seasoning into a pan and allow to simmer slowly for 15 to 20 minutes. Blend the flour with the remaining cold milk, stir into the pan with the leek, etc and cook for a minute or two.

# SCOTCH EGGS

*Cooking time:* 30 minutes   *Quantity:* 2–4 helpings

2 reconstituted dried eggs     little flour
8 oz sausagemeat               crisp breadcrumbs

METHOD: Hardboil the eggs as the instruction on page 69 then coat them with the sausagemeat. Form into neat shapes, dust with flour, then roll in breadcrumbs. Bake on a greased tin in the centre of a moderate oven.

Note: If you can spare an extra reconstituted dried egg coat the sausagemeat with this (or part of the egg) before coating with the breadcrumbs. When you have any fat to spare fry the Scotch Eggs instead of baking them.

# BRISKET OF BEEF

*Cooking time:* 2¼ hours   *Quantity:* 4 helpings

1 lb mixed vegetables           salt and pepper
  (carrots, turnips, parsnips)  a knob of dripping or
¼ lb stewing steak                margarine
a level tablespoon national     potatoes
  flour or oatmeal

METHOD: Wash and cut up vegetables. Cut meat into small pieces and dip in flour or oatmeal, salt and pepper mixed together. Heat fat in a large saucepan, brown meat on both sides, take it out, and put in layer of vegetables. Put back the meat, cover with the rest of the vegetables, and add boiling water to cover. Put on pan lid, simmer for 2 hours. Put in scrubbed potatoes half an hour before serving.

# BAKED STEAK WITH SLICED POTATOES

METHOD: Scrub and cut into ½ in thick slices, 2 lb potatoes. Parboil 10 minutes in salted water. Put half into a greased baking tin with a little sliced onion. Add 1 lb piece of stewing steak, cut thick, on top of this put a 'blanket' of sausage-meat, shaped to fit the steak. Cover with the rest of the potato slices. Thicken ½ pint of the potato liquid with a teaspoon each of gravy powder and flour; pour it on. Bake in a moderate oven 1 to 1½ hours. When half-cooked, brush the top potatoes with dripping and sprinkle with salt.

## MEAT ROLL

First of all soak a large slice of bread in milk. Now mix together ¼ lb minced veal, ¼ lb minced beef, ¼ lb sausage meat and a few minced bacon pieces. Add to them a small onion or one or two spring onions (if you can get them) sliced finely, a grated raw potato and salt and pepper to taste. Squeeze the milk out of the slice of bread and mash the bread into the meat mixture. If you can spare it, bind the mixture with a small beaten egg; otherwise use the milk in which the bread was soaked. If necessary, add enough white breadcrumbs to make the mixture firm enough to shape into a roll. Sprinkle thickly with browned breadcrumbs or medium oatmeal that has been toasted in the oven, put into a greased baking tin, cover with butter or margarine paper and bake in a good oven for an hour.

This roll can be served hot or cold. It looks most attractive when decorated with strips of anchovy or some sliced, cooked carrot sprinkled with a little chopped parsley.

## SPICED BEEF

3 to 4 lb boneless brisket or rolled thin flank. Mix together 1 teaspoonful each sugar, made mustard, salt, 2 tablespoonfuls vinegar and rub well into the meat, all over with back of a wooden spoon. Leave meat in dish, with 2 bayleaves, 4 cloves, ½ teaspoon peppercorns, for about 12 hours. Turn occasionally. Put the meat, with all its juices and spices into a pan, add 2 small onions (home pickled ones do nicely) sliced, and ½ lb sliced carrots and small bunch parsley. Just cover with water, put on lid and simmer slowly for 3 hours. The meat may be served hot, with the liquid thickened as gravy, or placed between two plates with a weight on top and left to get cold, the thickened liquid served as a cold sauce. If the oven is on, the meat can be cooked in a casserole; 4 hours at a very low heat.

# LANCASHIRE HOT POT

*Cooking time:* 2½ to 4 hours    *Quantity:* 6 helpings

¾ lb meat
2 carrots, sliced
1 onion or leek, if possible, sliced
3 lb potatoes, peeled and sliced

1 dessertspoon fat from the meat or dripping
½ pint vegetable stock
1 dessertspoon flour
pepper and salt

METHOD: Cut up meat into small pieces and place in a fireproof dish or casserole. Add sliced carrots and onion or leek, and pepper and salt. Add half the potatoes. Instead of slicing potatoes crack off lumps with a knife. Place the fat from the meat or the dripping on top. Put in a moderate oven with lid on for half an hour. Take out, add stock, blend 1 dessertspoon flour in a little water, pour into casserole. Add remainder of potatoes and sprinkle with salt and pepper. Cook in a moderate oven. Remove the lid for the last 20 minutes and cook until the potatoes are brown.

# MACARONI AND BACON DISH

*Cooking time:* 30 minutes    *Quantity:* 4 helpings

½ oz dripping or other fat
2 oz leek or onion, peeled and chopped
2 oz bacon, chopped
1 pint stock or water

6 oz macaroni
1 teaspoon salt
pinch pepper
watercress

METHOD: Melt the dripping or fat in a pan and fry the leek or onion and bacon until lightly browned. Add the stock or water and when boiling, add the macaroni and seasoning. Cook for about 20 minutes or until the macaroni is tender and the water is absorbed. Serve very hot garnished with watercress.

# PORK PASTIES

METHOD: Chop 1 leek. Place in a saucepan with ½ teaspoon fat cook slowly for ten minutes. Add 1 grated carrot, 6 oz sausagemeat, ½ teacup breadcrumbs and 1 dessertspoon gravy powder, with enough vegetable liquor to loosen. Mix well, then cook slowly for 10 minutes. Season, cool and use as a filling for pasties.

# STEAK AND POTATO PIE

*Cooking time:* 25 minutes    *Quantity:* 4 helpings

8 oz onions, sliced thinly
½ oz cooking fat or dripping
3 tablespoons flour
¼ pint water
1 tin stewed steak (16 oz size)

1 tin peas (8 oz size)
1 teaspoon salt
¼ teaspoon pepper
2 lb potatoes, cooked and
    mashed

METHOD: Fry the onions gently in the fat or dripping until tender; work in the flour. Add the water gradually and bring to the boil, stirring all the time; boil for 5 minutes. Add the steak, peas and seasoning and mix well. Place the mixture in a pie dish, cover with the mashed potato and brown under the grill or in a hot oven.

# BEEF OLIVE PIE

*Cooking time:* 1¾ hours    *Quantity:* 4 helpings

STUFFING
6 oz stale bread, soaked in
    water and then squeezed
    dry
2 tablespoons chopped suet
    or ¾ oz fat, melted
2 tablespoons chopped
    parsley
1 tablespoon chopped mixed
    herbs or 1 teaspoon dried
    herbs
1 teaspoon salt
¼ teaspoon pepper
4 tablespoons chopped onion

2 teaspoons lemon juice or
    lemon squash
FILLING AND TOPPING
1 lb stewing steak
½ oz dripping
¾ oz flour
¾ pint water or stock
1 teaspoon salt
pinch pepper
gravy browning
shortcrust or potato or
    oatmeal pastry made with 6
    oz flour, etc. see pages 52–
    53

METHOD: Mix the ingredients for the stuffing well together. Cut the meat into 8 thin slices about 3 by 4 inches. Spread a little stuffing on each slice of meat and roll up neatly. Make the remainder of the stuffing into about 8 small balls. Pack the olives and balls in a pie dish. Melt the dripping in a saucepan, add the flour and cook for a few minutes until brown. Add the water or stock, bring to the boil, stirring all the time and boil gently for 5 minutes. Season and colour with gravy browning. Pour the gravy into the pie dish. Roll out the pastry and cover the dish. Bake in the centre of a moderate oven for 1½ hours.

### RECIPE of the WEEK

### BAKED CARROT
### AND ONION PIE

**Cooking time:** 45 minutes
**Ingredients:** 1½ lb carrots, sliced, 6 oz turnips, sliced, 6 oz onion or leek, sliced, 2 oz bacon, chopped, 1 teaspoon salt, ¾ pint milk and vegetable stock, see method, 4½ tablespoons flour, pinch pepper, pinch ground nutmeg, 2 slices bread (cut 1 inch thick from a 2 lb loaf), diced, 2 tablespoons melted dripping or margarine. **Quantity:** 4 helpings

Boil the vegetables and bacon in a little salted water until tender. Strain the vegetables and bacon; keep the liquid for the sauce then measure out enough milk to give a total of ¾ pint of liquid. Place the cooked vegetables in a pie dish. Blend the flour with a little of the liquid, bring the rest of the liquid to the boil and pour on to the blended flour. Return to the saucepan, stir until it boils and boil gently for 5 minutes. Add the seasoning, pour the sauce over the vegetables in the dish. Cover with the bread and spoon the melted dripping or margarine over the top. Bake in a hot oven for 15–20 minutes until brown and crisp on top.

# The Butcher says..

'That's right, Mrs. Smith. We're getting a seventh of our meat now in corned beef—twopence in the 1s. 2d. as you might say. Lord Woolton's watching his stocks—he likes to be sure he's got a bit in hand. I don't mind telling you I was rather afraid the whole ration would be cut down. It's lucky for everyone there is this corned beef to help out with. Cold or hot, you can dish it up in a dozen different ways—and very tasty, too. No, Mrs. Smith, I don't want any points coupons, it's all part of the meat ration.'

## CORNED BEEF MOULD

**Preparation time:** 15 minutes
**Ingredients:** 2 to 4 oz corned beef, 4 oz soaked bread, 6 oz mashed carrot, mock horse-radish (4 tablespoons shredded swede, 1½ teaspoons mustard, 1½ tablespoons vinegar), chopped parsley, pepper and salt. **Quantity:** 4 helpings

Mix all the ingredients together. Press into basin and leave with plate and weight on top for about 4 hours. Turn out, cut into slices and serve with potato salad and watercress.

## AMERICAN MINCE

*Cooking time:* 30–35 minutes    *Quantity:* 4 helpings

6 oz corned beef, minced or finely chopped
8 oz cooked pearl barley
½ pint tomato pulp or white sauce, see page 69
1 teaspoon salt

¼ teaspoon pepper
1 oz cheese, grated
1 oz breadcrumbs
½ oz dripping or margarine
2 tomatoes (if available)

METHOD: Place the beef, barley, tomato pulp or white sauce, seasoning, cheese and breadcrumbs in layers in a greased pie dish. Finish with a layer of cheese and dot with the dripping or margarine. Bake in a moderate oven for 25 minutes. Slice the whole tomatoes and spread over the top. Return to the oven for a further 5–10 minutes.

## AMERICAN CORNED BEEF HASH

**Cooking time:** 50 minutes. Mix together 1 breakfastcup of chopped corned beef with the same quantity of diced raw potatoes and season with pepper. Put into a frying pan ½ teacup of vegetable water and a teaspoon or two of cooking fat or dripping. When the pan is hot put in the corned beef and potatoes, spreading them evenly. Dot with another teaspoon or two of fat over the top. Place a plate over the pan and cook quite slowly for about 45 minutes. A thick delicious crust will form on the bottom. Fold across and serve on a hot dish with cooked green vegetables. Pickled beetroot or cabbage is excellent with this dish.
NOTE: The pancake on page 36 is similar to this but uses cooked potatoes.

# CORNED BEEF WITH CABBAGE

*Cooking time:* 10–15 minutes    *Quantity:* 4 helpings

½ oz cooking fat
1 leek, sliced
1 lb corned beef, cut into
    small pieces
1 lb cooked potatoes, cut into
    small pieces

1 dessertspoon flour
½ small cup vegetable water
little made mustard, optional
1 cabbage, shredded
salt

METHOD: Heat the fat in a stout saucepan, add the leek and fry lightly. Put in the corned beef and potatoes, sprinkle with the flour and add the vegetable water with the mustard (if liked). Stir all together until very hot. Meanwhile cook the cabbage in a very little salted water with the lid on the pan. Drain and serve on a hot dish, topped with the meat mixture.

# HARICOT BEEF

*Cooking time:* 1 hour 45 minutes    *Quantity:* 4 helpings

8 oz haricot beans
1 lb corned beef, sliced
1 small cabbage, finely
    shredded (if available)
1 leek, chopped
few peppercorns

little salt
1 dessertspoon mustard
    powder
1 tablespoon gravy
    thickening
½ pint vegetable stock

METHOD: Soak the beans in water to cover for 24 hours then cook for 1 hour and strain. Put the beans, corned beef, cabbage and leek in layers in a dish, with the peppercorns and salt sprinkled between. Add the mustard and gravy thickening with the stock. Cover and cook in a slow oven for 45 minutes.

# CORNED BEEF RISSOLES

*Cooking time:* 20 minutes    *Quantity:* 2–3 helpings

4 oz corned beef
½ lb mashed potatoes
½ lb cooked mixed vegetables
4 oz wheatmeal breadcrumbs

seasoning
pinch mixed herbs
4 tablespoons brown sauce or
    vegetable water

METHOD: Flake the corned beef and mix with the mashed cooked vegetables and breadcrumbs. Season and add the mixed herbs. Bind the mixture with sauce or vegetable water, form into shapes. Bake in a quick oven.

# Let's talk about WARMING FOOD

*It isn't only hot meals that warm; although, of course, they are very comforting. There are foods that stoke your inner fires and, happily, three of the chief of them are cheap and easy to get. They are potatoes, oatmeal (soon to become more plentiful), national wheatmeal bread. These are also important health-protectors. Carrots, too, have some warmth-giving value, and they protect against colds and chills. Carrots also help you to see in the dark.*

## CORNED BEEF FRITTERS

*Cooking time:* 10 minutes   *Quantity:* 4 helpings

2 oz self-raising or plain flour
pinch salt
1 egg yolk or $\frac{1}{2}$ reconstituted
   egg
$\frac{1}{2}$ gill milk or milk and water
pinch dried mixed herbs

1 teaspoon grated onion
1 teaspoon chopped parsley
6 oz corned beef, finely
   flaked
1 oz clarified dripping or
   cooking fat

METHOD: Blend the flour with the salt, egg and milk or milk and water. Beat until smooth batter then add the herbs, onion, parsley and corned beef. Melt the dripping or fat in a frying pan and when really hot drop in spoonfuls of the batter mixture. Fry quickly on either side until crisp and brown. Serve as soon as possible after cooking.

## SAGE AND MINCE PUDDING

**Cooking time:** $1\frac{1}{2}$ hours **Ingredients:** Mix together 8 oz self-raising flour (or plain flour with 2 teaspoons baking powder), 1 lb grated raw carrots, 3 oz minced stewing steak, 2 tablespoons packet sage and onion stuffing, 1 finely chopped onion, 2 oz melted dripping or fat and seasoning to taste. This should form a stiff dough, but if too dry a little water may be added.

Grease a 2 pint basin, put in the mixture. Cover with a cloth or margarine papers and steam or boil for $1\frac{1}{2}$ hours. Serve with green vegetables and a good gravy. **Quantity:** 4 helpings

## POTATO AND CORNED BEEF PANCAKE

When you are offered corned beef instead of your cut of meat, do you know how to make it into a substantial dish? The great point is to keep it moist and utilise its fat to the best advantage. Here is a suggestion from America.

Mix lightly 1 breakfastcup of chopped corned beef with the same quantity of diced cooked potatoes, and season with pepper and salt. Pour into a pan $\frac{3}{4}$ to 1 gill milk or household stock and a teaspoon or so of clarified fat or dripping. When warmed turn in the meat and potatoes, spreading them evenly. Flick another two teaspoons of fat over the top. Place a plate over the pan and allow the pancake to cook quite slowly for about half an hour. A thick delicious crust will form on the bottom. Fold the pancake across and serve it up on a hot dish with sprouts or any other cooked green vegetable.

# SAUSAGES AND BEANS

*Cooking time:* 15–20 minutes    *Quantity:* 4 helpings

1 tin sausages (16 oz size)
1 tin beans in tomato sauce
  (16 oz size)
2 teaspoons mustard powder

2 teaspoons sugar
1 tablespoon bottled sauce*
1 tablespoon vinegar
1 lb potato, mashed

METHOD: Remove and keep the fat from around the tinned sausages; slice the sausages. Mix together the beans, mustard, sugar, sauce and vinegar and place in a shallow ovenproof dish. Cover with the sliced sausages and surround with mashed potato. Dot the potato with a little of the sausage fat and bake in a hot oven for 15–20 minutes or until brown.

*Use Worcester sauce or one similar in flavour.

# CORNED BEEF HASH

METHOD: Peel and grate 2 medium onions, dice 8 oz corned beef and 8 oz cooked potatoes, slice 8 oz tomatoes. Melt ½ oz dripping in a strong frying pan. Add the onions and fry gently until soft. Add the corned beef and potatoes, cook for several minutes, then add the tomatoes and a little seasoning. Cover the pan with a plate and cook very slowly for 15 minutes.

# CURRIED CORNED BEEF BALLS

*Cooking time:* 10 minutes    *Quantity:* 4 helpings

½ oz dripping or fat
1 tablespoon grated onion
1 teaspoon curry powder
6 oz corned beef, finely diced

½ teacup soft breadcrumbs
½ teaspoon Worcester sauce
little milk
½ teacup crisp breadcrumbs

METHOD: Heat the dripping or fat and fry the onion for 5 minutes. Stir in the curry powder, cook for 2 minutes with the onion, stirring well, then add the corned beef, soft breadcrumbs and Worcester sauce. Press the mixture into small balls, brush with the milk then roll in the crisp breadcrumbs. Either serve cold or heat under the grill, or in the oven if this is in use.

**My packed lunches are so monotonous. Can you suggest something for a change?**

We think you will like Bacon Turnovers.

### BACON TURNOVERS (2)

Grill 4 oz fat bacon rashers until the fat is brown and well frizzled. Pour off the liquid fat and set aside to get cold and congealed. When quite cold treat as lard. Rub it into 8 oz self-raising flour (or plain flour with 2 teaspoons baking powder). Season with pepper. Mix to a soft dough with water. Roll out and cut into rounds. Finely dice 8 oz cooked mixed vegetables, mince the grilled bacon, mix with the vegetables. Moisten with a little gravy. Put a spoonful of the mixture into the centre of each round, fold over, seal the edges, brush  with the remains of the fat and bake in a moderately hot oven for 25–30 minutes or until a golden appetising brown. These turnovers are delicious, cold or hot. See also page 26.

FOOD FACTS

# Vegetable Dishes

Home-grown vegetables were a very important part of our diet. We were encouraged to eat plenty of potatoes in place of bread, which used imported wheat, and for the valuable vitamins they contain. Carrots, parsnips and swedes were all used in a variety of recipes and green vegetables were very important and great emphasis was placed on cooking them correctly.

### RECIPE of the WEEK

#### *CARROT-CAP SALAD*

Every woman who values her good complexion should have this salad regularly.

Cook two or three good sized potatoes in their skins. When tender, strain without drying off to avoid making them floury. Slice and dice neatly; then dress in vinaigrette dressing (two parts of salad oil to one of vinegar, pepper and salt to taste) while they are still hot. Pile in a salad bowl lined with a few shredded lettuce leaves or watercress. Sprinkle with a little chopped chives or rings of spring onion and pile high with grated carrot. To make a more substantial dish, add one or two boned sardines or fillets of smoked herring.

# The Greengrocer says ..

What about some nice carrots this morning? There's a grand crop this year—thanks to the farmers. They do say that for keeping illness at a distance the carrot's a real blessing to all of us, young and old alike. Worth remembering this time of year. And they taste a treat, in my opinion, if you cook 'em cleverly and dish 'em nicely—my missus knows a dozen different ways. Even put them into puddings you can—and very good puddings they make too: you'd be surprised.

# POTATO PANCAKE

*Cooking time:* 10–15 minutes     *Quantity:* 4 helpings

1 lb cooked potatoes
¼ lb sausage meat
1 dessertspoon mint and
    parsley chopped together

1 dessertspoon mixed herbs
salt and pepper
milk
½ oz dripping

METHOD: Mash the potato with the sausage meat, add herbs, seasoning and milk to make a soft mixture. Heat dripping and spread potato mixture to cover the bottom of the pan. Fry until brown and crisp.

# SCALLOPED POTATOES (1)

*Cooking time:* ¾ hour     *Quantity:* 4 helpings

2 lb potatoes
2 tablespoons flour
1 pint milk and water or
    household milk

4–6 oz grated cheese
salt and pepper
2 tablespoons coarsely
    chopped parsley

METHOD: Scrape potatoes and cut into thin slices, blend flour with the milk, arrange potatoes in layers in a pie-dish, sprinkling each layer thickly with cheese, season with salt and pepper, moisten with milk. Finish with a layer of cheese, pour over the remaining milk and cover with a lid or greased paper. Bake in a moderate oven for ¾ hour. Sprinkle with 2 tablespoons of chopped parsley, serve with green vegetables or salad.

### *The Radio Doctor Says:*

'You may have heard what the greengrocer said when a critical customer asked if his vegetables contained vitamins. "If they do," he said, "they can easily be washed off." Well, they *can't* be washed off, but they *can* be cooked out, and that's a form of wastage.'

### *Song of Potato Pete*

Potatoes new, potatoes old
Potato (in a salad) cold
Potatoes baked or mashed or
    fried
Potatoes whole, potato pied
Enjoy them all, including chips
Remembering spuds don't come
    in ships!

# POTATO JANE

### *BAKED POTATOES*

When you have the oven on for baking day pop in some potatoes too. Bake in a moderate oven for 45 minutes. When they break under gentle pressure they are ready.

*Cooking time:* 45 minutes to 1 hour     *Quantity:* 4 helpings

1½ lb potatoes
½ leek, chopped
2 oz breadcrumbs

3 oz cheese, grated
salt and pepper
½–¾ pint of milk

METHOD: Put a layer of sliced potatoes in a fire-proof dish. Sprinkle with some of the leek, crumbs, cheese and seasoning. Fill dish with alternate layers, finishing with a layer of cheese and crumbs. Pour over the milk and bake in a moderate oven for 45 minutes, or steam in a basin for 1 hour. Serve with a raw vegetable salad.

# POTATO FINGERS

METHOD: Mix 1 oz flour with ½ lb mashed potato, season with salt and pepper. Bind, if necessary, with a little milk, or reconstituted dried egg. Shape into fingers, glaze with egg or milk, bake in a hot oven for about 10 minutes until brown and crisp.

# POTATO FLODDIES

These are real energy givers.

Scrub 2 potatoes and grate with a coarse grater over a bowl. Then add sufficient flour to form a batter. Season with salt and pepper. Melt a little dripping and make very hot in a frying pan. Drop the mixture into it. When brown on one side, turn and brown on the other. Serve with a little jam if you want it as a sweet dish. If you want it as a savoury, add a pinch of mixed herbs and a dash of cayenne pepper.

## POTATO BASKET

Scrub 1 lb potatoes and boil gently in a very little water. When they are nearly cooked, drain off the liquid reserving it for stock. Let them finish cooking in their own steam by covering them closely with a folded cloth under the lid and standing the saucepan at the side of the stove until they are floury. Peel and mash well. Add a beaten egg and mash again. Grease a cake tin and coat it with browned breadcrumbs. Press in the mashed potatoes to form a thick lining to the tin. Bake in a hot oven for about 10 minutes. Meanwhile dice 1 lb carrots, having cooked them for 15 minutes, and mix them with a sauce made from 1 oz dripping, 1 oz oatmeal and ½ pint milk or stock, and salt and pepper to taste. When the potato basket is cooked turn it out and fill it with the hot carrot mixture. Heat in the oven for a few minutes and serve piping hot. Enough for 4.

## POTATO CARROT PANCAKE

Well-seasoned mashed potato combined with cooked carrot makes a wholesome and savoury tasting pancake. Whip the mashed potato to a loose creamy consistency. Season well with pepper and salt and add some diced cooked carrots. Pan-fried slowly in a very little fat it develops a deliciously crisp crust, but it can be baked to a good brown in the oven if preferred.

# CHAMP

METHOD: Cook 2 lb potatoes allowing them to steam off and dry in the usual way. Cook 1 lb green vegetables in a very little water with the lid on the pan. If cabbage is chosen, shred it finely with a knife before cooking. Mash the potatoes with 1 teacup hot milk, beating well until quite smooth, then add the cooked vegetable and season with salt and pepper. Serve piping hot on hot plates with a pat of margarine on each portion

# SCALLOPED POTATOES (2)

METHOD: Scrub and scrape 1 lb potatoes, then cut them into fairly thin slices. Arrange in layers in a pie-dish or casserole, sprinkling each layer with flour seasoned with salt and pepper, and sliced spring onion. Pour over ½ pint milk, sprinkle the top with breadcrumbs and bake in a moderate oven for about one hour, or cook in a frying-pan covered with a plate for ½ to ¾ hour over low heat.

# Home-guards of health

Of course you don't want to be a food crank. But it is useful to know that there are certain homely foods that can do a marvellous job of protecting you and your family against illness.

Enlist these 'home guards' in your diet, and keep them regularly on duty!

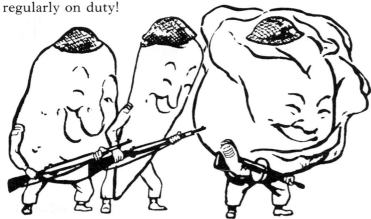

*Here are a few simple exercises:*

**1** Serve a good big helping of any green vegetables every day. Greens should be cooked quickly; served at once; keeping hot or warming up lessens their value.

**2** Serve, also, a good portion of root vegetables. Be sure that carrots are served several times a week. When cooking potatoes, boil or steam them in their skins for utmost health value.

**3** Give something raw and green every day. Sometimes it may be a salad of shredded cabbage heart or other tender greenstuff; or watercress or mustard-and-cress for tea; or plenty of chopped parsley in a sauce, on potatoes, or in a salad.

## PARSLEY POTATO CAKES

METHOD: Boil an extra pound of potatoes the day before you want to make the cakes. Mash these while hot, with a little milk. Season with salt and pepper.

Next day add a tablespoonful or two of chopped parsley and shape the mixture into little cakes. Cover these with brown breadcrumbs, and pan-fry in a little hot fat, or bake in the oven. The mixture should not be made wet. Serves 4 people.

*My skin is not as good as it used to be; I think it's lack of fruit.*

It's the Vitamin C in the fruit that is so good for your skin—and for your health. But you get exactly the same vitamin in vegetables. Remember, however, that you must have *extra* vegetable to make up for the missing fruit. Everyone needs at least 1,000 units of Vitamin C every day. Here is a brief list to guide you.

|  |  | Vitamin C Units |
|---|---|---|
| | *cooked* | |
| Spinach | 4 oz | 700 |
| Broccoli | ,, | 600 |
| Turnip Tops | ,, | 480 |
| Cabbage | ,, | 300 |
| Swedes | ,, | 260 |
| Potatoes | ,, | 240 |
| | *raw* | |
| Watercress | ½ oz | 150 |
| Spinach | ,, | 150 |
| Cabbage | ,, | 100 |
| Parsley | ,, | 70 |

*Note how much richer in Vitamin C are raw vegetables*

Then there are carrots. Although not a good source of Vitamin C, carrots provide other elements which clear the skin and improve its texture. A good plan therefore—and a plan for everyone who values health—is to have a raw vegetable salad (based on shredded cabbage heart or other green stuff, watercress and grated carrot); or cooked carrots, or an extra helping of green vegetables *as well as* your usual vegetables, every day.

# MARROW SURPRISE

*Cooking time:* 20 minutes   *Quantity:* 4 helpings

1 medium marrow
8 oz carrots, sliced
1 cup runner beans, sliced
salt
CHEESE SAUCE
1 oz margarine

2 tablespoons flour
½ pint household milk and
  vegetable stock
4 oz cheese, grated
salt and pepper

METHOD: Peel the marrow, unless garden fresh, remove the seeds and cut into large pieces. Put the carrots and beans in a saucepan of boiling salted water. Cover and cook until almost tender. Add the marrow, cook for 5 minutes. Serve with Cheese Sauce.

Melt the margarine in a saucepan, blend in the flour, cook for a few minutes, add the milk and vegetable stock to make a thick sauce, stir until smooth, add the grated cheese and seasoning. Pour the sauce over the marrow, carrots and beans. Brown under the grill. Serve with potatoes.

## Save those Orange Rinds!

Here's a new way to make use of orange peel. Grate it and mix a little with mashed potatoes. The potatoes will turn an exciting pink colour.

## The Radio Doctor Says:

'For the school child the potato should appear in every midday dinner. It gives energy. The large amounts one eats these days makes them a substantial source of Vitamin C. Potatoes are best steamed or baked in their jackets.

Let the plan be potatoes every day, one or two green vegetables most days, a yellow vegetable, particularly carrot—two or three times a week, and some raw green salad vegetable on most days.

## *PARSNIP CROQUETTES*

Mash 1 lb cooked parsnips with a fork until creamy. Make a thick sauce by melting 1 oz margarine in a saucepan, mixing in smoothly 1 oz flour, cooking together for a minute or two and then adding one small teacup water or vegetable stock in which one teaspoon of vegetable extract has been dissolved. Add 2 teaspoons breadcrumbs and cook for 5 minutes. Add this sauce to the parsnips, and salt and pepper to taste. When cold, divide into 10 or 12 parts and form into croquettes. Roll in browned crumbs or toasted oatmeal. Fry in a very little fat until golden brown on both sides; or form into a large roll, cover well with crumbs and bake in moderate oven for 20 to 30 minutes. Serve hot with gravy, or cold with salad.

# CHEESE BEANS

*Cooking time:* 2 hours   *Quantity:* 4 helpings

½ lb dried beans (soaked
  overnight)
2 oz grated cheese
1 tablespoon vinegar
2 teaspoons Worcester sauce

½ teaspoon made mustard
a good pinch of pepper and
  salt
1 to 2 tablespoons parsley
  and mint, chopped
  together

METHOD: Cook the beans without salt in the water in which they soaked. When the beans are tender, strain and keep two tablespoonfuls of bean water. Add all the other ingredients except herbs to this bean water and cook until cheese is melted. Toss the beans in the cheese sauce, put into a hot dish and sprinkle with chopped parsley and mint. Serve with a green vegetable and potatoes boiled in their skins.

To make Bean Roll, take ½ lb of beans, soak, cook and mash, add the other ingredients as above. Shape into a roll and serve with salad and a little home-made mayonnaise or use as a sandwich filling.

# Why is a potato like a lump of sugar?

Because a potato and a lump of sugar are both turned by your digestive system into exactly the same thing — glucose—fuel which your body 'burns' to give you energy and warmth.

Potatoes contain two important health-protecting vitamins and a little body-building material of very good quality.

## SCALLOPED VEGETABLES WITH BACON

*Cooking time:* 30 minutes   *Quantity:* 4 helpings

½ cabbage
3 or 4 carrots
1 leek
4 potatoes or any other
   vegetable
1 oz margarine

2 tablespoons national flour
   or 1 tablespoon fine
   oatmeal
2 or 3 slices bacon
browned bread crumbs

METHOD: Cook vegetables in a pint of water in a closely covered pan. Make thin white sauce with margarine, flour or oatmeal and vegetable water. Arrange vegetables in a fireproof dish, pour sauce over, lay bacon on top, sprinkle with breadcrumbs and crisp under grill.

Cheer up end-of-season potatoes. Boil peeled potatoes in fast boiling salted water with a teaspoonful of vinegar. Mash and cover with chopped parsley and mint or chopped watercress, or chopped carrot tops, or beat in raw vegetables or meat extract, or sprinkle with toasted oatmeal or browned crumbs.

Bake in jackets, split open, cover with grated cheese, return to the oven to brown (or grill for 1–2 minutes).

Cook large potatoes in their skins in boiling salted water. When they show signs of cracking, add cup of cold water; this will drive heat to centre of the potato and hasten cooking.

### RECIPE of the WEEK

#### WARTIME CHAMP

Here is a wartime version of the old Irish dish, Champ. Scrub and slice 1 lb potatoes and 1 lb carrots. Put in a saucepan with a teacupful of hot salted water and add a small cabbage finely shredded. Cover with the lid, cook steadily, giving an occasional shake until tender (about 15 minutes). The water should have just boiled away by then. Add a small teacupful of hot milk and mash well with a dash of pepper and more salt if necessary. Serve at once with a pat of margarine to each helping.

# How to keep the Vitamins in the Vegetables

Green vegetables must be cooked as quickly as possible, for slow cooking destroys their valuable vitamins. So always shred them with a knife. Spinach doesn't need shredding as it cooks so quickly.

Never soak green vegetables for a long time. Overlong soaking wastes valuable mineral salts. Just wash the greens thoroughly. But tight-hearted cabbage may be left in salted water for not more than half an hour.

If the outside leaves are too tough to serve, save them for soup. *The dark green leaves have more food value than the centre.*

In cooking green vegetables, use only just enough water to keep the pan from burning—usually a teacupful will do. Spinach needs no added water. Heat the water in the pan before you put in the shredded greens. Next sprinkle with a very little salt. *Now put the lid on the pan*—the greens are going to be 'steam-boiled,' and if it escapes the pan may go dry.

Cook steadily for about 10 to 15 minutes, shaking the pan occasionally. Drain off any liquid from the pan and save it for soup. If you can spare a teaspoon of margarine, add it to the greens and toss well before serving.

## TRY THESE FOR A CHANGE

**CABBAGE.** All sorts of additions may be made to steam-boiled cabbage. A few bacon rinds chopped small; or a few teaspoons of vinegar and a sprinkle of nutmeg or a shake of caraway seeds, and you have something novel and nice.

**TOPS.** Broccoli tops, turnip tops, and beetroot tops are all excellent if cooked as described above.

**RUNNER BEANS.** *Young* runner beans should be cooked whole, with just the tops and tails removed.

As a change from slicing the beans, try breaking them with the fingers into inch lengths. This saves a great deal of time and the flavour is better. Steam the broken beans or boil them in a very little salted water until tender (10 to 15 minutes). A teaspoon of fat added to the water makes them glisten and improves the taste.

Cold cooked runner beans are delicious in a salad. Mix a breakfastcup of cooked beans, ready chopped, with a breakfastcup of sliced cooked potatoes and a large lettuce neatly shredded. Decorate with sliced tomatoes or beetroot, nasturtium leaves or parsley.

At the end of the season let the older beans mature on the plant, shell them and dry the inside beans for winter use as haricots.

P's  for Protection Potatoes afford;
O's  for the Ounces of Energy stored;
T's  for Tasty, and Vitamins rich in;
A's  for the Art to be learnt in the Kitchen.
T's  for Transport we need not demand;
O's  for old England's Own Food from the Land;
E's  for the Energy eaten by you;
S's  for the Spuds which will carry us through!

Potatoes help to protect you from illness. Potatoes give you warmth and energy. Potatoes are cheap and home-produced. So why stop at serving them *once* a day? Have them twice, or even three times—for breakfast, dinner and supper.

# STUFFED MARROW

*Cooking time:* 50 minutes    *Quantity:* 4 helpings

stuffing as in Stuffed
  Cabbage below
1 medium marrow

salt
½ oz cooking fat, melted

METHOD: Peel the marrow and cut lengthways; remove the seeds. Cook in boiling salted water for 5 minutes, drain well. Put the two halves into a tin and fill with the stuffing. Brush with the melted fat. Cover the tin with a lid or greased greaseproof paper. Bake for 45 minutes in a moderate oven. Serve with brown gravy.

# STUFFED CABBAGE

*Cooking time:* 1 hour 5 minutes    *Quantity:* 4 helpings

1 medium cabbage
STUFFING
8 oz sausagemeat
1 onion, grated
4 oz soft breadcrumbs

1 tablespoon chopped parsley
pinch mixed herbs
1 teaspoon Worcester sauce
salt and pepper

METHOD: Put the whole cabbage into boiling salted water and boil for 5 minutes. Remove; retain ½ teacup of the liquid and carefully fold back the leaves, which will by now have softened. Mix all the stuffing ingredients together and put a little of the mixture between the leaves, folding them back as they are filled. Put into a casserole, adding ½ teacup of the vegetable water and covering first with a well greased paper and then the lid. Bake for 1 hour in a moderate oven. To serve, open out the leaves again.

## POTATO CHEESE

**Cooking time:** 25 minutes **Ingredients:** 2 lb old or new potatoes, salt and pepper, 6–8 oz cheese, grated, 2 tablespoons chopped parsley, 2 oz oatmeal. **Quantity:** 4 helpings

Peel or scrub potatoes, cut into small pieces and cook in a small quantity of boiling salted water until soft. Strain and mash in the pan. Mix in half the grated cheese, all the parsley, salt and pepper, turn the mixture into a shallow dish or baking tin, sprinkle the rest of the grated cheese and all the oatmeal over the surface. Put in a moderately hot oven or under a grill to brown. Serve with cabbage (cooked or shredded raw), or spinach.

### Bedtime Story

Once upon a time there were five housewives. Their names were Lady Peel-potatoes, the Hon. Mrs. Waste-fuel, Miss Pour-the-vegetable-water-down-the-sink, Mrs. Don't-like-uncooked-vegetables, and Mrs. Won't-eat-carrots. Don't let one of them put a nose in your kitchen.

## SAVOURY ONIONS

*Cooking time:* 1¼ hours   *Quantity:* 4 helpings

4 medium onions
salt and pepper
½ teacup soft breadcrumbs
1 teaspoon chopped sage

2 oz cheese, grated
1 egg or 1 reconstituted egg
½ oz margarine, melted

METHOD: Peel the onions, put into boiling salted water and cook steadily for 30 minutes. Lift the onions out of the liquid, save ½ teacup of this. Remove the centres of the onions, chop this finely and blend with the breadcrumbs, sage, cheese and egg. Season the mixture and fill the onion cases then put these into a casserole with the ½ teacup of onion stock. Brush the onions with the melted margarine. Cover the casserole and bake for 45 minutes in the centre of a moderately hot oven.

## BELTED LEEKS

*Cooking time:* 15 minutes   *Quantity:* 4 helpings

1 lb small leeks
salt and pepper

½ pint white sauce, see page 69
2 oz bacon rashers

METHOD: Prepare the leeks, leave whole and cook in boiling salted water until tender. Drain well, save some of the liquid to make the sauce. Put the leeks in a heated dish and top with the sauce. Grill the bacon, cut into narrow strips. Arrange as 'belts' over the leeks.

## TURNIP TOP SALAD

*Preparation time:* 15 minutes   *Quantity:* 4 helpings

4 oz turnip tops
4 oz white cabbage heart
2 oz raw beetroot

2 oz raw carrots
salad dressing
watercress for garnishing

METHOD: Grate or shred all the vegetables separately and arrange attractively on a large dish. Sprinkle with salad dressing and decorate with watercress. Make the salad dressing by adding vinegar, a little mustard, pepper and salt to a white sauce.

How about his Fruit Juice, Mother? Remember he's entitled to it under the new scheme.

# PATHFINDER PUDDING

*Cooking time:* 2 hours    *Quantity:* 4–6 helpings

SUET PASTRY
6 oz national flour
½ teaspoon salt
¾ teaspoon baking powder
1 oz suet, chopped or grated
1½ oz uncooked potato,
    shredded
water

FILLING
2 lb cooked parsnips, diced
4 oz cheese, grated
1 uncooked leek, sliced
½ teaspoon mustard powder
pepper
1 teaspoon salt

METHOD: Mix the flour, salt and baking powder, add the suet, potato and water to bind. Roll out three-quarters of the pastry to line a 2 pint greased basin. Mix the parsnips, cheese, leek, mustard, pepper and salt together. Put into the lined basin. Roll out the remaining quarter of pastry to form a lid. Put this on to the pudding, cover with an upturned saucer or greased greaseproof paper and steam for 2 hours.

## SALAD SUGGESTIONS

Well shredded spinach, heart of cabbage, leaves of spring greens, make a delicious salad base. And you've no idea until you try them how tasty young dandelion leaves can be. Choose young leaves, wash, chop finely and mix with any raw shredded root vegetables. A little sugar is a help in this kind of salad. Later on, you can use carrot tops, turnip tops, radish tops, and beetroot tops. The addition of any scraps of cold or 'points' meats, corned beef or fish make your salads still more substantial, nourishing and varied.

## *STUFFED TOMATOES*

Make the best use of fresh tomatoes when these are available. Cut a slice from each tomato, scoop out the pulp. Chop this finely. The quantities given are enough for 8 medium or 4 large tomatoes.
1. Make up ¼ pint thick well-seasoned white sauce. Add 2 oz grated cheese, 2 tablespoons chopped parsley and the tomato pulp. Spoon into the tomato cases. Serve cold or bake for 10 minutes in a moderately hot oven.
2. Blend 2 fresh eggs or 2 reconstituted dried eggs with the tomato pulp, 4 tablespoons soft breadcrumbs, 2 tablespoons chopped spring onions and a little seasoning. Spoon into the tomato cases. Bake for 10–15 minutes in a moderately hot oven.

# POTATO SALAD

*Cooking time:* 20 minutes    *Quantity:* 4 helpings

1½ lb potatoes, old or new
1½ oz flour
½ pint milk or milk and water
salt and pepper

1 tablespoon vinegar
1 tablespoon chopped parsley
1 tablespoon chopped mint
4 oz grated cheese

METHOD: Peel potatoes, cut into small pieces, cook in a small quantity of boiling salted water until just barely cooked. If old potatoes are used, cook in their skins and peel when cooked. While potatoes are cooking make the dressing. Blend the flour with a little milk to the consistency of thin cream. Boil the rest of the milk, and when boiling add the blended flour. Stir well over gentle heat till the sauce thickens, then add salt, pepper, vinegar, parsley and mint and ½ to 1 teaspoon of made mustard if you like it.

When the potatoes are cooked and strained, dice and while still hot mix with the dressing. Allow to become quite cold and serve on a bed of lettuce with grated cheese.

# Puddings

We found it was much more difficult to make puddings than it had been in the past, but with a little imagination we managed to conjure up appetising ends to the meal. We made good use of seasonal fruits and when cooking these sweetened the fruit with saccharin to save sugar, the crushed tablets were always added to the fruit after it was cooked.

# MAKING PASTRY

There are many ways of making pastry that do not use too much fat, include potatoes and oatmeal to give a change of flavour, the recipes are on this page. These foods are home grown and save shipping space. Substitute these pastries in any of the recipes that follow.

I saw three ships a-sailing
But not with food for me
For I am eating home-grown foods
To beat the enemy
And ships are filled with guns instead
To bring us Victory

## POTATO PASTRY

This is pastry that should be used a great deal as it helps to lighten the flour and makes our rations of fat go much further. Here are two versions.

**1** Sift 4 oz self-raising flour with a pinch of salt. Rub in 1½–2 oz cooking fat. Add 4 oz smooth mashed potato. Mix thoroughly then add a little water to bind. Roll out on a floured board and use as ordinary shortcrust pastry. It can be baked in a hot oven.
Note: This is a soft pastry.

**2** Sift 6 oz self-raising flour with a pinch of salt. Rub in 2–3 oz cooking fat, add 2 oz grated raw potato. Mix well and bind with water. Roll out on a floured board and use as ordinary shortcrust pastry. Bake as above. Note: This has a more interesting flavour than No. 1.

## OATMEAL PASTRY

Sift 6 oz self-raising flour with a pinch of salt. Rub in 2–3 oz cooking fat, then add 2 oz rolled oats. Mix with water and use as ordinary shortcrust pastry. Bake as potato pastry above.

# BAKEWELL TART

*Cooking time:* 40 minutes    *Quantity:* 4–6 helpings

shortcrust pastry made with 6 oz flour, etc. as Almond Flan, opposite
FILLING
2 tablespoons jam
2 oz margarine
2 oz sugar
1 teaspoon almond essence

1 egg or 1 reconstituted dried egg
2 oz self-raising flour or plain flour with ½ teaspoon baking powder
2 oz soft breadcrumbs
2 oz soya flour
2 tablespoons milk

METHOD: Make the pastry and line a flan ring on a baking sheet or a pie plate or sandwich tin. Spread with the jam. Cream the margarine, sugar and essence together; beat in the egg then add the flour or sifted flour and baking powder and remaining ingredients. Bake as the Almond Flan on this page but allow slightly longer cooking time if necessary. Serve hot or cold.

# MOCK APRICOT FLAN

METHOD: Line a large 9 inch pie plate or flan dish with shortcrust pastry or oatmeal pastry or potato pastry, see recipes left and right. Bake without a filling in a hot oven for 20–25 minutes until firm and golden.

Meanwhile grate 1 lb young carrots. Put into a saucepan with a few drops of almond essence, 4 tablespoons of plum jam and only about 4 tablespoons of water. Cook gently until a thick pulp. Spoon into the cooked pastry. Spread with a little more plum jam if this can be spared.
Note: The carrots really do taste a little like apricots.

# ALMOND FLAN

*Cooking time:* 35 minutes   *Quantity:* 4–6 helpings

SHORTCRUST PASTRY
6 oz self-raising flour or plain
  flour with $1\frac{1}{2}$ teaspoons
  baking powder
pinch salt
$1\frac{1}{2}$–2 oz cooking fat or
  margarine
water to mix
FILLING
1–2 tablespoons jam

1 oz margarine
$1\frac{1}{2}$ oz sugar
1 teaspoon almond essence
1 egg or 1 reconstituted dried
  egg
$1\frac{1}{2}$ oz plain flour
1 teaspoon baking powder
$1\frac{1}{2}$ oz semolina
$\frac{1}{2}$ teacup milk or milk and
  water

METHOD: Sift the flour or flour and baking powder and salt. Rub in the cooking fat or margarine, add enough water to make a firm rolling consistency. Roll out and line a flan ring on a baking sheet or a pie plate or sandwich tin; spread with the jam. Cream the margarine, sugar and essence together, beat in the egg. Sift the flour and baking powder. Stir into the creamed mixture, then add the semolina and blend in the milk or milk and water. Spoon into the pastry case. Bake in the centre of a moderately hot oven for 35 minutes or until firm, reduce the heat slightly towards the end of the cooking time if the pastry or filling is becoming too brown. Serve hot or cold.

## BRETON PEARS

**Cooking time:** $\frac{1}{2}$ hour. Make shortcrust pastry using 12 oz self-raising flour, pinch salt, 3 oz cooking fat and water to mix. Roll out and cut into 4 squares. Peel 4 ripe firm pears, take out as much core as possible with a sharp knife and fill the space with some kind of jam, apricot is particularly good. Place the pears on the pastry. Brush the edges of the pastry with water and seal these firmly around the pears. Bake in the centre of a moderately hot oven for 30–35 minutes.

# PRUNE FLAN

*Cooking time:* $1\frac{1}{4}$ hours   *Quantity:* 4–6 helpings

6 oz prunes, soaked overnight
  in water to cover
1 tablespoon golden syrup
$\frac{1}{2}$ teaspoon ground cinnamon
$\frac{1}{2}$ teaspoon mixed spice
1 oz margarine

few drops lemon essence
2 tablespoons soft
  breadcrumbs
shortcrust pastry made with
  6 oz flour, etc, see above

METHOD: Simmer the prunes until tender then lift from the water, cut the fruit into small pieces. Put into a saucepan with all the ingredients, except the pastry and stir over a low heat until well mixed. Allow to cool. Roll out the pastry, line a flan ring or a baking sheet or a pie plate or tin. Put in the prune mixture and bake in the centre of a moderately hot oven for 30 minutes. Serve hot or cold.

The liquid left from soaking the prunes can be thickened and served with the flan.

# CAKE OR PUDDING MIXTURE

*Cooking time:* 20 minutes or 1 hour    *Quantity:* 4 helpings

1 egg (1 level tablespoon of
   dried egg mixed with a
   tablespoon of water)
2 oz fat
2 oz sugar

4 oz national flour
½ teaspoon baking powder
a little milk or household
   milk

METHOD: Beat the egg. Cream fat and sugar, add egg and
lastly the flour mixed with the baking powder. Mix to a soft
consistency with a little milk. Spread in a tin and bake for 15 to
20 minutes. This mixture can be steamed in a basin for 1 hour
and served as a pudding with jam or custard sauce.

## BEETROOT PUDDING

Here is a new notion for using
the sweetness of beetroot to make
a nice sweet pudding with very
little sugar.

First mix 6 oz wheatmeal flour
with ½ teaspoon baking powder.
Rub in ½ oz fat and add 1 oz sugar
and 4 oz cooked or raw beetroot
very finely grated.

Now mix all the ingredients to
a soft cake consistency with 3 or 4
tablespoons of milk. Add a few
drops of flavouring essence if you
have it. Turn the mixture into a
greased pie dish or square tin and
bake immediately in a moderate
oven for 35–40 minutes. This
pudding tastes equally good hot
or cold. Enough for 4.

# STEAMED PUDDINGS

In many of these puddings you will find in some instances a
fairly high percentage of rising agent, i.e. baking powder
suggested with plain flour. This is because the war-time
national flour, while being nutritious, was heavy and needed
extra raising agent.

# RHUBARB SPONGE

*Cooking time:* ¾–1 hour    *Quantity:* 4 helpings

1½ lb rhubarb
2 tablespoons golden syrup
1½ oz margarine or cooking
   fat
3 tablespoons sugar
1 tablespoon dried egg

4 oz self-raising flour or plain
   flour and 2 teaspoons
   baking powder
pinch salt
milk or water to mix

METHOD: Wipe the rhubarb and cut into small pieces. Place
with the syrup in a pie dish. Cream the margarine or fat and
sugar and beat in the egg. Mix the flour or flour and baking
powder and salt, add to the creamed mixture alternately with
the milk or water to form a dropping consistency. Spread over
the fruit and bake in the centre of a moderate oven for ¾–1
hour, depending on whether a shallow or deep pie dish is used.

RECIPE of the WEEK

### APPLE AND
### BLACKBERRY ROLY

**Cooking time:** 30 minutes
**Ingredients:** potato pastry
as page 52, 1 lb cooking
apples, peeled, cored and
chopped, ⅓ lb blackberries,
2 oz sugar. **Quantity:** 4
helpings

Roll the pastry out to an
oblong shape. Spread with
the apples and blackber-
ries, sprinkle with the sugar and roll up. Seal the
ends of the roll, place on a
well-greased tin and bake
in a moderate oven for 30
minutes.

### GLAZED PEARS

**Cooking time:** ¾ to 1 hour **Ingredients:** 6 to 8 firm pears, 1 pint water, 2 good tablespoons raspberry or plum jam, ½ teaspoon vanilla essence, ½ teaspoon almond essence, 1 tablespoon sugar, few drops cochineal, optional, 2 teaspoons arrowroot or cornflour.

Method: This is a very good way to serve pears for one of the meals at Christmas time and British pears should be available. Peel the pears, try and keep them whole. Remove the core, if possible, with the tip of a sharp knife. Put the water, jam, essences and sugar into a saucepan, bring to boiling point. Add the pears and simmer steadily until tender. Keep turning the fruit in the liquid until well coated. Lift out of the liquid and tint this slightly with the cochineal, if you want a deeper colour. Measure the liquid, you should have ½ pint. Blend with the arrowroot or cornflour, return to the pan and stir over the heat until thickened. Spoon over the pears. Serve cold with Mock Cream, recipes on page 61. **Quantity:** 6–8 helpings

# PRUNE ROLY

*Cooking time:* 1 hour    *Quantity:* 4–6 helpings

| | |
|---|---|
| 8 oz national flour | 2 oz breadcrumbs |
| 2 teaspoons baking powder | 1 tablespoon syrup |
| pinch of salt | 2 teaspoons sugar |
| milk and water for mixing | ½ teaspoon cinnamon or spice |
| 2 to 4 oz prunes, cooked | 1 oz cooking fat |

METHOD: Blend flour, baking powder, salt. Mix to a soft consistency with milk and water. Roll out, spread with prunes, breadcrumbs, syrup, sugar and cinnamon. Form into a roll. Melt the fat in a roasting tin and when hot put in the roll, turning it in the fat. Bake for 1 hour in a moderately hot oven.

# RHUBARB CRUMBLE

*Cooking time:* 30 minutes    *Quantity:* 4 helpings

| | |
|---|---|
| 1 lb rhubarb | 4 oz plain flour |
| 2 tablespoons golden syrup | pinch salt |
| 1½ oz fat | 3 tablespoons sugar |

METHOD: Wipe the rhubarb and cut into small pieces. Simmer with the syrup until cooked and place at the bottom of a fireproof dish. Rub the fat into the flour, salt and sugar until like fine breadcrumbs and sprinkle over the stewed fruit. Bake in a moderate oven for 15–20 minutes.

# GINGER PUDDING

*Cooking time:* 1½ hours    *Quantity:* 4 helpings

| | |
|---|---|
| 6 oz plain flour | 3 oz sultanas or dates, chopped |
| 2 teaspoons bicarbonate of soda | 1 oz margarine |
| 2 teaspoons ground ginger | ½ pint milk |
| 2 tablespoons sugar | |

METHOD: Sift the flour, soda and ginger into a bowl, add the sugar and sultanas or dates. Boil the margarine and milk, pour into the bowl and mix well. Grease a 2 pint basin and put in the mixture, cover with greased, greaseproof paper and steam for 1½ hours. Serve with custard or a sweet sauce.

# SPICED COTTAGE PUDDING WITH LEMON SAUCE

*Cooking time:* 30 minutes    *Quantity:* 4 helpings

8 oz self-raising flour or plain
   flour with 4 teaspoons
   baking powder
pinch salt
2 tablespoons dried egg
3 oz fat

3 oz sugar
1 teaspoon ground cinnamon
$\frac{1}{2}$ teaspoon grated nutmeg
$\frac{1}{2}$ teaspoon mixed spice
approximately $\frac{1}{4}$ pint milk

METHOD: Mix the flour or flour and baking powder with the salt and dried egg. Rub the fat in well. Add the sugar with the spices; mix to a stiff consistency with the milk. Turn into a greased Yorkshire pudding tin about 8 × 6 inches. Bake in the centre of a moderately hot oven for 30 minutes. Cut in squares and serve hot with lemon sauce, below.

## LEMON SAUCE

*Cooking time:* 10 minutes    *Quantity:* 4 helpings

8 tablespoons lemon squash
water

3 teaspoons arrowroot
3 tablespoons sugar

METHOD: Make the lemon squash up to 1 pint with the water. Mix the arrowroot and sugar to a cream with a little of the liquid. Bring the rest of the liquid to the boil, pour on to the blended mixture and return to the saucepan. Stir until it comes to the boil and cook for 5 minutes.

## SOYAGHETTI

**Cooking time:** 2 hours **Ingredients:** 1 pint water, 3 oz soyaghetti, 1 pint milk or milk and water, 1 oz sugar, $\frac{1}{2}$ oz margarine, when possible. **Quantity:** 4–6 helpings

Bring the water to the boil, drop in the soyaghetti and cook for 20 minutes. Strain, if using milk and water in which to bake the soyaghetti, save some of this liquid. Put the cereal in a pie dish, pour over the liquid, add the sugar and margarine. If possible soak for several hours before cooking. Bake for approximately 2 hours in the centre of a very moderate oven. Soyaghetti is probably the best substitute for rice.

**Chocolate Soyaghetti:**
Ingredients as above but add $\frac{1}{2}$ oz cocoa or 1 oz chocolate powder. Proceed as above.

## PUDDING WITH CEREALS

During the past years several new cereals have made their appearance. With careful cooking, these are very good substitutes for the old familiar ones. Allow 1 oz of cereal per person.

# FARINOCA

*Cooking time:* 2 hours    *Quantity:* 4–6 helpings

3 oz farinoca
1 pint milk or milk and water

1 oz sugar
$\frac{1}{2}$ oz margarine, when possible

METHOD: Put the cereal in the pie dish, pour over the milk or milk and water, add the sugar and margarine. This cereal is undoubtedly better if soaked overnight before baking. When baking, put into the centre or near the bottom of a very moderate oven and cook for 2 hours.

Farinoca is a good substitute for tapioca.

# CARAMEL AND SEMOLINA MOULD

*Cooking time:* 15 minutes    *Quantity:* 4 helpings

| | |
|---|---|
| 2 oz sugar | 1 tablespoon apricot jam or |
| 4 tablespoons water | marmalade |
| 1 pint milk or milk and water | 3 oz semolina |

METHOD: Put the sugar and 2 tablespoons of water into a saucepan, stir until the sugar has dissolved, then boil until a golden caramel. Add the remaining water and heat until blended, cool slightly then pour into a basin or mould.

Meanwhile bring the milk or milk and water to the boil in a separate pan, add the jam or marmalade, whisk in the semolina and cook steadily for 10–15 minutes, stirring most of the time. Allow to cool and stiffen slightly, stir briskly then spoon over the caramel and allow to set. Turn out to serve.

# EGGLESS SPONGE PUDDING

*Cooking time:* 1¼–1½ hours    *Quantity:* 4–6 helpings

| | |
|---|---|
| 6 oz self-raising flour or plain flour with 1½ teaspoons baking powder | 1 tablespoon golden syrup |
| | ½ teaspoon bicarbonate of soda |
| 1½–2 oz margarine or cooking fat | 1 dessertspoon vinegar |
| 1½–2 oz sugar | milk to mix |

METHOD: Sift the flour or flour and baking powder, rub in the margarine or cooking fat, add the sugar and golden syrup. Blend the bicarbonate of soda with the vinegar, add to the other ingredients, with enough milk to make a sticky consistency. Put the mixture into a greased basin, allow room to rise. Cover with a plate or margarine paper. Steam for 1¼–1½ hours or until firm. Serve hot with fruit or jam.

VARIATIONS

A little golden syrup or jam could be put into the basin before adding the sponge mixture.

**Chocolate Sponge:**

Use 5 oz flour and 1 oz cocoa powder.

## *VICTORY SPONGE*

Grate 1 large raw potato and 2 medium raw carrots, mix in 1 breakfast cup breadcrumbs, 1 tablespoon self-raising flour, 2 tablespoons sugar, ½ teaspoon flavouring, such as vanilla or lemon. Thoroughly stir in 1 teaspoon baking powder. Put 2 or 3 tablespoons of jam in a heated basin, run it round to cover the inside. Cool. Put in the pudding mixture, tie on a cover of margarine paper, steam 2 hours.

# Based on Bread

The recipes on this page use bread in interesting ways to make puddings.

# POOR KNIGHT'S FRITTERS

*Cooking time:* few minutes    *Quantity:* 4 helpings

8 large slices of bread
little margarine

jam or golden syrup or thick
    fruit purée
little fat for frying

METHOD: Make sandwiches of the bread, margarine and jam or golden syrup or fruit. Cut into fingers and fry in a little hot fat. You can make nicer fritters if you dip the sandwich fingers into beaten reconstituted dried egg, mixed with a little milk, before frying. Top with sugar.

# DANISH APPLE PUDDING

*Cooking time:* 1 hour    *Quantity:* 4–6 helpings

2 lb apples, peeled and sliced
little water
4 saccharine tablets
few drops almond essence

½ oz margarine, melted
2 teacups breadcrumbs
2 tablespoons golden syrup

METHOD: Cook the apples in a little water until soft. Add the saccharine and almond essence, beat to a pulp with a fork. Grease a pie dish with the margarine. Sprinkle in a layer of crumbs, add a layer of apples. Continue like this until the dish is full, ending with breadcrumbs. Drip the syrup over the top and bake in the centre of a moderate oven for 1 hour.

# EVERY CRUMB COUNTS

*Never* throw away stale bread. Use it as breadcrumbs in savoury or sweet puddings. Bake strips of bread for rusks. Use crisped breadcrumbs as a breakfast cereal, or crush them for coatings. Soak, squeeze and beat up with a fork for sweet and savoury puddings, etc.

# CRUMBED PRUNES

*Preparation time:* 10 minutes    *Quantity:* 4 helpings

1 breakfastcup cooked prunes
1 breakfastcup crisped
    breadcrumbs

1 tablespoon sugar
½ pint thick custard

METHOD: Stone the prunes and cut them into small pieces. Mix with the crumbs and sugar. Put dessertspoons of the custard into individual fruit glasses, then portions of the prunes mixture, and top with custard. The sweet should be served as soon as possible after being prepared, so that the crisp crumbs and sugar contrast with the smoothness of the custard.

*We all liked Mrs. Parker, in the City, until we heard she wasted crusts (a pity!).*

## DUKE PUDDING

Soak 2 breakfastcups stale bread in cold water, squeeze as dry as possible, beat out lumps with a fork. Add 2 tablespoons fat or flaked margarine, 2 tablespoons sugar, 3 tablespoons any dried fruit, small teacup grated raw carrot, 1 teaspoon mixed spice. Stir 1 teaspoon bicarbonate of soda into a little milk and water (milk bottle rinsings will do) and blend well into the mixture. Spread evenly in a greased tart tin, sprinkle with a little sugar, bake in a moderate oven for 30 minutes.

# BREAD PUDDING

A Bread Pudding is an excellent way to use up bread. The recipe below can be varied in many ways, for example if you are short of dried fruit use a diced cooking apple or a little more marmalade. Slices of Bread Pudding are ideal to tuck into a packed meal box for a factory worker.

*Cooking time:* 1½ or 2 hours        *Quantity:* 4 helpings

| | |
|---|---|
| 8 oz stale bread | 2 oz dried fruit |
| 2 oz grated suet or melted cooking fat | 1 reconstituted dried egg milk to mix |
| 1 oz sugar | ground cinnamon or grated |
| 1 tablespoon marmalade | nutmeg to taste |

METHOD: Put the bread into a basin, add cold water and leave for 15 minutes then squeeze dry with your fingers. Return the bread to the basin, add all the other ingredients, with enough milk to make a sticky consistency. If the spice is added last you can make quite certain you have the right amount. Put into a greased Yorkshire pudding tin and bake in the centre of a slow oven for 1½ hours or steam in a greased basin for 2 hours.

# SUMMER PUDDING

*Preparation time:* 30 minutes        *Quantity:* 4 helpings

| | |
|---|---|
| 1 lb rhubarb | ½ pint water |
| 2 oz prunes (soaked overnight) | 8 oz bread |
| | 2 oz sugar |

METHOD: Stew rhubarb and prunes in the ½ pint of water in which the prunes soaked. Grease a cake tin or pudding basin and line the bottom and sides with fingers of bread, keep odd pieces for putting on top. Strain the juice from the fruit pulp. Soak the bread in the basin thoroughly with the juice. Fill the basin with alternate layers of fruit, sugar, and the trimmings of bread, packing it very tightly and finishing with a layer of bread. Pour over any remaining juice. Place a saucer and weight on top and leave overnight. Turn out and serve with custard.

## PADDED PUDDING

Make 1 pint custard sauce, using milk or milk and water but very little sugar; leave in the saucepan. Add 1 teacup fine stale breadcrumbs, 2 tablespoons jam and a few drops vanilla essence to the custard and continue cooking for 5 minutes. Spoon into 4 dishes, allow to cool and top with grated chocolate and Mock Cream as page 61.

# FRUIT SHORTCAKE

*Cooking time:* 15 minutes    *Quantity:* 4 helpings

PASTRY
8 oz self-raising flour with 2
   teaspoons baking powder
   or plain flour with 4
   teaspoons baking powder
pinch salt
1 oz cooking fat

1 dessertspoon sugar
water to mix
FILLING AND TOPPING
½ pint thick fruit purée
Mock Cream 1 or 2 as left
whole fruit

**The Ministry of Food wants your cooking secrets**

METHOD: Sift the flour and baking powder and salt together. Rub in the fat in the usual way, add the sugar. Mix to a rolling consistency with cold water. Roll out the pastry into two 7 in diameter rounds. Put on 2 lightly greased baking trays and bake near the top of a very hot oven for 15 minutes. Cool then sandwich with the fruit purée and a little Mock Cream. Top with the whole fruit and remaining cream. Serve when fresh.

## EGG CUSTARDS

You will find that dried eggs can be used in all your favourite custard recipes in place of fresh eggs. Reconstitute the egg or eggs carefully, blend with the other ingredients and cook in the usual way.

## FRUIT FOAM

**Cooking time:** 10–15 minutes
**Ingredients:** 1 lb fruit, prepared for cooking, little sugar to taste, Marshmallow Foam, as this page.
**Quantity:** 4 helpings

Cook the fruit with the sugar and as little water as possible. Allow to cool, then beat until a smooth pulp. Make the Marshmallow Foam. Allow the fruit to become quite cold then blend it with the Marshmallow Foam and spoon into glasses.

# MARSHMALLOW FOAM

*Preparation time:* 15 minutes    *Quantity:* 4 helpings

1 level teaspoon powdered
   gelatine
¼ pint water

1 tablespoon sugar
3 tablespoons powdered milk
few drops of flavouring

METHOD: Soften the gelatine with about 2 tablespoons of cold water. Heat the remainder of the water, pour over the gelatine and stir until dissolved. Add the sugar and gradually whisk in the milk powder. Continue whisking until the mixture is light and fluffy. Add the flavouring.

# FRUIT SEMOLINA

*Cooking time:* 20–25 minutes    *Quantity:* 4–6 helpings

1 lb fruit – apples, plums,
   rhubarb or mixed fruit
½ pint water

2 oz sugar
3 oz semolina

METHOD: Cook the fruit to a thick pulp, adding the water and sugar. It is not essential, but it will give a smoother sweet if it is then rubbed through a sieve. If not, beat until as smooth as possible. Bring the pulp again to the boil, whisk in the semolina and cook gently, stirring from time to time for a good 10 minutes.

## VANILLA MOUSE

Put 2 fresh eggs or reconstituted dried eggs into a basin with 1 oz sugar. Whisk over hot water until thick and fluffy. Remove from the water and continue whisking until cold. Make the Marshmallow Foam as opposite page, flavour it with vanilla essense. Gently blend the egg mixture into the Marshmallow Foam. Serves 4–6.

# DUTCH FLUMMERY

*Cooking time:* Few minutes   *Quantity:* 4 helpings

½ pint lemon squash
¾ pint water
½ oz powdered gelatine

2 reconstituted dried eggs or
  fresh eggs
2 oz sugar

METHOD: Put the squash and ½ pint of water into a saucepan and heat. Soften the gelatine with 2 tablespoons of water. Heat the remaining water and pour on to the gelatine. Add the eggs and sugar to the lemon mixture and cook slowly for 5 minutes. Remove the pan from the heat, add the dissolved gelatine, pour into a wet mould and allow to set.

# MOCK CREAM (1)

*Preparation time:* 5 minutes   *Quantity:* 2–4 helpings

1 oz margarine
1 oz sugar

1 tablespoon dried milk
  powder
1 tablespoon milk

METHOD: Cream the margarine and sugar. Beat in the milk powder and liquid milk.

# MOCK CREAM (2)

*Cooking time:* 5 minutes   *Quantity:* 2–4 helpings

1 tablespoon cornflour,
  custard powder or
  arrowroot

¼ pint milk
1 oz margarine
1 oz sugar

METHOD: Blend the cornflour or custard powder or arrowroot with the milk, tip into a saucepan and stir over a low heat until thickened, allow to cool. Cream the margarine and sugar until soft and light then very gradually beat in ½ teaspoon of the milk mixture. Continue like this until all the ingredients are mixed well. This makes a thick cream.
For a thin pouring cream use 1 teaspoon cornflour, custard powder or arrowroot.

**RECIPE of the WEEK**

### A SWEET FOR THE CHILDREN'S PARTY

Peel, core and cut ½ lb apples and simmer until tender in ½ teacup water. Sweeten with about 1 dessertspoon honey and flavour with cinnamon or ginger, whichever is liked. Whip the mixture until it is light and frothy. Add half a packet of tablet jelly – strawberry or raspberry is prettiest – and stir well, until it is thoroughly melted. When cool turn into a wet mould. Miniature meringues or ratafia biscuits make a simple decoration for this sweet.

## SPECIAL FROM BOURNVILLE

The recipes here form part of a special leaflet produced by Cadburys of Bournville on behalf of the Red Cross. It was sold for 1d. More of the delicious recipes are to be found on page 85.

## CHOCOLATE QUEEN PUDDING
Recipe from 'The Kitchen Front'

**Cooking time:** $\frac{3}{4}$–1 hour
**Ingredients:** 1 level teacup breadcrumbs, a small knob margarine, 1 level tablespoon sugar, $\frac{1}{2}$ pint milk, 2 level teaspoons, Bournville Cocoa, 4 tablespoons jam or jelly, 2 dried eggs, reconstituted, 1 teaspoon vanilla essence.
**Quantity:** 4 helpings

Put the breadcrumbs, margarine and sugar in a basin. Boil the milk, cocoa and half the jam and pour it over the breadcrumbs, stirring the mixure well together. Cover with a plate and leave half an hour. Beat eggs thoroughly. Spread a tablespoonful of jam over the bottom of a greased pie-dish. Add eggs and vanilla essence to the breadcrumb mixture. Pour the pudding into the pie-dish and bake about half to three quarters of an hour, in a moderately hot oven till set. Then spread the remaining jam over the top.

# CHOCOLATE SPONGE PUDDING

1 oz margarine
2 oz sugar
1 level tablespoon dried egg, dry
8 oz grated raw potato

6 oz flour
1 oz Bournville Cocoa
1 teaspoon baking powder
a pinch of salt
4 tablespoons milk

METHOD Cream fat and sugar together. Mix the dried egg with the raw potato and beat it into the fat and sugar. Mix flour, cocoa, baking powder and salt together and add to the creamed mixture, then stir in enough milk to make a soft dough. Put into a greased pudding basin and steam 1 hour or bake in a pie-dish in the oven 30 to 40 minutes.

# FRUIT CHOCOLATE CREAM

apple pulp or fruit in season
2 level tablespoons sugar or more to taste
1 level tablespoon Bournville Cocoa

1 heaped tablespoon flour
$\frac{1}{2}$ pint milk
Mock Cream, page 61

Put the fruit in the bottom of a glass dish or individual glasses. Mix sugar, cocoa and flour to a smooth paste with a little of the milk. Put the remainder on to boil and when boiling pour on to the blended cocoa and flour stirring well. Return to the saucepan, bring to the boil and cook about 8 minutes stirring continuously. Pour over the fruit and when cold top with mock cream. It is advisable to make the chocolate cream in a double pan or in a basin standing in a pan of boiling water.

# CHOCOLATE SAUCE

1 oz margarine
1 oz flour
$\frac{1}{2}$ pint milk

$1\frac{1}{2}$ oz sugar
$1\frac{1}{2}$ oz Bournville Cocoa
vanilla essence

Melt margarine in pan. Mix in flour, add milk gradually, then add sugar and cocoa which has been previously blended with a little milk. Bring to the boil stirring all the time. Allow to simmer 5 minutes. Flavour with vanilla and beat well.

# FOOD FACTS

## preparing for Christmas

Christmas begins in the kitchen and it isn't too soon to begin planning the best use of the Christmas rations now. So here are advance recipes for Christmas fare, all of them tested by practical cooks in the Ministry of Food kitchens.

### CHRISTMAS PUDDING WITHOUT EGGS

Mix together 1 cup of flour, 1 cup of breadcrumbs, 1 cup of sugar, half a cup of suet, 1 cup of mixed dried fruit, and, if you like, 1 teaspoon of mixed sweet spice. Then add 1 cup of grated potato, 1 cup of grated raw carrot and finally 1 level teaspoon of bicarbonate of soda dissolved in 2 tablespoons hot milk. Mix all together (no further moisture is necessary) turn into a well-greased pudding basin. Boil or steam for 4 hours.

## A GOOD DARK CHRISTMAS PUDDING

*Cooking time:* 4 hours then 2–3 hours   *Quantity:* 6 helpings

2 oz plain flour
½ teaspoon baking powder
¼ teaspoon salt
½ teaspoon grated nutmeg
¼ teaspoon ground cinnamon
1 teaspoon mixed spice
3 oz sugar
½–1 lb mixed dried fruit

4 oz breadcrumbs
2–4 oz grated suet or melted fat
1 oz marmalade
2 eggs or 2 reconstituted dried eggs
¼ pint brandy, rum, ale, stout or milk

METHOD: Sift the flour, baking powder, salt and spices together. Add the sugar, fruit and breadcrumbs and suet or fat. Mix with the marmalade, eggs and brandy, rum or other liquid. Mix very thoroughly. Put in a greased 2 pint basin, cover with greased paper and steam for 4 hours. Remove the paper and cover with a fresh piece and a clean cloth. Store in a cool place. Steam for 2–3 hours before serving.
Note: If the smaller quantities of suet or fat and fruit are used, the pudding should not be made more than 10 days before it is to be used. With the larger quantities you can make it a month before it is to be used.

## APPLE MINCEMEAT

Make mincemeat go further by blending it with grated or finely diced raw apples or with thick apple pulp.
If you have not been able to make, or obtain, mincemeat then flavour grated apple with plenty of spices and add a little mixed dried fruit or chopped cooked prunes or chopped raw dates. You then have a pleasant filling for the traditional Christmas tarts.

# Snacks & Supper Dishes

The sustaining snacks in this section were suitable for all meals of the day as well as supper time. There are ideas for lunch boxes too, as many people took packed meals with them to work. We were encouraged to eat a cooked breakfast, with everyone working so hard for the war effort they needed a good meal to start the day.

# HARD-TIME OMELETTE

*Cooking time:* 10–12 minutes    *Quantity:* 4 helpings

1½ oz cooking fat
4 medium potatoes, cooked
  and sliced or diced
2 small bacon rashers,
  chopped

3 eggs or reconstituted dried
  eggs
1½ tablespoons water
salt and pepper

METHOD: Heat the fat in a large frying pan or omelette pan. Fry the potatoes and bacon together until crisp and golden in colour. Beat the eggs with the water and seasoning. Pour over the potatoes and bacon and cook until set then fold and serve at once, or serve flat.

**POTATO CUTLETS FOR BREAKFAST**

These make an excellent start to the day; and one of the beauties of them is that you can prepare them the day before. Scrub 1½ lb potatoes and boil in their skins. When cooked, peel and mash them thoroughly. Scrape ½ lb carrots, boil till tender and mash. Mix the potatoes and carrots together, season with salt and pepper, then shape into cutlets. Dip in browned breadcrumbs, made by baking stale bread in the oven and crushing it. Next morning, place the cutlets in a greased tin and bake in a moderate oven for about 15 mins, or fry them in a very little hot fat.

# IRISH OMELETTE

*Cooking time:* 15 minutes    *Quantity:* 4 helpings

1 lb cooked potato
1 tablespoon chopped parsley
3 oz bacon, chopped
salt and pepper

4 eggs (4 level tablespoons
  dried egg mixed with 8
  tablespoons water)
¼ pint milk or household milk

METHOD: Slice the potatoes and mix with parsley, chopped bacon and seasoning. Put the mixture into a well-greased, pie-dish. Blend the eggs and milk, pour over the other ingredients and bake in a hot oven for 15 minutes.

**The Radio Doctor Says:**

Health rule for April. It's a good idea to cook potatoes in their jackets. The skin stops the precious Vitamin C from escaping and getting lost in the cooking water. Steaming potatoes is best of all. And never cook them twice.

# CRISP CRUST OMELETTE

*Cooking time:* 5–6 minutes    *Quantity:* 2–4 helpings

2 slices bread
1–1½ oz cooking fat
4 eggs or reconstituted dried
  eggs

2 tablespoons water
salt and pepper

METHOD: Cut the bread into small dice; heat the fat in the frying pan or omelette pan. Fry the bread until crisp and brown. Beat the eggs with the water and seasoning. Pour over the bread, cook until set then fold and serve.

# SPANISH OMELETTE

*Cooking time:* 10 minutes    *Quantity:* 2 helpings

2 eggs (2 level tablespoons
dried egg mixed with 4
tablespoons water)
1½ oz margarine or dripping
3 spring onions, chopped

8 oz shredded mixed
vegetables
2 tablespoons water
a pinch salt and pepper

METHOD: Beat the eggs. Heat the fat in a frying pan and fry the spring onion and vegetables until tender. Add the eggs, water, and seasoning, stir until the eggs are set, form into a roll, and serve immediately.

# SAVOURY SCONES

*Cooking time:* 10 minutes    *Quantity:* 8–10 helpings

4 oz national flour
4 oz medium oatmeal
1 teaspoon baking powder
½ teaspoon salt

2 oz shredded cheese
1 oz fat
household milk or milk and
water

METHOD: Mix dry ingredients and cheese, rub in fat and work enough milk or milk and water to make a really soft dough. Flatten out on floured board, cut in triangles, place on a greased sheet and bake in a hot oven till brown.

# POTATO SCONES

*Cooking time:* 20 minutes    *Quantity:* 8 scones

4 tablespoons self-raising
flour
1 teaspoon baking powder
½ teaspoon salt

1 tablespoon margarine or
cooking fat
4 tablespoons mashed potatoes
milk or household milk

METHOD: Mix together the flour, baking powder and salt, rub in the fat. Add the potato mashed until light and creamy. Mix all together with enough milk to make a soft dough. Roll out, form into rounds and cut into sections with a sharp knife. Brush the tops with milk, bake in a moderate oven for 20 minutes.

## BRIGHT BREAKFASTS SIMPLE—BUT DIFFERENT

Potato Floddies are quick to prepare and are especially appetising if cooked in the fat left over from bacon. Grate raw potatoes into a basin, Mix in enough flour to make a thick batter, season to taste, drop spoonsful of the mixture into a pan of hot fat. Fry on both sides.

Another novelty is slices of cooked carrot fried with bacon. Their cheery colour reminds you of 'bacon and tomatoes', but their flavour is new and delicious.

What about a cereal? Stale bread cut in cubes and baked, makes a crunchy, nourishing breakfast cereal. Use the heat left in the oven when you finish the main cooking.

# Rules for Using Dried Egg

**1** Store in a cool, dry place and replace the lid of the tin after use.

**2** To turn a dried egg into a fresh one, mix one level tablespoon of the powder with two tablespoons of water. This mixture equals one fresh egg.

**3** Now treat the egg as you would a fresh one. Don't make up more egg than is necessary for the dish you are making. Beat as usual before adding to other ingredients.

## SAUSAGEMEAT LOAF

*Cooking time:* 40 minutes    *Quantity:* 4–6 helpings

12 oz sausagemeat
4 oz corned beef, flaked
1 cooking apple, peeled and
  grated
1 teaspoon chopped sage
  or ½ teaspoon dried sage

1 onion, grated
1 tablespoon chutney,
  chopped finely
2 tablespoons crisp
  breadcrumbs

METHOD: Mix all the ingredients, except the breadcrumbs, together. Grease a loaf tin or pie dish, coat the bottom and sides with the crumbs. Put in the sausagemeat mixture and bake in the centre of a moderately hot oven for 40 minutes. Serve cold with salad or slice for a packed meal or serve hot with vegetables.

### "FADGE" FOR BREAKFAST

"Fadge" is both nourishing and filling for breakfast.

Boil some well-scrubbed potatoes, then peel and mash them while hot. When the mixture is cool enough to handle, add salt, and work in enough flour to make a pliable dough. Knead lightly on a well floured board for about 5 minutes, then roll into a large circle about ¼ inch thick. Cut into wedge shaped pieces and cook on a hot gridle, an electric hot-plate or on the upper shelf of a quick oven until brown on both sides, turning once.

## FISH PASTE

3 oz cooked fresh-salted cod
2 oz mashed potatoes
1 oz softened margarine

2 teaspoons Worcestershire
  sauce
pepper

METHOD: Flake the fish finely with a fork or put through the mincer and beat into the potato until the mixture is smooth and creamy. Then beat in the margarine and sauce and a little pepper. Use for sandwiches.

## SEMOLINA SOUFFLÉ

*Cooking time:* 45 minutes    *Quantity:* 4 helpings

¾ pint milk or milk and water
4 oz semolina
1 small onion, grated
salt and pepper
1 dessertspoon chopped
  parsley

2 oz cheese, grated
2 eggs or reconstituted dried
  eggs
2 or 3 tomatoes, sliced

METHOD: Bring the milk or milk and water to the boil; whisk in the semolina, add the onion and seasoning and cook steadily for 10 minutes over a low heat, stirring frequently. Add the parsley, cheese and eggs. Put the tomatoes at the bottom of a greased soufflé or pie dish. Top with the semolina mixture and bake for 30 minutes in the centre of a moderately hot oven. Serve as soon as cooked.

*Packed-Meal Menus*

Preparing packed meals is quite a job, now that so many of the sandwiches have vanished. But your family still expect something tasty in the dinner packet, and there's no need to disappoint them. Keep a corner of the larder for new and interesting sandwich finds and fillings and try some of the suggestions on these pages.

# TO HARDBOIL DRIED EGGS

Reconstitute the eggs; measuring the powder very carefully, see page 67, season lightly then pour into small greased basins or cups. Stand in a pan with a little boiling water and cook gently until set.

# MOCK CRAB

*Cooking time:* 4 minutes   *Quantity:* 2 helpings

½ oz margarine
2 eggs or 2 reconstituted
   dried eggs
1 oz cheese, grated

1 dessertspoon salad dressing
few drops vinegar
salt and pepper

METHOD: Melt the margarine in a saucepan, add the well beaten eggs. Scramble until half set then add the other ingredients. Serve as a sandwich filling or on hot toast or over mashed potatoes.

# SAUCY WAYS

A good sauce makes the simplest food more interesting. Try serving cooked vegetables with a white, cheese or parsley sauce. Use some of the vegetable stock in the sauce to save milk and give additional flavour. The Dutch sauce on page 72 is excellent with fish or it can be adapted to make a salad dressing.

# WHITE SAUCE

Use margarine or cooking fat for this or dripping.

METHOD: Heat 1 oz fat in a pan, stir in 1 oz flour, cook over a low heat then blend in ½ pint liquid (this can be all milk, milk and water, stock or all vegetable stock). Stir as the sauce comes to the boil and cook until thickened. Season to taste.
Cheese Sauce: Add 1–2 oz grated cheese to the thickened sauce.
Parsley Sauce: Add 1 to 2 tablespoons chopped parsley to the thickened sauce.

### SAVOURY SPLITS

These are delicious, filling things to have during a day's hard work or night watch.

Sift 6 oz plain flour with 2 level teaspoons baking powder and ½ teaspoon salt. Mix thoroughly with 4 oz sieved cooked potato (sieved, if possible, when still hot). Rub in 1 oz fat and blend to a soft dough with 4 tablespoons milk. Roll out to ½ in thickness on a well-floured board and cut into rounds. Glaze the tops with a little milk. Bake in a hot oven for 15 minutes. When cold, split the scones and fill with one of these mixtures.
**1** Finely diced cooked vegetables bound with a little white sauce.
**2** Finely diced cooked beetroots bound with horseradish or some other sharp sauce.
**3** Mixed vegetable curry.
**4** Shredded raw cabbage heart well mixed with mayonnaise and chopped parsley.

### SWEET SPLITS

If you like something in the sweet line, make your splits as above, but for the filling mix some cocoa and sugar (or honey) to a cream with milk. Then work into it a little creamed margarine.

# QUICK WELSH RAREBIT

*Cooking time:* 5 minutes    *Quantity:* 2 helpings

2 slices bread
1 teaspoon margarine
1 teaspoon chutney, or yeast
  extract

2 tablespoons grated
  cheese

METHOD: Toast the bread and spread with margarine and a thin coating of chutney, or yeast extract. Cover with grated cheese. Place under the grill till golden brown. Eat with a raw vegetable salad.

## *POTATO RAREBIT*

Used mashed potatoes as a basis for a rarebit. Beat the potatoes until soft and smooth; add a little milk if too stiff. The potatoes should be like a thick cream. Put in as much grated cheese as you can spare with seasoning to taste. Spread on hot toast and brown under the grill.

## *GOOD EATING*

How about these suggestions for new fillings?
**1** Shredded cheese and chutney or cooked beetroot.
**2** Cooked mashed potato, yeast extract and chopped parsley.
**3** Chopped grilled bacon and lettuce.
**4** Mashed sardines, pilchards, herring or haddock, mixed with shredded fresh carrot.
**5** Minced crisply cooked bacon rinds and toasted oatmeal.
**6** Fish paste and chopped parsley.
**7** Brawn, shredded swede and chutney.
**8** Vegetable or meat extract and mustard and cress.
**9** Chopped cold meat and mashed cooked vegetables with seasoning.
**10** American sausage meat and watercress.
You may think that some of these ideas will surprise the family, but they'll like them.

# OATMEAL CHEESE RAREBIT

*Cooking time:* 12 minutes    *Quantity:* 4–6 helpings

2 oz flour
$\frac{1}{2}$ pint water
2 oz toasted oatmeal or rolled
  oats*
2–3 oz grated cheese

1–2 teaspoons salt
$\frac{1}{4}$ teaspoon pepper
little made mustard
4–6 slices toast

METHOD: Blend the flour with a little of the water to make a smooth paste. Bring the remainder of the water to the boil and pour on to the blended flour, stirring well. Return to the pan and, stirring all the time, bring to the boil. Cook gently for 5 minutes then add the oatmeal, cheese and seasoning. Mix thoroughly and divide the mixture equally between the slices of toast. Brown under the grill.

* Spread the oats on to a flat tray and toast in a slow oven

# FARMHOUSE SCRAMBLE (1)

*Cooking time:* 10 minutes    *Quantity:* 2–3 helpings

$\frac{1}{2}$ oz margarine
8 oz mixed raw vegetables,
  finely grated

2 eggs or reconstituted dried
  eggs
salt and pepper

METHOD: Melt the margarine in a small pan; add the vegetables and heat until lightly cooked. Beat the eggs with a little seasoning and pour over the vegetables. Scramble lightly and serve with potatoes, as a sandwich filling or on hot toast.

Sandwich making is much easier if you dip the knife in boiling water before spreading the margarine.

Bread mustn't get mouldy now, so keep your bread bin in a dry, airy place. Wipe the bin out every day with a clean, dry cloth, and wash with soda and water once a week. Let new bread cool before putting it in the bin.

Plan your points and obey the rules
Just as you did with your football pools:
You'll find yourself an up-and-upper
At breakfast, dinner, tea and supper!

# CHEESE PANCAKES

*Cooking time:* 15 minutes    *Quantity:* 4 helpings

4 oz flour
1 teaspoon baking powder
2 eggs (2 level tablespoons dried egg mixed with 4 tablespoons water)

½ pint milk
4 oz grated cheese
salt to taste
fat for frying

METHOD: Blend the flour, baking powder and mixed eggs smoothly, add sufficient milk to make a thick, smooth batter. Beat for 10 minutes. Add rest of milk, the grated cheese and salt. Heat a little fat in the frying pan till smoking hot, pour in a thin layer of batter, fry until golden brown on both sides. Turn out, roll, serve with a sprinkling of shredded cheese. Continue until all the batter is used.

# CHEESE SAVOURY

*Cooking time:* 20 minutes    *Quantity:* 4 helpings

1 egg (1 level tablespoon dried egg mixed with a tablespoon water)
½ pint household milk

1 teacup breadcrumbs
4 oz grated cheese
pepper and salt to taste

METHOD: Beat egg with milk. Add the other ingredients. Pour into a greased dish and bake for 20 minutes in a moderate oven until set and brown.

# FARMHOUSE SCRAMBLE (2)

*Cooking time:* 15–20 minutes    *Quantity:* 4 helpings

2 lb mixed cooked vegetables
4 oz grated cheese
3 oz breadcrumbs
chopped parsley

2 eggs (2 level tablespoons dried egg, 4 tablespoons water)
pepper and salt

METHOD: Mix all the ingredients together. Melt a little dripping in a frying pan. When it is hot put in the mixture and spread it over the pan. Put on a saucepan lid and cook for about 20 minutes, shaking occasionally until it is brown. Turn out on a hot dish and serve it with lettuce or shredded cabbage. This dish is just as successful when baked in an oven, but add a little more liquid.

# What is the "Oslo Meal"?

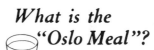

What is the "Oslo Meal"? This was a meal originally given as an experiment to school children, and its results in the health and development of the children were remarkable. It makes a satisfying main meal for the whole family —and its simplicity is a great point in its favour with busy housewives. It is salad, bread-and-butter, a glass of milk, *and a piece of cheese.*

## LOBSCOUSE

A quickly made dish, very popular with sailors. You'll like it, too! Melt a nut of margarine in a small saucepan, then add 3 oz grated cheese and about 2 tablespoonfuls milk. Stir over a low heat until the cheese is melting, then add two or three tinned or bottled tomatoes, cut in pieces and continue to cook gently until all ingredients are blended. Season with pepper and salt. Serve on a bed of piping hot mashed potato.

### The Radio Doctor Says:

'If I were allowed to say only three things on the Kitchen Front, I should say eat some raw green vegetables every day, I should praise milk and more milk and I should preach the virtues of the food which contains so much nutriment—cheese.'

### SALAD DRESSING FOR IMMEDIATE USE

Blend 1 level tablespoon household milk powder with 1 level tablespoon dried egg powder, $\frac{1}{2}$ teaspoon salt, a little pepper and dry mustard powder. Add just 1 tablespoon water and 2 tablespoons vinegar and mix until smooth then beat well. Note: It is important that no less than the above amount of vinegar should be used.

"'Household' milk? Why, ma, that's easy:
(Made this way it can't go cheesy.)
*First* the water, *then* the powder."
(Mothers never *quite* felt prouder!)

## DUTCH SAUCE

*Cooking time:* 10 minutes    *Quantity:* 1 pint

3 oz flour
1 pint milk or household milk or fish stock
3 teaspoons dry mustard
salt and pepper

1 egg (1 level tablespoon dried egg and 2 tablespoons water)
3 to 4 tablespoons vinegar

METHOD: Blend the flour with a little of the milk or fish stock. When smooth add the rest of the liquid and bring to the boil. Cook for 2 to 3 minutes, stirring all the time. Mix the mustard, salt and pepper with the egg and add to the sauce. Stir over a gentle heat, but do not let sauce boil again. Add the vinegar. Stir well and serve (the egg in this recipe is optional). You can use this sauce as Mayonnaise if fish stock is not used.

## EGG CHAMP

*Cooking time:* 20 minutes    *Quantity:* 4 helpings

1 lb potatoes
1 breakfastcup runner beans or any green vegetable
salt and pepper
$\frac{1}{4}$ pint milk

1 oz margarine
4 eggs (4 level tablespoons dried egg mixed with a tablespoon water)

METHOD: Scrub and scrape the potatoes and place in a small quantity of boiling salted water. Cook for 10 minutes and then add the sliced beans. When tender, drain, dry and mash the potatoes with sufficient milk to make smooth and creamy. Add the beans, season well, pile scrambled egg on top of the potato mixture and serve at once. To make the scrambled egg heat 4 tablespoonfuls of milk and the margarine in a pan, add the egg mixture, season and cook over a gentle heat until thickened.

### SUPPER SAVOURIES

**1** Potato Pasties are always a popular supper. Make a paste by mixing 4 oz mashed potatoes, 2 oz flour and 1 oz dripping with a little cold water. Roll out the paste fairly thin and cut it into rounds. Fill with a mixture of cold cooked vegetables, such as carrots, parsnips and beet. If you have a little cooked meat, so much the better. Mince it and add it to the vegetables seasoned to taste. Damp the edges of the pastry with cold water, fold over and seal. Cut a small hole in the top to let out the steam. Bake in a hot oven for 20 to 30 minutes. These are delicious eaten hot with vegetables and gravy, or, cold, they can take the place of sandwiches.

**2** Curried Potatoes make another favourite supper dish. Parboil 2 lb potatoes, and peel them into slices $\frac{1}{2}$ in thick. Make a mixture of 1 dessertspoon curry powder, 1 dessertspoon medium oatmeal and a little salt. Toss the potatoes in the mixture, then arrange in a greased fireproof dish or baking tin, dot with 1 oz dripping and bake in a moderate oven until browned (about 30 minutes).

# SORRY!

*There's no Kraft Cheese or Velveeta now being made!*

# CHEESE DUMPLINGS

*Cooking time:* 45 minutes  *Quantity:* 4 helpings

$1\frac{1}{2}$ lb potatoes, peeled
salt and pepper

2 reconstituted dried eggs
3 oz cheese, grated

METHOD: Cook the potatoes in boiling, salted water, drain and mash; do not add any liquid. Place over a low heat and season well. Add the eggs and 2 oz of the grated cheese. Shape into 8 or 10 round balls and roll in the remaining cheese. Place on a greased baking tin and bake for about 20 minutes in a hot oven until brown and crusty.

# CHEESE PUDDING

*Cooking time:* 30 minutes  *Quantity:* 4 helpings

$\frac{1}{2}$ pint milk or household milk
2 eggs (2 level tablespoons dried egg mixed with 4 tablespoons water)

4 oz grated cheese
1 breakfastcup breadcrumbs
salt and pepper
$\frac{1}{4}$ teaspoon dry mustard

METHOD: Add the milk to the egg mixture and stir in the other ingredients. Pour into a greased dish and bake for about 30 minutes in a moderately hot oven till brown and set.

# CHEESE SALAD

*Cooking time:* 10 minutes  *Quantity:* 4 helpings

1 medium sized cabbage
$1\frac{1}{2}$ oz flour
$\frac{1}{2}$ pint milk

salt
$\frac{1}{2}$ lb cheese, grated
nasturtium flowers

METHOD: Shred the cabbage finely. Blend the flour with a little cold milk, put the remainder on the boil. When boiling pour on to the blended flour, stirring well till smooth. Return to the pan and cook from 1 to 2 minutes. Add salt and grated cheese. Stir until cheese melts. Cool sauce, pour over the finely shredded cabbage, and serve decorated with nasturtium flowers.

# "Man-about-Kitchen"

Now that thousands of wives and mothers are helping in the factories, or evacuated to the country, many men are having to do their own cooking. No wonder they ask their women-folk for easy recipes! Here are a few suggestions.

'And if you don't mind prolonging the war, I know just where you can get...'

## PALETTE SALAD

*Preparation time:* 10 minutes   *Quantity:* 4 helpings

3 oz cabbage, shredded
4 oz cooked or raw beetroot, grated
2 oz raw parsnip, grated

1 oz raw leek, chopped
2 oz raw carrot, cut in thin strips

METHOD: Lay the shredded cabbage in an oblong dish. Arrange a border of beetroot around the edge of the dish with the other vegetables in strips.

### SPRING ON THE KITCHEN FRONT

Spring cleaning takes it out of you—and the only way to put it back is to see that you choose energy-making foods. Here is a meal that won't take much more time to get ready than a cup of tea but which will give you real staying-power.

All you need is one good-size *potato, seasoning, small nut of dripping, a thick frying-pan.*

Chop up the raw potato, melt the dripping in the frying-pan and then spread the potato all over the pan. Press it down firmly into the fat and season well. Then cover with a lid or plate and leave to cook very gently for about ¼ hour. So long as the pan is thick and the heat low, you can then leave it to cook itself. When you dish it up, the under-side of potato will be a golden brown.

## MOCK DUCK

*Cooking time:* 45 minutes   *Quantity:* 4 helpings

1 lb sausagemeat
8 oz cooking apples, peeled and grated

8 oz onions, grated
1 teaspoon chopped sage or ½ teaspoon dried sage

METHOD: Spread half the sausagemeat into a flat layer in a well greased baking tin or shallow casserole. Top with the apples, onions and sage. Add the rest of the sausagemeat and shape this top layer to look as much like a duck as possible. Cover with well greased paper and bake in the centre of a moderately hot oven.

## CHEESE SAUCE

*Cooking time:* 10 minutes   *Quantity:* 2 helpings

1 tablespoon flour
a little dry mustard
1 teacup milk

pepper
1 teaspoon salt
2 oz grated cheese

METHOD: Blend flour and mustard with a little milk and when smooth add the rest of the milk, bring to the boil, cook for 2 to 3 minutes, stirring all the time. Add seasoning and grated cheese, stir over a gentle heat until the cheese is melted.

# WHIT SALAD

*Preparation time:* 15 minutes    *Quantity:* 4 helpings

POTATO EGGS:
½ lb shredded carrot
2 oz grated cheese
¾ lb cooked mashed potatoes

SALAD:
¾ lb cooked, diced potato
1 small shredded cabbage or
    ½ lb spinach
½ lb shredded root vegetables
1 bunch watercress

DRESSING:
½ teaspoon salt
pinch of pepper
1 teacup milk
1 tablespoon vinegar
¼ teaspoon mustard
1 teaspoon sugar
1 teaspoon parsley and 1
    teaspoon mint, chopped
    together

METHOD: To make potato eggs, mix the carrots and grated cheese together and form into balls with a little potato if necessary. Cover the balls with a thick layer of potato and cut in halves. Arrange round the dish to look like hard-boiled eggs. Place the cooked diced potato in the centre of the dish. Add the chopped cabbage or spinach and shredded root vegetables. Decorate with watercress. Make the dressing by mixing all its ingredients together. Serve with the salad.

### The Radio Doctor Says:

'As for salad veg I don't mean a lettuce which looks as if it had loved and lost. Lettuce, in fact, is poor in Vitamin C. Go out for the cabbage leaves, the mustard and the cress, and all things raw and beautiful. Ring the changes with endive, chicory, and finely grated carrot, raw beetroot and young dandelion leaves.'

### Dig for your dinner

When salvage is all that remains of the joint
And there isn't a tin and you haven't a 'point'
Instead of creating a dance and a ballad
Just raid the allotment and dig up a salad!

## CARROT SANDWICHES FOR A CHANGE

**1** Add two parts of grated raw carrot to one part of finely shredded white heart of cabbage, and bind with chutney or sweet pickle. Pepper and salt to taste.
**2** Equal amounts of grated raw carrot, cabbage heart and crisp celery bound with chutney or sweet pickle. Pepper and salt to taste.
**3** Bind some grated raw carrot with mustard sauce, flavoured with a dash of vinegar.
**4** Cook diced carrot in curry sauce until tender enough to spread easily with a knife.

All these fillings taste their best with wholemeal bread.

# MOCK GOOSE

*Cooking time:* 1 hour    *Quantity:* 4 helpings

1½ lb potatoes
2 large cooking apples
4 oz cheese
½ teaspoon dried sage

salt and pepper
¾ pint vegetable stock
1 tablespoon flour

METHOD: Scrub and slice potatoes thinly, slice apples, grate cheese. Grease a fireproof dish, place a layer of potatoes in it, cover with apple and a little sage, season lightly and sprinkle with cheese, repeat layers leaving potatoes and cheese to cover. Pour in ½ pint of the stock, cook in a moderate oven for ¾ of an hour. Blend flour with remainder of stock, pour into dish and cook for another ¼ of an hour. Serve as a main dish with a green vegetable.

# Cakes & Baking

We could all manage without cakes, biscuits and scones but these helped to make meals more enjoyable. But the Ministry of Food used to remind us that it was important that all the family ate protective foods first before they enjoyed these home-made treats.

## EGGLESS SPONGE

*Cooking time:* 20 minutes    *Quantity:* 1 cake

6 oz self-raising flour with 1 *level* teaspoon baking powder or plain flour with 3 level teaspoons baking powder

2½ oz margarine

2 oz sugar

1 *level* tablespoon golden syrup

¼ pint milk or milk and water jam for filling

METHOD: Sift the flour and baking powder. Cream the margarine, sugar and golden syrup until soft and light, add a little flour then a little liquid. Continue like this until a smooth mixture. Grease and flour two 7 inch sandwich tins and divide the mixture between the tins. Bake for approximately 20 minutes or until firm to the touch just above the centre of a moderately hot oven. Turn out and sandwich with jam.

### Variation

*Eggless Queen Cakes:* Use the same recipe but only 6 tablespoons milk or milk and water. Spoon the mixture into about 12 large or 18 small greased patty tins and bake for 10–12 minutes in a hot oven.

## EGGLESS FRUIT CAKE

**Cooking time:** 1¼ hours **Ingredients:** 10 oz self-raising flour or plain flour with 3 teaspoons baking powder, 1 teaspoon mixed spice, pinch salt, 1 *level* teaspoon bicarbonate of soda, ½ pint well-strained weak tea, 3 oz margarine or cooking fat, 3 oz sugar, 3 oz dried fruit. **Quantity:** 1 cake

Grease and flour a 7 inch cake tin. Sift the flour or flour and baking powder, spice, salt and bicarbonate of soda together. Pour the tea into a saucepan, add the margarine or cooking fat, sugar and dried fruit. Heat until the fat and sugar melt, then boil for 2–3 minutes. Allow to cool slightly, pour on to the flour mixture, beat well and spoon into the tin. Bake in the centre of a moderate oven for 1¼ hours.

## ONE-EGG SPONGE

*Cooking time:* 15 minutes    *Quantity:* 1 cake

4 oz self-raising flour or plain flour with 2 teaspoons baking powder
1 oz margarine
2 oz sugar
1 tablespoon warmed golden syrup

1 egg or 1 reconstituted dried egg
½ *level* teaspoon bicarbonate of soda
4 tablespoons milk
little jam

METHOD: Grease and flour two 6 inch sandwich tins. Sift the flour or flour and baking powder. Cream together the margarine, sugar and golden syrup. Beat in the egg, then add the flour. Blend the bicarbonate of soda with the milk, beat into the creamed mixture. Spoon into the tins and bake above the centre of a moderate to moderately hot oven for approximately 15 minutes. Turn out of the tins, cool and sandwich together with a little jam.

# SYRUP LOAF

*Cooking time:* 30 minutes   *Quantity:* 1 loaf

4 oz self-raising flour or plain
   flour with 2 teaspoons
   baking powder
½ teaspoon bicarbonate of
   soda

pinch salt
2 tablespoons warmed golden
   syrup
¼ pint milk or milk and water

METHOD: Sift flour or flour and baking powder, bicarbonate of soda and salt. Heat the syrup and milk or milk and water, pour over the flour and beat well. Pour into a well greased 1 lb loaf tin and bake in the centre of a moderately hot to hot oven for 30 minutes or until firm.

# DRIPPING CAKE

*Cooking time:* 1 hour   *Quantity:* 1 cake

8 oz self-raising flour or plain
   flour with 4 teaspoons
   baking powder
pinch salt
1 teaspoon mixed spice
2–3 oz clarified dripping

2–3 oz sugar
3 oz mixed dried fruit
1 egg or 1 reconstituted dried
   egg
milk or milk and water to
   mix

METHOD: Sift the flour or flour and baking powder, salt and mixed spice. Rub in the dripping, if this is very firm grate it first. Add the sugar, fruit, egg and enough milk or milk and water to make a sticky consistency. Put into a greased and floured, 7 inch cake tin. Bake in a moderate oven about 1 hour.

## SPICE CAKE

**Cooking time:** 1½ hours
**Ingredients:** 4 oz dried fruit, 3 oz margarine or lard, 2 oz sugar, 1 teaspoon mixed spice, dusting of grated nutmeg, 1 teacup water, 8 oz self-raising flour or plain flour with 4 teaspoons baking powder, 2 oz golden syrup, 1 tablespoon milk, 1½ teaspoons bicarbonate of soda. **Quantity:** 1 cake

Put the fruit, margarine or lard, sugar, spices and water into a good-sized saucepan, bring to the boil. Simmer for 5 minutes and leave until quite cold. Turn into a bowl and fold in the flour or flour and baking powder. Warm the syrup with the tablespoon of milk in the saucepan, stir in the bicarbonate of soda, immediately blend with the rest of the ingredients. See that the soda is thoroughly mixed in or the cake will be streaky instead of richly brown all over. Turn into a greased cake tin and bake in a slow oven for 1½ hours.

***Saving Paper*** *Always save butter and margarine paper; they are just the thing for lining cake tins.*

# VINEGAR CAKE

*Cooking time:* 1 hour   *Quantity:* 1 cake

6 oz self-raising flour
3 oz margarine
3 oz sugar
¼ pint milk

1 tablespoon vinegar
½ teaspoon bicarbonate of
   soda
3–4 oz mixed dried fruit

METHOD: Sift the flour. Cream the margarine and sugar. Pour the milk into a large basin, add the vinegar and bicarbonate of soda; the mixture will rise and froth in the basin. Blend the flour and vinegar liquid into the creamed margarine and sugar then add the dried fruit. Put into a greased and floured 7 inch tin, bake in a moderate oven for 1 hour.

# DARK STICKY GINGERBREAD

*Cooking time:* 50 minutes    *Quantity:* 1 cake

6 oz self-raising flour or plain
  flour with 3 teaspoons
  baking powder
pinch salt
1 teaspoon bicarbonate of
  soda
1 teaspoon ground ginger
1 teaspoon ground cinnamon
  or mixed spice

1 tablespoon dried egg, dry
2 oz cooking fat or dripping
  or margarine or peanut
  butter
2 oz sugar
2 good tablespoons black
  treacle or golden syrup
1½ tablespoons milk
6 tablespoons water

METHOD: Line a tin about 7 by 4 inches with greased greaseproof paper or use margarine or cooking fat paper. Sift the dry ingredients into a mixing bowl. Put the fat (or alternatives), sugar, treacle or syrup into a saucepan, heat until melted, pour on to the dry ingredients, add the milk and beat well. Put the water into a saucepan in which the ingredients were melted and heat to boiling point, stir well to make sure no ingredients are wasted then pour on to the other ingredients and mix. Pour into the tin and bake in the centre of a very moderate oven for 50 minutes or until *just* firm. Cool in the tin for 30 minutes then turn out.

## Variations

If you want a dark gingerbread and have no black treacle, add 1 teaspoon gravy browning to the other ingredients.
*Moist Orange Cake:* Follow the recipe above; omit the spices and use marmalade instead of treacle or golden syrup.

## *WATER BISCUITS*

These are like the biscuits we used to buy before the war to serve with cheese.

Sift 8 oz plain flour and ½ teaspoon salt. Rub in 1 oz cooking fat and mix with water to make a firm dough. Knead well and roll out until paper thin. Cut into rounds or squares, put on to ungreased baking sheets and bake for 3–4 minutes towards the top of a very hot oven. The biscuits blister if they are rolled sufficiently thin.

# WELSH CAKES

*Cooking time:* 8–10 minutes    *Quantity:* Makes about 12

2 oz dripping
6 oz self-raising flour or plain
  flour and 3 teaspoons
  baking powder
¼ teaspoon ground nutmeg
2 oz sugar

2 oz mixed dried fruit
  (including some chopped
  dates or grated carrot)
1 reconstituted dried egg or 1
  fresh egg
1 tablespoon milk

METHOD: Rub the fat into the flour or flour and baking powder and add the spice, sugar and dried fruit. Mix to a stiff dough with the egg and milk. Treat the mixture as pastry and roll out to ¼ inch in thickness. Cut into 3 inch rounds. Preheat and grease a griddle or heavy frying pan. Put in the Welsh Cakes and cook for 4 minutes, or until golden brown on both sides.

# GINGER PARKIN

*Cooking time:* 50 minutes     *Quantity:* 1 cake

4 oz self-raising flour with 1
  teaspoon baking powder or
  plain flour with 3
  teaspoons baking powder
1 level teaspoon bicarbonate
  of soda
2 oz margarine or cooking fat
3 oz medium oat meal or
  rolled oats
1 oz sugar
2 tablespoons golden syrup
5 tablespoons milk

METHOD: Line a tin about 7 by 4 inches with greased greaseproof paper or use margarine or cooking fat paper. Sift the dry ingredients together, rub in the margarine or cooking fat, then add the oatmeal or rolled oats, sugar, golden syrup and milk and beat well. Spoon into the lined tin and bake in the centre of a moderate oven for 50 minutes or until firm.

### Variation

*Ginger Sponge Parkin:* Use 6 oz flour and omit the oatmeal or rolled oats. Reduce the liquid to 4 tablespoons. Bake as above and split the cake and fill with jam and a Mock Cream, page 61.

# GINGER AND DATE CAKE

*Cooking time:* 50 minutes     *Quantity:* 1 cake

7 oz self-raising flour or plain
  flour with 3 teaspoons
  baking powder
1 teaspoon bicarbonate of
  soda
1 teaspoon ground ginger
2 oz cooking fat, dripping or
  margarine
2 tablespoons golden syrup
1–2 oz sugar
2–3 oz dates, chopped
1 egg or 1 reconstituted dried
  egg
3 tablespoons milk or milk
  and water

METHOD: Line a tin about 7 × 4 inches with greased greaseproof paper or use margarine or cooking fat paper. Sift the dry ingredients together. Put the fat, dripping or margarine, syrup and sugar into a saucepan. Heat until melted. Add the dates and allow to stand for a few minutes then blend these ingredients and the egg with the flour mixture. Heat the milk or milk and water in the saucepan in which the fat was melted, stir well to make sure none of the ingredients are wasted. Pour on to the rest of the cake ingredients, beat well. Spoon into the tin and bake in the centre of a very moderate oven for 50 minutes. Cool in the tin for 20 minutes, then turn out.

---

**RECIPE of the WEEK**

## *FLAKED BARLEY CAKE*

**Cooking time:** 45–50 minutes **Ingredients:** 6 oz self-raising flour or plain flour with 3 teaspoons baking powder, ¼ teaspoon salt, 3 oz margarine, 3 oz sugar, 3 oz flaked barley, 4 tablespoons milk or water, 2 tablespoons jam. **Quantity:** 1 cake

Sift together the flour or flour and baking powder and salt. Rub in the margarine, add 2 oz of the sugar and the barley and mix to a stiff dough with the milk or water. Divide the mixture in half and shape into two equal sized rounds, about ½ inch thick. Put one round on a greased baking sheet and cover with jam. Place the other round on top, sprinkle with the rest of the sugar and bake in a hot oven for 20 minutes. Lower the heat to moderate and cook for a further 25–30 minutes until the cake is cooked through.

Reflect, whenever you indulge
It is not beautiful to bulge
A large, untidy corporation
Is far from helpful to the Nation

# ROCK BUNS

*Cooking time:* 10–12 minutes *Quantity:* 10–12 cakes

8 oz self-raising flour or plain flour with 4 teaspoons baking powder
½ teaspoon mixed spice, if desired
2 oz margarine or cooking fat or dripping
2 oz sugar

2 oz mixed dried fruit, chopped if required
1 egg or 1 reconstituted dried egg
milk or milk and water to mix
2 teaspoons sugar for topping

METHOD: Sift the flour or flour and baking powder and spice. Rub in the margarine, fat or dripping; add the sugar, dried fruit and the egg. Gradually add enough milk or milk and water to make a sticky consistency. Put spoonfuls on to one or two greased baking sheets. Sprinkle with the sugar and bake in a hot to very hot oven for 10–12 minutes.

## Variation
*Jam Buns:* Omit the dried fruit in the Rock Buns. Put the plain mixture on to baking trays. Make a dip in the centre of each cake with a floured finger and put in a little jam. Bake as above.

### HONEY OATMEAL BUNS

These nourishing buns are extremely popular in most homes. Try them on your family. This recipe makes 18 medium-sized or 12 larger buns.

Sift 4 oz white flour, 1 heaped teaspoon baking powder and some salt. Then rub in 2½ oz margarine or clarified cooking fat. When evenly mixed, add 4 oz fine oatmeal and a level teaspoon ground ginger. Mix a little beaten-up egg with 3 dessertspoons honey (loosened by slight warming if necessary) and mix to a stiff consistency with a fork. You may need a little milk here. Divide the mixture into roughly piled heaps. Bake in a hot oven for quick rising; then reduce the heat slightly for crisp, even browning. The whole baking should take about 20 minutes.

★  ★

### MAIDS OF HONOUR

**Cooking time:** 15–20 minutes
**Ingredients:** shortcrust pastry made with 6 oz flour, etc. see page 53, little jam, 1 oz margarine, 1–2 oz sugar, ½ teaspoon almond essence, 3 oz fine breadcrumbs, 2 tablespoons milk. **Quantity:** 12–15 tarts

Make the pastry, roll out thinly and line 12–15 patty tins, top with a little jam. Cream the margarine, sugar and almond essence, add the breadcrumbs and milk. Spoon the top over the jam and bake in the centre of a moderately hot oven until firm and golden.

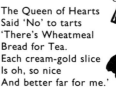

The Queen of Hearts
Said 'No' to tarts
'There's Wheatmeal
Bread for Tea.
Each cream-gold slice
Is oh, so nice
And better far for me.'

# ROLLED OAT MACAROONS

*Cooking time:* 15–20 minutes *Quantity:* 15–16 biscuits

3 oz margarine
2 oz sugar
½–1 teaspoon almond essence
1 tablespoon golden syrup

4 oz self-raising flour
4 oz rolled oats
milk to mix

METHOD: Cream the margarine, sugar, almond essence and syrup. Sift the flour, add to the creamed ingredients with the rolled oats. Mix thoroughly then add just enough milk to make the mixture bind together. Roll into 15–16 balls and put on to greased baking trays, allowing room to spread. Bake for 15–20 minutes or until golden brown in the centre of a moderate oven. Cool on the baking trays then remove.

# CARROT COOKIES

*Cooking time:* 20 minutes    *Quantity:* 12–15 cakes

1 tablespoon margarine
2 tablespoons sugar and a
  little extra for sprinkling
  on tops of the cakes
a few drops vanilla, almond
  or orange flavouring

4 tablespoons grated raw
  carrot
6 tablespoons self-raising
  flour or plain flour and ½
  teaspoon baking powder

(To get a full tablespoon of margarine or fat, plunge the spoon first into boiling water, then cut out the fat with the hot spoon. In this way, a piece of just the right quantity will be obtained.)

METHOD: Cream the fat and sugar together until it is light and fluffy. Beat in the flavouring and carrot. Fold in the flour or flour and baking powder. Drop spoonfuls of the mixture into small greased patty pans. Sprinkle the tops with sugar and bake in a brisk oven for about 20 minutes.

WE'VE A LOT TO TELL YOU....

OATMEAL

You will find hints and recipes for many simple and interesting ways to use us and other foods
. . . IN THE NEWS
read FOOD FACTS in the newspapers every week.
. . . ON THE AIR
listen to the Kitchen Front Talks at 8.15 am weekdays.

# FRUITY POTATO CAKES

*Cooking time:* 9–10 minutes    *Quantity:* 10–12 cakes

4 oz cooked potatoes
2 oz self-raising flour with ½
  teaspoon baking powder or
  plain flour with 1 teaspoon
  baking powder
1 oz margarine

1 oz sugar
1 tablespoon marmalade
1 oz dried fruit
TOPPING
sugar and mixed spice, if
  desired

METHOD: Mash or sieve the potatoes until light and floury; do not add any milk. Sift the flour and baking powder, mix with the potatoes. Cream the margarine, sugar and marmalade, then add the flour and potato mixture with the dried fruit. Mix together. Put on to a floured board and roll out with a floured rolling pin. Cut into 10–12 rounds or triangles.

Grease a heavy frying pan, solid electric hotplate or griddle with a greased paper. Heat for a few minutes then test by shaking on a little flour. The heat is correct when the flour turns golden brown within 1 minute. Put on the potato cakes. Cook for 2 minutes on either side then lower the heat and cook gently for another 5–6 minutes. Serve cold or hot.

The cakes can be sprinkled with a little sugar and mixed spice.

## BAKING POWDER DOUGHNUTS

**Cooking time:** 8–9 minutes **Ingredients:** 8 oz self-raising flour with 2 teaspoons baking powder or plain flour with 5 teaspoons baking powder, pinch salt, 2 tablespoons sugar, 2 tablespoons dried egg, dry, 4 tablespoons water, ¼ pint milk, 2 oz fat, sugar for coating. **Quantity:** 8–10 doughnuts

Sift together all the dry ingredients, gradually beat in the water and milk. Heat the fat in a large frying pan, drop in spoonfuls of the mixture. Cook quickly for 2 minutes on either side then lower the heat and cook more slowly for 4–5 minutes. Lift out of the pan, sprinkle with a little sugar. Serve hot or cold.

# RAISIN CRISPS

*Cooking time:* 20 minutes     *Quantity:* 24 biscuits

3 oz self-raising flour or plain flour with 1 teaspoon baking powder
1 tablespoon dried egg, dry
1 oz sugar

1 oz margarine
1 oz raisins, chopped
few drops almond essence
milk to mix

METHOD: Mix flour, dried egg and sugar together. Rub in the margarine, add the raisins, almond essence and enough milk to make a firm dough. Roll out thinly and cut into rounds (about 2 inches in diameter). Bake in the centre of a moderate oven for 20 minutes.

# HOW TO MAKE OATCAKES

Oatmeal, one of the finest foods for giving warmth and energy, is a 'must' for growing children. They will probably like it as Oatcakes, made this way.

Mix together 8 oz fine oatmeal, $1\frac{1}{2}$ oz self-raising flour and $\frac{1}{2}$ teaspoon salt. Add 1 tablespoon dripping, melted, and enough boiling water to bind. Roll out the mixture as thinly as possible in a little fine oatmeal. Cut it into triangles and bake on a greased tin in a fairly hot oven.

### OATMEAL BISCUITS

Mix $\frac{1}{4}$ lb flour, $\frac{1}{4}$ lb oatmeal, $\frac{1}{2}$ teaspoonful salt and $\frac{1}{2}$ teaspoon baking powder. Rub in 2 oz margarine, add 1 teaspoon sugar or syrup and mix to a stiff dough with milk or milk and water, half and half. Turn out on to a floured board and roll to about $\frac{1}{2}$ inch thickness. Cut into squares, place on a greased tin and bake in a moderate oven for 15 minutes.

### DROP SCONES

These are a favourite recipe in Scotland where they are known as Scotch Pancakes.

Sift 4 oz plain flour with 2 level teaspoons of baking powder and a pinch of salt. Add 1 tablespoon dried egg powder then beat in $\frac{1}{4}$ pint milk and 2 tablespoons water.

Grease and heat a heavy frying pan, electric solid hotplate or griddle. To test if the right heat, drop on a teaspoon of batter, this should turn golden brown on the bottom in 1 minute. Put the mixture in tablespoons on to the plate and leave until the top surface is covered with bubbles then turn and cook on the second side. The scones are cooked when quite firm.

# POTATO DROP SCONES

Rub 2 oz mashed potato into 4 oz flour and $\frac{1}{4}$ teaspoon salt. Make into a stiff batter with half a beaten egg and $\frac{1}{4}$ pint milk. Allow to stand for a time. Sift in a small teaspoon of cream of tartar and a small level teaspoon of bicarbonate of soda and $\frac{1}{2}$ oz sugar just before cooking. Cook in spoonfuls—as for Drop Scones—on a greased girdle or in a heavy frying pan. Serve with a little hot jam.

# COFFEE POTATO SCONES

Sift 6 oz plain flour, 2 level teaspoon baking powder and $\frac{1}{2}$ teaspoon salt into a basin. Mix thoroughly with 4 oz mashed potato. Rub in 2 oz fat with the tips of the fingers. Blend to a soft dough with $\frac{1}{2}$ teacup strong, milky, sweetened coffee. Roll out to $\frac{1}{2}$ inch thickness on a floured board and cut into rounds. Glaze the tops with a little milk. Bake on greased baking sheets in a hot oven for 15 minutes.

On this and the next 2 pages are a selection of recipes devised by Cadbury's which formed a leaflet which sold for 1d. in aid of the Red Cross. The rest of the recipes, which were for puddings, are on page 62.

## CHOCOLATE SQUARES

Melt 3 oz margarine with two tablespoons of syrup in a saucepan, mix in ½ lb rolled oats and a pinch of salt. Blend well, and put in a greased, shallow baking tin, flattening the mixure smoothly. Bake for half an hour to 40 minutes in a moderate oven. Take out, and whilst still hot, grate over it a tablet of chocolate. The chocolate will melt with the heat, and can be spread evenly with a knife. Cut into squares and lift out.

# CHOCOLATE LAYER CAKE

3 oz fat
1 tablespoon syrup or treacle
8 oz flour
½ teaspoon salt
1 good oz Bournville cocoa

1 teaspoon baking powder
½ teaspoon bicarbonate of soda
2 oz sugar
about ½ pint warm water

METHOD: Put fat and syrup into pan and dissolve. Mix all dry ingredients in basin and stir in melted fat and syrup, mix to a very soft consistency with warm water. Pour into two greased sandwich tins and bake about 30 minutes in a moderate oven. Turn cakes out and when cold, sandwich them with Mock Whipped Cream or chocolate spread.

*MOCK WHIPPED CREAM*
½ oz cornflour
¼ pint milk
1½ oz margarine

3 teaspoons sugar
few drops vanilla essence

METHOD: Mix cornflour to a paste with a little milk, heat remainder and when boiling add to the blended cornflour, stirring well. Return to saucepan bring to boil and cook 3 minutes. Cream the margarine and sugar. Whisk in the cornflour mixture gradually. Add vanilla essence.

*CHOCOLATE SPREAD*
1 oz Bournville cocoa
1½ tablespoons sugar

1 dessertspoon flour
½ cup milk

METHOD: Mix dry ingredients. Add the milk gradually and bring to the boil. Beat until quite smooth. Allow to cool.

# CHOCOLATE CAKE

6 oz flour
2 teaspoons baking powder
1 oz Bournville cocoa
2 oz fat
1 or 2 dried eggs, dry

2 oz sugar
3 saccharin tablets
a little milk and water
few drops vanilla essence

METHOD: Sieve flour, baking powder and cocoa together. Cream fat, egg and sugar. Add dry ingredients alternately with the saccharins dissolved in warm milk and water and essence and mix well. Bake in moderate oven about 50 minutes.

### CHOCOLATE BISCUITS

Melt 2 oz margarine and 1 tablespoon warmed syrup. Mix in 1 oz Bournville cocoa, 4 oz flour, 2 oz sugar, ¼ teaspoon bicarbonate of soda and 1 teaspoon vanilla essence. Beat well, roll out cut into squares, place on a baking sheet and prick. Bake in a moderate oven about 15 minutes. Sandwiched together with chocolate spread page 85.

## TEA-TIME FANCIES

2 oz fat
2 oz sugar
1 level tablespoon Bournville cocoa
1 dried egg, reconstituted

4 oz self-raising flour
1 level teaspoon baking powder
pinch of salt
about 2 tablespoons milk

METHOD: Cream fat and sugar, add cocoa and beat in the egg. Sift together flour, baking powder and salt and stir into the mixture alternately with a little of the milk until the consistency is soft and creamy. Put a spoonful of the mixture into greased and floured patty pans and bake about 20 minutes in a moderate oven. When cold slice off the tops, spread liberally with Mock Cream page 61 and replace tilted to show the filling.

### CHOCOLATE FLAVOURING

All the family will enjoy cakes and biscuits given a chocolate flavour, this is easily achieved as you will see from the recipes on the various pages.

## GLOSSY CHOCOLATE ICING

METHOD: Mix together 2 teaspoons melted margarine, 1 tablespoon cocoa powder, 1 tablespoon golden syrup and a few drops of vanilla essence.

## CHOCOLATE OAT CAKES

1 oz margarine and
1 oz cooking fat
8 oz self-raising flour
1 breakfastcup rolled oats

2 oz sugar
salt
1½ oz Bournville cocoa
milk and water

METHOD: Rub fats into flour. Add oats, sugar, salt and cocoa. Mix well adding a little milk and water to moisten. Roll out very thinly, cut into rounds and prick all over with a fork. Bake in a moderate oven about 15 minutes till golden brown.

# AMERICAN PIN WHEELS

PASTRY
8 oz flour
pinch of salt
¼ teaspoon bicarbonate of
  soda
½ teaspoon cream of tartar
or 1 teaspoon baking powder
2 oz margarine

milk to mix
CHOCOLATE MIXTURE
2 oz margarine
2 tablespoons sugar
1 dessertspoon Bournville
  cocoa
½ teaspoon vanilla essence

PASTRY: Put flour, salt, soda and cream of tartar in a bowl. Mix together, rub in margarine and bind to a stiff paste with milk.

CHOCOLATE MIXTURE: Cream margarine and sugar together, stir in cocoa, add essence, and if necessary a tablespoonful of milk; do not make too soft or the mixture will run during cooking. Roll out pastry into an oblong and spread with chocolate mixture. Roll up as for jam roll and cut into ¾ inch rounds. Pack into a baking tin and bake in a moderately hot oven 20 to 30 minutes.

★　　　★　　　★

# CHOCOLATE CAKE

2 oz margarine or cooking fat
2 oz sugar
few drops vanilla essence
1 tablespoon warmed golden
  syrup
5 oz self-raising flour or plain
  flour with 2 teaspoons
  baking powder

½ teaspoon bicarbonate of
  soda
1 oz Bournville cocoa
2 eggs or 2 reconstituted
  dried eggs
Milk or milk and water to
  mix
jam

METHOD: Cream together the margarine or cooking fat, sugar, vanilla essence and golden syrup. Sift the flour or flour and baking powder, bicarbonate of soda and cocoa. Add the eggs gradually to the creamed ingredients then the cocoa mixture and lastly enough milk or milk and water to make a soft consistency. Divide the mixture between two 7 inch greased and floured sandwich tins. Bake just above the centre of a moderate to moderately hot oven for 20–25 minutes or until firm to the touch. Cool and sandwich together with jam. The cake can be topped with Glossy Chocolate Icing, left.

## RECIPE of the WEEK

### STEAMED CHOCOLATE CAKE

**Cooking time:** 1½ hours
**Ingredients in a saucepan:** 1 breakfastcup milk, 2 tablespoons syrup, 2 oz margarine or lard
**Ingredients in a bowl:** 1 breakfast cup self-raising flour, 1½ tablespoons sugar, 2 tablespoons Bournville cocoa, 1 teaspoon bicarbonate of soda, 1 dessertspoon vinegar
**Quantity:** 1 cake
**Method:** warm ingredients in a saucepan, stirring them together. Meanwhile mix together ingredients in bowl mix very thoroughly. See that there are not any lumps of bicarbonate left. Pour warm sauce out of pan into bowl and stir all together adding vinegar. Pour mixture into a 7 in greased and floured cake tin, cover with greased paper and an inverted saucer. Steam for 1½ hours.
Note: One small gas jet will cook cake and a steamed pudding at the same time, one above the other.

# SCOTCH SHORTBREAD

This is an exceptionally economical recipe.

METHOD: Melt 2 oz margarine, add 4 oz plain flour and 1 oz sugar and mix well then knead with your fingers until the mixture binds together. Put on to an ungreased baking tin and press hard to form into a neat round about ½ inch in thickness. Mark into 6–8 sections; prick with a fork and bake in the centre of a moderate oven for 20 minutes.

# ICING
### (made with sugar and household milk)

4 level dessertspoons sugar
6 level tablespoons household
   milk, dry

2 tablespoons water
colouring
flavouring

METHOD: Mix sugar and milk powder together. Add water and beat till smooth. Add colouring and flavouring and spread on top of cake.

# GINGERBREAD MEN

*Cooking time:* 20 minutes   *Quantity:* 6–8 men

2 oz sugar or golden syrup
2 oz margarine
8 oz plain flour
½ level teaspoon mixed spice
2 level teaspoons ground
   ginger

few drops lemon substitute
1 level teaspoon bicarbonate
   of soda
1 tablespoon tepid water
little reconstituted egg
few currants

METHOD: Melt in a pan the sugar or syrup and margarine. Pour into a bowl, add some of the flour, the spices and lemon substitute. Stir well. Dissolve the bicarbonate of soda in the water, add to the mixture, continue stirring, gradually adding more flour. Finish the process by turning out the mixture on to a well-floured board. Knead in the remainder of the flour. Roll a small ball for the head, flatten it and place it on a greased baking tin, roll an oblong for the body and strips for arms and legs. Join these together with a little of the egg and put currants for the eyes. Continue like this until you have made 6–8 'men'. Cook in the centre of a moderate oven for 20 minutes. Cool then remove to a wire tray. Store in an airtight tin.

**RECIPE of the WEEK**

### UNCOOKED CHOCOLATE CAKE

This is a special treat for children who could make it themselves if they are old enough to heat food in a saucepan.

Put 2 oz margarine, 2 oz sugar and 2 tablespoons golden syrup into a saucepan. Heat gently until the margarine has melted and then remove from the heat. Stir in 2 oz cocoa powder and a few drops of vanilla essense then 6 oz crisp breadcrumbs. Mix well. Grease a 7 inch sandwich tin with margarine paper then put in the crumb mixture. Allow to stand for 4 or 5 hours then turn out carefully. Top with Glossy Chocolate Icing, made as the recipe on page 86.

# SIMNEL CAKE

*Cooking time:* 1 hour    *Quantity:* 1 cake

8 oz self-raising flour or plain
   flour with 4 teaspoons
   baking powder
pinch salt
1 teaspoon mixed spice
½ teaspoon ground nutmeg
½ teaspoon ground cinnamon
2 oz margarine or cooking fat

1½ oz sugar
8 oz mixed dried fruit,
   chopped
1 tablespoon golden syrup
1 tablespoon marmalade
¼ pint milk and water to mix
Mock Marzipan to decorate,
   right

METHOD: Sift the flour, baking powder if used, salt and spices together. Rub in the fat and add the sugar and fruit. Mix to a stiff consistency with the syrup, marmalade and milk and water. Turn into a greased 6 or 7 inch tin and bake in a moderate oven for 1 hour. When cold, cut in half, place a layer of Mock Marzipan between the two halves and decorate the top with the remaining paste.

## MOCK MARZIPAN

**Ingredients:** 2 oz margarine, 2 tablespoons water, 2–3 teaspoons ratafia or almond essence, 4 oz sugar or golden syrup, 4 oz soya flour

Melt margarine in the water, add essence and sugar or syrup then soya flour. Turn on to a board and knead well. Roll out; cut to a circular shape with the tin the cake was baked in. Smear the top of the cake with jam or jelly then cover with marzipan. The cake can be topped with icing as below.

Turn on your wireless at 8.15 every morning and listen to the Kitchen Front for useful tips and recipes.

## CHRISTMAS FANCIES

### CHOCOLATE COATING FOR YOUR CHRISTMAS CAKE

Mix together 3 tablespoons of sugar with 2 tablespoons of cocoa and 2 tablespoons of milk. Stir, in a stout saucepan, over a low heat until the mixture is thick and bubbly like toffee, then, while hot, pour it over your cake.

**A Christmassy sparkle** is easy to give to sprigs of holly or evergreen for use on puddings. Dip your greenery in a strong solution of Epsom salts. When dry it will be beautifully frosted.

# CHRISTMAS CAKE

*Cooking time:* 2 hours    *Quantity:* 1 cake

3 oz sugar
4 oz margarine
1 level tablespoon golden
   syrup
8 oz plain flour
2 teaspoons baking powder
pinch salt
1 level teaspoon mixed spice

1 level teaspoon ground
   cinnamon
2–4 reconstituted dried eggs
1 lb mixed dried fruit
½ teaspoon lemon substitute
   or essence
milk to mix

METHOD: Cream the sugar and margarine, add the syrup. Mix the flour, baking powder, salt and spices together. Add alternately with the eggs to the creamed mixture and beat well. Add the fruit, lemon substitute or essence and enough milk to make a fairly soft dough. Line a 7 inch tin with greased paper, put in the mixture and bake in a very moderate oven for 2 hours.

   This cake should keep about 2 months if stored in a clean, dry, airtight tin. Do not store until quite cold. Examine from time to time to make sure it is keeping all right.

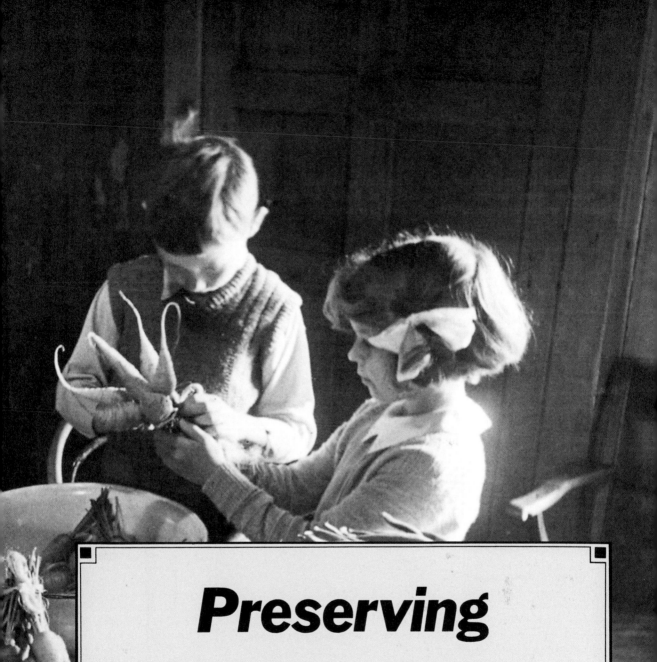

# Preserving

It is always a source of satisfaction and of pride to have one's own home-made jams, jellies and pickles. But when the Battle of the Atlantic was raging it was up to each one of us to preserve every ounce of home grown fruit and vegetables we could. So we searched our gardens and the fields and hedgerows for all the produce we could find and preserved them for the winter.

# Bottling without Sugar

. . . and if you follow these directions, it will be bottling without tears or fears. Home-grown fruits are grand ship savers and every ounce possible must be saved.

## OVEN METHOD

**1** Wash and drain jars.

**2** Pack fruit tightly, almost to top of jar.

**3** Place in a very low oven (gas mark $\frac{1}{4}$, 240 F) on cardboard or several thicknesses of paper. Jars should be covered with the lids (without rubber rings) to prevent fruit from burning.

**4** Leave in oven for $\frac{3}{4}$ hour to 1 hour (allow $1\frac{1}{4}$–$1\frac{1}{2}$ hours for apricots, pears and peaches) until fruit is cooked. Fruit shrinks in cooking so top up with fruit from one of the jars.

**5** Remove jars from oven one at a time, place on wooden table and cover fruit with boiling water.

**6** Tap jars to expel bubbles.

**7** Seal at once with rubber rings, lids and clips or screw-bands. The screw-bands should be tightened as jars cool.

**8** Test next day by removing screw-bands or clips. If seal is perfect you can lift jars by lids. Screw-bands should be dried, lightly greased and put on again loosely. Clips should not be replaced.

## TOP-OF-THE-STOVE METHOD

**1** Wash and drain jars.

**2** Pack jars tightly with fruit until almost full.

**3** Cover fruit with cold water, filling jars to overflowing.

**4** Fix on rubber rings (already soaked in cold water) and lids by clip or screw-bands. (Give screw-band a half-turn back to allow for expansion.)

**5** Take a fish kettle, zinc bath, bucket, or any pan deep enough for water to cover jars. Put a piece of wood or other packing in the bottom. The jars mustn't touch each other or the saucepan. Cover the jars with cold water.

**6** Bring the water very slowly to simmering point. (This should take $1\frac{1}{2}$ hours.) Simmer for 15 minutes. (Apricots, Pears and Peaches need 30 minutes.)

**7** Remove jars from saucepan. Place on wooden table, tighten screw-bands.

**8** Test next day as above.

Even more bottles and rings have been sent out to the shops this year than last—but demand is heavier too. Manufacture is still going on, so if you don't succeed in buying at the first attempt it is worth trying again. You may be able to use old rubber rings, but test them first for elasticity.

### HOW TO USE CAMPDEN TABLETS

**1** Dissolve Campden Tablets in cold or tepid water, allow 1 tablet to each $\frac{1}{2}$ pint of water.

**2** Pack the fruit into jars to within an inch of the top. Do not pack too tightly.

**3** Pour over the Campden solution until fruit is entirely covered. (Approximately $\frac{1}{2}$ pint of solution for each pound of fruit.)

**4** Seal at once with rubber rings, clips or screw-bands and glass lids.

**5** When fruit is required for use it must be boiled first in an open pan to get rid of preservative. This usually takes about 15 minutes.

**6** If metal covers are used, protect metal by fitting 2 or 3 layers of paper in lid.

# Preparing for Winter!

## APPLE RINGS

Here's a way of keeping apples that can be used for windfalls or blemished fruit. Wipe the apples, remove the cores and peel thinly. Cut out any blemishes. Slice into rings about $\frac{1}{4}$ inch thick. Steep the rings for 10 minutes in water containing $1\frac{1}{2}$ oz of salt to the gallon. Thread the rings on sticks or canes to fit across the oven or spread on trays. Dry very slowly until they feel like chamois leather. The temperature should not exceed 150°F. Turn once or twice during cooking.

Pears can be treated in the same way, but they must be cut in halves or quarters and spread on the trays.

## PARSLEY HONEY

*Cooking time:* $\frac{3}{4}$ hour    *Quantity:* 1 lb

5 oz parsley (including stalks)    1 lb sugar
$1\frac{1}{2}$ pints water    $\frac{1}{2}$ teaspoon vinegar

METHOD: Pick parsley and wash well. Dry. Chop stalks up roughly. Put into a pan with $1\frac{1}{2}$ pints of boiling water and boil until it reduces to a pint. Strain. Add 1 lb sugar and boil until syrupy (like honey) about 20 minutes, then add $\frac{1}{2}$ teaspoonful of vinegar. Pour into pots and cover. This jells by the next day, and tastes and looks like heather honey.

### HOW CAN I PRESERVE TOMATOES?

One way is to pulp them. Wash, and cut the tomatoes into quarters; and, if liked, add $\frac{1}{4}$ oz each of salt and sugar to every 2 lb tomatoes. Heat in a covered saucepan until quite soft. Rub the pulp through a sieve, return to the pan and bring to the boil. Have ready clean, hot jars. Fill the jars one at a time with the boiling hot pulp and seal it immediately before proceeding to next jar. Keep the pan on the heat all the time. Seal with four rounds of thin paper cut large enough to come well down the outside of the jars. Brush each round of paper with well-boiled paste and press, one above the other, tightly over the neck of the jar. Tie tightly with string while the paste is still wet.

Another method is to plunge the tomatoes, whole, into boiling water for half a minute, then into cold water. Peel them, put into screw-band or clip-top jars. Cover the tomatoes with brine made with $\frac{1}{2}$ oz salt to 1 quart water; add $\frac{1}{4}$ oz sugar, if liked. Put on the lids and sterilise in the same way as for bottled fruit but raise the temperature to 190°F in $1\frac{1}{2}$ hours and maintain for 30 minutes.

### Does Campden Solution Destroy Food Value in Fruits?

No. When required for use, of course, the fruits preserved by this simple method must be boiled to get rid of the preservative, but this  lowers the vitamin value only as much as ordinary cooking.

*Food for the picking*

Blackberrying is a traditional custom that most of us have enjoyed at one time or another. There are other Hedgerow Harvests too, that provide good things for the larder. So why not take the children and go a-harvesting? Be sure, however, that in their excitement they do not damage bushes or hedges, or walk through growing crops, or gather mushrooms in fields without getting the farmer's permission.

## GOOD JAMS AND JELLIES

Use the freshest fruit possible and try and pick or buy this when it is just ripe, but not over soft or bruised in any way. Use the amount of sugar recommended in reliable recipes if you want the jam or jelly to keep well. Each jar should contain 60% sugar content for perfect keeping quality, i.e. each 1 lb sugar should produce 1⅔ lbs jam or jelly. Cover the jars well and store in a cool dry place.

Several easy to make and less usual jams, marmalades and preserves are given.

Cooking or crab apples make a lovely jelly, so do other fruits with lots of flavour. There is no need to peel or core apples, simply cut them into pieces (you could use windfalls providing all bruised parts are cut away). To each 2 lb fruit allow 1 pint water. Simmer the fruit slowly to extract all the pectin then put through a jelly bag or several thicknesses of muslin to extract the juice. Measure this and allow 1 lb sugar to each 1 pint juice. Stir the heated juice and sugar until all the sugar has dissolved then boil rapidly until setting point is reached.

For a new flavour try mixing blackberries or rose hips with the apples.

**Elderberries** are delicious stewed with half-and-half apple; or made into jam with an equal quantity of blackberries. Wash and strip them from the stems.

**Sloes** look like tiny damsons. They are too sour to use as stewed fruit, but make a delightful preserve with marrow.

**Rowan-berries (Mountain Ash)** make a preserve with a pleasant tang, admirable to serve with cold meats. You can make the preserve of the berries alone, or with a couple of apples to each pound of berries.

**Hips and Haws** should not be picked until perfectly ripe. Hips—the berries of the wild rose, make a vitamin-rich syrup. Haws—the berries of the may-tree, make a brown jelly that is very like guava jelly.

**Nuts.** Cobnuts, walnuts, chestnuts and filberts are good keepers. Choose very sound well-coloured nuts. Remove them from their husks, spread them out and leave to dry overnight. Pack cobnuts and filberts tightly into jars or crocks and cover with an inch layer of crushed block salt. Pack walnuts and chestnuts in a similar manner but cover with sand instead of salt. Packed in this way your nuts should keep till Christmas. Beechnuts make good eating, too. Store them as you would cobnuts. Use as almonds.

**Mushrooms** are very easy to dry and make an excellent flavouring for winter soups and dishes. Small button mushrooms are best for drying. Gather them in the early morning; simply spread them out to dry in the air for a few days.

# ORANGE AND APPLE MARMALADE

Occasionally we are able to bring fresh oranges into the country for young children. Keep the peel and use it to make marmalade.

METHOD: Take the peel from 1 lb sweet oranges (this is 3–4 oranges). Shred this finely. Put into 2½ pints cold water and soak overnight. Simmer the peel in the water until tender and the liquid reduced. Add 1 lb peeled cooking apples (weight when peeled) to the peel and liquid. Simmer until the apples make a smooth purée.

Measure the apple and orange mixture. To each 1 pint pulp allow 1 lb sugar. Put the pulp and sugar back into the pan, stir over a low heat until the sugar has dissolved, then boil rapidly until setting point is reached. Put into hot jars and seal.

# ELDERBERRY AND APPLE JAM

*Cooking time:* about 1 hour     *Quantity:* about 6 lbs

3 lb elderberries          5 lb sugar
3 lb apples

METHOD: Remove berries from stalks and wash. Warm them to draw juice. Simmer for ½ hour to soften skins. Core apples and simmer until quite soft in another pan with very little water, pass through sieve or pulp well with wooden spoon, add apples to elderberries, reheat and add sugar. Stir until dissolved and boil rapidly until jam sets. Make first test for setting after 10 minutes. Put into hot jars and seal.

# BLACKBERRY AND APPLE JAM

*Cooking time:* ¾ hour     *Quantity:* about 5 lbs

Here is a favourite recipe:
1½ lb sour apples           4 lb firm blackberries
1 breakfastcupful water     4½ lb sugar

METHOD: Peel, core and slice the apples. Put in the preserving pan with the water and cook till quite soft. Add the blackberries and bring to the simmer. Simmer for 5 minutes, then add the sugar (warmed) and boil rapidly until setting point is reached. (Make first test after 10 minutes.) Put into hot jars and seal.

### Rose-Hip Syrup

This syrup is suitable for infants, very palatable and so rich in Vitamin C that 1 oz is sufficient for 1 month. It is 15–20 times as rich as orange juice.

2 lb rose hips, ripe and red, 1 lb 2 oz sugar

Wash hips and put into a stainless pan. Well cover with water and bring to the boil. Simmer until tender (about 10 minutes). Mash well with a wooden spoon. Put into a jelly bag made of flannel and squeeze out as much juice as possible. Return pulp to the saucepan and add as much water as at first. Bring to the boil and simmer for 5–10 minutes. Put back into jelly bag and squeeze again. Empty bag and wash it thoroughly. Mix the two lots of juice and pour into the clean jelly bag. Allow to drip overnight. A clean juice is now obtained free from the hairs that cover the seeds inside the fruit which might cause irritation if not removed.

Boil the juice down until it measures about 1½ pints, then add 1 lb 2 oz sugar. Stir until dissolved, boil for 5 minutes. Bottle while hot in perfectly clean hot bottles and seal at once. Small screw-capped bottles with rubber washers are suitable. A circle of rubber cut from an old hot water bottle or cycle inner tube, and boiled for 10 minutes to sterilise will do for a washer. The syrup should be stored in a dark cupboard.

A saltspoonful (15 drops) should be sufficient for an infant each day.

# They'll be welcome this winter

P EAS AND BEANS are very nourishing and they are easy to preserve and to store. *Drying* is the best method for peas and broad beans; *salting* is the best method for runner and French beans. Think how your family will enjoy these summer vegetables on a winter's day! Here is how to do it:

## Salting Beans

Salting is the best way of preserving runner or French beans. Use young fresh beans. Take a lb of cooking salt to 3 lb of beans. Wash the beans, dry, string them and, if large, break into pieces. Crush the salt with a rolling pin. Put a layer of salt about 1 inch deep into the bottom of a crock or jar. Press in a layer of beans, then another layer of salt $\frac{1}{2}$ inch deep, and so on. The secret of success is to pack the salt well down on the beans. Finish with a layer of salt 1 inch deep. Cover with paper and tie down. Leave for few days for beans to shrink. Add more beans and more salt until jar is full again. If beans are well covered with salt it doesn't matter how moist they are. Re-cover. Store in a dry cool place. Before use, wash beans thoroughly in hot water, then soak for 2 hours in warm water. Cook without salt.

**DRYING** Begin by dropping the peas or broad beans (shelled) into boiling water; boil for two or three minutes, drain. This improves the colour. Next, if you have time, 'pop' the skins off; the peas or beans then fall into halves and dry more quickly. All vegetables should be dried as quickly as possible, but be careful not to scorch them.

**IN THE OVEN** Spread the vegetables thinly on cake racks or trays made by nailing wooden slats together for frames, and tacking tightly stretched canvas or other open material across the bottoms (old curtain net will do). Put the trays in the oven (temperature not more than 150° Fahrenheit) and leave the door slightly open as this allows the moisture to escape. If you have a dial regulator, take no notice of it, but use the tap to adjust the heat, or you can use the heat left after baking, and so save fuel. In this case give the vegetables a good hour or so, then continue the next day. Several periods of such drying will do no harm.

**IN THE AIRING CUP-BOARD** Spread the vegetables on muslin, place on the hot water tank or on the hottest shelf in the cupboard and leave for several days with the door ajar.

***WHICHEVER METHOD YOU USE***, continue drying until the peas or beans are quite crisp. Then leave them for twelve hours to get cold. Store them in paper bags, or pieces of paper tied with string, in tins or jars. Look them over occasionally to see they're all right.

# MAKING GOOD PICKLES

Pickles and chutneys help to make meals more interesting so are worth making. Choose good quality vegetables for pickles. It is very important to have pure malt vinegar; this may be a little difficult to find, but it is worth while searching for it.

Cover pickles and chutneys carefully, never put metal tops directly on to the preserve, line the inside of a metal top with thick paper or cardboard; this prevents the top becoming rusty and spoiling the top of the contents of the jars.

★ **NOW—before you forget it—**
cut out this advertisement, put it up in your kitchen and make a start with your vegetable and fruit preserving. Think what a thrill it will be for your family in the dark days of winter when you serve such treats as summer peas, beans, pears, plums and apples of your own preserving.

## *PICKLED CUCUMBERS*

If the cucumbers are very small they can be left whole, but otherwise cut into convenient sized pieces.

Put into a brine made with 2 oz cooking salt to 1 pint cold water. Soak overnight. Allow 1 level tablespoon mixed pickling spices to each pint of vinegar. Boil vinegar and pickling spices for 15 minutes, strain and cool. Remove the cucumber from the brine, rinse well under the cold tap, then drain thoroughly. Pack into jars, pour over the cold vinegar and seal carefully.

# APPLE CHUTNEY

*Cooking time:* 45 minutes    *Quantity:* 3½ lb

| | |
|---|---|
| 8 oz onions, grated or finely chopped | 1 teaspoon pickling spices |
| ½ pint malt vinegar | 1 teaspoon salt |
| 2 lb apples, weight when peeled and chopped | 1 teaspoon ground ginger |
| | 12 oz sugar |
| | 2–4 oz dried fruit (if desired) |

METHOD: Put the onions into a saucepan with a little vinegar and simmer until nearly soft. Add the apples, spices tied up securely in a muslin bag, salt, ground ginger and just enough vinegar to stop the mixture from burning. Cook gently until the fruit is soft, stirring from time to time. Add the remainder of the vinegar and thoroughly stir in the sugar and dried fruit. Boil steadily until the chutney is thick. Remove the bag of pickling spices and pour the hot chutney into hot jars. Seal down at once.

# MUSTARD PICKLES

*Cooking time:* 15–20 minutes    *Quantity:* 2½ lb

| | |
|---|---|
| 2 lb mixed vegetables | 2 oz sugar |
| brine—see under Pickled Cucumber | 1 tablespoon flour or ½ tablespoon cornflour |
| 1 pint vinegar | 1 dessertspoon ground ginger |
| 1 tablespoon pickling spice | ½ tablespoon tumeric powder |

METHOD: Cut the vegetables into neat pieces. Soak overnight in brine. For quantities of brine, see Pickled Cucumbers, this page. Wash well under the cold tap and drain thoroughly. Boil the vinegar and pickling spice together. Mix all the dry ingredients with a very little vinegar until a smooth paste, pour over the strained hot vinegar and stir well. Return to the pan and cook until just thickened. Put in the vegetables and cook for 5 minutes. Put into jars and seal well.

# PICKLED ONIONS AND SHALLOTS

Remove outer skins from the onions or shallots, using a stainless knife to prevent their discolouring.

Soak in brine for 48 hours. For quantities see Pickled Cucumbers. Then proceed as for that recipe.

# Making Do

It was a challenge to all of us to 'make do' in every way, to save fuel and use our food wisely. We may not have been able to produce exactly the same dishes as we did before the war, but we could still keep our families well fed. The government gave us many ideas and dealt with various problems and many other people passed on their tips.

# 5 DISHES FROM 1 RECIPE

**Ingredients:** 1 level tablespoon dried egg (dry)*, 4 oz flour, pinch of salt, ½ pint of milk and water mixed. **Method:** Mix dry ingredients. Add sufficient liquid to make a stiff mixture. Beat well, add rest of liquid and beat again. *Dried eggs are new-laid shell eggs with shell and water removed.

## YORKSHIRE PUDDING

Make a knob of fat smoking hot in a tin and pour in the batter. Cook in brisk oven for 30 minutes.

## TOAD-IN-THE-HOLE

Use batter with sausages or meat left-overs. Cook for 30 minutes.

## SWEET PANCAKES

Make a knob of fat 'smoking' hot in frying pan. Cook each pancake separately (this makes 6 pancakes), browning on each side. Add jam while in pan; roll up.

## SAVOURY PANCAKES

Same as above, using fried onions or leeks, grated cheese or chopped cooked vegetables.

## BATTER PUDDING

Same as Yorkshire Pudding; omit salt, add sugar and fruit (dried apples or bottled plums). Cook and serve in baking dish.

# New ways with Carrots

'I can see why they tell us to eat a lot of home grown carrots', says Mrs. Harass 'but what else can you do with them except boil them?'

Carrots have many uses, not only in soups and stews but to sweeten puddings (they even take the place of apricots, as in the recipe on page 52) and in Cookies (page 83). They are delicious baked round a joint or in Carrot Jam (recipe opposite or in this Marmalade.

## CARROT AND SEVILLE ORANGE MARMALADE

This recipe has been tested by the Research Station at Long Ashton. It yields about 5½ lb of marmalade.

Wash 1¼ lb Seville oranges and squeeze out the juice. Collect all the pips into a muslin bag. Cut up the peel fairly coarsely and place it, with the juice and bag of pips, in a basin. Cover with 2 pints of water and leave overnight. Next morning, simmer gently until the peel is quite tender and the weight of pulp is 2½ lb. Remove the pips.

Cook 2 lb carrots (weighed after scraping) in a pint of water, in a covered saucepan until tender, and then mash well or rub through a wire sieve.

Add the carrot pulp and the water to the orange, bring to the boil, add 2 lb sugar and boil rapidly until of a fairly thick consistency (25 to 30 minutes).

As this marmalade contains little sugar it will not keep longer than a week or so, unless hermetically sealed. This may be done either by using fruit bottling jars or making an airtight seal to the jam jars with a synthetic skin which is now on the market. In either case the covered jars should be immersed while hot in a pan of hot water brought to the boil, and boiled for 5 minutes. The marmalade will then keep for months.

Every night our stout-hearted lorry drivers are risking their lives to bring you food. They don't let you down — so don't let them down by wasting food.

*Wholesome is as wholesome does...*

## CARROT JAM

When fruit is unobtainable and you have sugar for jam you can use carrots or swedes to eke out the fruit.

METHOD: Cook 8 oz peeled carrots in a little water until a smooth pulp. Cook 1 lb sliced cooking apples (weight when peeled) in $\frac{1}{4}$ pint water until a smooth pulp. Mix the carrot and apple pulps together. Measure this and to each 1 pint allow 1 lb sugar. Tip back into the saucepan, stir until the sugar has dissolved, then boil until stiffened. This never becomes as firm as a real fruit jam.

## HONEYCOMB TOFFEE

*Cooking time:* 8 minutes    *Quantity:* 6 oz

4 oz golden syrup
2 oz sugar (Demerara if possible)

2 level teaspoons bicarbonate of soda

METHOD: Boil the syrup and sugar together for about 5 minutes or until it is a rich brown colour. While still boiling stir in the bicarbonate of soda very quickly. Pour into a well-greased sandwich tin and allow to cool and set. When almost firm, loosen edges with a knife and turn out on to a wire tray. Break into pieces.

## SOME
### *Delicious Drinks*

Anyone can make them who has a garden or can easily get to the countryside.

### MINT TEA
Cover the bottom of a large jug with freshly gathered sprigs of mint. Pour on some freshly made weak tea or plain boiling water. Strain and serve. Make with dried mint in the winter using a little more than fresh mint. Strain well.

### BLACKBERRY LEAF TEA
Pick tender green leaves when dry if possible. Cut them up with a stainless knife. Spread them out and dry thoroughly in the shade or in an airy room; this may take four days or longer. Don't pick or dry them in the sun. Store in an airtight tin and turn them out fairly frequently to air and prevent going mouldy. Make just like ordinary tea. Or, if you like your tea strong, cook for five minutes after making. Serve without milk, add a little sugar if liked. Delicious and very like Indian tea.

### BARLEY WATER
Wash 2 oz barley, put into a pan with 2 pints of cold water. Simmer for 2 hours. Strain, add a little sugar and the juice from some sharp fruit such as rhubarb or redcurrants or lemon flavouring.

# WOOLTON PIE

*Cooking time:* about 1 hour     *Quantity:* 4 helpings

This pie is named after the Minister of Food—Lord Woolton. It is an adaptable recipe that you can change according to the ingredients you have available.

Dice and cook about 1 lb of each of the following in salted water: potatoes (you could use parsnips if topping the pie with mashed potatoes), cauliflower, swedes, carrots—you could add turnips too. Strain but keep ¾ pint of the vegetable water.

Arrange the vegetables in a large pie dish or casserole. Add a little vegetable extract and about 1 oz rolled oats or oatmeal to the vegetable liquid. Cook until thickened and pour over the vegetables; add 3–4 chopped spring onions.

Top with Potato Pastry or with mashed potatoes and a very little grated cheese and heat in the centre of a moderately hot oven until golden brown. Serve with brown gravy.

This is at its best with tender young vegetables.

**Listen to the
Kitchen Front
at 8.15
every morning**

## To-day's Scraps To-morrow's Savouries

You must make the best of every ounce of food you have. Even odds and ends left over from your meals mustn't be thrown away. Here are some suggestions for using-up:

**1** Chop up odd scraps of cold meat and bake in a batter.

**2** Left-over beans make splendid fillings for pastry turnovers.

**3** Use up cooked fish in a salad or as a sandwich filling.

---

**'What can I give baby instead of orange juice?'**
The juice squeezed from raw blackcurrants. Baby will need only half as much blackcurrant juice as orange. The Government is making arrangements this season for canning and bottling blackcurrant juice, so that it will be available next winter.

**'Can you give me a suggestion for a nourishing meatless meal?'**
Have a variant of the 'health meal' lately tried for school children, with excellent results to their health. Instead of meat and vegetables, they had wheatmeal bread and butter and salad, as much as they could eat, with cheese and a glass of milk. Instead of the cheese when you have used their ration give herring, or, when you can get pulses, cold lentil rissoles or pease pudding.

# WELSH MUTTON

*Cooking time:* 2 hours     *Quantity:* 4 helpings

For a meal for four people, get 1½ lb of scrag end of mutton. That costs 6d and is less than half one person's weekly ration. The other ingredients are:

| | |
|---|---|
| 4 large leeks | 1 pint of water |
| 3 carrots | salt to taste |
| 6 potatoes | |

METHOD: Cut up the mutton and put it in a saucepan with tepid salted water. Bring it to the boil. Take off the brown scum and simmer for an hour. Cut the leeks into 3-inch lengths, and add, with the cut-up carrots, to the pan, and simmer for half an hour. Then add the potatoes, peeled and quartered. Simmer for another 20–30 minutes.

# VICTORIA SANDWICH

*Cooking time:* 25 minutes    *Quantity:* 1 cake

2 oz of margarine
2 oz of sugar
2 dried eggs, used dry
5 oz of plain flour

2 tablespoons water
4 level teaspoons of baking
   powder

METHOD: Cream the fat and sugar and beat in the dried eggs. Mix the flour and baking powder and add them a little at a time to the creamed margarine and sugar, alternating with the water. Add a little milk if necessary but the mixture ought to be fairly stiff. Put into two greased tins and bake in a fairly hot oven. Turn out onto a wire rack. Sandwich together with one of the following fillings.

*Amusing little figures* cut from short-crust or biscuit dough, go down well. Roll the dough about ¼-inch thick. 'People' can be made by cutting small rounds for heads, larger for bodies, strips for arms and legs; pinch the various pieces of dough firmly together. Mark eyes, noses, mouths, with currants. If you can draw a little or have a friend who can, make thin cardboard 'patterns' of animals, lay them on the dough and cut round with a small sharp knife.

## WHITE ICING

**Cooking time:** 5 minutes **Ingredients:** 2 fluid oz water, 2 oz sugar, 2 oz milk powder. **Quantity:** Sufficient for 1 cake

Boil water and sugar together. Allow to go off the boil, then add the milk powder and mix well together. Use to cover 1 medium sized cake.

## VARIATIONS IN CAKE FILLINGS

*Cooking time:* 5 minutes    *Quantity:* to fill 1 cake

Here is the basic recipe for a cake filling which will not be either solid or runny, just thick enough to stay where it is meant to:

2 level tablespoons of dried
   egg
2 level tablespoons of flour
1 level tablespoon of sugar

5 level tablespoons of
   Household milk powder
1 pint of water

METHOD: Mix the dry things, including the milk powder dry (see that there are no lumps) and then blend to a smooth cream with some of the water. Bring the rest of the water to the boil and pour slowly on to the blended mixture; then put the whole lot back in the pan and boil, still stirring, for a couple of minutes. Beat it a bit as it gets cold and you will find you will have something you can reasonably call a cream.

Like that it won't taste very exciting, but there are hundreds of ways you can vary it and here are a few. You can make it taste of chocolate by adding 4 level tablespoons of cocoa before blending. The bottled flavours can be added at the end: then you can be sure of getting the taste you want. A few drops of vanilla is wonderful in chocolate cream, but hardly enough perhaps on its own. Lemon is good, or lemon and orange mixed. Or any of the fruit flavourings you like; or peppermint. Try making some chocolate and some peppermint and using them together; or putting peppermint filling inside a chocolate cake. But whatever kind you make, taste it when it is cooked and then sweeten to taste.

# After the War

It was wonderful when the strain of the war was over, but a fact many people do not appreciate was that food rationing continued for many years after the end of hostilities. Certainly some foods gradually became more plentiful and new foods, such as whale meat appeared. The advice from the Ministry of Food was still appreciated and so were the many broadcasts about food and recipes.

## SAVE THAT FAT

Many people know the trick of skimming the fat off the top of their stews when cold. But how many people know how to make best use of their fat?

Collect all the oddments of fat you can from frying pans, baking tins and stews. Melt and strain them all into a big bowl and wash them by pouring on some boiling water (you will need about a pint of water for 2 oz fat). When the liquid solidifies, lift off the solid fat and scrape the sediment off the bottom; it is now quite suitable for frying or roasting. Wise housewives will take this a step further. They will heat the fat up again until it stops bubbling. This means that it is quite free from moisture and will keep literally indefinitely. It can be used for anything, even cake making.

# PUMPKIN SOUP

*Cooking time:* about 45 minutes    *Quantity:* 4 helpings

1 onion
2 lbs pumpkin
water to cover
1 oz margarine

salt and pepper
milk as required
1 egg

METHOD: Chop up the onion. Peel the pumpkin, remove the seeds and slice. Place in a pan together with the onion and enough water to cover and cook until tender, then strain. Return to the heat, adding the margarine and salt and pepper to taste. Then add enough milk to make a nice creamy consistency and bring to a boil. When you feel it has cooked through enough, take off the heat and add a well-beaten egg. Serve.

# PEA PURÉE PANCAKES

*Cooking time:* 25 minutes    *Quantity:* 4 helpings

1 lb peas (fresh, dried or
    tinned)
½ teaspoon sugar
dab of margarine

1 dessertspoon chopped mint
salt and pepper
pancakes or fried croûtons
2 oz grated cheese

METHOD: Cook the peas until tender. Add a little sugar to the water as this brings out the flavour of the peas. Drain and mash the peas and then mix in the margarine, mint and seasoning. When you've made the pancakes spread the purée between two as though for a sandwich and serve with grated cheese. Alternatively you could serve the purée very hot in bowls like a soup adding croûtons. The croûtons are made by cutting bread into cubes and frying in very hot fat.

## SEVEN WAYS TO STUFF POTATOES

**Cooking time:** about 1¼ hours
**Ingredients:** 1 large potato per person, 2 tablespoons grated cheese per person, dab of margarine, a little milk, pepper and salt, filling. **Quantity:** 1 helping

Bake the potatoes in their jackets. When they are cooked cut a hole in the middle (a little bigger than a half crown) and scoop out the inside. Put the potato into a heated bowl with the cheese, margarine, milk and seasoning. Mash together. Then put back into the potato making a hollow so that it can be filled by any one of these: 1) scrambled eggs, 2) left-over mince, 3) left-over curry, 4) beans in tomato sauce, 5) left-over fish with some added flavouring, 6) sausage meat mixed with onion and sage, 7) scrambled egg mixed with some bacon. The potatoes are then returned to the oven to heat through. A lovely hot meal for winter.

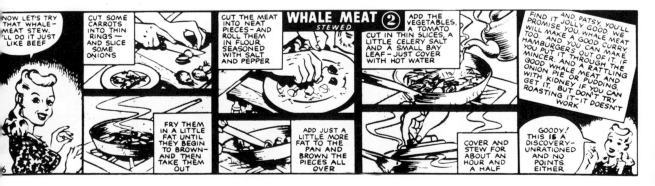

### MOCK OYSTER PUDDING

**Cooking Time:** 30 minutes
**Ingredients:** 5 medium soft roes, 2 oz dried breadcrumbs, ½ pint milk, 1 oz melted margarine, 2 dried eggs reconstituted, 1 teaspoon sugar, salt and pepper, a little nutmeg.
**Quantity:** 4 helpings

Rinse the roes, and drain well. Chop finely. Mix with the breadcrumbs, milk, margarine, eggs, sugar, seasoning and nutmeg. Turn into a greased piedish. Bake till golden brown in a moderately hot oven about 30 minutes.

# BAKED HERRING SANDWICH

*Cooking time:* 30 minutes    *Quantity:* 1 helping

herring
seasoning

margarine
2 slices bread

METHOD: Remove the scales, head and tail of the herring. Open it flat and clean out removing the bones. Then sprinkle lightly with salt and pepper. Spread the margarine on the bread (make a good coating) and then put the herring between the slices and bake in a hot oven until well browned. This should be served very hot and is ideal as a breakfast or supper dish.

# MUTTON MOULD

*Preparation time:* 10 minutes    *Quantity:* 4 helpings

2 cups cooked mutton
1 slice stale bread
2 cups any cooked vegetables
chopped parsley, lemon, thyme

chives or small onion, chopped
seasoning
dash Worcester sauce
½ pint thick white sauce

METHOD: Mince the mutton, bread and vegetables and then mix well. To this add the chopped herbs, onion, seasoning and Worcester sauce (or any other sauce). Stir in the white sauce making sure you keep the mixture as thick as possible. Spoon into a wet mould. It is ready to eat when cold and can be served with a salad or as a delicious sandwich filler. This recipe is a good way of using up those odds and ends as well as dealing with sometimes tough meat.

DON'T WASTE IT

# DEVON MILK

*Preparation time:* 30 minutes  *Quantity:* 4 helpings

¾ pint of thick sour milk
1 level tablespoon raspberry
   jam or stewed raspberries

1 dessertspoon sugar
a white of egg

METHOD: Strain the sour milk in a muslin so that the whey is drained and only the thick curd is left. Transfer this into a bowl and add the sugar and raspberry jam (or stewed raspberries). Lightly beat the egg white and then whisk this together with the rest of the ingredients and serve chilled in a glass dish.

### APPLE BUTTER

This spread makes a substitute for butter. After cutting out any damaged parts of the apples, wash and quarter them, but don't peel or core. Then place in a pan with enough water to cover and cook slowly until soft. After straining off juice rub the apples through a sieve. For every pound of pulp use ½ lb sugar. Add the sugar to the juice and bring to a boil, add pulp and continue to cook until the mixture is thick and smooth, remembering to stir to prevent catching. Pot into small jars and seal while hot. (Once opened it is better to use up quickly) Flavouring can also be added. For example the equivalent of an orange or lemon to 1 lb of pulp or even vanilla to taste; also quarter teaspoon of cinnamon or a few cloves could be added.

# RABBIT SURPRISE

*Cooking time:* 1½ hours  *Quantity:* 4 helpings

small rabbit
1½ pints of water
1 teaspoon of salt
½ pint of rice
fat for frying

1 onion or 3 spring onions
3 tomatoes
½ teaspoon of pepper
pinch of ginger or cayenne
½ pint brown gravy

METHOD: Bone the rabbit and cut into bite sized pieces. Boil up some salted water and pour in the rice and leave to cook for about 15 minutes. While you're waiting for it to cook you can be preparing the rabbit. Heat up the fat and gently cook the pieces of rabbit until a golden brown. Drain the cooked rice and to it add thinly chopped onion(s), sliced tomatoes, pepper and ginger or cayenne. Place a little of this mixture onto a greased casserole dish and then lay the rabbit on top. With the remainder of the rice mixture cover the rabbit add half a pint of gravy. Cover the casserole and cook gently for about an hour.

96

# RECIPE FOR CHOCOLATE

*Cooking time:* about 5 minutes     *Quantity:* ¾ lb

1 tin household milk
2 tablespoons cocoa or grated chocolate
2 oz sultanas

4 oz margarine
1 cup sugar
2 tablespoons milk (or may need a little more)

METHOD: Mix household milk, cocoa or chocolate and sultanas together. Heat margarine, sugar and milk in saucepan, pour into household milk mixture and mix well. Pour into a greased sandwich tin and leave to cool. Cut into pieces. It is ready to eat, but even better next day.

# GYPSY CREAMS

*Cooking time:* 10 to 15 minutes     *Quantity:* about 20

2 cups rolled oats
1 cup plain flour
½ cup sugar
1 teaspoon bicarbonate of soda

2 oz margarine
2 oz lard
1 tablespoon syrup
1 tablespoon water

METHOD: Mix the dry ingredients; melt the fat, syrup and water, without boiling, and add to the dry ingredients to form a stiff consistency. Make into small balls about the size of hazelnuts. Flatten slightly, and bake in a moderate oven for 10–15 minutes. When golden brown, cool on a wire tray. Sandwich together with a filling of butter icing, flavoured according to taste with chocolate, orange or vanilla. A little dried milk and syrup helps to stretch this filling.

## *HONEY CAKES*

**Cooking time:** about ¼ hour **Ingredients:** 1 level teaspoon sugar, 2½ margarine, 2 level tablespoons honey, 6 oz self-raising flour, 1 level teaspoon cinnamon. **Quantity:** 16 to 20

Beat together the sugar and margarine until the mixture is soft and creamy, then add the honey. Sift together the flour and cinnamon. Add to the creamy mixture with a spoon until it binds together then work it with your fingers until it is a soft smooth dough. Flour your hands, take off a piece of dough about the size of a large walnut and roll between the palms of hands until it is a smooth ball. Put on to a slightly greased tin and flatten slightly. Continue until all the dough has been used up. Bake in a moderately hot oven until the cakes are done—about 15 minutes.

98

# the
# VICTORY
## COOKBOOK

Marguerite Patten O.B.E.

# INTRODUCTION

The immediate period before Victory was certainly not a peaceful one. Fighting was intense both in Europe and in the Far East.

The Home Front, as we at home were known in Britain, continued to cope with the perils of flying bombs and rockets together with more personal worries. The problem of rationing had become a familiar one and people were managing well. We also became like squirrels, hoarding summer foods for the winter.

Seasonal fruits and tomatoes were bottled. Onions were a problem, too, for shipping space was far too valuable to import onions. so people dried as many as possible to give flavour to winter dishes.

The Women's Institutes and other organisations achieved wonderfully high standards when preserving fruits. They made jam, on behalf of the Ministry of Food and to the Ministry's specifications, to form part of the rations. The jars of bottled fruit put on show by them and those of us in the Food Advice Division of the Ministry were often artistically perfect - every piece of rhubarb would be the same length and beautifully packed. You would see jars of apple rings, with blackberries nestling in the centre of each apple ring.

Dig for Victory was a message observed by a very large percentage of the public. You could see vegetables growing among the roses and other plants in gardens, and some people even dug up all their flowers to plant a variety of vegetables and fruits instead.

In the country it was taken for granted that people would keep chickens, but many town dwellers decided to keep them, too, to give them fresh eggs and provide a chicken to cook from time to time. Some of my friends had invested in poultry, and a few had rabbits too. Many of the latter were never eaten, for they became family pets and no-one could bear to kill them.

## THE MINISTRY OF FOOD

The Ministry controlled the distribution of food during the war, and afterwards, and was responsible for giving out information on food rationing, and the wise use of all foods. The recipes and Food Facts leaflets published by the Ministry of Food enabled people to make the best use of the rations available and augment them with unrationed foods, such as potatoes, flour, oatmeal and seasonal vegetables. Much of the advice was given in a light-hearted manner. In addition to recipes and suggestions for new ways of incorporating more potatoes into the daily diet, for instance, the value of the vegetable was extolled by the symbol 'Potato Pete'. Children became interested in Potato Pete's friendly figure and advice and were more inclined to eat, and enjoy, potato dishes.

A Food Advice Division was established within the Ministry of Food to help ensure that the public kept fit on the rations and enjoyed the dishes they could make with the food available.

The headquarters staff in London were responsible for nutritional information and the recipes published by the Ministry. Throughout Britain Food Advice Centres were established, staffed by home economists, of whom I was one. We gave demonstrations in the Centres, and in market squares, hospital out-patient departments, works' canteens, large stores or any place where we could come into contact with people, for it was essential that everybody knew about the rations and any additional foods to which they were entitled.

In April 1940 Lord Woolton became Minister of Food and his name soon became very well-known. Although a recipe for the famous Woolton Pie, named after him, has already been given in my book on wartime cooking, We'll Eat Again, I have repeated it for, since that book was published, I have found that there are several versions, all of which are interesting.

## FOOD RATIONING

Not all basic foods were placed on the ration at one time; foods were introduced gradually:

**January 1940** - *rationing introduced. The foods placed on ration were: bacon, ham, sugar and butter.*

**March 1940** - *meat became a rationed food.*

**July 1940** - *tea, margarine, cooking fat and cheese made part of the ration.*

**March 1941** - *jam, marmalade, treacle and syrup all put on ration.*

**June 1941** - *distribution of eggs controlled.*

**November 1941** - *distribution of milk controlled.*

**July 1942** - *sweets put on ration.*

## WELFARE FOODS

The Vitamin Welfare Scheme was introduced in December 1941. Small children and expectant mothers received cod liver oil and concentrated orange juice (from America). These played a major part in ensuring that children grew up strong and healthy. Expectant and nursing mothers and small children were entitled to extra milk rations, too, as were certain invalids.

## WHAT WERE THE RATIONS?

These were the basic rations for one person per week. The ration book had coupons, covering the different ration foods, which were removed as the food was purchased. The basic rations varied slightly from time to time, as more or less of a certain food was available, but on the whole they were as follows:

BACON / HAM *4 oz (100 g) of either bacon or ham.*

MEAT *to the value of 1s 2d (6p in today's money). Sausages were not rationed but often difficult to obtain. Offal was originally not rationed but when supplies of meat*

were difficult it formed part of the ration. Canned corned beef and products like Spam generally formed part of the points system.

BUTTER *2 oz (50 g).*

CHEESE *2 oz (50 g). Sometimes this rose to 4 oz (100 g) and very occasionally to 8 oz (225 g). Vegetarians had extra cheese, for they surrendered their meat coupons.*

MARGARINE *4 oz (100 g).*

COOKING FAT *4 oz (100 g) but quite often this dropped to 2 oz (50 g). Dripping, sometimes mentioned in recipes, was scrapings from every frying pan or pot to obtain every spoonful of dripping. This was not available on rations.*

MILK *3 pints (1.8 litres), often dropping to 2 pints (1.2 litres). National Dried Milk (known as Household milk), which became available after December 1941, was a tin per 4 weeks.*

SUGAR *8 oz (225 g), which had to be used for cooking and jam-making too. When there were adequate supplies in the country the Ministry would release a little more for jam-making; this was available on the sugar coupon.*

PRESERVES *1 lb (450 g) very 2 months, so it was very important to supplement this (Jam, marmalade, with home-made preserves, golden syrup or treacle).*

EGGS *1 shell egg a week, if available, but frequently dropping to 1 shell egg every 2 weeks. From June 1942 dried eggs were available and the ration was a packet (containing the equivalent of 12 eggs) each 4 weeks.*

TEA *2 oz (50 g) per week. In December 1944 an extra tea allowance was introduced for 70-year-olds and over.*

SWEETS *12 oz (350 g) every 4 weeks.*

## THE POINTS SYSTEM

Each person was allowed 16 points per month and one had to choose how to use these points; for example, they allowed you to buy:

*1 can of meat or fish or*

*2 lb (900 g) dried fruit or*

*8 lb (3.6 kg) split peas or similar pulses.*

*Canned fruit was also available on points.*

## TO ADD TO THE RATIONS

National Dried Milk was a great help in augmenting the fresh milk ration. The flavour was not the same as fresh milk so it was mostly used in cooking. It was not the same as the milk powders produced to feed babies.

At first, we disliked dried egg intensely, mainly because we did not appreciate just how carefully one should reconstitute it. Quite quickly, though, we found that if you took just one absolutely level tablespoon of dried egg powder and carefully blended it with 2 tablespoons of water you had a very good product.

There were many recipes in which you could add the dried egg powder to the flour, or other ingredients, and not reconstitute it. In this case, you needed to add the 2 tablespoons of water to the rest of the liquid in the dish. As we got used to dried egg we found that most egg dishes could be made with it, including omelettes, scrambled eggs, Yorkshire Pudding batters, cakes of all kinds, even sponges and, surprisingly, a soufflé!

## EATING AWAY FROM HOME

By the end of 1944 it was estimated that about 9% of all food in Britain was consumed outside the home. There were approximately 147,000 catering establishments, serving 23,000,000 daily meals. They played an important part in supplementing the rations, as no ration cards or coupons had to be given up.

2000 British Restaurants were opened in towns and cities in Britain. The food was relatively inexpensive and comparable to good school dinners.

It was compulsory for factories to provide canteens. By the end of 1944 there were 30,500 in existence.

School meals were an essential part of catering and for many children were a real treat. By February 1945 1,850,000 school meals were served each day.

In addition to these places, restaurants of all kind were open. It was illegal to charge more than 5s 0d (25p) per meal, though large and expensive establishments were allowed to make cover charges.

# Helping hands...

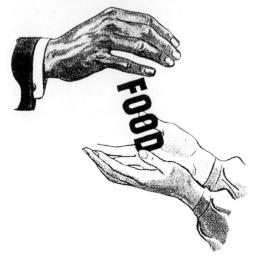

during cooking in the oven. Greaseproof bags were cut up to line cake tins.

FUEL Saving fuel was essential, so hay-box cookery became important.. A hay-box could be made from a large square biscuit tin or box with a well-fitting lid. Pads were made from hay, enclosed in cloth and fitted inside the base, the sides and lid of the container. Stews and soups were partially cooked in the oven, then placed inside the hay-box where they continued cooking, without using fuel.

Large vacuum flasks were often used in the same way to tenderize prunes or other dried fruit. The fruit would be well-soaked, half-cooked, then transferred to the flask to complete the cooking process.

The flasks were also used to keep soup hot; often left-over tea was strained from the teapot into a vacuum flask to be served later, so saving precious tea. It would be ready for people working late on ARP duties to take with them.

Steamers were used a great deal, for several kinds of food could be cooked over one pan of boiling water.

## MANAGING ON THE RATIONS

Today the medical profession and nutritionists claim that we were healthier in the days of rationing than we are today, when there is such an abundance of food available. So what kept us so healthy?

Before mentioning food I feel I must stress that our emotions at the time played a great part in keeping us going. We people at home could not let the forces down, we had to play our part too. Most people

## EXTRA BENEFITS

Some people were entitled to additional food. People doing extra heavy work and munition workers were allowed extra meat. Agricultural workers, who could not benefit from canteen facilities, were allowed an extra cheese ration

## EMERGENCY FEEDING

After bomb attacks, gas, electricity and water facilities were often out of action and homeless people had to be sheltered and fed. Mobile kitchens were rushed to bombed areas and W.V.S. and A.R.P. workers were there to give sympathy and provide plentiful cups of hot tea, coffee and food. Queen's Messenger Convoys were able to move around the area quickly to give help.

## DEALING WITH SHORTAGES

FOOD Because food was so important, during and after the war, it was an offence to waste any. In fact, if people were discovered wasting food, legal proceedings could be taken against them.

PAPER Paper was very scarce and we saved all wrappings from any fat and used it to cover food, especially

*We all liked Mrs. Parker, in the city, until we heard she wasted crusts (a pity!).*

worked very long hours in various jobs and also took part in voluntary activities in the ARP (Air Raid Precaution Services) and the WVS (Women's Voluntary Services) who were always there to help in times of emergency. Everyone in the Kitchen Front felt it was their duty to keep healthy to carry on.

Undoubtedly, our good health came from well-balanced meals, although probably few people realised they were good at the time, they seemed so horribly monotonous and catering was an endless problem.

In addition to the basic rations our meals were based on these unrationed foods:

BREAD (and flour-based foods). The National bread and flour were certainly not as light as we would wish and the flour did make baking more difficult (allied to the lack of fat, sugar and eggs for baking). The Ministry

## Yes madam—
## It's home-produced—

also introduced wholemeal bread and flour (generally known as wheatmeal), which had more flavour than the National white bread and flour. Oatmeal was also strongly recommended as part of a healthy diet, and was used in bread and biscuit recipes.

FISH - usually available in fairly small quantities only, unless you lived by the sea and were fortunate enough to have freshly caught fish.

VEGETABLES - this is where we augmented the small rations of meat, cheese and eggs. You may be surprised at the very generous amount of vegetables included in recipes in this book. Most people ate that amount to satisfy their appetites; even if they were not great vegetable lovers. Vegetables were eaten raw in salads and cooked, too. I am sure it was during the war years that the British learned how to cook vegetables correctly, so they retained flavour, colour and texture plus valuable mineral salts and vitamins.

FRUIT - which was in limited supply, particularly in wintertime. Citrus fruits (except for very rare, and small, amounts of fresh oranges which were only sold on children's ration books) were unknown, like other fruits that used to be imported. Adults had to get their intake of vitamins from raw vegetables; children from the excellent welfare foods supplied.

There were also limited supplies of canned fish and meat available on the points system, described on page 8, and small amounts of sausages, liver and other offal for which you generally had to form a queue at the butcher's shop.

Wartime food was not exciting, but we were not under-fed, nor were we hungry, as were people in many countries in Europe and other parts of the world. While rationing made it possible for everyone to be adequately fed, there is no doubt that we would all have been very unhappy indeed had we known in 1945 that rationing was to continue for several years to come - and would not finally come to an end until after the Coronation of our present Queen..

Although Victory Days celebrations and the food eaten then take up much of this book, I felt the British people deserved a tribute to their victory in coping with those years of rationing and food shortages. Therefore, the last chapter in this book covers the period from 1945 to the end of rationing in 1954, and includes the kind of recipes we used when various foods, such as oranges and other citrus fruits, bananas, extra kinds of cheese and many other ingredients gradually became available to use free of rationing again.

# FAMILY
# CELEBRATIONS

*Practically every household throughout Britain celebrated the Victory Days. The rations did not permit magnificent spreads of food but family cooks would certainly do their best to make everyday dishes look as festive as possible. Often, families were joined by overseas servicemen, especially Americans, at the celebrations.*

*The fact that VE Day and VJ Day came during the late spring and the summer was a great help, for it was easier to cater in summertime when there were homegrown tomatoes, lettuce, cucumber and other salad ingredients and an appreciable amount of summer fruits.*

*In this chapter I have concentrated chiefly on dishes for main meals, including the kind of soups, salads, fish, meat and vegetable dishes and the puddings that could have appeared on tables in all parts of the country on those two wonderfully happy days.*

# SOUPS

A meal during the years of rationing often included a soup and, for Victory celebrations, they would be an obvious choice as the first course of a celebration meal.

The recipes here give a variety of flavours and include soups suitable for a chilly or a beautifully hot day. They make good use of the variety of vegetables that are available during the various months of the year. A well-flavoured soup is a good start to any meal and helps to satisfy the appetite of hungry people.

## Onion Soup

PREPARATION TIME: 15 MINUTES

COOKING TIME: 40 MINUTES

QUANTITY: 4 HELPINGS

*When there are onions available do make this soup. If you have no onions in wintertime then try the recipe using leeks instead.*

**1 lb (450 g) onions, thinly sliced**
**1 oz (25 g) margarine or cooking fat**
  **or dripping**
**1½ pints (900 ml) beef or vegetable stock**
  **or water**
**little yeast extract**
**salt and pepper**
**4 small slices bread**
**1 oz (25 g) cheese, grated**

Cut the onion slices into smaller pieces. Heat the margarine or fat or dripping in a saucepan, add the onions and cook gently for 10 minutes, stirring most of the time. The onions should be golden in colour. Add the stock or water, with a little yeast extract to flavour, and seasoning. Cover the pan and simmer for 30 minutes or until the onions are soft.

Toast the bread, ladle the soup into soup plates or bowls, top with the toast and cheese and serve.

# Leek and Potato Soup

PREPARATION TIME: 20 MINUTES

COOKING TIME: 25 MINUTES

QUANTITY: 4 HELPINGS

**2 pints (1.2 litres) vegetable stock or water**
**4 medium leeks, thinly sliced**
**12 oz (350 g) potatoes, cut into**
  **½ inch (1 cm) dice**
**salt and pepper**
**2 tablespoons chopped parsley**
**little cayenne pepper (optional)**
**1 oz (25 g) margarine (optional)**

Bring the stock or water to the boil, add the leeks and potatoes and seasoning. Cover the pan and simmer for 25 minutes or until the vegetables are tender. Do not over-cook the soup or the leeks will lose colour.

Add the parsley, cayenne pepper and margarine, if you can spare this, at the end of the cooking time. The margarine is not essential but does improve the taste.

# Summer Beetroot Soup

PREPARATION TIME: 15 MINUTES

COOKING TIME: 10 MINUTES

QUANTITY: 4 HELPINGS

*Serve this excellent summertime soup hot or cold.*

**1 pint (600 ml) water**
**4 small or 2 medium cooked beetroot, skinned**
  **and coarsely grated**
**4 medium tomatoes, skinned and finely diced**
**4 tablespoons chopped spring onions**
**2 tablespoons chopped parsley**
**salt and pepper**

Bring the water to the boil, add the ingredients and cook gently for 10 minutes. Serve hot or allow the soup to become cold and well-chilled then serve.

*Variation: Use the same recipe in wintertime but sub-stitute a large finely chopped onion for the spring onions. Simmer this in the water for 10-15 minutes then add the beetroot and about 8 oz (225 g) bottled tomato purée and continue as in the recipe above. Omit the fresh tomatoes.*

# Green Pea Soup

PREPARATION TIME: 25 MINUTES
COOKING TIME: 30-35 MINUTES
QUANTITY: 4-6 HELPINGS

*When you have tender young peas do not waste the pods: use them to make a delicious soup.*

1½ lb (675 g) peas in pods
1 oz (25 g) margarine
2 small onions, chopped
1¼ pints (750 ml) water
1 sprig mint
salt and pepper
1 teaspoon sugar
**To garnish:**
chopped mint
chopped chives or parsley

Wash the peas, do not remove the peas from the pods but trim away any stalks and discard any damaged pods, using the peas from them. Heat the margarine in a pan, add the onions and cook gently for 5 minutes, so they do not become brown. Pour the water into the saucepan, bring to the boil, add the pea pods, mint, salt and pepper and sugar. Cook steadily for 20-25 minutes, or until the pods are very tender.

Rub the soup through a sieve, return to the saucepan, taste and add any extra seasoning required, then reheat for 5 minutes. Top with the freshly chopped herb garnish and serve.

*Variations: When the peas are older, use 12 oz (350 g) peas, without pods, and prepare the soup as above. Creamy Pea Soup: use 1 pint (600 ml) water and add ¼ pint (150 ml) milk or top of the milk or unsweetened evap-orated milk after the peas have been sieved and reheat.*

# Lentil Soup

PREPARATION TIME: 25 MINUTES
COOKING TIME: 1 HOUR
QUANTITY: 4-6 HELPINGS

8 oz (225 g) split lentils
2 medium onions, finely chopped
2 medium carrots, finely diced
1-2 bacon rashers, derinded and chopped
1½ pints (900 ml) water
1 tablespoon chopped parsley
1 teaspoon chopped fresh thyme or ½ tea
    spoon dried thyme
salt and pepper

Wash the lentils. If possible, soak them in cold water to cover for several hours, to reduce the cooking time. Strain the lentils and discard the soaking water. Put the lentils into a saucepan with the vegetables and bacon, including the rinds, for these add flavour. Add the water and herbs; season the soup lightly. Cover the pan and simmer for 1 hour. Remove the bacon rinds, taste the soup and add more seasoning, if required, then serve.

*Variations: Creamy Lentil Soup: use 1 pint (600 ml) water. Make a thin White Sauce with ½ oz (15 g) mar-garine, ½ oz (15 g) flour and ½ pint (300 ml) milk, blend into the soup just before serving and heat briefly. Leek and Lentil Soup: use 4 oz (100 g) lentils and 4 small sliced leeks. Add the leeks after the soup has been simmering 30 minutes. Omit bacon, if you wish. Note. To save fuel, cook the soup in a covered casse-role in the oven when in use. It takes about 1½ hours in a preheated oven, 160°C (325°F); Gas Mark 3.*

# A salad a day

all the year round

NUMBER TWELVE — MINISTRY OF FOOD LEAFLET

The seasonal salads here come from a Ministry of Food leaflet. Equivalents of the cup measures included in the recipes are: teacup is equivalent to ¼ pint (150ml) and a breakfast cup to ½ pint (300 ml).

'We used to think of a salad as just a pleasant little addition to cold meat,' says the Ministry of Food leaflet. 'Now that we have found out more about foods we have discovered how rich in value salads are. There is hardly a root or green vegetable that does not deserve a place in a salad. Use them raw whenever you can.

When making salads, touch the plants as little as possible. Keep in a cold place until needed; a saucepan with a well-fitting lid is excellent if placed on a cool floor.

Just before serving, wash carefully, shake off the water gently and dry the plants in a clean cloth or wire salad basket. Keep outside tough leaves for soups.

## VINAIGRETTE DRESSING

*Mix together 2 tablespoons salad oil, 1 tablespoon good quality vinegar, salt and pepper to taste, a little mustard and a pinch of sugar (optional). If liked, add chopped fresh herbs, such as parsley or thyme (or a pinch of dried herbs). Instead of herbs, try 1 or 2 crushed garlic cloves.*

## SPRING SALADS

(1) Make a thick bed of chopped raw cabbage heart in your bowl. In the centre pile a grated raw white turnip. Round this centre pile arrange smaller piles of grated raw carrot and grated raw beetroot (using a teacup of each). Decorate with radishes and parsley.

(2) Shred 8 oz (225 g) young turnip tops. Mix with 1 breakfastcup of diced cooked potatoes and 1 breakfastcup of diced cooked beetroot. Put into a bowl and decorate the top with 1 large grated carrot and sprigs of watercress and dandelion leaves.

(3) Young dandelion leaves make a delightful salad. Cut off the roots, wash the clusters of leaves well, dry in a cloth and toss in a Vinaigrette dressing (see box, left). Add a grated raw vegetable - carrot, parsnip or swede - and a few chopped spring onions.

## SUMMER SALADS

(1) Line a bowl with crisp lettuce leaves. Mix together 1 breakfastcup each of cooked peas, cooked diced potatoes and cooked diced carrots. Pile the mixture into the bowl and serve with mint sauce.

(2) Line a bowl with crisp lettuce leaves. Put in a breakfastcup cooked broad beans, a breakfastcup grated raw carrots and a medium-sized cucumber, diced. Decorate with a few nasturtium leaves and parsley.

(3) Mix together a breakfastcup of cooked runner beans cut into 1 inch (2.5 cm) lengths and a breakfastcup cooked diced potatoes and a large lettuce, shredded. Decorate with sliced tomato and a few chopped spring onions, if possible.

## AUTUMN SALADS

(1) Break a cauliflower into sprigs and steam them or boil them in a little salted water. When cold, arrange on a bed of lettuce with a breakfastcup of sliced cooked potatoes. Decorate with parsley and a sliced tomato.

(2) Allow 1 small cooked beetroot per person. Hollow out the centre and fill with a mixture of chopped apple

or pear and chopped celery, moistened with mayonnaise. Arrange the beets on a bed of salad greens and surround with little heaps of grated raw carrot, diced cooked potatoes and the beetroot centres, diced.

(3) Wash and dry young celery leaves. Toss them lightly in Vinaigrette dressing (page 16) and serve with diced cooked beetroot or grated raw beetroot.

## WINTER SALADS

(1) Make 3 tablespoons Vinaigrette dressing ( page 16) in a bowl. Put in 2 teacups grated raw cabbage heart and 1 teacup each diced cooked potatoes, diced raw apples and celery. Turn in the dressing with a wooden spoon. Decorate with watercress.

(2) Mix together 2 teacups grated raw cabbage heart, 2 teacups grated raw carrot and 1 teacup grated raw swede. Decorate with green celery tops and a little grated raw cauliflower.

(3) Line your bowl thickly with watercress, add 8 oz (225 g) chicory, cut into thin strips and mixed with 1 breakfastcup of grated raw beetroot. Serve with Vinaigrette dressing.

## Egg Mayonnaise

PREPARATION TIME: 10 MINUTES

COOKING TIME: 10 MINUTES

QUANTITY: 4 HELPINGS

**1 reconstituted dried egg or fresh egg**

**1 tablespoon milk**

**1 tablespoon salad oil**

**1 tablespoon vinegar**

**½-1 teaspoon made mustard**

**salt and pepper**

**pinch sugar (optional)**

Put all the ingredients in a basin, stand over a saucepan of hot, but not boiling, water and whisk until thick and

creamy. Remove from the heat and continue whisking as the mixture cools The mixture will keep in a covered jar in a cool place for several days. If it becomes rather thick, thin it with a little milk.

## Spiced Mayonnaise

PREPARATION TIME: 10 MINUTES

COOKING TIME: 10 MINUTES

QUANTITY: 4 HELPINGS

**2 reconstituted dried eggs**

**3 tablespoons salad oil**

**1-2 teaspoons Worcestershire sauce**

**1 tablespoon mushroom ketchup**

**1-2 tablespoons vinegar**

**½-1 teaspoon made mustard**

**salt and pepper**

Hard-boil the eggs (Cabbage Casserole, page 26). Rub them through a sieve, then add the rest of the ingredients gradually to give a smooth mixture.

*Variations: With shell eggs use the yolks only of 2-3 eggs. Use the chopped hard-boiled whites in the salad.*

*Creamy Egg Mayonnaise: hard-boil 2 reconstituted dried eggs (page 26). Rub through a sieve then gradually blend in 4 tablespoons top of the milk or better still unsweetened evaporated milk, if you can spare this. When smooth, beat in 1 tablespoon vinegar, ½-1 teaspoon made mustard, a little salt and pepper and a good pinch of sugar.*

*Herb Mayonnaise: To the Creamy Egg Mayonnaise add 1 peeled and crushed garlic clove and 2 tablespoons chopped mixed herbs (parsley, thyme, tarragon etc).*

---

### EGGLESS MAYONNAISE

*When eggs are not available or in very short supply, try this eggless mayonnaise. Mash one small cooked and skinned potato until very smooth, then add 1 teaspoon made mustard and 2 tablespoons vinegar (or to taste). Very slowly blend in 4 fl oz (125 ml) salad oil. Season with salt and pepper to taste.*

# FISH DISHES

These are some of the fish dishes that would be served during the period between VE and VJ Days.

Although fish was not rationed it was not available in large quantities and the selection of fish was limited. Many fishermen were serving in the Royal and Merchant navies. Often the fish had taken a long time to come from the coast to fish shops and, therefore, was not as fresh as it should be. This is why strong flavours, such as spices, were often used in fish dishes.

*Each time we serve a meal we stand in the limelight*

## Fish Roast

PREPARATION TIME: 10 MINUTES

COOKING TIME: 30 MINUTES

QUANTITY: 4-6 HELPINGS

*This is an excellent way of cooking a large piece of fish, or a whole fish, in the oven. When roasted it has an attractive brown and crisp skin.*

**2 lb (900 g) cod or fresh haddock,
   cut in one piece**
**8 oz (225 g) tomatoes, thickly sliced**
**salt and pepper**
**1 oz (25 g) cooking fat or dripping, melted**

Remove the fins from the fish and make about 4 shallow cuts across the top of the fish joint. Insert some of the tomato slices in the pockets made in the fish. Season the fish lightly and brush with the melted fat or dripping. Put into a roasting tin.

Preheat the oven to 200°C (400°F), Gas Mark 6 and bake for 30 minutes, basting with the small amount of fat or dripping in the tin once or twice. Add any tomato slices left to the roasting tin about 10 minutes before the end of the cooking time.

*Variation: Use finely chopped spring onions in place of the sliced tomatoes.*

## Swedish Herrings

PREPARATION TIME: 15 MINUTES

COOKING TIME: 25 MINUTES

QUANTITY: 4 HELPINGS

**4 herrings, cleaned
and filleted**
**1-2 teaspoons salt**
**2 tablespoons vinegar**
**2 tablespoons water**
**1½ tablespoons sugar**
**shake pepper**
**pinch ground cloves**
**2 tablespoons crisp browned breadcrumbs**

Rub the herring fillets with the salt, place in a baking dish, with the fillets slightly overlapping. Mix the vinegar, water, sugar, pepper and cloves together. Spoon over the herrings. Top with the crumbs.

Preheat the oven to 190°C (375°F), Gas Mark 5 and bake the fish, uncovered, for 25 minutes.

Serve hot with mixed vegetables or cold with salad.

## Devilled Pilchards

PREPARATION TIME: 15 MINUTES

COOKING TIME: 12 MINUTES

QUANTITY: 4 HELPINGS

*Canned pilchards are low on points and sustaining.*

**1 tablespoon mustard powder**
**1 tablespoon vinegar**
**1 tablespoon sugar**
**1 oz (25 g) margarine or dripping, melted**
**1 x 15 oz (425 g) can pilchards**
**1 small onion, finely chopped**
**1 bay leaf**
**4-6 cloves or good pinch ground cloves**
**¼ pint (150 ml) liquid (see method)**
**chopped fresh parsley, to garnish**

Blend the mustard with the vinegar, sugar and half the melted margarine or dripping. Lift the pilchards from the can, split and spread with the mustard mixture then fold over again. Save the liquid from the can.

Place the fish in the grill pan, or a suitable dish, and put under a preheated grill for a few minutes while making the sauce.

Heat the remaining margarine or dripping, add the onion and cook for 2 minutes, put in the bay leaf and cloves. Tip the liquid from the can into a measure, add enough water to give ¼ pint (150 ml). Pour over the onion and simmer 5 minutes. Remove the bay leaf and cloves. Spoon the sauce over the fish and return to the grill for 5 minutes. Garnish with parsley and serve.

# Fish and Tomato Bake

PREPARATION TIME: 15 MINUTES

COOKING TIME: 30 MINUTES

QUANTITY: 4 HELPINGS

*The tomatoes in this dish keep the fish beautifully moist. No fat is needed in the dish at all.*

**1 lb (450 g) tomatoes, sliced**

**1 teaspoon sugar**

**salt and pepper**

**2 tablespoons chopped parsley**

**2 tablespoons chopped spring onions**

**½ teaspoon chopped thyme or ¼ teaspoon dried thyme**

**4 white fish cutlets**

**3 tablespoons crisp browned breadcrumbs**

Preheat the oven to 180°C (350°F), Gas Mark 4. Place half the sliced tomatoes in a flat layer at the bottom of a shallow casserole or large pie dish.

Blend the sugar, seasoning, parsley, spring onions and thyme together. Add a sprinkling of this mixture to the tomatoes. Arrange the fish cutlets in a layer over the tomatoes, and flavour them with some more of the herb mixture. Cover with the remaining tomatoes and the last of the herb mixture. Top with the breadcrumbs and bake in the preheated oven for 30 minutes.

Serve the fish bake hot with seasonal vegetables, including a green leaf vegetable, if possible.

*Variation: When fresh tomatoes are not available use bottled tomato purée.*

# Scalloped Herrings

This is a good way to use up leftover fish and potatoes.

Bone, skin and flake 2 small cooked herrings; mix into ½ pint (300 ml) white sauce. Grease a shallow dish and sprinkle over it 2 tablespoons breadcrumbs. Spoon the fish mixture into the dish and top with 8 oz (225 g) mashed potato. Sprinkle on another 2 tablespoons breadcrumbs and dot with ½ oz (15 g) margarine. Bake in a hot oven, 200°C (400°F) Gas Mark 6 for about 25 minutes, until browned on top.

## Fish Soufflé

PREPARATION TIME: 20 MINUTES

COOKING TIME: 40 MINUTES

QUANTITY: 4 HELPINGS

*A soufflé is an ideal dish for a special celebration. You can make this, even if you have no fresh eggs, for reconstituted dried eggs are an acceptable alternative.*

**8 oz (225 g) white fish**
**I oz (25 g) margarine**
**I oz (25 g) flour**
**¼ pint (150 ml) milk or fish stock**
**few drops anchovy essence (optional)**
**3-4 reconstituted dried eggs or fresh eggs**
**salt and pepper**

Preheat the oven to 190°C (375°F), Gas Mark 5. Grease a 6-7 inch (15-18 cm) soufflé dish or a small casserole with a little margarine.

Make sure the fish is free from skin and bone. While cooked fish can be used, a stronger favour is given if you use uncooked white fish. Either mince or chop it, then pound it very well. If using cooked fish flake it finely.

Heat the margarine in a saucepan, stir in the flour, then gradually add the milk or stock. Stir or whisk briskly as the sauce comes to the boil and becomes very thick. Add the anchovy essence, if using. Blend the fish with hot sauce then remove the pan from the heat.

With dried eggs: reconstitute the eggs in the usual way and whisk into the fish mixture, season to taste.

With fresh eggs: separate the yolks and whites. Whisk the yolks into the fish mixture, season to taste. Whisk the egg whites until they stand in peaks, do not over-whip them, for that makes a dry soufflé. Fold into the other ingredients.

Spoon the mixture into the soufflé dish and bake for 30 minutes, or until well-risen and golden in colour. Serve at once.

# MEAT DISHES

When a family was planning a Victory Celebration Meal, everyone would probably save their meat ration coupons to buy a good-sized joint (they would manage without meat for many days to do this).

The meat ration was 1s 2d worth per person per week (6p in modern money) for a family of 4 people over a period of 2 weeks. A recipe list from a Ministry of Food leaflet suggesting how the meat ration could be best used over the two weeks, was based on the family's buying just one joint in that time; for the second week, dishes such as Fillets of lamb, based on breast of lamb, or Stuffed marrow were suggested.

At the time this leaflet was published liver, which had previously been included on the meat ration due to a shortage of other meats, was just taken off the ration, as supplies has improved.

## LIVER AND BACON HOT-POT

PREPARATION TIME: 25 MINUTES

COOKING TIME: 45 MINUTES

QUANTITY: 4-6 HELPINGS

*When not on the ration liver was greatly in demand; people would queue at the butcher's shop, hoping the supply would last until it was their turn to be served. This dish would often be served with dumplings, cooked separately from the hot-pot.*

**I lb (450 g) lambs' liver**
**salt and pepper**
**3 bacon rashers**
**I tablespoon flour**
**8 oz (225 g) carrots, thinly sliced**

Put the liver into a pan of cold salted water, bring just to the boil, then drain, saving about ½ pint (300 ml) of the water. When cool, slice the liver thinly.

Grill the bacon, then derind and chop it.

Season the flour and coat the liver and bacon. Pack the meat into a casserole with the carrots and the reserved ½ pint (300 ml) stock. Cover the casserole, put it in a preheated oven, 180°C (350°F) Gas Mark 4 and bake for 35-40 minutes.

If liked, make dumplings to serve with the hot-pot.

## FILLETS OF LAMB

PREPARATION TIME: 30 MINUTES

COOKING TIME: 1 HOUR PLUS 15 MINUTES ON THE SECOND DAY

QUANTITY: 4 HELPINGS ON 2 DAYS

*Here, two breasts of lamb are used to give two meals, each providing small portions for 4 people.*

**2 flaps of breast of lamb**

**salt**

**2-3 carrots, sliced**

**1 small turnip, sliced**

**1 bay leaf**

**2-3 peppercorns**

**blade of mace**

**few parsley stalks**

**little mint sauce**

**little made mustard**

SHOW YOUR BOOK PLEASE

Trim away the surplus fat from the breasts, then score round the small bones with a sharp knife. Do not remove the bones. Place the meat in a pan of boiling salted water with the vegetables and the herbs, tied in muslin. If fresh herbs are not available use ½-1 teaspoon mixed dried herbs.

Cover the pan and simmer gently for 1 hour, when the meat should be tender and easy to loosen from the bones. Put the meat on a board and remove the bones.

Spread both inner sides of the meat with the mint sauce and mustard. Set one breast of meat in a straight-sided baking tin, then place the second breast over it, with the coated side inside. Press well together, keep in position with a second tin, well weighted down. Leave in a cool place overnight in this position.

Meal 1 Cut half the breasts into neat thin fingers and serve cold with salad and mixed vegetables.

Meal 2 Cut the remaining lamb into neat fingers, coat in batter or egg and breadcrumbs and fry in a little hot fat until crisp and brown.

RECIPE of the WEEK

### *Mock Goose*

PREPARATION TIME: 25 MINUTES

COOKING TIME: 1 HOUR

QUANTITY: 6-8 HELPINGS

Among the many war-time recipes for making Mock Duck and Mock Goose, this one, which could used either mutton or lamb, was ideal for special occasions.

*1 leg of mutton or lamb, boned*
*For the stuffing:*
*2-3 medium onions or 4 large leeks, finely*
*    chopped*
*2 small cooking apples, peeled, cored and*
*    chopped*
*3 oz (75 g) breadcrumbs*
*2-3 teaspoons chopped sage or*
*    1-1½ teaspoons dried sage*
*1 oz (25 g) margarine, melted*
*salt and pepper*

Spread the boned meat out flat. Blend all the stuffing ingredients together. Put over the meat, then roll up and form into the shape of the body of a goose. Tie securely. Weigh the joint to calculate the cooking time and roast it as usual.

## VEGETABLE
## AND KIDNEY PIE

PREPARATION TIME: 30 MINUTES

COOKING TIME: 55 MINUTES

QUANTITY: 4 HELPINGS

**2-3 lb (1-1.5 kg) mixed vegetables**

**salt and pepper**

**1-2 tomatoes, if available**

**4 oz (100 g) ox kidney or 2 sheep's kidneys**

*For the gravy:*

**1½ oz (40 g) flour, preferably wheatmeal**

**1 pint (600 ml) vegetable stock**

**1 teaspoon yeast extract or vegetable extract**

**Wheatmeal pastry (page 23)**

Peel and dice root vegetables, pod peas and cut beans into small pieces. Put the root vegetables and any other vegetables that are not young and tender, into boiling lightly salted water and cook for 10 minutes only; strain and save the vegetable water for the gravy. Slice the tomatoes, if using, and mix with the other vegetables.

Skin the ox or sheep's kidney(s), remove the core. Cut into very thin slices. Put into a little well-seasoned water and simmer for 15 minutes, then strain.

Pack the kidney and vegetables in layers in a 2-3 pint (1.2-1.8 litre) pie dish. Blend the flour with the vegetable water and extract then cook steadily until a thickened gravy. Pour gravy to cover the vegetables into the pie dish, saving the rest to serve with the meal. Allow to cool before covering the filling with pastry.

Make the pastry and use to cover the pie.

Preheat the oven to 190°C (375°F), Gas Mark 5 and bake the pie for 45 minutes. Lower the heat slightly after 30 minutes if the pastry is becoming a little too brown. Serve hot with the rest of the gravy.

*Variation: If using lamb's kidneys there is no need to pre-cook them; simply skin, core and dice finely.*

## VEGETABLE MINCE

PREPARATION TIME: 30 MINUTES

COOKING TIME: 40 MINUTES

QUANTITY: 4 HELPINGS

*This Ministry of Food recipe illustrates how a small amount of meat and a generous amount of vegetables could provide a satisfying meal.*

**1 lb (450 g) small potatoes**

**1-1½ lb (450-675 g) carrots**

**salt and pepper**

**1 lb (450 g) green peas**

**1 oz (25 g) dripping or fat**

**1 large tomato, sliced**

**1 large onion, or equivalent spring onions**

**4-6 oz (100-175 g) minced beef**

**½ oz (15 g) flour**

**little vegetable stock**

Put the potatoes and carrots into boiling salted water and cook steadily for 20 minutes then add the peas and continue cooking for a further 15 minutes.

Meanwhile heat the dripping in a pan, add the tomato and onion(s) and cook gently for 10 minutes, add the minced beef, blend with the vegetables and stir with a fork to keep the meat crumbly. Stir over a low heat for a further 10 minutes then add the flour and enough vegetable stock to make a sauce-like consistency. Season the mixture, bring to the boil and cook gently for 5-10 minutes. Dish up the vegetables in a deep hot dish and top with the mince.

## MINCE-STUFFED MARROW

PREPARATION TIME: 25 MINUTES

COOKING TIME: 1 HOUR

QUANTITY: 4 HELPINGS

**3 oz (75 g) bread, preferably wheatmeal**

**¼ pint (150 ml) water**

**4 spring onions, if possible, chopped**

**2 teaspoons chopped fresh herbs or**

**½ teaspoon mixed dried herbs**

**4-6 oz (100-175 g) raw minced beef**

**salt and pepper**

**1 medium marrow**

**1 oz (25 g) dripping or fat**

Put the bread into a basin, add the water. Leave to soak for 5 minutes then beat until smooth, add the chopped spring onions (if available), the fresh or dried herbs, minced beef and seasoning.

Wipe the marrow. Cut into half, lengthways, scoop out the seeds and fill with the stuffing. Put the two halves together, tie firmly with tape or string.

Preheat the oven to 180°C (350°F), Gas Mark 4 and melt the dripping or fat in a roasting tin. Add the marrow and turn around in the hot fat. Bake for 1 hour, basting from time to time with the fat in the tin.

Serve with mixed vegetables.

*Variation: Add extra ingredients to this basic recipe: 2 skinned and chopped tomatoes, 4 oz (100 g) sliced mushrooms, 4-8 extra spring onions (or use 1-2 onions, chopped and cooked for 5 minutes in hot fat).*

---

### *Wheatmeal Pastry*

*Wheatmeal flour makes very good pastry but, because it is a little heavier than white flour, you should add a small amount of baking powder.*

*Blend 8 oz (225 g) plain wheatmeal flour with ½ teaspoon salt and 1 teaspoon baking powder.*

*Rub in 2 oz (50 g) margarine or cooking fat or dripping then add enough water to make a rolling consistency, although one that is slightly softer than when making pastry with white flour.*

*Roll out and use as in the individual recipe.*

# BLANQUETTE OF CHICKEN

PREPARATION TIME: 30 MINUTES

COOKING TIME: 2½ HOURS

QUANTITY: 4-6 HELPINGS

*Most war-time chickens were elderly, with plenty of fat, which would be rendered down to use in cooking.*

**1 boiling fowl**

**3 onions or leeks, left whole**

**4 medium carrots, left whole**

**1 turnip, diced**

**salt and pepper**

**small bunch of mixed herbs or ½ teaspoon**
   **dried mixed herbs**

*For the sauce:*

**1 oz (25 g) margarine (see method)**

**1 oz (25 g) flour**

**¼ pint (150 ml) milk**

**½ pint (300 ml) chicken stock**

**1 or 2 reconstituted dried or**
   **fresh eggs**

**chopped parsley**

Put the chicken into a large saucepan with the vegetables. Add sufficient water to cover and a little seasoning. Add the herbs, securely tied in muslin. Bring the liquid to boiling point, cover the pan and simmer for 2½ hours, or until the chicken is tender.

Towards the end of the cooking time make the sauce. If you are very short of margarine, omit it and rely on the fat in the chicken stock to give the right flavour to the sauce. Measure out the stock from the pan in which the chicken is cooking, then strain it..

If using margarine: heat in a pan, stir in the flour then add the milk and most of the stock and bring to the boil and cook until thickened. If not using margarine: blend the flour with the milk and most of the stock, bring to the boil and cook until thickened. Remove the pan from the heat so the sauce is no longer boiling.

Beat the dried or fresh egg(s) with the remaining cold stock, whisk into the sauce and simmer gently for 2 or 3 minutes.

Serve the chicken and vegetables with the sauce.

*Variation: use the cooked chicken and sauce to make a chicken mould. Dice the chicken meat and pack into a mould. Dissolve 2 teaspoons gelatine in the hot sauce, pour over the chicken and leave to set.*

# BLACK PUDDING HOT-POT

PREPARATION TIME: 20 MINUTES

COOKING TIME: 1 HOUR

QUANTITY: 4 HELPINGS.

**8 oz (225 g) black pudding**

**8 oz (225 g) potatoes, thinly sliced**

**8 oz (225 g) carrots, thinly sliced**

**1 large onion, if available, finely chopped**

**1 teaspoon chopped sage or**
   **½ teaspoon dried sage**

**1 oz (25 g) flour**

**1 teaspoon gravy powder**

**¾ pint (450 ml) water**

**salt and pepper**

Skin the black pudding and cut into ¼ inch (5 mm) slices. Arrange a layer of sliced potatoes in a greased casserole, then a layer of black pudding and carrots. Blend the onion and sage, sprinkle half into the casserole. Add another layer of carrots then the black pudding and chopped onion and sage. End with a layer of sliced potatoes. Blend the flour, gravy powder and water together in a pan and stir over heat until thickened, add a little seasoning. Pour over the ingredients in the casserole and cover with a lid. Preheat the oven to 180°C (350°F), Gas Mark 4 and bake the casserole for 1 hour.

This nutritious casserole is good served with sliced cooked beetroot.

☆ ☆ ☆ ☆ ☆ ☆ ☆ ☆ ☆ ☆ ☆ ☆ ☆ ☆ ☆ ☆ ☆ ☆ ☆ ☆ ☆ ☆ ☆ ☆ ☆ ☆ ☆ ☆ ☆ ☆ ☆ ☆ ☆

# *Sheep's Head Roll*

PREPARATION TIME: 45 MINUTES COOKING TIME: 2½-3 HOURS QUANTITY: 6-8 HELPINGS

*If you have never cooked sheep's head before you will be delighted at the amount of meat you can obtain from it and the tasty flavour of the roll. The vegetables make the meat go further, as well as adding flavour.*

| | |
|---|---|
| **I sheep's head** | **I tablespoon chopped** |
| **salt and pepper** | **mixed herbs or** |
| **I tablespoon vinegar** | **½ teaspoon mixed dried herbs** |
| **2 dried cloves or** | **I lb (450 g) turnips, diced** |
| **pinch ground cloves** | **I lb (450 g) carrots, diced** |
| **I blade of mace** | **4 oz (100 g) brown breadcrumbs** |
| **pinch ground cinnamon** | **4 oz (100 g) flour** |
| **I garlic clove, chopped** | |

Soak the sheep's head in salted water for a short time, remove and put into a saucepan with cold water to cover. Bring the water to the boil, then discard it. This is known as 'blanching' and it gives a better colour and flavour to the meat.

Tie the head in a cloth, this makes sure the delicate brains, which are so nourishing, are kept with the head in cooking. Return the head to the saucepan with fresh water to cover, and the vinegar, spices, herbs and vegetables. Season lightly. Cover the pan and simmer steadily for 1½-2 hours, or until the head is sufficiently tender to remove the meat.

Strain the stock and put the head and vegetables on one side. Remove the meat from the head and thinly slice the tongue. Keep this separate. Mince or finely chop the rest of the meat, blend with the softened vegetables, the breadcrumbs and the flour. Season to taste.

Press the meat mixture into a long strip with floured hands, arrange the sliced tongue down the centre and then form into a roll. Either wrap this in margarine paper and a cloth or put into a large greased jam jar. Steam for 1 hour.

Allow to become cold, then unwrap or turn out of the jar, slice and serve with salad.

*Variations: Coat the cooked roll with browned breadcrumbs before serving.*

*Add a little tomato ketchup or Worcestershire sauce to the meat mixture to give additional flavour.*

*Although the roll is generally served as a cold dish it is equally good hot with a gravy, made from some of the stock used in cooking the beef.*

☆ ☆ ☆ ☆ ☆ ☆ ☆ ☆ ☆ ☆ ☆ ☆ ☆ ☆ ☆ ☆ ☆ ☆ ☆ ☆ ☆ ☆ ☆ ☆ ☆ ☆ ☆ ☆ ☆ ☆ ☆ ☆ ☆

# VEGETABLE DISHES

Vegetables became very important during the years of shortages and most people found adventurous ways of cooking them. For celebration meals, trouble would be taken to make them as interesting as possible.

## CHEESE, TOMATO AND POTATO LOAF

PREPARATION TIME: 30 MINUTES

COOKING TIME: 35 MINUTES

QUANTITY: 4 HELPINGS

1 lb (450 g) cooked new potatoes

12 oz (350 g) tomatoes

1 oz (25 g) margarine

1 oz (25 g) flour

7½ fl oz (225 ml) milk or milk and vegetable stock

3 oz (75 g) cheese, grated

salt and pepper

*To coat the tin:*

½ oz (15 g) margarine

1 oz (25 g) crisp fine breadcrumbs

Cut the potatoes into slices about ⅓ inch (7.5mm) thick. Cut the tomatoes into slightly thicker slices. Heat the margarine in a saucepan, add the flour, then the milk, or milk and vegetable water, stir or whisk briskly as the sauce comes to the boil and thickens. Remove from the heat, add the cheese and seasoning.

Grease a 2 lb (900 g) loaf tin or use an oval casserole and coat with the breadcrumbs. Preheat the oven to 180°C (350°F), Gas Mark 4.

Arrange about a third of the potatoes in a neat layer in the container, cover with a little sauce and half the tomatoes. Put in half the remaining potatoes, with the rest of the sauce and tomatoes. Add a final layer of potatoes. Cover the dish with margarine paper and bake in the preheated oven for 30-35 minutes. Turn out and serve hot with a salad.

## CABBAGE CASSEROLE

PREPARATION TIME: 20 MINUTES

COOKING TIME: 35 MINUTES

QUANTITY: 4 HELPINGS

*It often surprises people to know it was possible to hard-boil dried eggs. Obviously they did not look like a proper egg, for white and yolk were mixed together, but they tasted perfectly pleasant.*

2 tablespoons dried egg powder and 4 tablespoons water, or 2 fresh eggs

½ pint (300 ml) water

salt and pepper

1 small cabbage, shredded

salt and pepper

½ oz (15 g) margarine

1 tablespoon flour

¼ pint (150 ml) milk

4 oz (100 g) cheese, thinly sliced

2 tablespoons fine, crisped breadcrumbs

Reconstitute the eggs by blending the powder with the 4 tablespoons of cold water. Pour into a greased cup or small basin, cover with margarine paper and steam over boiling water for 10 minutes. If using fresh eggs, boil them for 10 minutes, then crack and remove the shells. Slice the dried or fresh eggs neatly.

While the eggs are cooking bring the ½ pint (300 ml)

water to the boil, add a little salt and shake of pepper, then put in the cabbage and cook for 5 minutes, then strain. The cabbage liquid can be saved as vegetable stock, for soup or vegetable dishes. Heat the margarine, stir in the flour and then the milk; bring to the boil and cook until thickened; season to taste.

Put a layer of the cabbage into a greased casserole, top with a layer of sliced cheese and half the sliced eggs. Add a second layer of cabbage, cheese and eggs and then a final layer of cabbage. Top with the white sauce, then the breadcrumbs. Do not cover the casserole.

Preheat the oven to 180°C (350°F), Gas Mark 4 and bake the casserole for 25 minutes.

## BEETROOT FRICASSEE

PREPARATION TIME: 20 MINUTES

COOKING TIME: 5-10 MINUTES

QUANTITY: 4-6 HELPINGS

**1 oz (25 g) margarine**

**1 lb (450 g) cooked beetroot, peeled and cut into 1 inch (2.5 cm) dice**

**1 medium onion, finely chopped**

**1 teaspoon flour**

**3 tablespoons vinegar**

**2 tablespoons water**

**salt and pepper**

**3 tablespoons chopped parsley**

Heat the margarine in a saucepan, add the rest of the ingredients, except the parsley. Mix thoroughly and heat for 5-10 minutes only, add half the parsley, stir to blend. Top with the rest of the parsley and serve.

This fricassée is particularly good served with fish dishes, especially white fish.

*Variation: Cucumber Fricassée: If you can spare cucumbers use them, peeled and diced, instead of the diced beetroot. You will need the same amount of cucumber as beetroot.*

## POTATO RING

PREPARATION TIME: 20 MINUTES

COOKING TIME: 45 MINUTES

QUANTITY: 4 HELPINGS

*Good taste demands I keep my jacket on*

**3 large potatoes**

**1 tablespoon flour**

**1 tablespoon chopped parsley or**

**1 teaspoon chopped mixed herbs**

**salt and pepper**

**1 oz (25 g) cooking fat or dripping, melted**

Preheat the oven to 180°C (350°F), Gas Mark 4. Scrub, but do not peel, the potatoes. Grate on a coarse grater then mix with the flour, parsley or mixed herbs and salt and pepper to taste.

Form into a ring shape on a flat baking tray or ovenproof serving dish. Brush with the melted fat or dripping and bake for 45 minutes.

When cooked, fill the centre with a mixture of cooked seasonal vegetables.

## CURRIED CARROTS

PREPARATION TIME: 20 MINUTES

COOKING TIME: 20 MINUTES

QUANTITY: 4-6 HELPINGS

**2 lb (900 g) carrots, sliced**

**salt and pepper**

**1 oz (25 g) cooking fat or dripping**

**2 medium onions, finely chopped**

**1 oz (25 g) flour**

**1 tablespoon curry powder, or to taste**

**2 oz (50 g) sultanas**

**1 tablespoon chutney**

Put the carrots into 1 pint (600 ml) boiling salted water and cook steadily for 10 minutes or until just tender.

Meanwhile, start to make the sauce. Heat the fat or

dripping in a pan, add the onions and fry steadily for a few minutes, until tender. Add the flour and curry powder, blend with the onions and cook for 1 minute.

Strain the carrots, keep hot in a warmed serving dish. Measure out ¾ pint (450 ml) of the carrot liquid, blend with the flour and onion mixture. Bring to the boil and stir over the heat until thickened, then add seasoning, sultanas and chutney. Blend well and simmer for 5 minutes. Pour over the carrots and serve.

## SUMMER VEGETABLE PIE

PREPARATION TIME: 35 MINUTES

COOKING TIME: 45-50 MINUTES

QUANTITY: 4-6 HELPINGS

*This pie is excellent made with early, quite small root vegetables and tomatoes.*

**1 lb (450 g) carrots, sliced**

**8 oz (225 g) turnips, cut into ½ inch (1.5 cm) dice**

**8 oz (225 g) parsnips, cut into ½ inch (1.5 cm) dice**

**8 oz (225 g) onions, finely chopped**

**¾ pint (450 ml) water**

**salt and pepper**

**1 lb (450 g) tomatoes, sliced**

**2 oz (50 g) margarine**

**1½ oz (40 g) flour**

**¼ pint (150 ml) milk**

**2 oz (50 g) cheese, grated**

**2 large slices of bread, 1 inch (2.5 cm) thick**

Put the carrots, turnips, parsnips and onions into the water, add salt and cook until just tender, do not overcook. Strain and keep ½ pint (300 ml) of the stock.

Arrange the mixed vegetables with the sliced tomatoes in a 2½ pint (1.5 litre) greased pie dish. Preheat the oven to 190°C (375°F), Gas Mark 5.

Heat 1 oz (25 g) margarine in a saucepan, stir in the flour, then add the milk and vegetable stock. Bring to the boil and stir or whisk until thickened and smooth. Add seasoning to taste. Remove from the heat and stir in the cheese. Spoon over the vegetables.

Cut the bread into 1 inch (2.5 cm) dice. Put on top of the vegetable mixture. Melt the remaining margarine and spoon over the bread. Bake in the preheated oven for 20-25 minutes or until the topping is crisp and brown. Serve hot.

## TOMATO CHARLOTTE

PREPARATION TIME: 15 MINUTES

COOKING TIME: 30 MINUTES

QUANTITY: 4 HELPINGS

*This recipe can be served as a light main dish topped with grated cheese, or as a vegetable with meat or fish, in which case omit the cheese.*

**salt and pepper**

**2 teaspoons sugar**

**1¼ lb (55 g) tomatoes, thinly sliced**

**4 oz (100 g) breadcrumbs**

**2 tablespoons chopped parsley**

**2 tablespoons chopped chives or spring onions**

**1 oz (25 g) margarine or dripping melted**

Preheat the oven to 180°C (350°F), Gas Mark 4. Grease a 1½ pint (900 ml) pie dish. Blend a little seasoning with the sugar and sprinkle over the tomatoes. Arrange layers of breadcrumbs and tomatoes in the dish, ending with breadcrumbs. Add most of the parsley and chives or spring onions to the tomato layers but save a little for garnish. Top with the margarine or dripping and bake for 30 minutes. Sprinkle with the parsley and chives or spring onions; serve hot.

*Variation: Add 1½-3 oz (40-75 g) grated cheese to the breadcrumb topping or chopped spring onions or chopped fresh parsley.*

# Puddings

Puddings were a very essential part of most meals for they helped to satisfy hungry people. In summer most people based their puddings on seasonal fruits. In cold weather steamed puddings were popular.

## Marmalade Pudding

PREPARATION TIME: 25 MINUTES

COOKING TIME: 1½ HOURS

QUANTITY: 4-6 HELPINGS

*This recipe for a very satisfying pudding is an ideal way to use up stale bread.*

**1 oz (25 g) margarine**
**¼ pint (150 ml) milk or milk and water**
**4 oz (100 g) bread**
**1 oz (25 g) self-raising or plain flour**
**1 teaspoon baking powder**
**1 oz (25 g) sugar**
**3 tablespoons marmalade**
**1 reconstituted or fresh egg**

Heat the margarine with the milk, or milk and water. Crumble the bread into a basin, add the hot milk and melted margarine, blend well, then allow to stand for 10 minutes. Sift the flour and baking powder into the bread mixture, then add the sugar, half the marmalade and the egg. Beat well until you have a smooth mixture.

Grease a 1½ pint (900 ml) pudding basin, put the rest of the marmalade at the bottom of the basin, then add the pudding mixture. Cover with margarine paper and steam for 1½ hours. Turn the pudding out and serve it with custard (page 38).

## Bird's Nest Pudding

PREPARATION TIME: 25 MINUTES

COOKING TIME: 1¼ HOURS

QUANTITY: 4 HELPINGS

*Tapioca was the preferred cereal for this pudding.*

**2 oz (50 g) tapioca**
**1 pint (600 ml) milk, or milk and water**
**1-2 oz (25-50 g) sugar**
**4 medium cooking apples, peeled and cored**
**8 teaspoons jam or bramble jelly**

Put the tapioca, milk and sugar into a saucepan, stir over a low heat until the mixture thickens, then cook for 10 minutes.

Place the apples in a large pie dish. Preheat the oven to 160°C (325°F), Gas Mark 3. Fill the centre of the apples with the jam or jelly. Pour the thickened milk pudding around the apples and bake in the preheated oven for 50-60 minutes, or until the apples are tender.

## Mocha Foam

This is like a mousse. It may be served by itself or as a topping on a plain cake or dessert.

*¼ pint (150 ml) moderately strong coffee*
*1 teaspoon gelatine*
*1 tablespoon cocoa powder*
*1 oz (25 g) sugar*
*3 tablespoons dried milk powder*

Put 3 tablespoons of the cold coffee into a basin and add the gelatine. Allow to stand for 2 minutes then melt over a pan of hot, but not boiling, water. Heat the rest of the coffee, add the cocoa powder, sugar and dissolved gelatine. Gradually whisk in the dried milk powder (make sure there are no lumps) and continue whisking until light and fluffy.

# Fruit Amber

PREPARATION TIME: 25 MINUTES

COOKING TIME: 40 MINUTES, BUT SEE METHOD

QUANTITY: 4 HELPINGS

*This is a very good way to make a special pudding with a relatively small amount of fruit. If you can spare fresh eggs then the pudding can have a meringue on top.*

**12 oz (350 g) fruit**

**little water (see method)**

**1-2 oz (25-50 g) sugar, or to taste**

**2 oz (50 g) soft breadcrumbs**

**2 reconstituted dried eggs**

**¼ pint (150 ml) milk**

Heat the oven to 160°C (325°F), Gas Mark 3. Prepare the fruit. Apples should be peeled, cored and sliced; plums can be halved and stoned.

If using very firm fruit, such as apples or plums, pre-cook them for a short time in a saucepan with 2-3 tablespoons water and sugar to taste. The fruit should be almost, but not quite, cooked, then it should be mashed to make a purée.

With soft fruit all you need to do is mash this, without pre-cooking, to make a purée.

Blend the sugar with the fruit, if this has not been used in cooking, add the breadcrumbs and mix well. Whisk the eggs and milk together and add to the other ingredients.

Grease a 1½ pint (900 ml) pie dish, add the fruit mixture and bake in the preheated oven for 35 minutes, or until firm. Serve as soon as possible after baking.

*Variation: If using 2 fresh eggs, add the yolks only to the fruit mixture. Bake the pudding as above. When it is firm, lower the heat to 150°C (300°F), Gas Mark 2. Whisk the 2 egg whites until stiff, fold in 2 oz (50 g) sugar. Spoon over the pudding and bake for 25 minutes or until golden in colour. Serve hot.*

**RECIPE of the WEEK**

# Toffee Apple Pudding

PREPARATION TIME: 25 MINUTES

COOKING TIME: 2 HOURS

QUANTITY: 4-6 HELPINGS

This was a steamed pudding to serve for a special treat or on a special occasion.

*For coating the basin:*

*1 oz (25 g) margarine*

*2 tablespoons brown sugar*

*For the pudding:*

*8 oz (225 g) self-raising flour or plain flour sifted with 2 teaspoons baking powder*

*pinch salt*

*2 teaspoons sugar*

*2 oz (50 g) margarine*

*water to bind*

*1 lb (450 g) cooking apples, peeled, cored and thinly sliced*

*sugar to sweeten*

*2 tablespoons water*

Spread the margarine for coating inside a 2 pint (1.2 litre) basin, then add the sugar, making sure this adheres to the margarine.

Sift the flour, or flour and baking powder, with the salt and sugar into a bowl. Rub in the margarine, then add sufficient water to make a soft dough. Roll out three-quarters of the dough and use to line the basin. Add the apples, a little sugar and the water. Damp the edges of the pastry with water. Roll out the remaining pastry to form the lid, place over the filling and seal the edges firmly.

Cover with margarine paper and a cloth and steam over rapidly boiling water for 1 hour, then lower the heat and cook steadily for a further hour. Turn out and serve hot with custard ( page 38).

☆  ☆  ☆  ☆  ☆  ☆

## THRIFTY CHRISTMAS PUDDING

PREPARATION TIME: 35 MINUTES

COOKING TIME: 2½ HOURS PLUS ANOTHER 1 HOUR

QUANTITY: 6 HELPINGS

*I demonstrated this recipe just before Christmas 1944. The rolled oats give a nutty texture and the carrots help to save sugar as well as improve the colour of the mixture.*

**3 oz (75 g) bread, weight without crusts**
**¼ pint (150 ml) water**
**3 oz (75 g) plain flour**
**1½ teaspoons baking powder**
**½ teaspoon mixed spice**
**½ teaspoon ground cinnamon**
**3 oz (75 g) rolled oats**
**3 oz (75 g) carrots, finely grated**
**3 oz (75 g) margarine, melted**
**3 oz (75 g) sugar, preferably brown**
**8 oz (225 g) mixed dried fruit**
**2 fresh or reconstituted dried eggs**

Break the bread into small pieces, put into the cold water and leave for at least 20 minutes then beat with a fork until smooth. Sift the flour with the baking powder and spices, add to the bread with the rest of the ingredients and mix thoroughly.

Grease a 2½ pint (1.5 litre) basin, spoon in the mixture. Cover carefully with margarine paper then a cloth or greaseproof paper and steam over boiling water for 2½ hours. Remove the damp covers, leave to dry then replace on the pudding. Store in a cool place for 2-3 days only. On Christmas morning, steam for 1 hour. Traditionally, the pudding would be served with Sherry Custard or Hard Sauce.

☆  ☆  ☆  ☆  ☆  ☆

## CHRISTMAS CHOCOLATE LOG

PREPARATION TIME: 20 MINUTES

COOKING TIME: 12-15 MINUTES

QUANTITY: MAKES 1 CAKE

*While the National flour made it impossible to produce a really lighter sponge, this was quite acceptable.*

**3 reconstituted dried eggs or 3 shell eggs**
**3-4 oz (75-100 g) sugar, preferably caster**
**3 oz (75 g) self-raising flour or plain flour sifted with ¾ teaspoon baking powder**
**1 oz (25 g) margarine, melted**
*For the filling:*
**little jam**
*For the coating:*
**2 oz (50 g) margarine**
**4 oz (100 g) icing sugar, sifted**
**1 tablespoon cocoa powder, sifted**

Preheat the oven to 190°C (375°F), Gas Mark 5. Line a Swiss Roll tin approximately 9 x 11 inches (23 x 28 cm) with greased greaseproof paper.

Put the eggs and most of the sugar into a bowl and whisk until thick and creamy. Sift the flour, or flour and baking powder, twice to lighten it. Fold gently into the egg and sugar mixture, then fold in the margarine. Spoon into the prepared tin. Bake in the preheated oven for 12-15 minutes, or until firm to a gentle touch.

Sprinkle a sheet of greaseproof paper with the rest of the sugar. Turn the sponge out on to this, remove the cooking paper. Spread with the jam and roll firmly. Leave until cold.

Cream the margarine for the filling until soft, add most of the icing sugar and all the cocoa. Mix thoroughly then spread over the roll, mark ridges with a fork to look like a tree trunk. Sprinkle the last of the icing sugar over the log. Decorate the serving plate with fresh holly.

# STREET PARTIES

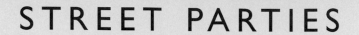

Street parties were the most popular way of celebrating the Victory Days in 1945. Some parties were exclusively for children, with adults waiting on table. Other parties would be for everyone living in the street, often with the visiting milkman, postman, air-raid wardens or anyone known to the inhabitants asked to join in. There were also special street parties for the elderly.

The typical street party recipes given here are in relatively small quantities, for volunteers would undertake either to make some of the dishes needed or to donate a precious pat of fat, a little of their tea ration or a pot of jam.

People who were children in 1945 have told me that they had ice cream at their street party – the first time they had ever tasted it. Sometimes it could have been home-made, but relatively few people had refrigerators in the 1940s, so it seems it must have come from caterers or shops that either had refrigerators or made the ice cream with available ingredients in old-fashioned ice-cream makers. There is a wartime ice cream recipe on page 39, suitable for making in a refrigerator or an ice-cream maker.

## children's party fare
······· ✰ hints ✰ ideas ✰ recipes ✰ ·······

### MENU FOR CHILDREN'S STREET PARTIES

Sandwiches (this page)

Sausage Rolls (page 42)

Selection of cakes, tarts and biscuits

Jellies (page 38)

Ice cream, if available (page 39)

Lemon and orange squash

Milk and/or tea

### MENU FOR CHILDREN'S AND ADULTS' STREET PARTIES

Sandwiches (this page)

Victory Scotch Eggs ( page 35)

Beef Shortcakes ( page 35)

Selection of cakes, tarts and biscuits

Jellies for the children ( page 38)

Ice cream, if available (page 39)

Celebration Trifle (page 38)

Lemon and orange squash

Beer and cider

Milk and tea

### MENU FOR THE ELDERLY

Home-made soup (pages 14-15)

Ham and Beef Roll (page 36)

or selection of cold meats

Various salads (pages 16-17)

Celebration Trifle ( page 38)

Fruit salads

Orange and Date Cake ( pages 36-7)

Beer and other drinks

Tea

## SANDWICHES

These are some of the sandwich fillings that could be made to celebrate VE and VJ days in 1945. Foods such as salmon would be canned and were purchased on the points system. Two tips for sandwich making:

To make margarine go further, cream it with a little warm (not too hot) milk; this also enables it to be spread more easily and sparingly.

Cut the loaf lengthways, to save time, then cut the long slices into smaller pieces when the sandwiches have been made.

### FOR YOUNGER CHILDREN

Jam and Mock Lemon Curd (page 39) were favourite sweet fillings. Potted meat or fish were usual savoury ones. In addition there could be:

Mock banana sandwiches: cook parsnips until very soft; drain well then mash until very smooth with a few drops of banana essence and a little sugar.

Cheese and date spread: blend finely grated cheese and mix with chopped dates.

Cheese and carrot: blend equal quantities of grated raw carrot and grated cheese; moisten with a little milk or one of the mayonnaise recipes on page 17.

Egg sandwiches: scramble reconstituted or fresh eggs in a little margarine, cool, blend with mayonnaise (see page 17) and put on shredded lettuce or watercress.

### FOR ADULTS AND OLDER CHILDREN

Pilchard and cucumber: mix mashed pilchards and finely diced or grated cucumber, serve on lettuce or shredded cabbage heart. For salmon and cucumber, use salmon in place of pilchards.

Salad sandwiches: mix sliced tomatoes, cucumber, lettuce and top with mayonnaise (page 17).

Spiced beef: flake corned beef finely, mix with a little finely chopped mustard pickle and serve on shredded red or green cabbage.

# Victory Scotch Eggs

PREPARATION TIME: 20 MINUTES

COOKING TIME: 40 MINUTES

QUANTITY: MAKES 8 HALVES

*This is a special version of the well-known savoury. When making these to serve as one of the savoury dishes for a Victory Party you can cut the halved eggs into smaller pieces so they go further.*

**4 shell eggs**
**2 oz (50 g) cheese, grated**
**1 tablespoon Mayonnaise (page 17)**
**1 lb (450 g) sausagemeat**
**To coat:**
**little reconstituted dried egg or**
    **shell egg or milk**
**2 oz (50 g) crisp breadcrumbs**

Boil the shell eggs for 10 minutes, then shell and cut in halves across the eggs. Cool sufficiently to handle then carefully remove the egg yolks. Mash these in a basin, then add the cheese and mayonnaise. Spoon into the white cases and press the egg halves together firmly.

Divide the sausagemeat into 4 portions, wrap around the eggs, seal the joins very firmly. Brush with a little egg or milk then coat with the crisp breadcrumbs.

Preheat the oven to 190°C (375°F), Gas Mark 5. As the oven is heating put in a greased baking tray to become very hot. Put the Scotch Eggs on the hot tray and bake in the preheated oven for 30 minutes. To serve, cut into halves or quarters. Garnish with lettuce.

*Variations: Omit the cheese and mayonnaise to make the usual Scotch Eggs.*

*Use reconstituted dried eggs, steaming them in 4 very small cups. Mash the cooked eggs, add the cheese and mayonnaise. Shape into rounds then coat with the sausagemeat and continue as the recipe.*

# Beef Shortcakes

PREPARATION TIME: 25 MINUTES

COOKING TIME: 25 MINUTES

QUANTITY: 12 TO 16 SHORTCAKES

*These shortcakes are equally good hot or cold. If serving hot prepare the filling while the shortcakes are baking. Split the shortcakes, add the filling and serve as soon as possible. If serving cold, then cool both the shortcakes and the filling before putting them together.*

**For the shortcakes:**
**12 oz (350 g) self-raising flour or plain flour**
    **sifted with 3 teaspoons baking powder**
**½ teaspoon salt**
**1 teaspoon mustard powder, if available**
**2 oz (50 g) margarine or fat**
**milk, or milk and water, to bind**
**For the filling:**
**1 oz (25 g) margarine**
**1 oz (25 g) plain flour**
**¼ pint (150 ml) milk**
**4 tablespoons left-over gravy, if available**
**8-10 oz (225-300 g) corned beef**
**1 teaspoon Worcestershire sauce**
**salt and pepper**

Preheat the oven to 220°C (425°F), Gas Mark 7. Lightly grease a baking tray.

Sift the flour, or flour and baking powder, with the salt and mustard powder. Rub in the margarine or fat then bind to a soft consistency with the milk, or milk and water. Roll out the dough to ¾ inch (1.5 cm) thick and cut into 12-16 rounds. Put on to the baking tray and cook for 12-15 minutes, or until quite firm.

Heat the margarine for the filling, stir in the flour, then add the milk and stir briskly as the sauce comes to the boil and thickens. Add the gravy; if none is available see the suggestions below.

Flake the corned beef, add to the sauce with the

Worcestershire sauce and a little seasoning.

Split the shortcakes, spread the bottom halves with the filling, then cover with the top halves.

*Variations: When no gravy is available add 2 fresh skinned and chopped tomatoes or 2 well-drained chopped bottled tomatoes or use a little extra milk or vegetable stock in the sauce.*

*Instead of corned beef finely chop or mince any cooked meat you have.*

*If serving the shortcakes cold, put a layer of crisp lettuce or shredded cabbage heart on the shortcake before adding the filling.*

## Ham and Beef Roll

PREPARATION TIME: 20 MINUTES

COOKING TIME: 2 HOURS

QUANTITY: 4-6 HELPINGS

**4 oz (100 g) fat ham, minced**
**I lb (450 g) lean beef, minced**
**2 oz (50 g) soft breadcrumbs**
**I teaspoon finely chopped sage or ½ teaspoon dried sage**
**I reconstituted dried or fresh egg**
**salt and pepper**
**little flour, for shaping and coating**

Blend all the ingredients but the flour together, form into a roll with floured hands. Put into a floured cloth or cover with margarine paper.

Steam for 2 hours then serve hot with gravy and seasonal vegetables or cold with salad.

## Ginger Honey Buns

PREPARATION TIME: 15 MINUTES

COOKING TIME: 12-15 MINUTES

QUANTITY: 12-14 CAKES

**8 oz (225 g) self-raising flour or plain flour sifted with 2 teaspoons baking powder**
**½-I teaspoon ground ginger**
**2 oz (50 g) margarine**
**2 oz (50 g) sugar**
**2 tablespoons clear honey**
**2 oz (50 g) sultanas or other dried fruit**
**I fresh or reconstituted dried egg**
**little milk or milk and water**

Preheat the oven to 200°C (400°F), Gas Mark 6. Grease 2 baking trays. Sift the flour, or flour and baking powder, with the ginger. Rub in the margarine, add the sugar, honey, dried fruit, and egg. Mix well. Gradually add enough milk, or milk and water, to make a sticky dough that stands up in peaks. Put spoonfuls on the baking trays and bake in the preheated oven for 12-15 minutes, until golden and firm. Cool on a wire rack.

## Orange and Date Cake

PREPARATION TIME: 15 MINUTES

COOKING TIME: 50 MINUTES

**2 oz (50 g) margarine or cooking fat**
**2 oz (50 g) sugar**
**3 tablespoons orange marmalade**
**few drops orange essence**
**4 oz (100 g) dates, finely chopped**
**7 oz (200 g) self-raising flour, or plain flour sifted with 1¾ teaspoons baking powder**
**I teaspoon ground ginger**
**4 tablespoons milk or water**
**½ teaspoon bicarbonate of soda**
**I reconstituted dried or fresh egg**

Preheat the oven to 160°C (325°F), Gas Mark 3. Grease and flour an oblong tin measuring about 7 x 4 inches (18 x 10 cm).

Put the margarine or cooking fat, sugar, marmalade and essence into a saucepan and stir over a low heat until melted. Remove the saucepan from the heat, add the dates to the hot mixture and allow it to stand for 15 minutes.

Sift the flour, or flour and baking powder, with the ginger, add the melted ingredients and dates then mix well. Pour the milk, or water, into the saucepan, stir to absorb any of the melted ingredients, add the bicarbonate of soda then pour on to the rest of the ingredients. Lastly add the egg. Beat well and spoon into the prepared tin. Bake the cake in the preheated oven for 50 minutes or until firm. Cool in the tin for 20 minutes then turn out on to a wire rack to cool completely.

# Eggless Ginger Cake

PREPARATION TIME: 20 MINUTES

COOKING TIME: 20 MINUTES

QUANTITY: 1 CAKE

**6 oz (175 g) self-raising flour or plain flour sifted with 1½ teaspoons baking powder**
**½-1 teaspoon ground ginger**
**2 oz (50 g) margarine or cooking fat**
**2 oz (50 g) sugar**
**6 tablespoons milk**
**¾ teaspoon bicarbonate of soda**
**2 teaspoons vinegar**

Grease and flour a 7-8 inch (18-20 cm) cake tin. Preheat the oven to 190°C (375°F), Gas Mark 5.

Sift the flour, or flour and baking powder, with the

ginger into the mixing bowl. Rub in the margarine or fat, add the sugar and milk.

Blend the bicarbonate of soda with the vinegar: the mixture will bubble. Beat into the cake mixture. Spoon into the tin and bake for 20 minutes.

Serve the cake when fresh.

## Celebration Trifle

PREPARATION TIME: 30 MINUTES

COOKING TIME: 15 MINUTES

QUANTITY: 8 HELPINGS

**8 sponge squares ( pages 44-5)**
**3-4 tablespoons jam**
**¼ pint (150 ml) sweet sherry**
**1 can or bottle of fruit in syrup**
**1 packet fruit jelly or 1 x recipe jelly (right)**
**2 pints (1.2 litres) thick custard (right)**
**sugar to taste**
***To decorate:***
**whipped evaporated milk (page 39) or Mock Cream (page 39)**
**glacé cherries**
**angelica**

Split the sponge cakes, then sandwich them together with jam. Put into a large serving bowl.

Pour the sherry into a jug, open the can of fruit, strain enough of the syrup into the sherry to give about 7½ fl oz (225 ml). Spoon this over the sponge cakes. Chop the well-drained fruit finely and add to the sponge cakes. Measure any syrup left from the can of fruit and mix this with the liquid in which to dissolve the jelly or make a jelly from fruit squash (see right). Pour the warm jelly over the cakes and leave until set.

Make the custard. Sweeten to taste and allow to cool, whisking once or twice as it cools, so a skin does not form. Pour over the jelly and cover. When quite cold decorate with the suggested decorations.

# Jelly

PREPARATION TIME: 10 MINUTES

NO COOKING

QUANTITY: 4 HELPINGS

**⅔ pint (400 ml) water**
**1 oz (25 g) sugar**
**½ oz (15 g) gelatine***
**⅓ pint (200 ml) fruit squash**
***** **this would be one sachet of today's gelatine**

Heat a little of the water with the sugar until this has dissolved. Pour 2 or 3 tablespoons of cold water into a basin, sprinkle the gelatine on top. Allow to stand for 2-3 minutes then dissolve over hot, but not boiling, water. Blend with the hot sugar and water. Add the rest of the cold water and the fruit squash. Rinse out a basin or mould in cold water, add the jelly and leave until set.

*Variations: Jelly Cream: use slightly less water than given above, i.e. ½ pint (300 ml) only if using fruit squash(but ¾ pint (450 ml) if using a jelly tablet). Allow the jelly to stiffen slightly then add a good ¼ pint (150 ml) whipped evaporated milk (see page 39).*

*Milk Jelly: soften then dissolve ½ oz (15 g) gelatine in 4 tablespoons water; when cold add 1 pint (600 ml) less 4 tablespoons milk and a little flavouring essence. Make a fruit-flavoured jelly; when cold and beginning to stiffen whisk in 3 tablespoons dried milk powder.*

# Egg Custard

Reconstitute 2 dried eggs. Beat with 1 oz (25 g) sugar until smooth. Add ½ pint (300 ml) milk for a thick custard or ¾-1 pint (450-600 ml) milk for a thinner custard. Cook over hot water, whisking all the time until smooth and thickened. Add a little vanilla essence to flavour.

# To Whip Evaporated Milk

METHOD 1. Put the can of milk into a saucepan then add enough water to cover it. Boil the water briskly for 15 minutes. Check it covers the can throughout this time. Allow the can of milk to cool, open it and whisk it.

METHOD 2. To give a stiffer texture: boil the can of milk in water. At the end of 15 minutes open it carefully, protecting your hands, as it may spurt out. Pour the hot milk into a bowl. Soften 1 teaspoon gelatine in 2 tablespoons cold water then add to the very hot evaporated milk and blend thoroughly. Chill the mixture for several hours, or even overnight, then whisk briskly.

# Mock Creams

Blend 1 tablespoon cornflour, arrowroot or custard powder (whichever is available) with ¼ pint (150 ml) milk. Pour into a saucepan and stir over a low heat until thickened. Allow to become absolutely cold.

Cream 1 oz (25 g) butter or margarine with 1 oz (25 g) sugar (icing sugar is best, if available). Very gradually beat teaspoons at a time of the thickened cornflour and milk mixture into the creamed fat and sugar. The more it is beaten the lighter it becomes. For a thin cream use just 1 teaspoon cornflour ,or arrowroot or custard powder.

Recipe 2: Soften 2 teaspoons gelatine in 2 tablespoons cold water then dissolve over a pan of very hot water. Allow to become quite cold, but not set.

Cream 2 oz (50 g) butter or margarine and 2 oz (50 g) sugar (icing sugar, if possible). Gradually beat the cold gelatine into the creamed ingredients.

For a thinner cream gradually add 2 tablespoons milk after the gelatine has been incorporated.

# Mock Lemon Curd

Blend 1 teaspoon cornflour with 4 tablespoons lemon squash and 3 tablespoons water. Pour into a saucepan, add 1 oz (25 g) margarine, 1 oz (25 g) sugar and a pinch of citric or tartaric acid. Stir over a low heat until the mixture thickens and becomes clear. This should take about 10 minutes. Remove the curd from the heat. Stir the mixture as it cools to prevent a skin forming.

# Home-made Ice Cream

PREPARATION TIME: 20 MINUTES PLUS FREEZING TIME
COOKING TIME: 15 MINUTES FOR MAKING THE CUSTARD AND BOILING THE EVAPORATED MILK.
QUANTITY: 6 HELPINGS

**½ pint (300 ml) custard (made as page 38 or with custard powder), sweetened to taste**
**1 can evaporated milk, whipped (see above)**
**flavouring (see method)**

Blend together the cold custard and the whipped evaporated milk. Add a flavouring (see below) and put into the freezing compartment of a refrigerator set at its coldest position; freeze until 'mushy'. Take out, beat hard then return to the freezing compartment to continue freezing.

*Flavourings: Chocolate: blend 1-1½ tablespoons sifted cocoa powder into the hot custard. Add a few drops of vanilla essence, too.*

*Coffee: add 1-2 tablespoons coffee essence to hot custard or make the custard with part milk and part liquid coffee.*

*Fruit: omit custard and add ¼-½ pint (150-300 ml) thick sweetened fruit purée to the whipped evaporated cream.*

*Vanilla: add 1 teaspoon vanilla essence to hot custard.*

# CHILDREN'S CELEBRATIONS

Children were very fortunate during the Victory celebrations, for they often attended many parties, including street parties, family parties and special children's events at school or in their own homes. In some cases children had remained evacuated to safer areas throughout the war, so they, like members of the Forces, were returning home. Sometimes parties were made more elaborate by encouraging the children to go in fancy dress.

The menus for these parties would be mostly sweet foods, cakes and biscuits, with sausage rolls, or other simple savouries, and there would be sandwiches of various kinds. You will find typical recipes of the period for all these in this chapter.

Among the most usual desserts for children were jelly (made as on page 38) and blancmange. Blancmange powders were available but, as the years went by, they tended to have very synthetic flavours. If fresh milk was scarce the blancmange would be made either with diluted evaporated or condensed milk (both sold on points) or with the powdered household milk.

# ..Shoot straight, Lady

## MAKING PASTRY

It was very difficult to make good pastry during the war years, for not only was fat scarce but the flour became much heavier in texture. Some of the ways in which cooks compensated for the lack of fat are given here. Cooks who had used plain flour for pastry, now often chose self-raising flour to give a lighter texture.

## SHORTCRUST PASTRY

PREPARATION TIME: 10 MINUTES

COOKING TIME: AS IN THE RECIPES

QUANTITY: DEPENDS UPON THE RECIPE

**8 oz (225 g) plain or self-raising flour**
**pinch salt**
**4 oz (110 g*) fat - margarine and lard mixed or**
**cooking fat or good dripping**
**cold water to bind**
**\* use this metrication to give the classic pro-**
**portions of half fat to flour**

Sift the flour and salt into a mixing bowl. Rub in the fat until the mixture is like fine breadcrumbs. Add sufficient water to make a dough with a firm rolling consistency.
*Variations: These low-fat pastries were best eaten hot.*
*Low-fat Shortcrust: use self-raising flour and 2 oz (50 g) fat. Bind with milk instead of water, if possible, to add a little more fat to the mixture.*
*Oatmeal Shortcrust: omit 2 oz (50 g) flour and add 2 oz (50 g) fine oatmeal or rolled oats instead. This is very good*

when using only 2 oz (50 g) fat. Bind with water or milk to make a pleasantly 'nutty' flavoured pastry.
*Potato Shortcrust: rub 2 oz (50 g) fat into 4 oz (110 g\*) flour and a good pinch of salt. Add 4 oz (110 g\*) very smooth potato, mashed without any extra liquid or fat. Mix well, then add cold water or milk to make a firm rolling consistency. Very little liquid should be required.*

## SAUSAGE ROLLS

PREPARATION TIME: 20 MINUTES

COOKING TIME: SEE METHOD

QUANTITY: 6-14

In pre-war days flaky pastry would have been used to make these rolls but in 1945 this had become a memory, for it required such a high proportion of fat.

**Shortcrust Pastry made with 8 oz (225 g)**
**flour, etc (see recipe above)**
**8 oz (225 g) sausagemeat**
**little milk, to glaze**

Preheat the oven to 200°C (400°F), Gas Mark 6. The Shortcrust Pastry makes excellent sausage rolls, as do the variations and the American Baking Powder Pastry on page 43, if you can serve the rolls hot or warm. The more economical pastries tend to become rather hard when cold.

Roll out the pastry and cut into two strips, about 5 inches (13 cm) wide and 14 inches (35.5 cm) long. Moisten the sides of the pastry with a little water.

Place the sausagemeat in the centre of each strip. Fold the pastry to enclose this and seal the edges firmly.

For small sausage rolls cut each strip into 6-7 portions, for larger ones into 3-4 portions only. Make 2 slits on top of each roll and brush with milk. Put on to a baking sheet. Bake in a preheated oven, allowing the small rolls 20 minutes and the larger ones 25-28 minutes.
*Variation: If sausagemeat is scarce blend each 6 oz (175 g) with 2 oz (50 g) seasoned mashed potato.*

## AMERICAN BAKING POWDER PASTRY

PREPARATION TIME: 15 MINUTES

COOKING TIME: AS SPECIFIC RECIPES

QUANTITY: AS SPECIFIC RECIPES

*This is a very low fat pastry which must be eaten as soon as possible after baking.*

**8 oz (225 g) self-raising flour with 1 teaspoon**
**baking powder or plain flour with**
**3 teaspoons baking powder**
**pinch salt**
**1-2 oz (25-50 g) margarine or cooking fat**
**1 tablespoon sugar, for sweet dishes**
**water to bind**

Sift the flour and baking powder with the salt, rub in the margarine or cooking fat until the mixture is like fine breadcrumbs. Add the sugar if required. Gradually blend in sufficient cold water to make a rolling consistency. Bake the pastry as soon as possible.

## CHOUX BUNS

PREPARATION TIME: 10 MINUTES

COOKING TIME: 25-30 MINUTES

QUANTITY: 12-15

*Choux pastry was regarded as a pre-war luxury until people realised it could be made with dried eggs. For special occasions, Mock Cream or fruit fillings would be used.*

## USING AMERICAN BAKING POWDER PASTRY

*These dishes use the amount of pastry given on this page.*

### SAVOURY DISHES

*Sardine Fingers: roll out the pastry as thinly as possible, cut into two oblong pieces. Mash 2 large cans of sardines in tomato sauce (obtainable on points). Spread over the bottom piece of pastry and top with the other piece. Bake in a preheated oven, 200°C (400°F), Gas Mark 6, for about 25 minutes, or until firm, then cut into 24 fingers.*

*Cheese and Carrot Fingers: follow the recipe above but blend 4 oz (100 g) grated cheese with 4 oz (100 g) grated raw carrots and a very little mayonnaise (page 17) or milk. Use as the filling and bake as above.*

*Beef and Tomato Fingers: follow the recipe above but mash 8 oz (225 g) corned beef with 2 skinned and chopped tomatoes (or use 2-3 tablespoons tomato ketchup instead). Use as the filling and bake as above.*

### SWEET DISHES

*Apple Fingers: follow the recipe above but use thick apple pulp, sweetened with honey plus 2-3 tablespoons chopped dates, as the filling. Bake as above.*

*Jam or Marmalade Fingers: use jam or marmalade as the filling. Dust the cooked slices with sifted icing sugar.*

**¼ pint (150 ml) water**
**1-2 oz (25-50 g) margarine**
**1 teaspoon sugar**
**2½ oz (65 g) plain flour**
**pinch salt**
**2 reconstituted dried or fresh eggs**
**Mock Cream (page 39), to fill**
**Chocolate Icing (page 47), for topping**

Preheat the oven to 200°C (400°F), Gas Mark 6. Grease 2 baking trays.

Put the water and margarine into a saucepan, heat until the margarine has melted, remove from the heat.

Sift the flour and salt and add to the pan. Stir briskly to blend then return to a very low heat and stir until the mixture forms a ball and leaves the inside of the saucepan quite clean around the base and sides. This stage is important.

Allow the mixture to cool thoroughly. Beat the eggs well and gradually beat into the flour mixture; you may not need quite all of the second egg, for the mixture should have a sticky consistency.

Put 12-15 heaps of the pastry on the trays and bake for 25-30 minutes until well-risen, golden and quite firm. Cool away from a draught. Split the buns, if there is any slightly uncooked mixture inside remove it.

When quite cold fill with Mock Cream and top with the Chocolate Icing.

*Variations: Top the buns with sifted icing sugar, if available, instead of Chocolate Icing.*

*Eclairs: make finger shapes instead of heaps on the trays. Bake for about 20-25 minutes.*

## BABY DOUGHNUTS

PREPARATION TIME: 10 MINUTES

COOKING TIME: 6-7 MINUTES FOR EACH BATCH

QUANTITY: ABOUT 18 SMALL DOUGHNUTS

*These are really rather like thick fritters, but children enjoyed their sugary taste.*

**8 oz (225 g) self-raising flour or plain flour sifted with 2 teaspoons baking powder**

**I reconstituted dried or fresh egg**

**I oz (25 g) margarine, melted**

**I oz (25 g) sugar**

**¼ pint (150 ml) milk or milk and water**

**2 oz (50 g) cooking fat or dripping, for frying**

**1½ oz (40 g) sugar, to coat**

Sift the flour, or flour and baking powder, into a bowl. Add the other ingredients, except the fat and sugar, and blend well until a very thick smooth batter.

Heat half the cooking fat or dripping in a frying pan, add about 9 small spoonfuls of the batter, cook steadily for 3-3½ minutes then turn over and cook for the same time on the second side. To test if cooked press firmly with the back of a knife, the doughnuts should feel firm.

Lift the doughnuts out of the pan, cool and then roll in some of the sugar.

Repeat this process with the rest of the batter, fat and sugar.

## WHISKED SPONGE SLAB

PREPARATION TIME: 15 MINUTES

COOKING TIME: 12-15 MINUTES

QUANTITY: I CAKE

*This is an ideal sponge to bake as a large fairly flat cake, that can be cut up into small squares to make decorated cakes for small children.*

*If eggs are not available, see the Eggless 'Sponge' below. While dried eggs did not make as good a sponge as fresh eggs, the result was very palatable.*

**3 oz (85 g*) self-raising flour or plain flour sifted with I teaspoon baking powder****

**3 reconstituted dried or fresh eggs**

**4 oz (110 g*) sugar, use caster if possible**

**\* use this metrication**

**\*\* This generous amount of baking powder was because of the heavy wartime flour; reduce this to ¼ teaspoon with today's flour.**

Preheat the oven to 190°C (375°F), Gas Mark 5. Line a Swiss Roll tin, about 12 x 8-9 inches (30.5 x 20-23 cm) with well-greased margarine paper or greaseproof paper, if you have any available.

Sift the flour, or flour and baking powder, and leave it in the kitchen on a plate while whisking the eggs;, this will help to lighten the sponge.

Put the eggs and sugar into a mixing bowl and whisk hard until the mixture thickens. With dried eggs you get a better result if the bowl is placed over a pan of hot, but not boiling, water and the ingredients whisked until they thicken, then the bowl removed from the heat and the eggs and sugar whisked until cold.

Fold the flour, or flour and baking powder, into the whisked eggs and sugar. Pour into the tin and bake until firm to the touch, this takes approximately 12-15 minutes. Lift from the tin and place on a wire cooling tray.

*Variations: Iced Sponge Cakes: cover the top of the sponge with Glacé Icing (page 47). Allow this to set then cut the cake into small squares.*

*Each cake can be topped with a small sweet to make them look pretty or the icing can be 'feathered'.*

*Sponge Sandwich: grease and flour two 6½-7 inch (16.5-18 cm) sandwich tins, or line them with greased margarine paper. Divide the mixture between the tins and bake for about 15 minutes. Cool for 2-3 minutes then turn out. Sandwich together with jam or jam and Mock Cream ( page 39) and top with Glacé Icing.*

*Swiss Roll: Make and bake 1 recipe quantity of the Whisked Sponge Slab. Turn the sponge on to sugared paper, remove the cooking paper, spread with warm jam and roll firmly.*

# EGGLESS 'SPONGE'

PREPARATION TIME: 10 MINUTES

COOKING TIME: 15 MINUTES

QUANTITY: MAKES 1 CAKE

*Eggless recipes were very much in demand. Although this is not a true sponge the flavour is very acceptable. It can be used in the same way as the Whisked Sponge Slab recipe and variations above.*

**3 oz (85 g\*) margarine**

**4 oz (110 g\*) sugar**

**1 tablespoon golden syrup**

**6 oz (175 g) self-raising flour sifted with**

**1 teaspoon baking powder or plain flour**

**sifted with 2½ teaspoons baking powder**

**¼ pint (150 ml) milk or milk and water**

**\* use this metrication**

Preheat the oven to 190°C (375°F), Gas Mark 5. Line a Swiss Roll tin, about 12 x 8-9 inches (30.5 x 20-23 cm) with well-greased margarine paper or greaseproof paper, if you have any available.

Cream the margarine, sugar and syrup until soft and light. Fold in the sifted flour and baking powder with the milk, giving a smooth mixture.

Spoon into the tin and bake for 15 minutes or until firm to the touch.

*Variation: Eggless 'Sponge' Sandwich: divide the mixture between two 6½-7 inch (16.5-18 cm) sandwich tins. Preheat the oven to 180°C (350°F), Gas Mark 4 and bake for 18-20 minutes. Cool for about 5 minutes in the tins then turn out on to a wire rack. When cold sandwich together with jam. The top can be dusted with sugar or covered with Glacé Icing (see page 47).*

## GLACE ICING

*This is also known as Water Icing. Icing sugar could be purchased as part of the sugar ration.*

Sift the sugar if it has lumps and blend with a little water. The icing can be flavoured with essence or sifted cocoa or chocolate powder or coffee essence or liquid coffee.

## CHOCOLATE ICINGS
### *with chocolate*

Melt 4 oz (100 g) plain chocolate in a basin over hot water, add ½ oz (15 g) margarine and 1 teaspoon water. Stir well then cool slightly and use as an icing.

This gives enough icing for a very thin layer in the centre of the Choux Buns.

### *without chocolate*

Warm the syrup slightly, so you do not use too much.

Blend 2 tablespoons of warm golden syrup with 2 tablespoons sifted cocoa powder and ½ oz (15 g) melted margarine. Flavour with vanilla essence.

## SPONGE BISCUITS

PREPARATION TIME: 15 MINUTES

COOKING TIME: 10-12 MINUTES

QUANTITY: 18-20 BISCUITS

*These were ideal for very small children. They could be served plain or iced or sandwiched together with jam.*

**2 reconstituted dried or fresh eggs**

**2-3 oz (50-75 g) sugar**

**2½ oz (65 g) self-raising flour or plain flour**
  **sifted with ½ teaspoon baking powder**

**few drops vanilla essence**

Preheat the oven to 200°C (400°F), Gas mark 6. Grease 2-3 baking trays well.

Put the eggs and sugar into a bowl and whisk over hot water until thick and creamy. Remove from the heat and whisk until cold. Sift the flour, or flour and baking powder. Fold into the eggs with the vanilla essence.

---

### *Feathering*

*Iced cakes of any kind were a treat for it was illegal for bakers to produce iced cakes. You could ice cakes at home if you had the ingredients.*

*Make the Glacé Icing (left). For a thick layer over the sponge slab on pages 44-5, make a double quantity.*

*Spread the top of the sponge with most of the icing, do not allow it to set.*

*Add a little sifted cocoa or a few drops of colouring to the rest of the icing and use it either to pipe lines across the cake or dip a skewer in the icing and form lines. Take the back of a knife and drag these lines towards you.*

*Use the knife to pull them away from you, so giving the feathered effect.*

---

Drop small spoonfuls on to the trays, allowing plenty of space for the mixture to spread during baking.

Cook for 10-12 minutes until pale golden in colour and firm in texture. Remove from the baking trays on to a wire rack. When quite cold store in an airtight tin. They keep well for several days.

*Variations: Top the biscuits with a little Glacé Icing or Chocolate Icing (left).*

*Sandwich pairs of biscuits together with jam.*

## OATY BISCUITS

PREPARATION TIME: 20 MINUTES

COOKING TIME: 15 MINUTES

QUANTITY: 24 BISCUITS

**4 oz (115 g\*) margarine or cooking fat**

**3 oz (85 g\*) sugar**

**7 oz (200 g) fine oatmeal or rolled oats**

**5 oz (150 g) self-raising flour or plain flour**
  **sifted with 1¼ teaspoons baking powder**

**pinch salt**

**1 reconstituted dried egg or fresh egg**

**little milk**

**\* use this metrication**

Preheat the oven to 180°C (350°F), Gas Mark 4. Grease 2 baking trays well.

Cream the margarine, or cooking fat, and sugar until soft and light, add the oatmeal, or rolled oats, and mix well. Sift the flour, or flour and baking powder, with the salt, add to the oat mixture with the egg. Mix very thoroughly before adding the milk, for the drier the biscuit dough the better the biscuits.

Gradually stir in enough milk to make a firm dough. Knead the dough and roll out on a floured board until about ¼ inch (5 mm) in thickness. Cut into small shapes and put on to the baking trays. Bake for 15 minutes or until firm and golden. Cool on the baking trays.

Store in an airtight tin, away from other biscuits.

## SPICED BISCUITS

Preparation time: 25 minutes

Cooking time: 10 minutes

Quantity: 30 biscuits

**2 oz (50 g) lard or cooking fat**
**2 oz (50 g) sugar**
**1 tablespoon golden syrup**
**6 oz (175 g) plain flour**
**½ teaspoon bicarbonate of soda**
**pinch ground cinnamon, or to taste**
**pinch ground ginger, or to taste**
**little water**

Preheat the oven to 160°C (325°F), Gas Mark 3. Grease 2 baking trays.

Cream the lard, or fat, with the sugar and syrup. Sift the flour with the bicarbonate of soda and spices. Add to the creamed ingredients. Mix very well and then add just enough water to make a firm dough. Turn out on to a lightly floured board, roll out until just ¼ inch (5 mm) in thickness. Cut into 30 rounds. Place on the baking trays and bake 10 minutes.

Cool the biscuits on the baking trays.

> ## Crumb Sponge
>
> As nuts were unavailable this way of using crisp breadcrumbs was sometimes recommended for making a 'nutty' textured sponge. Use the same ingredients as for the Whisked Sponge Slab on page 44 but substitute 3 oz (85 g★) crisp fine breadcrumbs for the flour.
>
> The mixture does not rise as well but it does give an interesting texture. You can fold 1 small teaspoon baking powder into the whisked eggs and sugar before adding the crumbs to make a lighter texture. Flavour the mixture with a few drops of almond essence.
>
> ★ use this metrication

## CARROT BUNS

Preparation time: 15 minutes

Cooking time: 12-15 minutes

Quantity: 12 buns

*It is important that the carrots are freshly grated and not put into water before use*

**8 oz (225 g) self-raising flour or plain**
**flour sifted with 2 teaspoons baking**
**powder**
**3 oz (75 g) margarine or cooking fat**
**3 oz (75 g) sugar**
**4 tablespoons finely grated raw carrot**
**2 tablespoons sultanas (optional)**
**1 reconstituted dried or fresh egg**
**little milk or water**

Preheat the oven to 220°C (425°F), Gas Mark 7. Grease 2 baking trays.

Sift the flour, or flour and baking powder, into a mixing bowl, rub in the margarine or cooking fat, add the sugar, carrots, sultanas and egg. Mix well then add sufficient milk or water to make a sticky consistency.

Put 12 small heaps on the baking trays and cook for 12-15 minutes or until firm and golden in colour.

minutes then lower the heat and continue steaming for a further 50 minutes. Turn out and serve with custard.

*Variations: In 1939, when the Board of Education Booklet was prepared, dried eggs were not available. A reconstituted dried egg could be used instead of a fresh egg.*

*For a lighter pudding increase the eggs to 2. Instead of the syrup or jam or curd or marmalade put soaked, but not cooked, dried prunes or figs in the basin or use peeled, cored and sliced cooking apples.*

*Add 3-4 oz (75-100 g) raisins or sultanas or chopped dates to the flour mixture before mixing with the egg and milk and water.*

## PATRIOTIC PUDDING

PREPARATION TIME: 20 MINUTES

COOKING TIME: 1½ HOURS

QUANTITY: 4-6 HELPINGS

*This well known steamed pudding appeared first in the recommendations for feeding children at school dinners in a Board of Education booklet in 1939.*

**8 oz (225 g) self-raising flour or plain flour**
**    sifted with 2 teaspoons baking powder**
**pinch salt**
**3-4 oz (75-100 g) margarine or cooking fat**
**3 oz (75 g) sugar**
**1 egg, beaten**
**milk and water to mix**
**3-4 tablespoons golden syrup, jam,**
**    lemon curd or marmalade**

Sift the flour, or flour and baking powder, with the salt into a mixing bowl. Rub in the margarine or fat, add the sugar, the egg and enough milk and water to make a soft dropping consistency (like thick whipped cream). Put the syrup or other ingredients, then the pudding mixture into a well greased 1-1½ pint (600-900 ml) basin, cover with margarine paper or greased greaseproof paper and steam over rapidly boiling water for 40

## JELLIED TRIFLE

PREPARATION TIME: 10 MINUTES

NO COOKING

QUANTITY: 4-6 HELPINGS

*This was another favourite pudding with children at their school dinners. It would not have been served on either VE or VJ Days for schools were closed in celebration of the former day and on their annual summer holiday in August. It may well have been served in the days that followed these historic events. It appealed to children who did not like custard, for although it was served with custard this could be refused if desired.*

**1 pint (600 ml) jelly (see page 38)**
**4-6 oz (100-175 g) stale plain cake**
**4-6 oz (100-175 g) fresh fruit such as dessert**
**    apples or plums or soft fruit or 3-4 oz (75-**
**    100 g) dried fruit, such as cooked prunes or**
**    apple rings or stoned dates**

Make the jelly, as page 38, and allow it to become cold. Crumble the cake into small pieces. Dice or slice the fruit, if necessary. Add the crumbled cake and the prepared fruit to the jelly. Spoon into a bowl or individual dishes and leave until set. The trifle may be served with cold custard, if liked.

# VOLUNTARY SERVICES CELEBRATIONS

*The many thousands of people who volunteered to help the war effort by taking on service work, often in addition to their everyday work, had every right to celebrate in grand style, for their work had not only been invaluable, but was unremitting. Many of them had regularly risked their lives during and after air raids in towns and cities throughout Britain.*

*For the ARP services, the Women's Institute, with its branches all over the country, the WVS and the many groups of essential workers, including ambulance drivers and fire brigade crews, as well as the many more I have not been able to mention in this chapter, VE and VJ Days were wonderful reasons for celebration.*

## THE ARP SERVICE

ARP (Air Raid Precaution Service) volunteers were on duty before, and during, air raids. They often had to rescue people from bombed buildings and this was done without thought of their own lives.

Many old and young people who worked hard all day did duty at night-time as fire watchers. Their job was very important because they were the people who would spot the first fires and give immediate warning. Harrods store in London, for instance, had its own ARP organisation, totalling 700 people, including Control Officers, Senior Pickets, Permanent Pickets, Wardens, Fireguards, Women's Civil Defence Services, Harrods Firemen and Auxiliary Firemen, Special Police and other staff.

The following recipes, from a booklet issued by the WVS on Communal Feeding in War Time, were the kinds of food offered to ARP workers at centres and canteens established in all large towns to give people hot drinks, food and a welcome brief period of leisure.

## QUICK SNACKS

These were the kind of 'easy-to-eat' snacks weary ARP workers would have snatched in a brief respite from duty. Hot drinks, especially tea, cocoa or coffee, were often their greatest need.

## CHEESE DREAMS

Make one or two sandwiches of bread, margarine and grated, or sliced, cheese. A little chutney could be included, if available. Dip the sandwiches in a beaten reconstituted dried or fresh egg mixed with 1-2 tablespoons milk, and fry in hot cooking fat until crisp and golden brown. Serve with salad.

## CHEESE POTATOES

Bake large potatoes and split into halves. Scoop out the centre pulp, mix with grated cheese and seasoning. Return to the potato skins. Reheat and serve.

RECIPE of the WEEK

## CHEESE PUDDING

PREPARATION TIME: 10 MINUTES

COOKING TIME: 30 MINUTES

QUANTITY: 3-4 HELPINGS

½ pint (300 ml) milk
1 oz (25 g) margarine
2 oz (50 g) soft breadcrumbs
1 reconstituted dried or fresh egg
3 oz (75 g) cheese, grated
salt and pepper

Pour the milk into a saucepan, add the margarine and heat until the margarine melts. Remove from the heat; add the breadcrumbs and allow to stand for 15 minutes.

Whisk the egg and add to the breadcrumb mixture with the cheese and seasoning. Mix well.

Preheat the oven to 190°C (375°F), Gas Mark 5. Pour the cheese mixture into a greased 6-7 inch (15-18 cm) soufflé dish or 1 pint (600 ml) pie dish. Bake for 30 minutes or until well-risen and golden brown. Serve at once with a green vegetable.

## BEANS ON TOAST

Heat canned beans and serve on hot toast. They can be topped with a fried egg.

## TOMATOES ON TOAST

Halve, season and fry tomatoes, put on to hot toast and top with grilled or fried sausages.

## HERB OMELETTE

Beat 2 reconstituted dried or fresh eggs. Season and add about 1 tablespoon chopped mixed herbs or 1 teaspoon dried herbs.

Heat 1 oz (25g) margarine or cooking fat in a pan. Add the egg mixture and cook until set at the bottom then tilt the pan so the top liquid egg runs underneath and continue cooking until set.

Fold, away from the handle, and serve. The omelette could be filled with crisp chopped bacon or grated cheese or cooked tomatoes.

## SPANISH OMELETTE

Dice 2 cooked potatoes, finely chop a small onion, heat 1 oz (25 g) margarine and heat the vegetables. Add the seasoned eggs and cook until firm. Do not fold.

### IN THE COUNTRY

The Women's Institute members were a very important group, for they tackled various wartime jobs in the countryside and played a vital role in village life. They helped with agricultural work, and the preserves they made for Britain with local fruit became part of the official jam ration. In many cases, they were related to farmers or farm workers and cooked for the Land Army workers and the farmers. A typical selection of country dishes have been included in the chapter on Country Celebrations.

### ESSENTIAL WORKERS

Ambulance crews and the Fire Brigade members worked both night and day to deal with the many accidents caused by the war, as well as carrying out their everyday commitments.

### THE WVS

The WVS (Women's Voluntary Service) was created just before the war, and its members did an enormous range of jobs during the war. A book entitled 'The Story of the WVS', sadly now out of print, gives a very clear picture of their work and importance during, and after, the war.

The service, always known as the WVS, was formed in 1938. When it became apparent that there was going to be a war in the foreseeable future, the Dowager Lady Reading approached the then Home Secretary, Sir Samuel Hoare, with a view to recruiting women to help in work connected with Air Raid Precautions. Sir Samuel wanted a force of a million standing by.

It says much for Lady Reading's remarkable gift for leadership and for her ability to convince women that even if they only gave a few hours service a week it would make an incalculable difference to the course of events, that so many women dropped their colanders and ran. Starting with a membership of five, by the end of its first year the WVS was 300,000 strong.

Their first wartime job was to help with the evacuation of city children and mothers to safer areas. They became volunteer drivers to all departments, served endless meals at Emergency Feeding Centres after air-raids, manned canteens for Air Raid Wardens and in various Service Clubs throughout Britain. They later extended this to become partners to NAAFI in some combat zones. They even set up club rooms in Paris and Brussels after the successful D Day landings led to victory in Europe.

Post-war acknowledgement of the wonderful work done by the WVS both during the war and afterwards - and which the organisation is still doing - came in 1966, when the Queen honoured the WVS by adding 'Royal' to its title, since when the service's full name has been Women's Royal Voluntary Service.

It is certain that WVS celebrations for both VE and VJ Days would be enjoyed by an enormous number of people in Britain and in other countries where these women were doing such invaluable and cheerful work. The recipes included in this chapter come from a WVS wartime handbook of recipes and other WVS collections of recipes and cooking hints collected by local WVS groups.

## CREAM OF PARSNIP SOUP

PREPARATION TIME: 25 MINUTES

COOKING TIME: 35-40 MINUTES

QUANTITY: 4-5 HELPINGS

*This is particularly good in summertime when parsnips are young, sweet in flavour and very tender.*

1 lb (450 g) parsnips, peeled and
   minced or grated
4 oz (100 g) onions or leeks, finely chopped
2 bacon rinds
2 pints (1.2 litres) stock or water
salt and pepper
1 oz (25 g) flour
¼ pint (150 ml) milk
chopped parsley, to garnish

Put the parsnips, onions or leeks and bacon rinds into a saucepan with the stock or water. Bring to the boil, season to taste, cover the pan and boil steadily until the vegetables are tender. Blend the flour gradually with the milk, add to the soup, stirring well to prevent any lumps forming. Remove the bacon rinds, add any extra seasoning required. Garnish with the parsley.

## TOMATO SOUP

PREPARATION TIME: 20 MINUTES

COOKING TIME: 30-35 MINUTES

QUANTITY: 4-5 HELPINGS

*One of the many tasks undertaken by the WVS was to collect and supply fresh vegetables to mine sweepers and other small ships around the coasts of Britain, the crews of which had no opportunity of gathering these for themselves. WVS womenn were therefore used to finding vegetables and fruit, so for Victory celebrations would undoubtedly make this soup, which was a favourite with old and young. It was an ideal summertime soup, for fresh tomatoes would be readily available for several months.*

¾ oz (20 g) dripping
1 small carrot, sliced
1 small potato, sliced
1 small onion, sliced
2 bacon rinds
2½ pints (1.5 litres) stock or water
12 oz (350 g) tomatoes, halved
salt and pepper
2 oz (50 g) flour
1 teaspoon sugar

Heat the dripping in a saucepan and fry the carrot, potato, onion and bacon rinds for a few minutes. Boil most of the stock or water, add to the ingredients in the saucepan with the tomatoes and a little seasoning. Cover the pan and boil gently until the vegetables are tender. Mash with a wooden spoon or put through a sieve. Return to the saucepan. Blend the flour with the rest of the stock or water, which should be cold. Add to the pan and stir over the heat until thickened. Adjust the seasoning and add the sugar.

## COD AND TOMATO FISH CAKES

PREPARATION TIME: 25 MINUTES

COOKING TIME: 25-30 MINUTES

QUANTITY: 4-5 HELPINGS

*The good amounts of tomato, onion and parsley help to make up for the rather small proportion of fish in these fish cakes.*

½ oz (15 g) cooking fat
1 small onion, finely chopped
1 large tomato, finely chopped
1½ lb (675 g) cooked potatoes, mashed
8 oz (225 g) cooked fish, flaked
salt and pepper
1 tablespoon chopped parsley
2 oz (50 g) crisp breadcrumbs, to coat

DIG FOR VICTORY

G.E. 1045

# GUINNESS for STRENGTH

Heat the fat and add the onion and tomato, cook until a soft purée. Blend with the mashed potatoes, fish, seasoning and parsley. Form into 8-10 round cakes. Coat in the crisp breadcrumbs.

Preheat the oven to 190°C (375°F), Gas Mark 5. Grease and heat a baking tray. Put the fish cakes on this and bake for 15-20 minutes, or until crisp and brown.
*Variation: Fry the cakes in hot fat, if available.*
*For a better coating, dust the fish cakes with seasoned flour, brush with beaten egg and coat in the crumbs.*
*When more fish is available use only 12 oz (350 g) mashed potato and the same weight of cooked fish.*

## SALMON LOAF

PREPARATION TIME: 25 MINUTES

COOKING TIME: 1 HOUR

QUANTITY: 4-5 HELPINGS

**6 oz (175 g) canned pink salmon**
**nearly ¼ pint (150 ml) milk (see method)**
**3 oz (75 g) stale bread**
**4 tablespoons cold water**
**½ oz (15 g) margarine, melted**
**3 oz (75 g) cooked potatoes, mashed**
**½ tablespoon chopped parsley**
**salt and pepper**
**½ tablespoon vinegar**

Open the can of fish and pour the liquid into a measure, add enough milk to make ¼ pint (150 ml). Break the bread into small pieces, put into a basin, add the water, soak for about 15 minutes, then squeeze dry.

Flake the salmon, then mix all the ingredients together, put into a greased 1 lb (450 g) loaf tin or oblong casserole. Cover with greased greaseproof paper. Preheat the oven to 180°C (350°F), Gas Mark 4. Bake for 1 hour. Serve hot or cold.
*Variation: The loaf can be steamed for 1 hour instead of being baked.*

## CORNISH PASTIES

PREPARATION TIME: 30 MINUTES

COOKING TIME: 30 MINUTES

QUANTITY: 4-5 HELPINGS

*In the original WVS recipe for these favourites, there are hints on making the pasties quickly, not individually, but as the recipe has been adapted for a small number of helpings it now allows for making the more traditional individual pasties.*

**Shortcrust Pastry made with**
**1 lb (450 g) flour etc. (page 42)**
*For the filling:*
**4 oz (100 g) minced beef**
**1 medium onion, finely chopped**
**8 oz (225 g) turnips, finely diced**
**2 oz (50 g) carrots, finely diced**
**little stock**
**salt and pepper**
**little milk, to glaze**

Preheat the oven to 190°C (375°F), Gas Mark 5. Make the pastry as on page 42, roll out and cut into 4 or 5 large rounds.

Mix the ingredients for the filling together, moisten with a very little stock and season to taste. Put spoonfuls of the filling into the centre of each pastry round. Brush the edges of the pastry with water, bring these together and flute them to make the traditional pastie shape. Brush with a little milk.

Put the pasties on a greased baking sheet and bake in the preheated oven for 30 minutes.
*Variations: Use one of the alternative kinds of pastry on pages 23 and 43 instead of Shortcrust Pastry.*
*When more meat is available use 8 oz (225 g) minced beef, 8 oz (225 g) finely diced potato with 2 chopped onions and omit the other vegetables.*

# RAISED PORK PIE

PREPARATION TIME: 40 MINUTES

COOKING TIME: 2 HOURS

QUANTITY: 8-10 HELPINGS

**For the pastry:**

**1 lb (450 g) plain flour**

**1 teaspoon salt**

**4 oz (100 g) cooking fat or**
**well clarified dripping (see below)**

**½ pint (300 ml) water**

**For the filling:**

**1 lb (450 g) pork sausage meat**

**6 oz (175 g) fat bacon, minced**

**2 medium onions, finely chopped**

**1 tablespoon chopped mixed herbs or ½ tea-**
**spoon dried mixed herbs**

**salt and pepper**

**To glaze:**

**1 reconstituted dried or fresh egg**

**1 tablespoon water**

Sift the flour and salt into a mixing bowl, keep in a warm place. Put the cooking fat or dripping into a saucepan with the water. Heat until the fat or dripping has melted. Pour on to the flour and mix well. Keep warm until using this.

Blend all the ingredients for the filling together.

Knead the pastry until a smooth pliable paste. Roll out two-thirds and line the base and sides of a 7-8 inch (18-20 cm) cake tin, preferably one with a loose base. Put in the filling. Damp the edges of the pastry. Roll out the remaining dough to make a lid, press in position.

Make a slit in the centre of the pastry covering, for the steam to escape during baking. Any pastry left can be made into leaf shapes to decorate the pastry. Beat the egg with the water and brush over the pastry.

Preheat the oven to 180°C (350°F), Gas Mark 4 and bake the pie for 2 hours. Serve cold with salad.

*Variation: If fresh pork is available use half finely diced lean pork and half sausage meat.*

## CLARIFYING DRIPPING

Put the dripping in a saucepan with cold water to cover. Bring gradually to the boil, removing any scum. Strain into a bowl and cool. When cold, carefully lift off the fat which has set on top of the water and scrape the bottom. Heat the fat gently in a saucepan until all the water in it has evaporated. The clarified fat is now ready for use for frying or baking.

## WVS SPECIAL SANDWICH FILLINGS

### WATERCRESS AND SALMON

Blend the boned salmon from a small can with 1-2 tablespoons vinegar, 4 oz (100 g) chopped watercress, 6 oz (175 g) mashed potatoes, 4 oz (100 g) finely chopped leek and salt and pepper to taste.

### SAVOURY EGG AND BACON

Heat 1 oz (25 g) margarine in a pan, add 2 oz (50 g) chopped spring onions, 2 oz (50 g) finely chopped cooked bacon, and heat for a few minutes. Reconstitute 4 dried eggs or use fresh eggs, beat with 6 tablespoons milk, pour into the pan, add a little salt and pepper and cook gently until the eggs have set, stirring occasionally. Allow to become cold.

### PILCHARD AND LEEK SPREAD

Blend 8 oz (225 g) canned pilchards in tomato sauce with 2 oz (50 g) finely chopped leeks, 2 oz (50 g) chopped parsley, 8 oz (225 g) mashed potatoes, 1 tablespoon vinegar and salt and pepper to taste.

## RHUBARB SNOW

PREPARATION TIME: 20 MINUTES

COOKING TIME: 20 MINUTES

QUANTITY: 4-5 HELPINGS

*Golden syrup was one of the most valuable wartime commodities and was often used in place of sugar. It was included on the points system.*

**12 oz (350 g) rhubarb**

**1-2 tablespoons water**

**3 oz (75 g) golden syrup.**

**½ pint (300 ml) milk**

**1½ oz (40 g) semolina**

**few drops lemon essence**

Cut the rhubarb into small pieces, put into a saucepan. Add the water (use 2 tablespoons if rhubarb is not very ripe) and the syrup. Cook until a thick pulp.

Pour the milk into a second saucepan, whisk on the semolina, add the lemon essence. Bring to the boil, then stir over a low heat for 10 minutes. Allow to cool for a few minutes then tip into a bowl. Add the rhubarb pulp. Leave until cool but not set and beat vigorously until a frothy mixture. Spoon into a serving bowl.

*Variations: When both sugar and syrup are scarce cook the fruit with just the water then add crushed saccharine tablets to the hot cooked fruit.*

## SUMMER PUDDING

PREPARATION TIME: 20 MINUTES

COOKING TIME: 10 MINUTES

QUANTITY: 4-5 HELPINGS

**1½ lb (675 g) soft fruit, a mixture of red and**

**black currants or other summer fruits**

**3-4 tablespoons water**

**sugar or golden syrup, to sweeten**

**8-10 oz (225-300 g) stale bread**

Put the prepared fruit into a saucepan with the water (use the 4 tablespoons of water if the fruit is very firm) and sugar or syrup to sweeten. Cook only until the fruit is soft, do not allow it to become a pulp.

Cut the bread into thin slices and line a 1-1½ pint (600-900 ml) basin with most of this (save enough for the top covering). Fill with the fruit and some of the juice. Cover with the remaining bread.

Put a plate and light weight on top of the pudding and leave to stand for about 12 hours. Turn the pudding out carefully and serve with the remaining juice and custard (page 38).

## APPLE AND DATE SLICE

PREPARATION TIME: 25 MINUTES

COOKING TIME: 30-35 MINUTES

QUANTITY: 8-10 HELPINGS

*This was the nearest one could get to flaky pastry with rather less fat than the classic recipe and the somewhat heavier flour of the 1940s.*

**For the pastry:**

**1 lb (450 g) self-raising flour or plain flour**

**sifted with 2 teaspoons baking powder**

**½ teaspoon salt**

**8 oz (225 g) cooking fat or margarine**

**water, to bind**

**For the filling:**

**1 lb (450 g) cooking apples, peeled,**

**cored and minced or grated**

**8 oz (225 g) breadcrumbs**

**8 oz (225 g) cooking dates, minced**

**or finely chopped**

**1-2 teaspoons mixed spice**

**2 oz (50 g) margarine or**

**cooking fat, melted**

**To glaze:**

**1 reconstituted dried or fresh egg**

**1 tablespoon water**

Sift the flour, or flour and baking powder, and salt into a bowl. Add the fat to the flour and cut into small pieces with one or two knives. Blend with the water to make a soft pliable dough.

Put the dough on to a floured surface and roll out then fold over, as though making puff pastry, i.e. bring up the bottom third of the dough and bring down the top third. Cover lightly and stand in a cool place for 30 minutes then roll out and fold again. Give a final rolling to make a large oblong shape. Divide this into two equal pieces.

Preheat the oven to 190°C (375°F), Gas Mark 5. Put half the pastry on to a large flat baking tray.

Mix all the ingredients for the filling together. Spread over the pastry on the baking tray. Keep the filling away from the extreme edges of the pastry. Moisten the edges with the beaten egg, mixed with the water. Cover with the second oblong of pastry. Seal the edges. Brush the top with the egg and water. Bake in the preheated oven for 30-35 minutes or until the pastry is golden brown. Cut into fingers and serve hot or cold. *Variations: When fat is scarce use the economical pastry recipe on page 43. You will need a total weight of pastry of 1½ lb (675 g).*

## EGGLESS CHOCOLATE BUNS

PREPARATION TIME: 15 MINUTES

COOKING TIME: 15-20 MINUTES

QUANTITY: 12-15 MINUTES

**8 oz (225 g) self-raising flour or plain flour**
   **sifted with 2 teaspoons baking powder**
**1 oz (25 g) cocoa powder**
**3 oz (75 g) sugar**
**7½ fl oz (225 ml) hot water**
**1 tablespoon golden syrup**
**1 teaspoon bicarbonate of soda**
**few drops vanilla essence**
**3 oz (75 g) margarine, melted**

Preheat the oven to 180°C (350°F), Gas Mark 4. Grease 12-15 patty tins. Sift the flour, or flour and baking powder, with the cocoa, add the sugar.

Pour the hot water into a good-sized container, add the syrup and bicarbonate of soda. This fizzes and makes the liquid rise rapidly. Add to the cocoa mixture with the essence and margarine.

Spoon into the tins and bake for 15-20 minutes or until firm to the touch. Remove from the tins on to a wire cooling rack.

## RAISIN AND SPICE BUNS

PREPARATION TIME: 10 MINUTES

COOKING TIME: 15 MINUTES

QUANTITY: 12 BUNS

*In these quickly made cakes the dried egg powder was generally added to the flour. It was however essential to add the 2 tablespoons water to the mixture before adding any extra milk or water.*

**8 oz (225 g) self-raising flour or plain flour**
   **sifted with 2 teaspoons baking powder**
**1 tablespoon dried egg powder**
**1 teaspoon mixed spice**
**2 oz (50 g) margarine or cooking fat**
**3 oz (75 g) sugar**
**3-4 oz (75-100 g) raisins**
**2 tablespoons water**
**milk or milk and water to bind**

Preheat the oven to 220°C (425°F), Gas Mark 7. Grease 2 flat baking trays.

Sift the flour, or flour and baking powder, with the dried egg and spice. Rub in the margarine or cooking fat, add the sugar, raisins, water and enough milk or milk and water to make a sticky dough. It should stand in soft peaks when a knife is pulled through the mixture in the bowl.

Put spoonfuls on to the prepared trays and bake for

15 minutes, or until golden brown and firm. Remove on to a wire cooling tray.

*Variation: Oaty Raisin and Spice Buns: omit 2 oz (50 g) flour and use 2 oz (50 g) rolled oats instead. Sift ½ teaspoon baking powder with the self-raising flour or still use 2 teaspoons baking powder with plain flour.*

# Let's talk about FOOD

## HINTS FROM THE WVS

The WVS passed on in its various food booklets many practical hints, most of them based on using every last ounce of food, since nothing must be wasted in wartime. Here are some of them.

### BICARBONATE OF SODA IN STEWED FRUIT

A little bicarbonate of soda added to the fruit while stewing will neutralise some of the acid and the fruit will then need less sugar. Use ½ teaspoon bicarbonate of soda to 1 lb (450 g) fruit. Stir it in slowly at the end of the cooking time. Note, though, that this tip is not suitable for use in jam making.

### USING SARDINE OIL

The oil left over from a can of sardines could be utilised in the following ways:

1. Used in place of salad oil in a vinaigrette or French dressing with a fish salad.

2. Use for frying: (a) potato cakes; (b) a slice of bread to serve with potato or fish cakes; (c) fish cakes.

3. Use it for binding flaked fish and sauce for a Fish Pie.

## USING VEGETABLE WATER

The water used for cooking vegetables, which retains some of the vegetables' vitamins, should be used in the following ways:

1. For gravy, make a thick sauce and thin down with fresh vegetable water just before serving.

2. Do the same thing with soups: that is, make them fairly thick so that as the vegetables are strained, the liquor can be added to the soup to give it additional flavouring and Vitamin C.

3. When serving Cauliflower au gratin, use the liquor the cauliflower has been cooked in to make the white sauce. Use for macaroni cheese as well.

### HELPING THE SUGAR RATION ALONG

Stretch the sugar ration is by making full use of sweetened condensed milk and dried fruit.

Use honey and syrup, instead of sugar, to sweeten stewed fruit. Add them either before or after cooking.

Honey and syrup may also be used to replace up to half the sugar used in jam and marmalade: if your recipe needs 3 lbs (1.25 kg) sugar, you could use instead half that amount of sugar and 1½ lb (759 g) honey or syrup. Honey or syrup may be used in bottling fruit, too, but the flavour will be noticeable.

## Making the MOST OF THE SUGAR

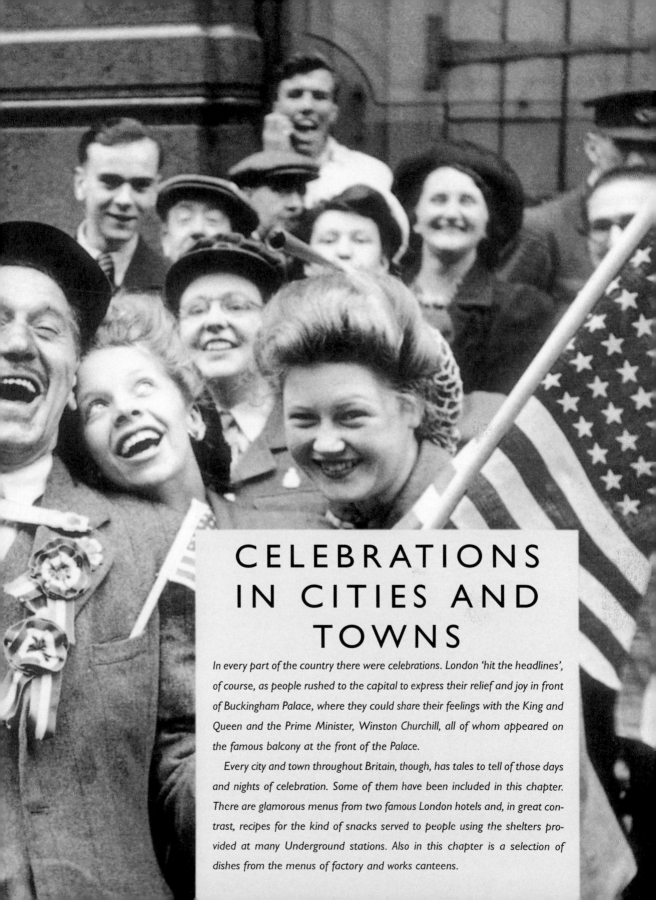

# CELEBRATIONS IN CITIES AND TOWNS

In every part of the country there were celebrations. London 'hit the headlines', of course, as people rushed to the capital to express their relief and joy in front of Buckingham Palace, where they could share their feelings with the King and Queen and the Prime Minister, Winston Churchill, all of whom appeared on the famous balcony at the front of the Palace.

Every city and town throughout Britain, though, has tales to tell of those days and nights of celebration. Some of them have been included in this chapter. There are glamorous menus from two famous London hotels and, in great contrast, recipes for the kind of snacks served to people using the shelters provided at many Underground stations. Also in this chapter is a selection of dishes from the menus of factory and works canteens.

# FACTORY CELEBRATIONS

Factories were situated throughout the land, of course, but most were in or on the outskirts of cities and towns, so the workers had to cope with the danger of air-raids as well as excessively hard work.

As a member of the Food Advice Division in the Ministry of Food, I had the opportunity to visit various factories and to talk to the workers during meal breaks about war-time recipes.

Factory workers, both men and women, worked incredibly hard, in day and night shifts, especially in armament and aircraft factories. Breaks in the work schedule, in the canteens or round tea trolleys on the factory floor, were cheerful interludes, usually with music as a form of relaxation.

The days following VE and VJ Days must have been full of celebration in the canteens and canteen cooks would certainly have done their best to embellish the standard menus. The recipes that follow have been selected from standard factory canteen menus, though quantities have been reduced.

## Meat Pudding

PREPARATION TIME: 30 MINUTES

COOKING TIME: 2½ HOURS

QUANTITY: 4 HELPINGS

*Even by the end of the war, in canteens it was not always possible to have just steak and kidney as a filling but this recipe is typical of the kind of savoury meat pudding that would be served.*

*For the pastry:*

**7 oz (200 g) plain flour, wholemeal if possible**

**3 oz (75 g) rolled oats or fine oatmeal**

**2½ teaspoons baking powder**

**salt and pepper**

**2-3 oz (50-75 g) suet, grated**

**water, to bind**

*For the filling:*

**8 oz (225 g) stewing steak**

**4 oz (100 g) liver or ox-kidney, if available (see method) or 4 oz (100 g) cooked haricot beans or cooked dried peas**

**4 oz (100 g) sliced onions or leeks**

**4 oz (100 g) sliced carrots**

**2 tablespoons chopped parsley**

Mix the flour, oats, baking powder, seasoning and suet together then add enough cold water to make a dough with a soft rolling consistency. Roll out; use about three-quarters to line a 1½-2 pint (900-1200 ml) pudding basin. Dice the meat(s) finely; if there is no liver or ox-kidney use the beans or peas for extra protein.

Mix with the other ingredients for the filling and season well. Add 3-4 tablespoons water. Moisten the edges of the pastry then roll out the remaining dough to form a lid. Put in position, cover with margarine paper or greased greaseproof paper and steam for 2½ hours. Serve with brown gravy and mixed vegetables.

*Variations: If suet is not available rub cooking fat or dripping or margarine into the flour.*

*Vegetable Pudding: in many homes when there was no meat left, a similar pudding would be made filled with as many different vegetables as possible.*

## Haricot Stew

PREPARATION TIME: 20 MINUTES

COOKING TIME: 35 MINUTES

QUANTITY: 4 SERVINGS

*In canteens, just as much as in the home, fresh meat had to be augmented with corned beef and plenty of vegetables. This stew can be varied according to the vegetables in season. Leeks were used a great deal, often to take the place of onions, which were difficult to get at certain times of the year.*

**2 oz (50 g) dripping**
**I large leek, thinly sliced**
**2 oz (50 g) plain flour**
**I½ pints (900 ml) vegetable stock**
**I lb (450 g) mixed vegetables, diced**
**salt and pepper**
**4 oz (100 g) cooked haricot beans**
**4 oz (100 g) corned beef, diced**

Heat the dripping in a large pan, add the leek and fry until brown. Blend in the flour and then the stock. Bring to the boil and cook, stirring, until thickened then add the mixed vegetables with seasoning to taste.

Cover the pan and simmer the stew until the vegetables are almost tender. Add the haricot beans and corned beef and simmer for 10 minutes to heat through.

## Toad In The Hole

PREPARATION TIME: 15 MINUTES

COOKING TIME: 35-40 MINUTES

QUANTITY: 4 HELPINGS

*Canteen meals often included sausages and this was one of the favourite ways of serving them.*

**I oz (25 g) dripping or cooking fat**
**I lb (450 g) sausages**
***For the batter:***
**5 oz (150 g) plain flour**
**pinch salt**
**I tablespoon dried egg powder**
**2 tablespoons water**
**½ pint (300 ml) milk or milk and water**

Preheat the oven to 200°C (400°F), Gas Mark 6. Put the dripping or cooking fat into a Yorkshire Pudding tin, heat for a few minutes, add the sausages and turn around in the fat then cook for 5 minutes.

Now raise the oven setting to 220°C (425°F), Gas Mark 7. Blend the ingredients for the batter together: this is slightly less thin than for an ordinary Yorkshire Pudding batter, to make it more satisfying. (When using dried egg to make a batter, the dried egg powder was generally mixed with the flour and salt, then the water added to the liquid. This saved time.)

Pour the batter over the hot sausages and bake for 25-30 minutes, or until well risen and golden brown. Lower the heat slightly towards the end of the cooking time, if necessary.

*Variations: Use a fresh egg and omit the 2 tablespoons water. Substitute Lentil sausages (recipe on page 66). Sweet Batter Pudding: often a batter, similar to the one above, was baked and served with hot jam or golden syrup as a pudding. Use the recipe above or the more usual one of only 4 oz (110 g\*) flour to 1 egg and ½ pint (scant 300 ml) milk or milk and water.*
*\*use this metrication.*

## Lentil Sausages

*The following ingredients give 1 lb (450 g), or about 8 lentil sausages.*

Cook 3 oz (75 g) split lentils with a chopped leek or onion, a good tablespoon of finely chopped sage and a generous amount of seasoning in water to cover until a thick soft purée.

Blend with 1 tablespoon soya or ordinary flour, a little chopped parsley and 8 oz (225 g) very smooth mashed potato. Form into sausage shapes. Coat in a beaten reconstituted dried or fresh egg and fine breadcrumbs. Fry, grill or bake until golden brown.

If using in place of ordinary sausages in Toad In The Hole (page 65) omit the coating.

## Bread Pudding

PREPARATION TIME: 25 MINUTES

COOKING TIME: 1¼ HOURS

QUANTITY: 4-6 HELPINGS

*A Bread Pudding is an ideal way of using up stale bread and it has always been extremely popular in this country, both as a hot pudding with custard or served cold instead of a cake. The marmalade makes up for the grated lemon and orange rinds and crystallized peel that would have been included in a good Bread Pudding in the days before the war.*

**8 oz (225 g) stale bread**

**water (see method)**

**2 oz (50 g) suet, shredded or margarine or**
 **cooking fat, melted**

**2 oz (50 g) sugar**

**½-1 teaspoon grated or ground nutmeg**

**pinch mixed spice**

**1-2 tablespoons marmalade**

**3-4 oz (75-100 g) mixed dried fruit ( see**
 **method)**

**1 reconstituted dried or fresh egg**

**little milk or milk and water**

Break the bread into small pieces and put into a basin, add enough cold water to cover. Leave for 30 minutes then squeeze the bread hard to extract any surplus moisture. Put the bread into a basin, add the rest of the ingredients. The dried fruit could be all of one kind or a mixture of fruits; chopped, soaked, but not cooked, dried prunes give a good flavour. Add just enough milk or milk and water to make a sticky consistency.

The pudding can be baked or steamed, if it is being served as a hot pudding, but if it is to be served cold, it is better to bake it.

If steaming, put the pudding mixture into a greased 1½-2 pint (900-1200 ml) basin. Cover with margarine paper and steam for 1½ hours.

If baking the pudding, grease a 7 inch (18 cm) cake tin. Put in the mixture. Preheat the oven to 180°C (350°F), Gas Mark 4 and bake for 1-1¼ hours, or until firm. If serving as a cake, cool in the tin then cut into squares and top with a little sugar before serving.

## Apple Fruit Cake

PREPARATION TIME: 25 MINUTES

COOKING TIME: 1¼ HOURS

QUANTITY: 1 x 8 INCH (20 CM) CAKE

*Teatime breaks were very important for workers in factories and cakes and buns were usually available. When apples were plentiful this was a popular cake.*

**12 oz (350 g) self-raising flour or plain flour**
 **sifted with 3 teaspoons baking powder**

**4 oz (100 g) margarine or cooking fat**

**4 oz (100 g) sugar**

**½-1 teaspoon ground cinnamon**

**8 oz (225 g) cooking apples, peeled, cored**
 **and diced, weight when prepared**

**3 oz (75 g) sultanas or raisins**

**1 reconstituted dried or fresh egg**

**milk as required**

**1 oz (25 g) brown sugar, for topping**

Preheat the oven to 180°C (350°F), Gas Mark 4. Grease and flour an 8 inch (20 cm) cake tin.

Sift the flour, or flour and baking powder, into a mixing bowl, rub in the margarine or cooking fat, add the sugar, cinnamon, apples, sultanas or raisins and the egg. Mix very thoroughly. If necessary, add a little milk but the mixture must be a sticky consistency, i.e. it should stand up in peaks when handled with a knife.

Spoon the mixture into the cake tin, smooth flat on top and sprinkle over the brown sugar. Bake for 1¼ hours or until golden brown and firm; reduce the heat slightly after 50 minutes, if necessary. Cool for 10 minutes in the tin then turn out on to a wire cooling rack. Eat the cake when freshly baked.

## CITY CELEBRATIONS

VE Day was a public holiday in Britain, so factories and shops, as well as schools, were closed. Plenty of people were working, however - like the Glasgow bus clippie waving her cap so happily in the picture on this page.

In London, where there were parades and much excitement, the world-famous Harrods department store carried out the Government's wish by opening its Food Halls and Bank, both brilliantly lighted while the rest of the store was in darkness, for several hours on VE Day morning.

Queues formed round the store from an early hour, according to the store's staff magazine, the Harrodian Gazette. 'Inside the store good spirits and tolerance were much in evidence and customers showed every co-operation,' noted the Gazette. 'Everyone was in high spirits, much shaking of hands and mutual congratulations were in evidence... It was just another of those days which none of us will ever forget.'

Despite the rationing, still very much in force of

course, the store had on sale that morning fresh fish and juicy steaks and was able to provide coffee and a cold lunch for all its staff who were on duty in the store.

THE **V** 1945

# GARDEN PARTY

WILL BE HELD AT

**THE HARRODIAN CLUB, MILL LODGE, BARNES**

ON

Saturday, 7th July

## THE GREATEST SOCIAL EVENT OF THE YEAR

Comic Competitions - Dancing - Concert - Tennis - Cricket
Bowls - Baseball - Sports

SEE THE PUNCH AND JUDY SHOW
SWINGS AND ROUNDABOUTS
ALL THE FUN OF THE FAIR

All Harrodians and Staff of Allied Houses are cordially invited to bring their friends with them to this Family Gathering

Hutchings & Crowsley, Printers, 117 Fulham Road, SW3

## RESTAURANT MEALS

During and after the war food rationing brought great problems to restaurants and hotels everywhere. The leading chefs, who had been used to cooking with the best ingredients in the world, now had to make appetising and sustaining food out of limited resources. Designated First Class establishments were allowed a little leeway in catering matters and they were allowed to make a house charge.

In London at the Savoy Hotel, where the head chef was François Latry until 1942, one of the most famous dishes of the war was created by him in honour of the Minister of Food, Lord Woolton. This was, of course, Woolton Pie, for which there are many recipes; sadly, François Latry did not leave a written recipe for his original creation. My interpretation of how it might have been cooked at the Savoy starts on this page.

It is interesting to see the kinds of food served in first class hotels and restaurants during this period. The menu reproduced on page 70 comes from the famous London restaurant, Simpsons, just down The Strand from the Savoy,. and is the one they served on VE Day. Although it was a menu in celebration of a very important event, the meal's fixed price of 5s 0d (25 p), the legal maximum price for all restaurant meals, could not be increased.

The Savoy Hotel, for their official Victory In Europe Dinner on May 8th 1945, produced the following elegant menu:

The first course choice was La Tasse de Consommé Empire, or La Crème Marche Triomphale, or La Couronne de Crousacés des Vainqueurs.

This was followed by Le Poulet des Héros Alliés, with Le Velouté Champ d'Honneur and Les Feuilles de Rosée Aube de Bonheur.

For sweet, guests were offered Les Pêches Glacées de la Victoire and Les Friandises de la Paix.

The Dorchester hotel had no record of special VE Day dinners but sent me some of their wartime menus which show how imaginative their chefs had to be with sparse rations and low prices.

## Welsh Rarebit

PREPARATION TIME: 15 MINUTES

COOKING TIME: 5-6 MINUTES

QUANTITY: 4 HELPINGS

*This version of Welsh Rarebit was one I sampled, for it was served in the Silver Buffet restaurant at Harrods, where I so often had my lunch. It was carefully prepared, the potatoes really were beautifully smooth and the mixture was carefully seasoned to compensate for the relatively small amount of cheese used.*

**6 oz (175 g) cooked potatoes**
**1 oz (25 g) margarine, melted**
**4-6 oz (100-175 g) cheese, grated**
**little milk**
**salt and pepper**
**1 teaspoon made mustard, or to taste**
**few drops Worcestershire sauce**
**4 slices of bread**

Mash the potatoes until they are absolutely smooth, blend with the margarine and three-quarters of the cheese then gradually add enough milk to make a creamy consistency. Stir in the rest of the ingredients.

Toast the bread, spread with the rarebit mixture, top with the remaining cheese and place under a preheated grill until piping hot and bubbling. Serve at once.

## Woolton Pie

*Most people have their own interpretation of this recipe. Basically, it is made with mixed vegetables, a sauce and a topping, which could be pastry or potatoes. I am sure the original Woolton Pie, created at the*

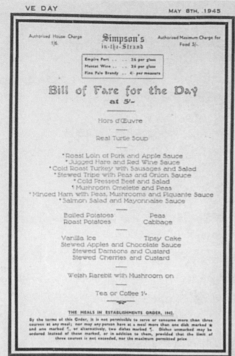

VE DAY            MAY 8TH, 1945

### Simpson's
in-the-Strand

Authorised House Charge 1/6       Authorised Maximum Charge for Food 5/-

Empire Port ... 1/6 per glass
Muscat Wine ... 1/6 per glass
Fine Pale Brandy ... 4/- per measure

## Bill of Fare for the Day
at 5/-

Hors d'Œuvre

Real Turtle Soup

\*Roast Loin of Pork and Apple Sauce
\*Jugged Hare and Red Wine Sauce
\*Cold Roast Turkey with Sausages and Salad
\*Stewed Tripe with Peas and Onion Sauce
\*Cold Pressed Beef and Salad
\*Mushroom Omelette and Peas
\*Minced Ham with Peas, Mushrooms and Piquante Sauce
\*Salmon Salad and Mayonnaise Sauce

Boiled Potatoes       Peas
Roast Potatoes       Cabbage

Vanilla Ice       Tipsy Cake
Stewed Apples and Chocolate Sauce
Stewed Damsons and Custard
Stewed Cherries and Custard

Welsh Rarebit with Mushroom on

Tea or Coffee 1/-

THE MEALS IN ESTABLISHMENTS ORDER, 1942.

By the terms of this Order, it is not permissible to serve or consume more than three courses at any meal; nor may any person have at a meal more than one dish marked \* and one marked ¶, or alternatively, two dishes marked ¶. Dishes unmarked may be ordered instead of these marked, or in addition to them, provided that the limit of three courses is not exceeded, nor the maximum permitted price

---

Savoy Hotel, looked most enticing and tasted very good too.

Prepare a mixture of vegetables, such as parsnips, potatoes, leeks, carrots and any other vegetables in season. Take time and trouble to cut them into uniform shapes, such as short fingers.

Cook lightly in a little boiling water, so they retain texture and flavour. Put into a dish. Top with an interesting sauce. I imagine the Savoy might well have made a special Cheese Sauce, flavoured with herbs.

The covering might have been beautifully piped potatoes, topped with a little grated cheese, so they became brown and shining when the pie was baked for about 30 minutes in the oven.

SAVOY HOTEL

## CELEBRATIONS
## IN THE SHELTERS

There can be few people who celebrated the end of the war more whole-heartedly than those who had spent so much time in the air-raid shelters. Home owners throughout Britain had erected Anderson and Morrison shelters or had relatively safe places in their houses to go at the time of the air-raids.

In London there were periods when day after day, night after night, bombs fell all over the city. This is when the crowds went to the underground shelters at tube stations. No fewer than 177,000 people were recorded as having taken shelter from the blitz in the tubes on September 17, 1940. This number fell, stabilising for a time at about 60,000 per night, then increased again when the blitz came back in 1943-44. Often troops, who were moving across London at night time, sheltered in these tube stations too.

In all, 79 deep tube platforms were permitted for use as shelters. As the years went by, proper sanitary arrangements, better lighting and facilities were arranged by the Government.

Food was provided and sold by J. Lyons of Cadby Hall and its serving was organised by the Tube Refreshment Service, which employed between 400 and 500 women. The food was delivered to the packing depots at the end of each line. At 1 p.m. each day the Tube Refreshment trains were loaded and, as the trains ran through, the bins were dropped off at a service point on each platform. At 4 p.m. wash boilers were switched on and by 6 p.m. tea and cocoa were served to the shelterers along the platform. Wherever possible, hot drinks were served again in the morning before people left for work or home.

Even on VE-night 12,000 people were at the Underground Tube stations and in the deep shelters.

The recipes that follow give a idea of the food that was sold to the shelterers and which they would have enjoyed on VE-night.

# COLD MEAT PASTIES

PREPARATION TIME: 25 MINUTES

COOKING TIME: 20 MINUTES

QUANTITY: 4 PASTIES

*This recipe comes from a wartime book published by McDougalls. The high amount of Worcestershire sauce, which may be reduced, if liked, is typical of recipes of the era, as people tried to put as much flavour as possible into fairly flavourless food.*

**Shortcrust pastry made with 8 oz (225 g) flour etc. (page 42)**

***For the filling:***

**8 oz (225 g) cold meat, minced**

**1 small onion, minced or chopped**

**2 tomatoes, sliced**

**2 tablespoons chopped cooked carrots or other vegetables**

**2 tablespoons Worcestershire sauce**

**2 tablespoons gravy or water**

**salt and pepper**

**1 reconstituted dried egg or fresh egg, if available, to glaze**

Preheat the oven to 200°C (400°F), Gas Mark 6. Grease a baking tray.

Roll out the pastry and cut it into four rounds. Brush the edges with water or a little beaten egg. Mix the ingredients for the filling together and put in the centre of each round. Bring the edges together, pinch well and trim into flutes between the finger and thumb.

Make a slit in the side of the pastry with a pointed knife. Brush with beaten egg, if liked. Place on the baking tray and bake in the preheated oven for 20 minutes.

# VEGETABLE PASTIES

Follow the recipe for Cold Meat Pasties above, but fill the pastry with about 1 lb (450 g) lightly cooked diced vegetables, such as onions, carrots, turnips, potatoes and swede. 1-2 chopped uncooked tomatoes give extra flavour. Use less Worcestershire sauce and a little tomato ketchup to flavour.

## SAVOURY POTATO PASTIES

Follow the recipe for Cold Meat Pasties but make a filling with 12 oz (350 g) diced cooked potatoes, 2 finely chopped cooked onions, 1-2 oz (25-50 g) grated cheese, 1 teaspoon finely chopped sage or ½ teaspoon dried sage and 2-3 finely chopped fresh or well-drained bottled tomatoes.

## APPLE TURNOVERS

PREPARATION TIME: 25 MINUTES

COOKING TIME: 25-30 MINUTES

QUANTITY: 4 TURNOVERS

**Shortcrust pastry made with 10 oz (300 g) flour etc. (page 42)**

**2 teaspoons semolina**

*For the filling:*

**1 lb (450 g) apples, peeled, cored and thinly sliced**

**1-2 oz (25-50 g) sugar**

**1-2 oz (25-50 g) sultanas, if available**

**pinch ground ginger(optional)**

Preheat the oven to 200°C (400°F), Gas Mark 6. Grease a baking tray.

Roll out the pastry and cut it into four rounds. Brush the edges with water. Sprinkle the semolina over the centre of the pastry; this absorbs the juice from the apples and helps to keep the pastry crisp.

Blend the ingredients for the filling together. Put on one side only of each round. Damp the edges of the pastry with water and fold the pastry over the apple filling. Seal the edges firmly together and flute them with a finger and thumb.

Place on the baking tray and bake in the preheated

oven for 20 minutes, then lower the heat to 180°C (350°F), Gas Mark 4 and cook for a further 10 minutes to make sure the fruit is tender.

*Variation: If using bottled apple slices, drain them very well before using. The fruit needs a little less cooking so allow 20-25 minutes only in the oven.*

## CURRANT BUNS

PREPARATION TIME: 30 MINUTES, PLUS PROVING

COOKING TIME: 12-15 MINUTES

QUANTITY: 12-15 BUNS

*Yeast cookery was much more popular among country-dwellers than those living in towns, although gradually they began to appreciate the fact that yeast buns were wonderfully low in fat content. The dried yeast described in the method below was the type that was available in 1945.*

**½ oz (15 g) fresh yeast or ¼ oz (7 g or ½ tablespoon) dried yeast**

**1-2 oz (25-50 g) sugar**

**7½ fl oz (225 ml) water**

**12 oz (350 g) plain flour**

**pinch salt**

**1-2 oz (25-50 g) margarine or cooking fat**

**2 oz (50 g) currants**

*To glaze:*

**2 tablespoons water**

**2 tablespoons sugar**

For fresh yeast, cream the yeast with a teaspoon sugar. Warm the liquid until tepid, then add to the yeast.

If using dried yeast, dissolve 1 teaspoon of the sugar in the tepid liquid, add the dried yeast, leave for 10 minutes then use as fresh yeast.

Add a sprinkling of the flour to the yeast liquid, then leave it in a warm place until the surface is covered with bubbles.

Meanwhile, sift the flour and salt into a mixing bowl, rub in the margarine or cooking fat, add the rest of the

sugar and the currants then the yeast liquid. Mix the ingredients together then turn on to a floured board. Knead the dough well. To tell if it is sufficiently kneaded press with a floured finger: the impression comes out when the dough is ready to prove (rise).

Return the dough to a clean bowl, cover and leave in a warm place for about 1½ hours, or until just double in size.

Turn out, knead again and cut into 12-15 portions. Form into rounds. Put on to lightly greased baking trays. Cover lightly and leave to prove again for about 20 min-

utes or until well-risen. Preheat the oven to 220°C (425°F), Gas Mark 7. Bake the buns in the preheated oven for 12-15 minutes or until golden brown and firm.

Heat the water and blend with the sugar; brush over the buns when cooked to glaze them.

*Variation: Swiss Buns: form the dough into about 15-18 finger shapes. Bake as above, but do not glaze the buns. When they are cold, cover the tops with Glacé icing (page 47).*

*If using modern dried yeast, add it to the flour The strict routine for wartime dried yeast is unnecessary.*

# THE FORCES
# VICTORY

No one who can remember the day the Second World War was declared in September 1939 will forget how one by one the leaders of the Commonwealth countries pledged their support. They were our Allies in the fight.

Although the USA did not enter the war until after the Japanese attack on Pearl Harbor in December 1941, individual Americans came over to form the Eagle Squadron of the RAF. Often, too, you would see people wearing the standard uniforms of the British forces, then notice a flash on their arm which showed they were Polish, Czech, Norwegian, French or some other nationality.

The celebrations in every Allied country when the war was ended were wholehearted. If the country had been occupied by the enemy the people had to celebrate in spirit, rather than with a lavish meal, for they were desperately short of food. To pay tribute to all the Allied forces, this chapter gives famous dishes from some of the countries from where these brave men and women came. Sadly, lack of space prevents the inclusion of each and every country.

## GUILDHALL CELEBRATIONS

The archives of the Guildhall show that special cele-brations were given by the Corporation of London for prominent war-time officers of His Majesty's and Allied forces when they were presented with the Freedom of the City. Although details of the occasions have been carefully recorded, and dinners were held at the Guildhall, there are no details of the menus. In view of the food shortages at the time it is fairly certain that the meals would have been somewhat spartan. Famous names in the Guildhall records include General Eisenhower, who was honoured with an address and a sword of honour on 12 June 1945; General Montgomery (known often as Monty and created Viscount Montgomery of Alamein), who was given the Freedom of the City in July 1946; and Lord Louis Mountbatten (later Earl Mountbatten of Burma), on 10 July 1946.

A luncheon was given at the Guildhall for the officers and ratings of HMAS *Australia* on 17 July 1945 and, a year later, in August 1946, for officers and men of the French Navy.

## AFRICA

There are four recipes typical of Africa. For South Africa I have chosen one of their interesting traditional stews made with mutton or lamb, known as Bredie. This is very good with sweet potatoes, a favourite vegetable in Africa. My husband served for a short time towards the end of the war in West Africa at Accra, Kano, and Maidugari, so I am including a recipe for the dish he enjoyed in celebration of VE Day in West Africa. There is also a recipe from Rhodesia (now Zimbabwe), and one from Kenya.

## BREDIE

PREPARATION TIME: 30 MINUTES

COOKING TIME: 1¼ OR 2 HOURS (SEE METHOD)

QUANTITY: 4-6 HELPINGS

*This is a traditional South African stew made with mutton or lamb. The traditional flavouring for this stew comes from a flower known as waterblommetjie, which is only available in South Africa. Rosemary makes a good substitute, however. As mutton is rarely available in Britain these days, I have given lamb in the ingredients. If mutton is used, the stew will need to be cooked for rather longer.*

**2 breasts of lamb, weighing about**
   **3 lb (1.3 kg) or 8 lamb chops**
**pinch ground ginger, optional**
**salt and pepper**
**1-2 teaspoons brown sugar (see method)**
**1 oz (25 g) flour**
**1-2 tablespoons oil (see method)**
**2 medium onions, thinly sliced**
**1 medium cooking apple, peeled,**
   **cored and sliced**
**1 lb (450 g) tomatoes, skinned and chopped**
**½ pint (300 ml) lamb stock**
**1-2 teaspoons chopped rosemary ,or**
   **½ teaspoon dried rosemary**

Cut the breast of lamb into small pieces, or ask the butcher to do this for you. Blend the ginger, if used, with the seasoning, sugar and flour. (Use the larger amount of sugar with the fatter breast of lamb.) Coat the lamb with the mixture.

Heat the oil in a large frying pan. (Use the smaller amount of oil with breast of lamb, or, if there is a fair amount of fat, on the lamb chops.) Fry the meat in the hot oil until golden on both sides, then remove from the pan on to a plate. Add the onions and apple and turn in any oil remaining in the pan until they are slightly golden in colour.

Return the meat to the pan with the tomatoes, stock and rosemary, stir well, then put the lid on the saucepan. If this is a poor fit place a piece of foil underneath, as it is important that the small amount of liquid does not boil away. Simmer for 2 hours for breast of lamb, or 1½ hours for lamb chops.

## CHICKEN CHOP

PREPARATION TIME: 35 MINUTES

COOKING TIME: 2 HOURS

QUANTITY: 4-6 HELPINGS

*When VE Day was declared my husband was the Commanding Officer of three staging posts for the RAF in West Africa and he celebrated this splendid occasion with one of his favourite meals from this part of the world - a good curry.*

**1 chicken, weighing 4 lb (1.8 kg)**

**1 small lemon**

**2 tablespoons groundnut or sunflower oil**

**2 small onions, chopped**

*To flavour the curry:*

**1 large red chilli pepper or**

  **½ teaspoon chilli powder**

**¼ teaspoon cayenne pepper**

**½ teaspoon turmeric**

**2 tablespoons grated fresh ginger**

**½ pint (300 ml) stock**

**½ pint (300 ml) coconut milk (see note)**

**1 x 2 inch (5 cm) piece cinnamon stick**

**salt and pepper**

**4 oz (100 g) fresh dates (weight when stoned)**

Cut the chicken into small joints; grate the lemon zest and squeeze out the juice. Heat the oil and fry the chicken with the onions until pale golden. Remove from the pan. Chop the red chilli pepper and mix it (or the chilli powder) with the cayenne, turmeric and ginger. Add to the pan, then blend in the chicken stock. Return the chicken and onions to the pan with the lemon rind and half the lemon juice.

Put the coconut milk, cinnamon stick, seasoning and dates into the pan. Stir well to blend. Cover the pan tightly, lower the heat and simmer for 2 hours. Remove the cinnamon and add more lemon juice if required. Serve with rice, a sweet chutney and a few extra dates.

Note: to make coconut milk at home, either: (1) add 3 oz (75 g) creamed coconut to ½ pint (300 ml) boiling water and stir until dissolved; or (2) put 2 oz (50 g) desiccated coconut in a container, add ½ pint (300 ml) boiling water. Allow to stand until cold then strain and use the liquid.

## STUFFED AUBERGINES

PREPARATION TIME: 25 MINUTES

COOKING TIME: 40 MINUTES

QUANTITY: 4 HELPINGS

*In Kenya, as in many parts of Africa, aubergines (often called garden eggs) are very plentiful.*

Wash 2 large aubergines and cut in half lengthways. Scoop out the pulp and dice this. Fry a finely chopped onion in a little fat, add the aubergine pulp, 2 skinned and chopped tomatoes, 8 oz (225 g) minced lamb, 2 oz (50 g) breadcrumbs and seasoning. Put into the aubergine shells. Top with crisp breadcrumbs and a little melted butter.

Bake for 30 minutes in a preheated oven, set to 190°C (375°F) Gas Mark 5.

## *Banana Pudding*

PREPARATION TIME: 15 MINUTES

COOKING TIME: 15-20 MINUTES

QUANTITY: 4 HELPINGS

*This simple-to-make fruit pudding is a favourite in Zimbabwe (formerly Southern Rhodesia).*

Peel 4 large bananas and put them into a buttered dish. Top with the juice of 1 large orange and 2 tablespoons of brown sugar.

Cover with 2 oz (50 g) freshly grated coconut and bake in a preheated oven, set to 190°C (375°F), Gas Mark 5 for 15-20 minutes.

*Variation: Desiccated coconut could be used instead of the freshly grated nut.*

## AUSTRALIA AND NEW ZEALAND

Undoubtedly one of the foods that returning members of the Australian and New Zealand Forces would have been given was a really good steak or even the Carpet Bag version. New Zealanders would doubtless appreciate these, too, or would have chosen a succulent leg of roast lamb or hogget (year-old lamb).

A Pavlova would have been the inevitable dessert in both countries. This delicious light sweet, based on egg whites and named after the ballerina Anna Pavlova, is one of their most prized dishes.

If friends were dropping in for a cup of tea or morning coffee to meet the returning men or women, they would no doubt have been given the very light authentic scones known as Gems and the chocolate-coated Lamingtons - both favourite recipes of Australia and New Zealand.

## *Gems*

PREPARATION TIME: 15 MINUTES

COOKING TIME: 10 MINUTES

QUANTITY: MAKES 12

*These small sweet scones are famous in Australia where they were baked in special gem irons, much cherished by their owners. Deep patty tins can be used instead. Gems freeze well.*

**4 oz (110 g\*) self-raising flour or plain flour**
    **sifted with 1 teaspoon baking powder**
**pinch salt**
**1½ oz (40 g) butter**
**1½ oz (40 g) caster sugar**
**1 egg - size 2 or 3**
**4 fl oz (120 ml\*) milk**
**\*use this metrication**

Preheat the oven to 200°C (400°F), Gas Mark 6. Grease 12 gem irons or deep patty tins. Place in the oven to become very hot. Sift the flour, or flour and baking powder, and salt. Cream the butter and sugar until soft and light, beat the egg with the milk. Fold into the creamed mixture together with the flour.

Spoon into the hot irons or tins and bake for 10 minutes, or until well risen and firm. Remove on to a wire cooling rack.

## Pavlova

*"Cawfee?"*

PREPARATION TIME: 25 MINUTES
COOKING TIME: 50 MINUTES
OR SEE NOTE
QUANTITY: 6 HELPINGS

**4 egg whites**
**8 oz (225 g) caster sugar**
**1½ level teaspoons cornflour**
**1½ teaspoons white vinegar**
**1 teaspoon vanilla essence**

Brush one or more baking trays with a few drops of oil, or use non-stick trays or line trays with baking parchment. Make a circle of the required size on the baking parchment. The secret of a Pavlova with the crisp outside but soft, rather like a light-textured marshmallow inside, is to put the meringue shape into an oven preheated to a higher temperature then immediately alter this to the lower setting. As the heat drops in a gas oven quickly, a higher setting can be used than in an electric oven. Preheat an electric oven to 180°C (350°F), then lower to 150°C (300°F); preheat a gas oven to Mark 7 then lower to Mark 2.

Put the egg whites into a large bowl. Whisk by hand or with an electric mixer until stiff; you should be able to turn the bowl upside down without the mixture falling out. Do not whisk until the egg whites are dry and crumbly. Blend the sugar and cornflour; beat into the egg whites a tablespoon at a time. Fold the vinegar and essence into the meringue. Spoon or pipe into a flan shape. Place in the preheated oven, as described above. Lower the heat and bake for approximately 50 minutes, or until crisp on the outside and a pale beige colour. Cool in the oven with the heat turned off, then fill (see suggestions below).

The Pavlova does not store well.

Australian Filling: blend the pulp of passion fruit with whipped cream and use in the Pavlova, top with a little more passion fruit pulp.

New Zealand Filling: blend whipped cream with peeled and diced kiwifruit, top with more sliced kiwifruit. In 1945 this fruit was known as Chinese Gooseberries.

Note: for a crisp texture throughout, omit the vinegar and cornflour. Make the meringue, shape the Pavlova but preheat the oven to 90-110°C (200-225°F), Gas Mark S or ¼. Slightly quicker baking sets the outside and gives a stickier centre, in which case set the oven to 110-120°C (225-250°F), Gas Mark ¼-½. Bake for 3-4 hours. This Pavlova stores well in an airtight tin.

## Lamingtons

*These chocolate-coated sponge cakes are a great favourite in both Australia and New Zealand.*

Make the sponge mixture as the Victoria Sandwich on page 107 with 6 oz (175 g) butter or margarine etc.

Bake in an 8 inch (20 cm) square tin in a preheated oven, set to 180°C (350°F), Gas Mark 4 for 20-25 minutes. Allow to cool then cut into 16 squares.

Insert a skewer into each square and dip in chocolate icing (see below) then coat in desiccated coconut.

## Chocolate Icing

Blend 8 oz (225 g) sifted icing sugar with 1 oz (25 g) cocoa powder, put into a saucepan with 2 tablespoons water, few drops vanilla essence and ½ oz (15 g) butter. Heat until a flowing consistency. Use the icing before it has time to stiffen.

## THE USA AND CANADA

In many American homes there might well have been two Thanksgiving dinners in 1945. One in November, the month the event is generally celebrated, and the second, a very special celebration, in either May for VE Day or August for VJ Day.

The main dish for the real Thanksgiving is roast turkey and the most popular dessert a Pumpkin Pie. As both the Victory Days took place in spring to summertime, when soft fruit was available, I have included a recipe for the American well-loved Strawberry Shortcake instead of the pie.

Roast turkey is so well known, I have included another American favourite dish of the era - Chicken Maryland. This became extremely popular in Britain during the late 1950s and early 1960s.

Canadians love dishes with maple syrup and Maple Pancakes would be a wonderful welcome home dish.

## CHICKEN MARYLAND

*This combination of fried chicken, sweetcorn fritters and fried bananas was a great favourite.*

Coat 4 tender chicken joints with seasoned flour then beaten egg and crisp breadcrumbs. Fry for approximately 15 minutes in hot fat or oil until golden brown and cooked.

Keep hot while frying the sweetcorn fritters (see below) and bananas.

Peel 4 bananas, coat in seasoned flour and fry for a few minutes.

## SWEETCORN FRITTERS

Blend 2 oz (50 g) self-raising flour with a little seasoning, 1 egg and 3 tablespoons milk. Add 6 oz (175 g) drained canned or cooked sweetcorn kernels.

Fry in hot fat or oil until brown and firm. Drain on absorbent paper.

## MAPLE PANCAKES

*Canadians, like Americans, enjoy these at most times of the day.*

Make a batter with 4 oz (110 g*) flour, pinch salt, 2 eggs and 14 fl oz (500 ml) milk. Cook in the usual way and top with a generous helping of maple syrup.

A slightly thicker batter can be used to make waffles. *use this metrication.

## STRAWBERRY SHORTCAKE

PREPARATION TIME: 20 MINUTES

COOKING TIME: 10 OR 15-20 MINUTES

QUANTITY: 4-6 HELPINGS

*There are many recipes for shortcakes, this one is not only a popular one in America, but it would have been the most usual in 1945, for the people in that country were rationed for fats, and this particular recipe uses relatively little.*

**For the shortcake mixture:**

**3 oz (85 g*) butter or margarine**

**8 oz (225 g) self-raising flour or plain flour**
**    sifted with 2 teaspoons baking powder**

**4 oz (100 g) caster sugar**

**1 egg - size 1 or 2**

**milk, to bind**

**For the filling:**

**1 lb (450 g) strawberries**

**sugar to taste**

**little butter**

***use this metrication**

Preheat the oven to 220°C (425°F), Gas Mark 7. Lightly grease a large baking tray. Sift the flour, or flour and baking powder. Rub the butter or margarine into the flour, add the sugar. Beat the egg, add to the flour mixture with sufficient milk to make a soft rolling consistency. Roll, or pat out, the dough until ¼ inch (0.5 cm) thick and cut into 8-12 rounds for smaller individual short-cakes. If making one large shortcake, divide the dough into equal halves and form each into an 8 inch (20 cm) round. Place on the baking tray and put in the pre-heated oven. Bake small shortcakes for about 10 minutes and large ones for 15-20 minutes, or until they are well risen, firm and brown.

Slice most of the strawberries and add sugar to taste. Save a few whole berries for decoration. When the shortcakes are cool, sandwich together with a little butter and the sliced strawberries. Top with the whole fruit. Serve the shortcakes when freshly made, with cream or yogurt or fromage frais.

*Variation: Omit the butter when sandwiching the short-cakes together, use sliced strawberries only, top with whipped cream and serve with the coulis below.*

## STRAWBERRY COULIS

Heat 2 oz (50 g) caster sugar with 1 tablespoon lemon juice and 1 tablespoon water until dissolved. Sieve or liquidize 1 lb (450 g) of strawberries. Blend with the syrup. Serve cold or heat for a short time. Do not overcook or you will lose the fresh fruit flavour.

### FAR EAST

VJ Day in August 1945 brought the fighting in the Far East to an end. This had involved a vast number of the Allied forces fighting the Japanese. Many people, including both those in the armed forces and civilians, had been taken prisoner. It is not hard to imagine their relief when the fighting ended with the capitulation of Japan.

Oriental dishes were little known in Britain at that time but they have, of course, become great favourites since. On the following pages are three recipes from the Far East. It is doubtful if Service personnel sampled them at the time, since they had relatively little to eat, especially those who had been prisoners of war.

## Sin Tim Yue

*This Chinese dish is very easily prepared. Use a firm-fleshed fish.*

Cut 1½ lb (675 g) white fish into 1.5 inch (3.5 cm) pieces. Dry well and coat in a good tablespoon cornflour seasoned with salt and pepper.

Cut 4 oz (100 g) green beans and about 8 spring onions into small pieces; peel and crush 2 garlic cloves.

Deseed a red pepper; drain 2 oz (50 g) canned bamboo shoots and 2 oz (50 g) water chestnuts; cut these, and the pepper, into matchstick pieces.

Heat 1½ tablespoons vegetable oil in a wok or large frying pan and cook the fish until golden in colour. Lift on to a hot dish and keep hot.

Add another 1½ tablespoons oil to the pan and fry the prepared vegetables for 3-4 minutes.

Blend 1½ teaspoons cornflour with 2 tablespoons soy sauce, 2 tablespoons white wine, 1 tablespoon lemon juice, 1 tablespoon caster sugar and 1 or 2 teaspoons chopped fresh ginger.

Pour over the vegetables, stir over a low heat until thickened. Spoon over the hot fish and serve with cooked bean sprouts.

## Marta Pulao

*On VE Day in May 1945 my brother, an officer in the Merchant Navy, was on a ship bound for India with military equipment. On VJ Day he was in Bombay with the ship loaded ready for a Malaysian invasion which fortunately did not happen, due to Japan's capitulation. The ship's crew had changed to Indians and this may well be one of the dishes they would have eaten on the important day.*

Soak 6-7 oz (175-200 g) Patna rice in cold water for 1 hour. Heat 1½ oz (40 g) ghee (clarified butter) and add 6 cloves, 2 small pieces of cinnamon, ½ teaspoon turmeric and a teaspoon caraway seeds. Fry in the ghee for 2 minutes to bring out the flavours. Drain the rice, add to the pan with a little salt and 8 oz (225 g) shelled peas.

Mix well and cook gently for 4-5 minutes then add 2 pints (1.2 litres) boiling water. Allow the rice mixture to reach boiling point then cover the pan tightly and cook for about 30 minutes. This goes well with all meat and vegetable dishes.

## Shrimps in Lime and Coconut Sauce

PREPARATION TIME: 15 MINUTES PLUS MARINATING

COOKING TIME: 6 MINUTES

QUANTITY: 4 HELPINGS

*This recipe, which is typical of East Asian dishes, is included in tribute to the many people who suffered great deprivation at Singapore and in that region.*

**1 large or 2 small limes**

**1 lb (450 g) peeled prawns or shrimps**

**½ pint (300 ml) coconut milk (see below)**

**1 tablespoon sunflower oil**

**2 teaspoons light soy sauce**

**salt and pepper**

**little chopped lemon grass or parsley, to garnish**

Grate the top zest from the limes and squeeze out enough juice to give 2 tablespoons, or a little more if preferred. Blend the fish with the lime zest. Cover and leave in the refrigerator for an hour so the lime flavour penetrates the shellfish.

Make the coconut milk: the simplest and best way for this recipe is to pour ½ pint (300 ml) boiling water over 2 oz (50 g) desiccated coconut. Leave until cold then put into a liquidizer to make a smooth liquid. You can also heat 3 oz (75 g) creamed coconut in ½ pint (300 ml) water until dissolved and use this.

Heat the oil, toss the shellfish in it for 1 or 2 minutes, then add the coconut milk, soy sauce and lime juice. Season to taste and heat thoroughly, but do not allow the mixture to boil.

Top with the lemon grass or parsley and serve with cooked rice.

## OCCUPIED EUROPE

The following recipes represent the countries, many of whose people served with Allied forces or were resistance fighters, in various parts of Europe. In Russia returning troops would be facing devastation in many of their towns and villages but would know that their country was once again free of occupying troops after VE Day. Solyanka is one of their most delicious soups and a Borshch is both economical and full of flavour.

Czechoslovakia, Poland, Hungary and Norway had known the horrors of German occupation. Sadly, none of these countries was to enjoy complete freedom immediately after VE Day in 1945; they had to wait for a long time for this to come. The underground movement in the occupied countries and the bravery of their people who fought alongside the Allies was greatly admired.

The recipes from these countries which I have included

here are all very easy to make and give several new ways with vegetables.

My sister married a Norwegian and has sent me the information about this country at the time of VE Day.

# *Solyanka*

PREPARATION TIME: 25 MINUTES

COOKING TIME: 20-25 MINUTES

QUANTITY: 6 HELPINGS

*This is a wonderful fish soup that is sufficiently sustaining to make a complete meal. Although the ideal choice of fish is given in the ingredients, the fish can be varied according to what is available.*

2 tablespoons oil

1 onion, finely chopped

2 small carrots, neatly diced

2 small potatoes, neatly diced

2 pints (1.2 litres) fish stock

salt and pepper

1 bay leaf

1 lb (450 g) lightly cooked salmon

8 oz (225 g) lightly cooked white fish

2 large pickled cucumbers, thinly sliced

1 tablespoon capers

1 lemon

*To garnish:*

¼ pint (150 ml) soured cream or yogurt

1 tablespoon chopped parsley

dill sprigs

green olives, stoned

6 lemon slices

Heat the oil in a saucepan, add the onion, carrots and potatoes and cook for 5 minutes, stirring from time to time. Add the fish stock, season lightly, then add the bay leaf and simmer for 10 minutes.

Cut the fish into 1-1½ inch (2.5-3.5 cm) pieces, add to the soup with the cucumbers and capers. Heat gently for 5-10 minutes. Halve the lemon, discard the pips, then scoop out the pulp and add to the soup.

Pour into soup bowls, top with the soured cream or yogurt, parsley, dill, olives and lemon slices.

## Borshch

*This can be made quickly with cooked beetroot but the flavour is much better if an uncooked one is chosen. This recipe gives 4-6 helpings.*

Peel and grate a large raw beetroot, grate about 8 oz (225 g) carrots. Peel and slice an onion and garlic clove, skin and chop 2 large tomatoes; chop 1 celery stick.

Put all the vegetables into 2 pints (1.2 litres) of beef stock, add 1-2 tablespoons vinegar and 1-2 tablespoons lemon juice with salt and pepper to taste. Simmer for about 1½ hours.

Top each serving with soured cream.

*Variation: If using cooked beetroot simmer the other vegetables for about 35 minutes, add the peeled and grated cooked beetroot and cook for 10 minutes then serve topped with the soured cream.*

## Pacuszki z Kartofli

*These Polish Potato Pancakes are delicious. This recipe will make 4-6 servings.*

Boil about 1½ lb (675 g) potatoes, strain, sieve and mash until very smooth.

Separate 3 eggs and gradually beat into the potato mixture the 3 egg yolks, ½ pint (300 ml) milk, a little ground cinnamon and sugar to taste.

Whisk the 3 egg whites until stiff and fold them into the mixture.

Heat butter in a frying pan and fry spoonfuls of the mixture for 2 or 3 minutes then turn over and cook on the other side for the same time.

Serve as soon as possible after cooking, topped with cooked berry fruits or with hot jam.

## Letscho

PREPARATION TIME: 20 MINUTES

COOKING TIME: 50 MINUTES

QUANTITY: 4 HELPINGS

*This Hungarian dish is a pleasant change from the more familiar French Ratatouille.*

**2 medium onions, thinly sliced**

**2 oz (50 g) lard or cooking fat**

**2-3 green peppers, deseeded and sliced**

**4 large tomatoes, skinned and sliced**

**salt and pepper**

Separate the onion slices into rings. Heat the lard or fat and cook the onions until tender but not brown. Add the sliced peppers and tomatoes with a little seasoning. Cover the pan and cook gently for 35-50 minutes.

Serve as a separate course or with meat or fish.

## Kulajda

PREPARATION TIME: 20 MINUTES

COOKING TIME: 30 MINUTES

QUANTITY: 4 HELPINGS

*This Czechoslovakian dish is an original potato soup, for when it is almost ready to serve an egg is added for each person. These are heated sufficiently to set lightly, so you eat a whole egg with your soup.*

**1 lb (450 g) potatoes, weight when**
  **peeled and diced**

**1¼ pints (750 ml) water**

**salt and pepper**

**1-2 teaspoons caraway seeds**

**1 medium onion, finely chopped**

**3-4 oz (75-100 g) mushrooms, finely diced**

**1 tablespoon flour**

**½ pint (300 ml) single cream**

**4 eggs**

**1 teaspoon lemon juice or vinegar**

Put the potatoes into a rather wide saucepan with the water, seasoning, caraway seeds and onion. Simmer for 10 minutes, then add the mushrooms. Cover the pan and simmer for a further 15 minutes, or until the potatoes are soft. Blend the flour with the cream, whisk into the hot, but not boiling soup, heat very gently until the soup is hot again.

Carefully break the eggs into the soup and cook for a few minutes until they are lightly set. Finally stir in the lemon juice or vinegar.

Spoon an egg and some soup into individual soup cups or soup bowls.

## NORWAY

The picture on this page shows the jubilation felt throughout Norway on VE Day 1945. Nothing could stop the happiness of Oslo's inhabitants - not even an armed German soldier.

This scene was typical of all the freed countries of occupied Europe in 1945.

In Norway by 1945 the inhabitants were on the verge of starvation, for the Germans sent the best food back to Germany. There was no tea or coffee, and all kinds of weird substitutes such as the dried leaves of various bushes or dried apple peel were used. Leather was very scarce and many people wore shoes which they had made out of paper or fish skins.

Even people living in flats tried to keep a few rabbits or chickens to eke out the meagre food supplies.

# *Blotkake*

PREPARATION TIME: 15 MINUTES

COOKING TIME: 30 MINUTES

MAKES: 1 CAKE

*This light cake, smothered with whipped cream and berry fruit, often lingonberries or cloudberries, is a popular feature of Norwegian celebrations, so would have been made in Norway just as soon as all the ingredients were available.*

**4 eggs**
**8 oz (225 g) caster sugar**
**2 oz (50 g) plain flour**
**2 oz (50 g) potato flour, or more plain flour**
**1 teaspoon baking powder**
*For filling and topping:*
**½-¾ pint (300-450 ml) whipping cream**
**berry fruits**

Preheat the oven to 180°C(350°F), Gas Mark 4. Grease and flour or line a 9 inch (23 cm) round cake tin.

Whisk the eggs and sugar until thick and creamy. Sift the flour(s) with the baking powder, and fold into the egg mixture. Spoon into the tin and bake for 30 minutes or until firm to a gentle touch.

Cool for a time, then turn out. When cold, cut into 3 layers. Whip the cream. Fill and top the cake with the cream and berries.

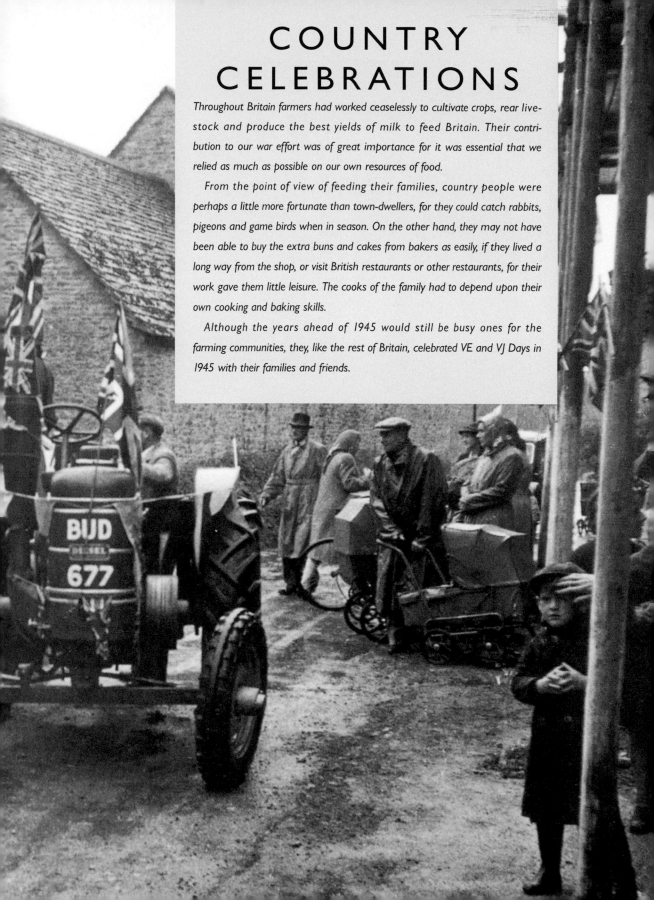

# COUNTRY CELEBRATIONS

Throughout Britain farmers had worked ceaselessly to cultivate crops, rear live-stock and produce the best yields of milk to feed Britain. Their contri-bution to our war effort was of great importance for it was essential that we relied as much as possible on our own resources of food.

From the point of view of feeding their families, country people were perhaps a little more fortunate than town-dwellers, for they could catch rabbits, pigeons and game birds when in season. On the other hand, they may not have been able to buy the extra buns and cakes from bakers as easily, if they lived a long way from the shop, or visit British restaurants or other restaurants, for their work gave them little leisure. The cooks of the family had to depend upon their own cooking and baking skills.

Although the years ahead of 1945 would still be busy ones for the farming communities, they, like the rest of Britain, celebrated VE and VJ Days in 1945 with their families and friends.

For a healthy, happy job
Join the
WOMEN'S
LAND
ARMY
For details:
CLIVE UPTTON
APPLY TO NEAREST W.L.A. COUNTY OFFICE OR TO W.L.A. HEADQUARTERS 6 CHESHAM ~~PLACE~~ STREET LONDON S.W.1
Issued by the Ministry of Agriculture and the Ministry of Labour and National Service

## THE WOMEN'S LAND ARMY

One of the hardest-working groups of women in the country was the Women's Land Army. They replaced the younger male farm and agricultural workers, who were serving in the Forces or in factories on essential work. The women's days were long and full of hard physical effort; it was amazing how young girls, who had little, if any, experience of the hard work of farming in all weathers, managed so well. Victory meant they could return to their homes, though many continued to work on the land after the war was over.

Much less well-known than the Women's Land Army, the Women's Timber Corps (WTC), known as the Lumberjills, numbered more than 6,000 members at its peak. They tackled every sort of job connected with wood and trees; they drove tractors and locomotives, hauling loads of timber up and down impossible gradients. They measured and felled trees and loaded endless telegraph poles, pitprops, railway sleepers and potential packing cases and charcoal.

## KIDNEY AND BACON SOUP

PREPARATION TIME: 25 MINUTES

COOKING TIME: 55 MINUTES

QUANTITY: 4-6 HELPINGS

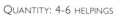

*This is a very satisfying soup, nutritious enough to make a light meal. As most farmers kept pigs they would be able to use the kidneys plus their allowance of bacon in it.*

**2 pig's kidneys, skinned and finely diced**

**1 oz (25 g) flour**

**salt and pepper**

**3 bacon rashers, derinded and chopped**

**2 medium leeks, thinly sliced**

**4 oz (100 g) mushrooms, sliced**

**1½ pints (900 ml) water**

**3 slices of bread**

**2 tablespoons chopped chives**

Remove any gristle from the kidneys. Blend the flour and seasoning and coat the kidneys in this. Heat the bacon and bacon rinds in a saucepan, add the kidneys and cook gently for 5 minutes, then add the leeks and mushrooms, with the water. Stir well to blend, then lower the heat and simmer for 45 minutes, or until the kidneys are tender. Remove the bacon rinds.

Toast the bread and cut it into ½ inch (1.5 cm) dice. Serve the soup with a topping of the toasted croûtons and chopped fresh chives.

## PARSLEY PUDDING

PREPARATION TIME: 25 MINUTES

COOKING TIME: 2 HOURS

QUANTITY: 4 HELPINGS

*Parsley gives a very special flavour to this savoury pudding. Never waste the stalks of parsley, they can be used in soups and stews, for they give even more flavour than the leaves.*

**For the pudding:**

**8 oz (225 g) self-raising flour or plain flour sifted with 2 teaspoons baking powder**

**½ teaspoon salt**

**2 oz (50 g) raw potato, grated**

**2 oz (50 g) suet, finely chopped or grated**

**water, to bind**

**For the filling:**

**2 bacon rashers, derinded and chopped**

**sprinkling of gravy powder**

**8 tablespoons finely chopped parsley leaves**

Grease a 1½ pint (900 ml) pudding basin. Sift the flour, or flour and baking powder, with the salt, add the potato and suet then enough water to make a dough with a soft rolling consistency.

Roll out the pastry and use nearly three-quarters to line the base and sides of the basin.

Add the filling ingredients, then roll out the remaining pastry to form a lid; moisten the edges of the pastry with water, put the pastry round in place and seal the joins. Cover with margarine paper and/or a cloth and steam for 2 hours. Allow the water under the steamer to boil briskly for the first hour, then lower the heat for the remaining period.

*Variations: for Steak and Parsley Pudding: use 8 oz (225 g) finely diced stewing steak instead of the bacon.*

*Bacon, Onion and Parsley Pudding: follow the recipe but add 2 sliced onions to the ingredients.*

## RABBIT STEW

PREPARATION TIME: 30 MINUTES

COOKING TIME: 2 HOURS

QUANTITY: 4-6 HELPINGS

**1 rabbit, cut into joints**

**1 tablespoon vinegar**

**1 oz (25 g) flour**

**salt and pepper**

**1-2 oz (25-50 g) dripping or cooking fat**

**2 bacon rashers, derinded**
  **and chopped, if available**

**2 medium onions, sliced**

**3 medium carrots, sliced**

**1 pint (600 ml) water or chicken stock**

**¼ pint (150 ml) dry cider**

**½ tablespoon chopped tarragon or**
  **½ teaspoon dried tarragon**

**Dumplings (page 93)**

**2 tablespoons chopped parsley**

Put the rabbit to soak in cold water with the vinegar for 30 minutes. Remove and dry well. Mix the flour with the seasoning and coat the rabbit joints in this. Heat the dripping or cooking fat with the bacon rinds, add the rabbit and cook steadily for about 10 minutes, or until

golden brown in colour. Remove from the pan, add the bacon, onions and carrots and cook for 5 minutes then return the rabbit to the pan with the water or stock, stir as the liquid comes to the boil and thickens slightly. Add the cider and the tarragon.

Cover the pan and simmer gently for about 1½ hours. Check there is sufficient liquid in the pan, if not add a little more water or stock and bring to the boil. Add the uncooked dumplings, made as in the recipe on page 93, and cook for a further 20 minutes. Remove the bacon rinds and sprinkle over the chopped parsley before serving the stew.

*Variations: Chicken Stew: use a not-too-fat chicken instead of rabbit. There is no need to soak the jointed chicken. The cooking time will be about the same as the rabbit if it is a fairly elderly fowl. If the chicken is younger, then reduce the cooking time by about 15 minutes.*

*Pigeon Stew: use 3 large or 6 smaller pigeons. There is no need to soak these before cooking. Halve the birds then proceed as in the recipe. If the pigeons are young, reduce the cooking time by about 15-20 minutes.*

### RENDERING DOWN CHICKEN FAT

Allow the chicken stock to become quite cold then carefully take the fat from the top of the liquid. Put this into a saucepan, cover with cold water and bring the water to the boil. Pour into a bowl and leave in a cool place.

Lift the fat from the top of the liquid. Any impurities or tiny pieces of food will be in the liquid at the bottom of the bowl. The chicken fat can be used in cooking.

### USING CHICKEN STOCK

The stock in which the chicken was cooked is excellent as a basis for soups. Store it carefully and use as soon as possible.

## DUMPLINGS

PREPARATION TIME: 15 MINUTES

COOKING TIME: 15-20 MINUTES

QUANTITY: 4-6 HELPINGS

*Dumplings were one of the dishes that were frequently made, for they helped to satisfy people's appetites and so 'eke out' precious meat.*

*Grated raw potato was used in this type of pastry as well as in shortcrust pastry to give a good texture with the minimum of fat.*

**8 oz (225 g) self-raising flour or plain flour**
   **sifted with 2 teaspoons baking powder**
**good pinch salt**
**2 oz (50 g) suet, finely chopped or grated**
**2 oz (50 g) raw potato, grated**
**water, to bind**

Sift the flour, or flour and baking powder, with the salt, add the suet and potato. Mix well then gradually add enough cold water to make a soft rolling consistency.

Divide the mixture into about 16 and roll into balls with lightly floured hands.

Drop the dumpling balls into boiling salted water and cook briskly for 10 minutes then lower the heat and cook more slowly for a further 5-10 minutes, until the dumplings have risen well. Lift out of the water with a perforated spoon and serve.

*Variations: Instead of the suet, use 1-2 oz (25-50 g) margarine or cooking fat in the dumplings. Rub this into the flour, or flour and baking powder, and salt.*

*Savoury Dumplings: flavour the mixture with chopped parsley, chives or sage or a little dried herbs. These are very good served by themselves and just sprinkled with grated cheese.*

*Mustard Dumplings: add a generous amount of mustard powder to the flour; Mustard Dumplings are particularly good with cooked chicken or rabbit.*

*Sweet Dumplings: add 1-2 tablespoons sugar to the mixture after adding the suet, or other fat. Boil in water, or if you have soft fruit left from cooking fruit dilute this with water and cook the dumplings in it.*

*If you can spare 1-2 tablespoons marmalade add this to the mixture before mixing with the water.*

*Top sweet dumplings with a very little sugar before serving with cooked fruit or by themselves.*

## Prune Sponge

PREPARATION TIME: 25 MINUTES

COOKING TIME: 1½ HOURS

QUANTITY: 4-6 HELPINGS

*This is a very good pudding, for the prunes become plump with steaming. If you soak the prunes in weak left-over tea, rather than water, they will have a very rich flavour.*

**8-12 prunes, soaked overnight**
**8 oz (225 g) self-raising flour or plain flour**
   **sifted with 2 teaspoons baking powder**
**½ teaspoon mixed spice**
**½ teaspoon grated or ground nutmeg**
**1 oz (25 g) margarine or cooking fat**
**1-2 tablespoons golden syrup**
**6 tablespoons milk or milk and water**

Grease a 1½ pint (900 ml) basin. Drain the soaked prunes and arrange at the bottom of the basin.

Sift the flour, or flour and baking powder, with the spices, rub in the margarine or cooking fat, add the golden syrup and the milk, or milk and water. Spoon into the basin, cover with margarine paper and steam for 1½ hours.

Turn the steamed pudding out and serve it with a custard sauce (see page 38).

# Bread and Butter Pudding

PREPARATION TIME: 20 MINUTES

COOKING TIME: 1-1¼ HOURS

QUANTITY: 4-6 HELPINGS

*The Celebrations for VE and VJ days in 1945 might well have been the time when the farmer's wife or whoever did the cooking at the farm would decide to make a real Bread and Butter Pudding with butter and shell eggs - a rare extravagance.*

**4 large slices of bread**
**approximately 2 oz (50 g) butter**
**3 oz (75 g) sultanas**
**3 eggs**
**2 oz (50 g) sugar**
**1 pint (600 ml) milk**
***For the topping*:**
**sprinkling of sugar**
**little grated or ground nutmeg**

Spread the bread with the butter and then cut into neat squares. Put into a 2 pint (1.2 litre) pie dish. Add the sultanas. Beat the eggs with the sugar. Warm the milk, pour over the beaten eggs then strain over the bread and butter. Allow to stand for at least 30 minutes.

Preheat the oven to 150°C (300°F), Gas Mark 2. Sprinkle the sugar over the top of the pudding together with the nutmeg. Bake for 1-1¼ hours or until just firm.
*Variations: For a very crisp brown topping raise the oven heat to 180°C (350°F), Gas Mark 4 for the last 5-8 minutes.*
*Jam Bread and Butter Pudding: Spread the bread and butter with Victoria plum or apricot jam or with marmalade before cutting it into squares.*
*Use 3 reconstituted dried eggs instead of fresh eggs.*

## TURN WASTE INTO DELICACIES!

# Fruit Crisp

PREPARATION TIME: 25 MINUTES

COOKING TIME: 40-45 MINUTES

QUANTITY: 4 HELPINGS

**1 lb (450 g) fruit, weight when prepared, i.e. peeled or stoned**
**2-3 tablespoons water (see method)**
**1 oz (25 g) sugar**
***For the topping:***
**1 oz (25 g) margarine or cooking fat**
**1 oz (25 g) sugar**
**1 tablespoon golden syrup**
**4 oz (100 g) rolled oats**

Preheat the oven to 180°C (350°F), Gas Mark 4. Grease a 1½ pint (900 ml) pie dish. Put the fruit into the pie dish with the water and 1 oz (25 g) sugar. If using ripe soft fruit, use only about 1 tablespoon water. Cover the pie dish and bake firm fruits for 10-15 minutes and soft fruits for 5-10 minutes.

Put the margarine or cooking fat into a saucepan, add the sugar and syrup. Stir over a low heat until the ingredients have melted. Remove from the heat and stir in the rolled oats. Blend thoroughly then spread over the fruit in a flat layer.

Bake in the preheated oven for 30 minutes, or until the topping is golden brown. Serve hot or cold.

# Cheese and Apple Cake

PREPARATION TIME: 20 MINUTES

COOKING TIME: 30-35 MINUTES

QUANTITY: 1 CAKE

*Farmers and their employees were allowed extra cheese since it was not possible for them to obtain canteen meals or get to British restaurants. The small amount of cheese in this cake gives it a most interesting flavour. It should be eaten when freshly baked and even slightly warm.*

## PLUM CHARLOTTE

*Preparation time: 25 minutes, Cooking time: 40 minutes,*
*but see method, Quantity: 4 helpings*

1 lb (450 g) fruit, weight when prepared,
i.e. peeled or stoned

3 oz (75 g) sugar

8 oz (225 g) bread

2 oz (50 g) margarine or suet

Cut apples into slices, halve and stone plums but leave soft fruit whole. It is advisable to cook the firm fruits for about 5 minutes in a saucepan with 1 oz (25 g) of the sugar and very little water. Soft fruit is better if not pre-cooked.

Make the bread into fairly coarse crumbs by pulling it into pieces with your fingers. If using margarine, melt it, add the crumbs and turn around in the hot margarine until coated and slightly brown. If using suet, grate it finely and mix with the crumbs. Add the remaining sugar to the bread.

Preheat the oven to 180°C (350°F), Gas Mark 4. Put half the crumb mixture into a greased 1½ pint (900 ml) pie dish and then add the fruit. Cover with the rest of the crumb mixture. Bake in the preheated oven for 35 minutes or until the crumb topping is very brown and crisp.

10 oz (300 g) self-raising flour or plain flour
   sifted with 2½ teaspoons baking powder
pinch salt
3 oz (75 g) margarine or cooking fat
   or dripping
1 oz (25 g) sugar
2 oz (50 g) Cheddar cheese, grated
¼ pint (150 ml) milk
*For the topping:*
4 dessert apples, peeled, cored
   and thinly sliced
2 oz (50 g) sugar, preferably brown
½ teaspoon ground cinnamon
1 oz (25 g) margarine, melted

Preheat the oven to 190°C (375°F), Gas Mark 5. Sift the flour, or flour and baking powder, with the salt into a mixing bowl, rub in the margarine, cooking fat or dripping, add the sugar and cheese. Mix well, then gradually blend with the milk. Turn the mixture on to a lightly floured board and knead lightly then form into an oblong to fit into an ungreased 7 × 10 inch (18 × 25 cm) Swiss Roll tin. Arrange the apple slices on top of the dough. Blend the sugar and cinnamon and sprinkle over the apples, then brush with the melted margarine.

Bake for 30-35 minutes or until firm. Cool for a few minutes then remove from the tin. Cut into fingers.

## Summer Fruit Crumble

PREPARATION TIME: 20 MINUTES

COOKING TIME: 35 MINUTES

QUANTITY: 4-6 HELPINGS

*Fruit Crumbles became popular during the years of rationing when the scarcity of fat made it difficult to produce good pastry for fruit pies and tarts.*

*A crumble made with lovely summer fruits, such as black and red currants, raspberries or loganberries, makes a splendid special occasion pudding which is economical to make.*

1½ lb (675 g) mixed summer fruits
   (see above)
2 oz (50 g) sugar
*For the crumble topping:*
6 oz (175 g) flour, plain if possible
3 oz (75 g) margarine
3-4 oz (75-100 g) sugar

Preheat the oven to 180°C (350°F), Gas Mark 4. Prepare the fruits and put into a 2 pint (1.2 litre) pie dish. Add the sugar but there is no need to add water if the fruits are ripe and juicy.

Cover the pie dish and heat the fruit in the oven for about 5 minutes only, then take out of the oven.

Put the flour into a mixing bowl, rub in the margarine, add the sugar and sprinkle evenly over the top of the fruit. Do not cover the dish. Bake for 30 minutes or until the topping is golden brown and crisp.

*Variations: The amount of margarine can be reduced to 2 oz (50 g) and the sugar to 2 oz (50 g) also, but the amount of sugar in the recipe helps to give a really crisp topping.*

*If using firm plums or sliced apples add a little water and cook for 10-15 minutes, or until the fruit begins to soften slightly before adding the crumble topping.*

*If short of sugar add a little dried fruit or marmalade to help sweeten the fruit or use a sugar substitute.*

## Family Currant Cake

PREPARATION TIME: 20 MINUTES

COOKING TIME: 50 MINUTES OR 1 HOUR

QUANTITY: 1 CAKE

**8 oz (225 g) self-raising flour or plain flour
sifted with 2 teaspoons baking powder**

**4 oz (115 g\*) margarine or cooking fat**

**4 oz (115 g\*) sugar, preferably soft light
brown**

**1 reconstituted dried egg or fresh egg**

**6 oz (175 g) currants**

**5 tablespoons milk**

**\* use this metrication**

Grease and flour a 6-7 inch (15-18 cm) round cake tin or 1½-2 lb (675-900 g) loaf tin. Preheat the oven to 180°C (350°F), Gas Mark 4.

Sift the flour, or flour and baking powder, into a mixing bowl, rub in the margarine or cooking fat, add the sugar, beaten egg and the currants. Mix well, then gradually stir in the milk and mix again.

Spoon into the cake or loaf tin. Bake until firm. When baked in a loaf tin the cake will take approximately 50 minutes but about 1 hour in the round tin. Cool for a few minutes then turn out on to a wire cooling rack.

## Dripping Cake

PREPARATION TIME: 15 MINUTES

COOKING TIME: 1 HOUR-1 HOUR 10 MINUTES

QUANTITY: 1 CAKE

*Dripping was a highly prized ingredient, because it was a very flavourful form of fat which had many uses. If a family had saved their meat coupons to have a joint of beef the drippings from the roasting pan would be saved, clarified (see page 57) and allowed to become cold to use in baking.*

**8 oz (225 g) self-raising flour or plain flour
sifted with 2 teaspoons baking powder**

**pinch salt**

**4 oz (100 g) clarified dripping (page 57)**

**3 oz (75 g) sugar**

**1 reconstituted dried or fresh egg**

**5 oz (150 g) dried fruit**

**6 tablespoons milk**

Preheat the oven to 180°C (350°F), Gas Mark 4. Grease and flour a 6 inch (15 cm) cake tin. Sift the flour and salt into a mixing bowl, rub in the dripping, then add the rest of the ingredients.

Spoon into the cake tin and bake for 1 hour-1 hour 10 minutes, or until firm. Turn out on to a wire cooling rack. The richness of dripping made this economical cake keep moist for some time.

*Variation: Use cooking fat instead of dripping.*

## Mock Almond Paste

*Many cakes benefit from the addition of an icing or a topping like this almond paste. The recipe comes from a leaflet, produced by the manufacturers of Stork margarine, for an iced Victory Cake.*

Sieve 4 oz (110 g - use this metrication) dried potato powder and 1 heaped tablespoon dried egg powder together.

Put 2 oz (50 g) margarine, 4 1/2 tablespoons (about 3 oz/75 g) granulated sugar and 2 tablespoons water into a saucepan. Stir over a low heat until the margarine and sugar have melted, which should take 3 - 5 minutes. Add the potato powder and egg and stir well. Keep the heat low and continue to stir for about 3 minutes, or until thick and smooth.

Remove from the heat and stir in 1 tablespoon almond essence. (The original recipe added 1 teaspoon vanilla essence as well.) Cool, knead and roll into a round to fit the top of an 8 inch (20 cm) cake. The Almond Paste will keep for up to 4 weeks.

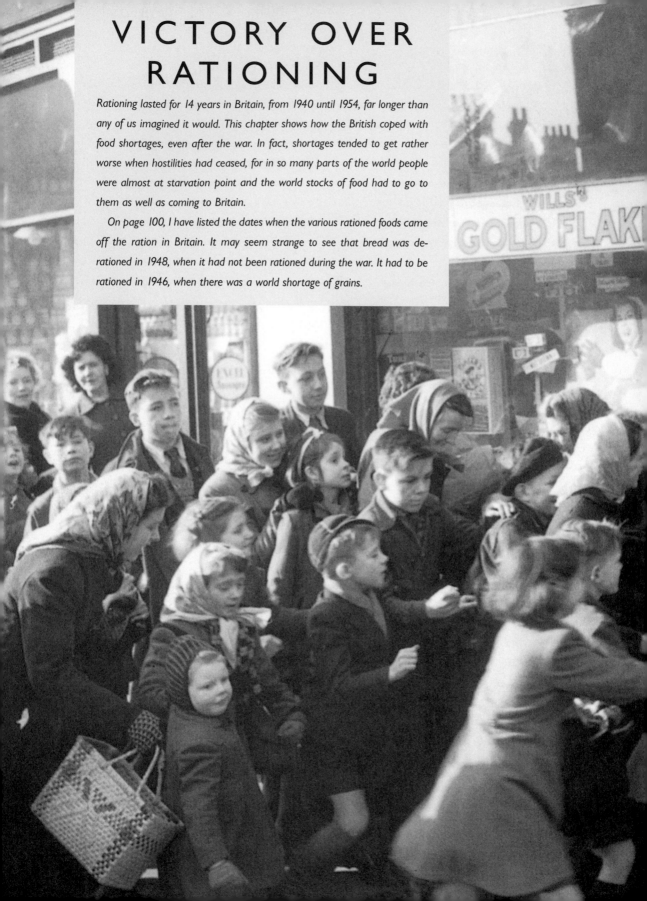

# VICTORY OVER RATIONING

*Rationing lasted for 14 years in Britain, from 1940 until 1954, far longer than any of us imagined it would. This chapter shows how the British coped with food shortages, even after the war. In fact, shortages tended to get rather worse when hostilities had ceased, for in so many parts of the world people were almost at starvation point and the world stocks of food had to go to them as well as coming to Britain.*

*On page 100, I have listed the dates when the various rationed foods came off the ration in Britain. It may seem strange to see that bread was de-rationed in 1948, when it had not been rationed during the war. It had to be rationed in 1946, when there was a world shortage of grains.*

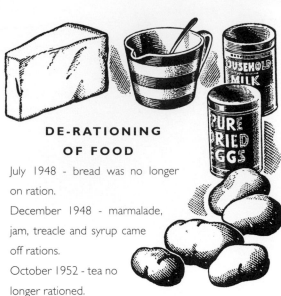

## DE-RATIONING OF FOOD

July 1948 - bread was no longer on ration.

December 1948 - marmalade, jam, treacle and syrup came off rations.

October 1952 - tea no longer rationed.

February 1953 - sweets came off ration.

March 1953 - distribution of eggs no longer controlled, they were off the ration.

April 1953 - now possible to obtain cream, which had been unobtainable during the years of rationing.

September 1953 - sugar came off the ration.

May 1954 - butter, margarine, cooking fat and cheese free from rationing.

June 1954 - meat no longer rationed. Ration books were now no longer required.

### 1946

During this year there were fears of a world famine and, for the first time, bread was rationed in Britain. Oatmeal had been a very important food during the whole of the war period; now, with a shortage of bread, it was used even more.

Rice was no longer imported; quantities of cereals for animal feed were reduced. The hopes for increased rations of meat, bacon and eggs were not realised.

The government did make this year, however, a special increase of 1½ lb (675 g) sugar on each ration book to allow for Christmas cooking. Sweeter cakes and puddings and even sweetmeats could be made.

### 1947 TO 1949

The meat ration was reduced from 1s 2d (6p) to 1s 0d (5p). Canned meat and unrationed offal, like tripe, were eagerly bought.

Although the rations were severe, many foods that had not been brought into this country before were beginning to appear. I well remember Brazil nuts being obtainable for Christmas 1947. More unusual vegetables, such as red and green peppers, were also coming into the shops.

The official Ministry information shows no special increases of any foods for Christmas that year but there was extra sugar for jam-making over a four-week period during the summer. Bread and preserves were de-rationed in 1948.

There were sparse supplies of oranges, from which people could make real marmalade, rather than one based upon apples and carrots, as in the past.

BBC Television had been resumed. I did the cooking in the first BBC Women's magazine programme in November 1947 and continued doing this throughout the fifties and early sixties.

On 24 April 1947 the Home Secretary publically confirmed that there was still much valuable work being done by the WVS. Their soup recipe on page 104 is very appropriately named in view of the work they were doing then, and still do, to help the elderly. The service was honoured by the word Royal being added to its title by the Queen in 1966. So today it is the WRVS.

### 1950 TO 1954

During this period the various basic foods gradually became de-rationed, as I have noted above, and it was now much easier to plan meals, for so many other foods were appearing in the shops. There were better supplies of fish, vegetables, fruit and poultry.

In 1952 I was able to demonstrate a fairly basic pre-war Christmas Pudding and Cake on BBC TV. These recipes were repeated in 1953; then in 1954 I was able to show viewers the recipes I still use to this day: you will find them on pages 108-9.

Much of my work on television during the early 1950s was on basic cooking, demonstrating how to cook interesting fish and vegetable dishes and, when meat came off the ration, choose the correct cuts of meat and appetising dishes using these. There was great interest in baking. When rationing ended it seemed that everyone wanted to make perfect cakes, particularly Victoria Sandwiches.

## THE MINISTRY OF FOOD

It was still very important for the Ministry to control foods and to give help to people. The Food Advisers still continued their work, appearing at Agricultural Shows and other venues and also giving demonstrations to young women leaving the services, who were now cooking for the first time.

## Suffolk Rusks

PREPARATION TIME: 10 MINUTES

COOKING TIME: 18-20 MINUTES

QUANTITY: MAKES 24 RUSKS

**8 oz (225 g) self-raising flour or plain flour**
  **sifted with 2 teaspoons baking powder**
**pinch salt**
**1½ oz (40 g) margarine**
**1 tablespoon caster sugar, optional**
**¼ pint (150 ml) milk**

Preheat the oven to 200°C (400°F), Gas Mark 6. Sift the flour, or flour and baking powder, and salt, rub in the margarine, add the sugar. Blend with enough

> ## Don't waste bread by letting it get stale

milk to make a soft rolling consistency. Roll out to ¾ inch (2 cm) in thickness. Cut into 12 rounds. Put on an ungreased baking tray; bake for 8 minutes, or until firm enough to handle. Remove from the oven, lower the heat to 180°C (350*°F), Gas Mark 4. Cut each round in half horizontally. Place the cut side downwards on to baking trays. Bake for 10 minutes, or until golden brown and crisp.

*Variation: do make these with butter when possible.*

## Cobs

PREPARATION TIME: 5-6 MINUTES

COOKING TIME: 10 MINUTES

QUANTITY: 10-12 HELPINGS

*These are an excellent substitute for bread. They are made in minutes and must be eaten fresh. They freeze well.*

**8 oz (225 g) self-raising four or plain flour**
  **sifted with 2 teaspoons baking powder**
**pinch salt**
**1 oz (25 g) margarine**
**approximately ¼ pint (150 ml) milk**

Preheat the oven to 230°C (450°F), Gas Mark 8. Lightly grease a baking tray. Sift the flour, or flour and baking powder, and salt into a bowl. Rub in the margarine. Add enough milk to make a soft binding consistency - the mixture must not be too stiff, but rather sticky. Divide the dough into 10-12 portions and roll into balls with floured hands. Place on the baking tray and cook for 10 minutes, or until they feel firm, are golden brown in colour and crisp. Eat the cobs when freshly baked.

*Variation: like the Suffolk Rusks, these are excellent when made with butter instead of margarine.*

## OATMEAL

I have taken the following information from a special Ministry of Food leaflet of the period.

'Oatmeal is such an important food that the Government has undertaken to subsidise it. There are plentiful supplies of oatmeal and rolled oats at a price which is within reach of all.

'Scotland gives us oatmeal, the most valuable of our cereals, more nourishing even than wholemeal flour. Oatmeal is one of the simple foods on which our forefathers lived and throve. The cakes that King Alfred burned were, in all probability, oaten cakes and, for many a century, oatmeal played an important part in the countryman's daily diet. During the last hundred years other cereals have tended to oust it from the Englishman's table but today it is coming into its own once again.

'Why is oatmeal valuable? Because it not only builds our bodies and gives us energy but also helps to protect us from illness. Oatmeal contains even more of that elusive Vitamin B1 than wholemeal bread and far and away more than white flour. That is one reason why it is a "protective food". Another is that it gives us the elements that make bone and blood.'

## Oatmeal for thickening soups and stews

To 2 pints (1.2 litres) of soup or stew add 1½-2 oz (40-50 g) oats. Fine, medium or coarse oatmeal should be added about 30 minutes before the end of the cooking time, but rolled oats need be added only 10 minutes before the end. Stir well to blend then simmer steadily after adding the oats. Stir from time to time to prevent the mixture sticking.

## Oatmeal instead of nuts

Toast oatmeal or rolled oats on a tray in an oven preheated to 180°C (350°F), Gas Mark 4 for about 15 minutes or under a preheated grill for 6-8 minutes, or until golden in colour. This makes it tasty and digestible to sprinkle over fruit and individual sweets instead of chopped nuts.

## Oatmeal Scones or Farls

PREPARATION TIME: 15 MINUTES

COOKING TIME: 12-15 MINUTES OR 10 MINUTES

QUANTITY: 12 SCONES

*These scones, or farls, can be cooked in the oven or on a griddle (a bakestone). They are equally good as a savoury or sweet scone. The extra baking powder used is to compensate for the weight of oats.*

**8 oz (225 g) rolled oats or medium oatmeal**
**2 oz (50 g) self-raising flour sifted with 1 teaspoon baking powder or plain flour sifted with 1½ teaspoons baking powder**
**good pinch salt**
**1-1½ oz (25-40 g) margarine or cooking fat**
**1-2 oz (25-50 g) sugar for sweet scones**
**approximately ¼ pint (150 ml) milk**

Put the oats into a mixing bowl, sift the flour, baking powder and salt into the bowl. Rub in the margarine or fat, add the sugar, if using this, and enough milk to make a fairly firm rolling consistency.

Roll out the dough on a board coated with a little flour until approximately ½ inch (1 cm) thick, if baking the scones, but slightly less than that if cooking on the griddle. Cut into small rounds or triangles.

If baking the scones: preheat the oven to 220°C (450°F), Gas Mark 7. Lightly grease a baking tray. Add the scones and bake for 12-15 minutes.

If cooking on a griddle: grease then preheat the griddle. To test if this is the right heat shake on a little flour, it should turn golden in colour within I minute but no shorter a time.

Put the scones on the griddle, cook steadily for 5 minutes, turn over and cook for the same time on the second side.

Lift the scones on to a clean teacloth, placed on a wire cooling tray, and cover with the cloth. This keeps the scones pleasantly moist.

*Variations: To give an attractive appearance to the scones brush the tops with a little milk and sprinkle with a small amount of rolled oats before baking. This is not suitable when cooking the scones on the griddle.*

*Cheese Scones: these are very good for a packed meal. Use just I oz (25 g) margarine or cooking fat and add 2 oz (50 g) or even 3 oz (75 g) grated cheese, if you can spare it. Sift a little pepper and dry mustard powder with the flour and baking powder as well as the salt.*

*Fruit Scones:if you have any dried fruit to spare add about 2 oz (50 g) to the flour mixture.*

*Oatmeal Treacle Scones: omit the sugar and add I-2 tablespoons black treacle. You will need a little less milk.*

## RECIPES FROM FOOD FIRMS

As well as the Ministry of Food, many food firms also supplied recipes for the public. The following recipes were given by Omo, Batchelors and Stork. They are not quite as originally printed, for I have inserted the metric measures, preparation time, etc. The quantities of ingredients and method are as the original recipes.

Local authorities also helped to give people imaginative ideas for their meals .

# Potato and Cheese Fritters

PREPARATION TIME: I5 MINUTES

COOKING TIME: 5-6 MINUTES

QUANTITY: 4 HELPINGS

*For the batter:*

**3 oz (75 g) plain flour**

**I teaspoon baking powder**

**¼ pint (I50 ml) milk and water**

**2 Oxo cubes or I heaped teaspoon fluid Oxo**

**little Worcestershire sauce**

**2 oz (50 g) cheese, grated**

**salt and pepper**

**3 large cooked potatoes, new potatoes are ideal, if small use 6, sliced**

*For frying:*

**little cooking fat or dripping**

Blend the flour, baking powder and milk and water to make a smooth batter. Add the Oxo, Worcestershire sauce, half the cheese and a little seasoning.

Dip the sliced potatoes into the batter. Heat the fat or dripping and drop the potato slices into the hot fat. Fry them on both sides until golden. Sprinkle with the remaining grated cheese and serve hot.

# Cheese and Lentil Pie

PREPARATION TIME: 30 MINUTES

COOKING TIME: 50 MINUTES

QUANTITY: 4 HELPINGS

**8 oz (225 g) lentils**

**½ tablespoon chopped onion, leek or chives**

**2 Oxo cubes or I heaped teaspoon fluid Oxo**

**½ pint (300 ml) water**

**salt and pepper**

**6 oz (175 g) cheese, grated**

**I lb (450 g) mashed potatoes**

**little dripping**

Soak the lentils overnight in cold water to cover. Drain then put them into a pan with the onion, leek or chives, the Oxo cubes or fluid Oxo and the ½ pint (300 ml) water. Cover the pan tightly and cook until the lentils are fairly dry. Season and mix with the cheese.

Preheat the oven to 200°C (400°F), Gas Mark 6. Spoon the lentil mixture into a 2 pint (1.2 litre) greased dish. Top with the mashed potatoes. Add the dripping in small pieces and bake for 20 minutes.

*Variation: Use haricot beans instead of lentils. As these take longer to tenderize, you should increase the amount of water to 1 pint (600 ml).*

## Green Pea Torte

QUANTITY: FOR 3 OR 4 PEOPLE

Make pastry using 2½-3 oz (65-75 g) flour, rub in 1½ oz (40 g) fat, mix with a very little milk or water. Roll very thinly in a strip.

Place on a greased baking tin or sheet and bake for 10 minutes in a quick oven, 200°C (400°F), Gas Mark 6. Meanwhile, heat a tin of Batchelors Peas.

Lift the cooked pastry from the baking sheet on to a hot dish. Cover the pastry with hot peas, sprinkle with grated cheese, place under the grill for 1 minute and serve at once.

## Old Folks Soup

PREPARATION TIME: 30 MINUTES

COOKING TIME: 40 MINUTES

QUANTITY: 4-5 HELPINGS

*The work of the WVS may have changed somewhat since wartime and the period immediately after the war, but they continue to give wonderful help to people, including the old and less fit. This is typical of the kind of satisfying meal in a soup they offer to old folks, perhaps in a Meals on Wheels lunch.*

**1 oz (25 g) dripping or cooking fat**

**2 oz (50 g) carrots, sliced**

**2 oz (50 g) turnips, diced**

**1 medium onion, finely chopped**

**1 leek, thinly sliced**

**1 small celery stick, finely chopped**

**1½ oz (40 g) flour**

**2 pints (1.2 litres) stock**

**salt and pepper**

**6 oz (175 g) sausages or sausagemeat**

Melt the dripping or cooking fat in a saucepan, add the vegetables and fry gently for a few minutes. Add the flour and blend with the vegetables, then pour in the stock. Stir briskly as the liquid comes to the boil and the soup thickens. Season to taste.

Cook until the vegetables are nearly tender. Meanwhile, skin the sausages, if using, and form the meat into small balls with floured fingers. Drop into the soup and simmer for 15 minutes.

## Piquant Tripe

Wash 1 lb (450 g) dressed tripe in cold water then put into a saucepan with sufficient fresh water to cover, a bay leaf and a little seasoning. Cover the pan, bring to the boil and simmer gently for 1½ hours.

Remove the tripe from the pan, cut into small pieces. Save ½ pint (300 ml) of the liquid.

Heat 1½ oz (40 g) margarine in a pan, stir in 2 oz (50 g) flour, add the tripe liquid and ½ pint (300 ml) milk. Stir constantly as the sauce comes to the boil and thickens.

Add the tripe and heat, then add 3 tablespoons chopped gherkins and 2 teaspoons mustard blended with 1 tablespoon vinegar. Heat gently, being careful not to let the sauce boil, before serving the tripe.

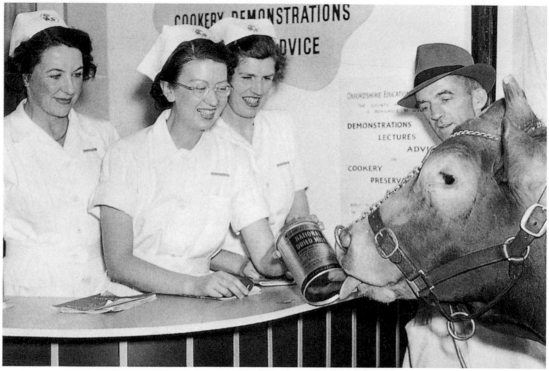

## Stuffed Pigeons

*In the early 1950s when grain was so very precious there was a plague of pigeons, who were eating it.*

*Farmers asked me to demonstrate pigeon dishes to persuade the public to make use of this very edible but, at the time, tiresome bird.*

Halve young pigeons lengthways; remove as many bones as possible; spread sausagemeat against the cut side, then coat in beaten egg and crisp breadcrumbs.

Fry in hot fat until crisp and brown all over; lower the heat and continue cooking for 10-15 minutes. Serve with creamed potatoes and a green vegetable.

### RETURN OF FRUIT

The return of oranges, lemons and other citrus fruits and bananas was one of the most exciting things, for these made such a difference to our lifestyle.

Before fresh bananas became available dried bananas were on sale. These were dark brown, rather chewy in texture and sweet. They were very pleasant if sliced and cooked in a little lemon-flavoured sugar syrup or chopped and added to a steamed pudding mixture with other dried fruit. Many people ate them as a snack.

Two recipes that follow make use of citrus fruit.

## Banana Cream

PREPARATION TIME: 10 MINUTES

NO COOKING IF CUSTARD MADE

QUANTITY: 4 HELPINGS

*This was a delicious dessert that became possible when bananas came back*

**3 large ripe bananas**

**2 tablespoons cold water**

**½ oz (15 g) gelatine***

**¼ pint (150 ml) custard (page 38)**

**½ pint (300 ml) evaporated milk, whipped (page 39)**

**sugar, to taste**

**\* this would be one sachet of today's gelatine**

Mash the bananas until a pulp. Pour the water into a basin, add the gelatine and allow to stand for 2 minutes then dissolve over hot, but not boiling, water. Add to the warm custard with the bananas, blend together.

Leave in a cool place until the mixture begins to stiffen then fold in the whipped evaporated milk with sugar to taste.

Spoon into glasses and chill well.

## Canary Pudding

PREPARATION TIME: 20 MINUTES

COOKING TIME: 1½ HOURS

QUANTITY: 4 HELPINGS

**3 oz (75 g) margarine**

**4 oz (100 g) caster sugar**

**2 teaspoons finely grated lemon rind**

**2 reconstituted dried or fresh eggs**

**4 oz (100 g) self-raising flour or plain flour**
   **sifted with 1 teaspoon baking powder**

**2 tablespoons lemon juice**

Cream the margarine, sugar and lemon rind until soft and light. Beat the eggs lightly and add gradually to the creamed mixture. Sift the flour, or flour and baking powder, and add to the other ingredients with the lemon juice.

Grease a 1½ pint (900 ml) basin, put in the mixture, cover with greased greaseproof paper and steam over boiling water for 45 minutes then lower the heat and steam more gently for a further 45 minutes.          .

Serve with Lemon Sauce (see below).

## Lemon Sauce

Put 2 oz (50 g) sugar and ¼ pint (150 ml) water into a small saucepan with 2 teaspoons very finely grated lemon zest.

Stir over a low heat until the sugar dissolves.

Blend 1 teaspoon cornflour with 2 tablespoons lemon juice. Add to the ingredients in the saucepan and stir over a low heat until the sauce thickens and becomes clear.

## Cheese and Haddock Soufflé

PREPARATION TIME: 15 MINUTES

COOKING TIME: 30-35 MINUTES

QUANTITY: 4 HELPINGS

*As fresh eggs became more plentiful, eventually being de-restricted in March 1953, many enthusiastic cooks turned their attention to making soufflés, for they felt that this was the dish for which fresh eggs were essential. Although the result is certainly better with shell eggs, soufflés can be made with dried eggs very happily. Cream, which had been unavailable right through the years of rationing, became available again from April 1953 - just in time for the Queen's Coronation1.*

**1 oz (25 g) butter or margarine**

**1 oz (25 g) flour**

**¼ pint (150 ml) milk**

**3 tablespoons extra milk or cream**

**3 eggs**

**1 egg white**

**4 oz (100 g) mature Cheddar cheese, grated**

**4 oz (100 g) cooked smoked haddock,**
   **finely flaked**

**salt and pepper**

Preheat the oven to 190°C (375°F), Gas Mark 5. Grease a 6-7 inch (15-18 cm) soufflé dish.

Heat the butter or margarine in a saucepan, stir in the flour, then add the milk and cream, if using this. Whisk hard as the sauce comes to the boil and thickens. Remove from the heat.

Separate the eggs. Add the egg yolks to the sauce, put the whites with the extra egg white. Blend the cheese and fish with the other ingredients in the saucepan. Add seasoning to taste. Whisk the whites

until they stand in soft peaks, and fold carefully into the cheese and fish mixture.

Spoon into the soufflé dish and bake in the pre-heated oven for 30-35 minutes, or until well risen and golden brown. Serve at once.

*Variation: This soufflé can be made with dried eggs. Reconstitute 3 or 4 eggs in the usual way and add to the sauce in exactly the same way as fresh eggs. You have no whites to whisk separately. The soufflé will rise well, but will not be quite as light as when fresh eggs are chosen.*

## Victoria Sandwich

PREPARATION TIME: 25 MINUTES

COOKING TIME: 20 MINUTES

QUANTITY: MAKES 1 SPONGE CAKE

*Most cooks wanted to achieve a perfect Victoria Sandwich and, in the 1950s at various fêtes and shows, there were countless competitions for this*

*sponge cake. The old-fashioned method of using the eggs instead of weights was still used; this made absolutely certain the fat, sugar and flour exactly matched the weight of the eggs (in their shells).*

**6 oz (175 g) butter or margarine**

**6 oz (175 g) caster sugar**

**3 eggs - size 1 or 2**

**6 oz (175 g) self-raising flour or plain flour
    sifted with 2 teaspoons baking powder**

***For the filling and topping:***

**jam**

**caster sugar**

Preheat the oven to 180-190°C (350-375°F), Gas Mark 4-5. Ovens vary appreciably and it is wise to use the lower setting the first time you make this sponge cake. Grease and flour or line two 7½-8 inch (19-20 cm) round sandwich tins.

Cream the butter or margarine and sugar until soft and light. Whisk the eggs and gradually beat into the creamed mixture, adding a little of the flour if the mixture looks like curdling. Sift the flour, or flour and baking powder, and fold into the other ingredients.

Spoon into the tins and bake side by side in the preheated oven for approximately 20 minutes or until firm to the touch. Cool in the tins for a few minutes then invert on to a folded teacloth on the palm of your hand then invert on to a wire cooling rack. This ensures that the top of the delicate cake is not marked by the tray.

When cold, sandwich together with jam and top with a sprinkling of caster sugar.

## Christmas Cake of 1954

PREPARATION TIME: 35 MINUTES

COOKING TIME: SEE METHOD

QUANTITY: MAKES 1 CAKE

*This is the cake that has won so much praise over the years from people who make it. Ovens vary a great deal and this is particularly obvious when baking rich fruit cakes, such as this one, so test carefully and check baking as indicated in the method.*

**12 oz (350 g) plain flour**

**1 teaspoon ground cinnamon**

**1 teaspoon mixed spice**

**4 oz (110 g*) candied peel, chopped**

**2 lb (900 g) mixed dried fruit, preferably 1 lb (450 g) currants, 8 oz (225 g) sultanas, 8 oz (225 g) seedless raisins**

**2-4 oz (50-110 g*) blanched almonds, chopped**

**4 oz (110 g*) glacé cherries, chopped**

**4 large eggs**

**4 tablespoons milk, sherry, brandy or rum**

**finely grated rind 1 lemon**

**finely grated rind 1 orange (optional)**

**8 oz (225 g) butter or margarine**

**8 oz (225 g) sugar, preferably dark moist brown sugar**

**1 tablespoon black treacle or golden syrup**

**\* use this metrication**

Preparing the tin: this is a rich Christmas cake that should ideally be made at least one month before Christmas. It gives the right amount of ingredients for a 9 inch (23 cm) round or 8 inch (20 cm) square cake. Prepare the tin carefully. Line the bottom of the tin with a double round of brown paper and cover this with a double thickness of lightly greased greaseproof paper. Line the sides of the tin with greased greaseproof paper. Tie a deep band of brown paper around the outside of the tin.

Preparing the cake: sift together all the dry ingredients. Mix together the peel, fruit, almonds and cherries (if these are slightly sticky then mix with a little of the flour). Blend the eggs with the milk, sherry, brandy or rum. Cream together the lemon and orange rinds with the butter or margarine, sugar and treacle or golden syrup until soft. Do not over-beat: this cake does not need much beating. Gradually blend in the egg mixture and sifted dry ingredients. Stir in all the fruit. Put the mixture into the tin, smooth flat on top, then press with damp knuckles to help keep the cake moist on top.

Bake in the centre of a moderate oven, 160°C (325°F), Gas Mark 3 for about 1½ hours then lower the oven to cool 140-150°C (275-300°F), Gas Mark 1-2 for

about another 2 hours. Baking times for rich fruit cakes like this vary considerably according to the particular oven, so test it carefully.

To test rich fruit cakes: After the first third of the cooking time the cake should still be very pale in colour. If darkening too much, lower the oven temperature rather sooner than indicated above. Test again at the end of the second third of the cooking time. The cake should still be fairly soft on top but a good golden colour;, if becoming too dark then lower the heat still further. To test if completely cooked at the end of the cooking time, check that the cake has shrunk away from the sides of the tin then listen very carefully. An uncooked rich fruit cake makes a distinct humming noise. When completely cooked it is absolutely silent. *Variation: Add 4 oz (110 g\* - use this metrication) finely diced uncooked apricots and 2 oz (50 g) ground almonds to the above mixture.*

## Christmas Pudding of 1954

PREPARATION TIME: 40 MINUTES
COOKING TIME: 6-8 HOURS THEN 2-3 HOURS
QUANTITY: 10-12 HELPINGS

**4 oz (110 g\*) fine soft breadcrumbs**
**2 oz (50 g) flour, preferably plain**
**4 oz (110 g\*) shredded suet**
**4 oz (110 g\*) moist brown sugar**
**8 oz (225 g) seedless or stoned and chopped raisins**
**4 oz (110 g\*) sultanas**
**4 oz (110 g\*) currants**
**2 oz (50 g) dried apricots, finely chopped**
**1 oz (25 g) dried prunes, stoned and finely chopped**
**4 oz (110 g\*) mixed candied peel, chopped**
**2 oz (50 g) glacé cherries, chopped**

**2 oz (50 g) cooking apple (weight when peeled), grated**
**2 oz (50 g) carrots (weight when peeled), grated**
**2 oz (50 g) blanched almonds, chopped**
**½ teaspoon grated lemon rind**
**½ teaspoon grated orange rind**
**¼-½ teaspoon ground nutmeg**
**½-1 teaspoon mixed spice**
**¼-½ teaspoon ground cinnamon**
**2 large eggs**
**1½ teaspoons lemon juice**
**1½ teaspoons orange juice**
**1½ teaspoons black treacle**
**4 tablespoons stout or ale**
**½ wineglass brandy or rum**
**\* use this metrication**

Mix all the ingredients together. I like to leave the uncooked pudding mixture standing overnight, so that the flavours blend better. It also allows all members of the family to stir the mixture and wish.

Grease two 2½ pint (1.5 litre) or one 4½ pint (2.5 litre) basins; put in the mixture. Cover well with greased greaseproof paper and foil. A Christmas Pudding does not rise in the same way as a light sponge pudding but it swells in cooking so never fill the basin too full. If you press the mixture down firmly you can cut neater slices of the cooked pudding, but my recipe gives a crumbly pudding rather than a solid one.

Steam each pudding for 6-8 hours depending upon the size; take off the damp covers at once; cool the puddings, then put on dry covers. Store the pudding in a cool dry place.

On Christmas Day, steam the pudding for another 2-3 hours before serving.

# *Post-War*
# KITCHEN

**W**HILE WE WERE still thinking longingly in the years from 1945 of good pre-war succulent roast joints and tender steaks, there were slight changes in attitude about the kind of food we wanted. People from many nations had been in Britain, either serving in the forces or here as refugees; they had met British people and told them about their national dishes. Then, too, British men and women had served in the armed forces in many countries and they had gleaned some knowledge of various foreign cuisines. Gradually, as we moved into the 1950s, more people started to holiday abroad. All of these factors made us more willing to accept new kinds of food and different types of cooking side by side with our own traditional fare.

Most people had been grateful to the Ministry of Food for its work during the war years. The Ministry had given practical information and recipes in newspapers, on the radio and in demonstrations throughout the country. It had helped people make the best of the restricted foods available. The people at the Ministry felt, quite rightly, that they had kept the population at home healthy during the war years. They now decided that they should continue to guide and advise us on what we should, or should not, eat in the years ahead. The Ministry's experts published *The A.B.C. of Cooking* for general sale and monthly booklets entitled *Food and Nutrition* for use by educational establishments.

After a year or so of such work many people became disenchanted with the Ministry's continual advice and there were mutterings about Britain being turned into a 'nanny-state'. People wanted restrictions lifted and rationing to end as speedily as possible so that they would to be able to buy just what they wanted and not what they were told was good for them.

It was not just the attitude to food that had changed with the war. Although many men and women from the forces were happy to return to their peacetime occupations, others were less willing to do so. In spite of the dangers of war, they had seen new countries and had experienced a more exciting life which they wanted to find at home. Perhaps the greatest change was in the status of what is often called 'the average housewife'. During the war, mothers frequently had to be lone parents while fathers were serving abroad. Women found they had managed the problems of running

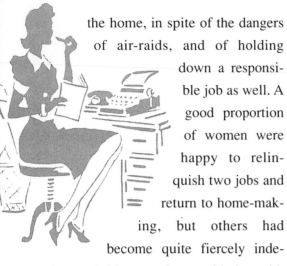

the home, in spite of the dangers of air-raids, and of holding down a responsible job as well. A good proportion of women were happy to relinquish two jobs and return to home-making, but others had become quite fiercely independent and this caused some friction with returning husbands. It also meant that many women had become accustomed to planning meals to accommodate their jobs. The need for Britain to regain our exports meant that there were jobs available for most people who wanted them.

Many new developments for the home, especially the kitchen, were also a help for women wishing to have a job as well as run a home. Electric mixers, liquidizers (blenders) and pressure cookers made the preparation of food easier and cooking quicker. Refrigerators altered shopping habits, for perishable foods could be stored for longer periods. All of these had an effect upon the choice of recipes. Deep freezers were known in America but Britain had to wait a little longer for them.

The years from 1945 onwards were full of changes on the international and national scene. I mention some of the most important of them in the introduction to each year. Britain grieved at the death of the much loved George VI in 1952 but also rejoiced at and were thrilled by the pageantry and splendour of the Coronation of his daughter Elizabeth II in 1953.

The development of television by the BBC meant that many of these events could be seen by the public as they happened. During the war years the radio had given news, information and entertainment but how much greater was the impact of television! As more and more homes had a television set, there was a noticeable effect upon the way evening meals were served and one heard a lot about TV meals served on trays so no time need be spent away from watching the magic screens. Television gradually prevented people going to the cinema or to other outside entertainments as regularly as they once had done.

*"My turn to scrape the dish"*

## NOTES ABOUT THE RECIPES

Although many of the recipes in *Marguerite Patten's Post-War Kitchen* are economical, since they are the original ones demonstrated in the years when many foods were still rationed, you will find their flavour is good, for people were much more discerning and critical of dishes after the war ended.

*Ingredients* in the recipes are given in both imperial and metric amounts although, of course, in the years covered by this book metrication was unknown in Britain.

*Oven temperatures* have been carefully tested. If you have a fan oven you will need to reduce the setting slightly when baking cakes and pastry. Consult your manufacturer's handbook.

*Spoon measures* are level in all cases. If the word 'level' is introduced into a recipe it means special care must be taken when filling the spoon.

## THE INGREDIENTS USED

*Eggs* were scarce right up to the time when they were derationed (in 1953) so we used dried eggs a great deal of the time. I have retained reconstituted dried eggs in several recipes for authenticity, but most of my readers will want to use fresh eggs: they are interchangeable in all recipes.

*Flour* for several years after the ending of the war was dark and heavy and needed an excessive amount of baking powder. I have adapted the recipes for use with today's much more refined flour.

I have found it fascinating to recall these important years for this book and I hope that its reader will be equally interested.

*Marguerite Patten*

## RECONSTITUTING DRIED EGG POWDER

One had to be very careful about reconstituting dried eggs during the war. Quite quickly, however, we found that if measurements were accurate, the egg powder made an acceptable substitute. To make one egg, measure one absolutely level tablespoon of dried egg powder. Put it in a cup or basin, then gradually add 2 tablespoons cold water. Stir well until smooth.

# ★1945★

THE CELEBRATIONS THAT marked the ending of the Second World War went on throughout this year; pictures of the street parties and some of the many celebrations will be found in my companion book *The Victory Cookbook.*

It was a great tragedy that American President Roosevelt died in April so could not share in the rejoicings.

The summer of 1945 ended the wartime Coalition Government. A general election brought Labour to power under the leadership of Clement Attlee. Lord Woolton was no longer Minister of Food but his name would long be remembered for his work on the Kitchen Front and also for the dish that bore his name, Woolton Pie, a mixture of seasonal vegetables.

In July of this year the blackout ended amid scenes of great excitement. A well-known song of the war years had a line that read: 'We're going to get lit-up when the lights go on in London' – and no doubt many people did!

No-one expected rationing to be alleviated during 1945, for it was realized that the populations of most of the countries of Europe were starving and their needs must come before those of the British people. Our ships had to bring men and materials back from the various theatres of war, so the transport of any extra food had to take second place. Aid from America, which had helped Britain so much in the previous years, was diverted to the countries previously conquered by Germany and Japan.

The joy felt with the return of many servicemen and women to their homes and the ending of the ever-present fear about hostilities abroad, and attack at home, made rationing almost bearable for most of the population, though there were some rumblings of discontent about the high-handed attitude of shopkeepers, many of whom had lost the habit of wooing customers. People were beginning to feel that the Government must move quickly to make more interesting foods available.

Making preserves of various kinds for the winter months was even more popular than in past years. Many people found they had spare time now that fire-watching and other ARP (Air Raid Precautions) duties were no longer necessary.

Although when the war ended there was no increase in the amount of rationed foods, the kind of recipes I was asked to demonstrate changed quite a lot. Obviously, people were much more relaxed and life lost the terrible feeling of imminent danger. Many people began to invite friends to their home for coffee in the morning or for afternoon tea and wanted recipes for economical home-made biscuits and cakes. I have included some of these recipes in this chapter, as well as a few of the more spartan dishes that would have been served in 1945.

In August of this year it was stated in the press that one million servicemen would be demobilised by December. The same report added that another million people would be released from munition work. The Government urged any men who had worked in the mines to return when possible as it was imperative that Britain increased its coal production.

In November General Charles de Gaulle, who had formed the Free French Forces, was elected to be the new President of France.

## BREAKFAST DISHES

Breakfast was still a very important meal in the 1940s and now that nights disturbed by air-raids were over, there was no doubt that young and old were much more wide-awake to enjoy the first meal of the day. Ready-cooked cereals, such as cornflakes, were popular although regular supplies of a specific cereal might be erratic and people had to be content with an alternative. Porridge was served in many homes, for oatmeal and rolled oats were basic foods that were generally in good supply.

The term 'muesli' was not known by the public at this time but, as can be seen in the Food Facts below, the Ministry of Food were suggesting a 'Swiss Breakfast' which was exactly the same thing. The semolina porridge, also below, was not popular.

---

### FOOD FACTS

## Using your points for BREAKFAST DISHES

*Savoury Potato Cakes*

WHAT to give the men-folk and the children for breakfast is a problem in many households. A small, well-planned outlay of points will help you to give the family a good hot meal for starting off the day. The recipes here are kitchen-tested.

**Swiss Breakfast** *(for 4)*
*4 oz. barley flakes or kernels; 4 tablesps. milk; ½ lb. grated apple; 1-2 level tablesps. sugar.*
Soak the barley flakes or kernels overnight in barely enough water to cover. In the morning, beat up well with the other ingredients. This is a delicious change from porridge.

**Savoury Potato Cakes** *(for 4)*
*1 lb. left-over mashed potato; 1 tin sardines (4½ oz. size); 2 level tablesps. chopped parsley; 1 level teasp. salt; ¼ level teasp. pepper.*
Mix all ingredients well together. Turn on to a board and shape into 8 cakes. Brown under grill on both sides, or bake in a moderate oven till firm and brown.

**Semolina Porridge** *(for 4)* *4-6 oz. semolina; 2 level teaspoons salt; 2 pints liquid (1 pint or less milk, and remainder in water).*
Blend the semolina and salt with a little of the cold liquid. Bring the remainder to the boil and pour on to the blended semolina. Return to the pan and boil gently for 15-20 minutes, stirring well to prevent it burning. (If thick porridge is preferred use the larger amount of semolina.)

**Fried Pilchards on Fried Bread** *(for 4)* *1 tin pilchards, 15-oz. size; 4 slices of bread; fat for frying if necessary.*
Fry the pilchards till brown on both sides. They should be sufficiently oily to fry without extra fat. Remove from the pan and keep hot. Add a little extra fat if necessary, to fry the slices of bread till golden brown on both sides. Divide the pilchards on to the 4 slices of fried bread and serve hot.

**CUT THIS OUT AND KEEP IT**

ISSUED BY THE MINISTRY OF FOOD, LONDON, S.W.1.          FOOD FACTS No. 331

---

## Breakfast Quickies

The bacon ration was small and people were always trying to find ways to make it go further, for bacon was still a favourite breakfast food. Where quantities are given the dish gives 4 helpings.

**Bacon Fritters:** These are a good way to eke out a small amount of bacon. Fry 2 bacon rashers then cut into small pieces. Make a batter with 2 oz (50 g) self-raising flour, a pinch of salt, 1 reconstituted dried egg (page 10) or a fresh egg and 5 tablespoons milk or milk and water. Add the bacon and season to taste.

Drop spoonfuls into a little hot fat and fry until crisp and brown on either side.

**Cheese Fritters:** Follow the recipe for Bacon Fritters above but use grated cheese instead of bacon. These are excellent with cooked tomatoes.

**Herring Roes:** Coat soft or hard herring roes with a little seasoned flour, and fry in hot fat. If no fat is available for frying, put the roes on a plate with a tablespoon or two of milk and seasoning. Cover and steam for 10 minutes. Serve on hot toast.

**Kippers:** These can be grilled, fried or steamed but the easiest method of cooking is to put them in a large dish, pour over boiling water, cover the dish and leave for 5 minutes.

**Kipper Scramble:** To make 1 or 2 kippers go further, flake the cooked flesh from the skin and bones. Mix the flesh with 2 or 3 reconstituted dried eggs (page 10) or fresh eggs. Season lightly. Heat 1 oz (25 g) margarine in a pan, pour in the egg mixture and scramble lightly.

The flesh from cooked bloaters, smoked haddock or white fish could be used instead.

## EGGY BREAD

*Preparation time: 5 minutes*
*Cooking time: 4 minutes*
*Quantity: 4 helpings*

This was a good way of making 2 eggs serve 4 people. It appealed very much to children, particularly those who were not over-fond of a whole boiled or fried egg. This is the original recipe, using reconstituted dried eggs (see page 10), but you could use fresh eggs instead. Remember to reconstitute the dried eggs carefully, making sure there are no lumps.

    2 level tablespoons dried egg
       powder
    4 tablespoons water
    salt and pepper
    4 large slices bread
    1 oz (25 g) fat

Reconstitute the egg powder with the water (page 10) and add seasoning to taste. Pour on to a flat dish.

Dip the slices of bread in the egg until well coated, making sure all the egg is used. Do not leave the bread soaking for too long for this makes it soggy and inclined to break.

Melt the fat in a large frying pan and cook the coated bread until golden on both sides and the egg is firmly set. Serve at once.

---

## BACON AND POTATO CAKES

*Preparation time: 10 minutes*
*Cooking time: 8 minutes*
*Quantity: 4 helpings*

This was a good way of making 1 or 2 bacon rashers go a long way. They added flavour to the potato cakes. The rinds would be fried until very crisp then broken into small pieces and added to the mixture or saved for a garnish on soups or stews.

The Ministry of Food advisers always stressed 'cook extra potatoes to use in savoury or sweet dishes'. The timings for this recipe depend upon the potatoes being ready cooked.

    1 or 2 bacon rashers, derinded
    12 oz (350 g) cooked potatoes
    1–2 tablespoons milk
    1 tablespoon chopped parsley
    salt and pepper
    1 tablespoon flour
    little fat, if necessary

Fry the bacon rashers and rinds until very crisp, and chop into small pieces. Mash the potatoes and add enough milk to make a fairly firm mixture with the bacon, parsley and seasoning. Form into 4 large or 8 small round cakes. Lightly coat the cakes in the flour then fry them until crisp and brown on both sides in the bacon fat remaining in the pan. If there is very little then melt a small knob of cooking fat in the pan before adding the cakes.

Serve with cooked halved tomatoes or a few heated bottled tomatoes.

## MAIN MEALS

In the days of air-raids many families had their main meal in the middle of the day, for the evenings and nights could be very disturbed. Now that there was no fear of unwelcome interruptions people could enjoy an evening meal if they so wished. These are some of the popular dishes of 1945.

☆ ☆ ☆ ☆ ☆ ☆ ☆ ☆ ☆ ☆ ☆ ☆ ☆ ☆ ☆ ☆ ☆ ☆ ☆ ☆

### CURRIED VEGETABLE SOUP

*Preparation time: 25 minutes*
*Cooking time: 12–22 minutes (see method)*
*Quantity: 4 helpings*

Root vegetables were a staple part of the British diet during the whole year. Raw carrots and turnips became part of vegetable salads. Onions were scarce during the winter months but became more readily available out of season after the war ended. Much work had been done by the Ministry of Food to educate the public to the fact that cooking vegetables for the minimum time retained the maximum amount of vitamins and mineral salts as well as flavour and texture.

2 medium carrots
1 small turnip
1 small parsnip
2 onions
2 potatoes
2 tomatoes
1 oz (25 g) margarine or cooking fat
1 tablespoon flour
2 teaspoons curry powder,
  or to taste
1¼ pints (750 ml) water
salt and pepper
¼ pint (150 ml) milk

Peel the vegetables. The tomatoes should be skinned. For speedy cooking, grate the vegetables coarsely; otherwise cut them in small neat dice. Chop the tomatoes. Melt the fat in a saucepan, add the onions and cook gently for 5 minutes then stir in the flour and curry powder. Add the water, bring to the boil then put in the remaining ingredients except the tomatoes and milk. Cook for 10 minutes if the vegetables are grated or for 15–20 minutes if cut into dice. Add the tomatoes and milk and heat for a few minutes.

### CUCUMBER SOUP

*Preparation time: 10 minutes*
*Cooking time: 15 minutes*
*Quantity: 4 helpings*

'Dig for Victory' had been a slogan throughout the war years so a large percentage of the population had become good at growing vegetables. Home-grown cucumbers were highly prized.

1 medium cucumber
1 oz (25 g) margarine
1 medium onion or bunch spring onions,
  finely chopped
1 pint (600 ml) water
salt and pepper
2 teaspoons finely chopped mint
½ pint (300 ml) milk

It is better to remove most of the peel from the cucumber as it gives a very bitter taste to the soup. You can leave on about ½–1 inch (1.25–2.5 cm) to add to the colour of the soup. Dice or grate the cucumber pulp, and finely chop the small amount of skin. Heat the margarine in a saucepan, add the onion(s) and cook gently for 5 minutes. Add the water, bring to the boil then put in the cucumber, seasoning and mint. Simmer for 8 minutes then add the milk and heat for 2 minutes.

#### VARIATIONS
The soup can be rubbed through a sieve.
Use unsweetened evaporated milk instead of the ordinary milk.

#### MODERN TOUCHES
Use single cream instead of milk.
Liquidize the soup.

# FOOD FACTS

## WHAT TO HAVE FOR SUPPER?

*HERRINGS are just about the tastiest fish you can get!*

### HERRINGS AMERICAINE

*Preparation time: 15 minutes*
*Cooking time: 25 minutes*
*Quantity: 4 helpings*

There was a spate of recipes using the term 'Americaine' when the war ended, for America had been our good friend and ally. Greaseproof paper was almost unobtainable, so the wrappings of margarine and other fats were carefully hoarded.

**For the stuffing:**
1 oz (25 g) margarine
1 medium onion, grated
    or finely chopped
2 medium tomatoes,
    chopped
2 oz (50 g) soft breadcrumbs
1 tablespoon chopped parsley
1 reconstituted dried egg
    (see page 10) or fresh egg

salt and pepper

**To cook the herrings:**
4 herrings, heads removed
    and boned
½ tablespoon margarine,
    melted

Heat the margarine for the stuffing, add the onion and cook for 5 minutes. Mix in the other stuffing ingredients. Put the stuffing into the herrings and place in a baking dish. Top with the half tablespoon melted margarine. Cover the dish with a lid or with margarine paper. Bake for 25 minutes in a preheated oven set to 190°C (375°F), Gas Mark 5. Serve hot or cold with vegetables or salad.

### SAUSAGES IN CIDER

*Preparation time: 5 minutes*
*Cooking time: 20 or 35 minutes*
*(see method)*
*Quantity: 4 helpings*

The sausages obtainable during this period of the 1940s were singularly lacking in meat and flavour and often difficult to obtain, so it meant a queue at the butcher's. Sausages were unrationed, so gave another main dish. This was a good way to impart some taste to them.

1 lb (450 g) sausages
1 oz (25 g) cooking fat
    or margarine
1 onion, thinly sliced
2 dessert apples, cored and sliced
½ pint (300 ml) cider
salt and pepper

Prick the sausages. Melt the fat in a frying pan then add the sausages and cook steadily for 5 minutes, turning them so they brown on all sides. Stir in the onion and cook for 2 minutes then add the rest of the ingredients. Cover the pan and simmer for a good 10 minutes. Serve with mashed potatoes and cabbage.

If more convenient, brown the sauages in the frying pan, add the onions, as above, then transfer to a casserole. Heat the apples with the cider in the frying pan then spoon over the sausages. Cover the dish and bake for 25 minutes in a preheated oven set to 190°C (375°F), Gas Mark 5.

### CHEESE AND TOMATO CHARLOTTE

*Preparation time: 15 minutes*
*Cooking time: 30 minutes*
*Quantity: 4 helpings*

This recipe is a good way of using up various rather hard pieces of cheese.

4 large slices bread
2 oz (50 g) cooking fat or
    dripping (see Variations, right)
1 pint (600 ml) jar bottled
    tomatoes
6 oz (175 g) cheese, grated
1 medium onion, finely
    chopped or grated
1 tablespoon chopped parsley
salt and pepper

**For the sauce:**
liquid from tomatoes
water (see method)
1 level tablespoon cornflour
1 tablespoon chopped chives
1 tablespoon chopped parsley
1 teaspoon made mustard
few drops Worcestershire sauce

Cut the bread into neat fingers of uniform size. Melt the fat or dripping in a frying pan and fry the bread until brown and crisp on both sides.

Drain the tomatoes, retaining the liquid. Mix the tomatoes with the cheese, onion, parsley and seasoning.

Preheat the oven to 190°C (375°F), Gas Mark 5. Put half the bread into a pie dish or casserole. Top with the cheese and tomato mixture then the rest of the fried bread. Bake for 20–25 minutes.

Meanwhile, make the sauce. Measure the tomato liquid and add enough water to make up to ½ pint (300 ml). Blend with the cornflour. Pour into a saucepan and stir over a medium heat until thickened. Add the herbs, mustard, Worcestershire sauce and any extra seasoning required. Serve the sauce separately.

**VARIATIONS**

If short of fat or dripping, crisp the bread in the oven before making this dish. Use fresh tomatoes instead of bottled ones. Cook until tender then strain and continue as in the recipe.

BISCUITS *would* KEEP YOU GOING...

# SUMMER BEETROOT SOUP

*Preparation time: 15 minutes*
*Cooking time: 10 minutes*
*Quantity: 4 helpings*

This soup is particularly good when young cooked beetroot are available. Yeast extract (Marmite) was used to add flavour to many dishes for this was often available in 1945.

about l0 oz (300 g) cooked beetroot, peeled and grated or finely chopped
bunch spring onions, chopped
1½ pints (900 ml) water
½ teaspoon Marmite, or to taste
salt and pepper
1 teaspoon vinegar

Put all the ingredients into a saucepan, being sparing with the salt for the yeast extract is salty. Simmer for 10 minutes.

**VARIATION**
Omit the Marmite and use a stock cube instead.

**A MODERN TOUCH**
Serve the soup topped with yogurt.

# TRIPE MORNAY

*Preparation time: 20 minutes*
*Cooking time: 1 hour*
*Quantity: 4 helpings*

Tripe has always been an acquired taste in Britain, and is more popular in the north of England than in the south. It was unrationed meat, so many people would seize the opportunity to buy it on the rare occasions it was available.

1 lb (450 g) tripe
water (see method)
2 medium onions,
    thinly sliced
salt and pepper
few drops vinegar

**For the sauce:**
1 oz (25 g) margarine
1 oz (25 g) plain flour
¼ pint (150 ml) milk
2 oz (50 g) cheese, grated

Wash the tripe in plenty of cold water then cut into neat 2 inch (5 cm) squares. Put into a saucepan; cover with cold water. Bring the water to the boil, strain the tripe and discard the liquid. This is 'blanching' the meat, to give it a better colour and flavour.

Place the tripe and onions in a saucepan, add just enough water to cover, a little seasoning and the vinegar. Cover the pan and simmer for 4–5 minutes. Strain the tripe and onions, retaining 7 fl oz (200 ml) of the liquid from the pan.

In a separate pan, heat the margarine for the sauce, stir in the flour, then the milk. Bring to the boil and cook until thickened. Spoon the tripe, onions and reserved liquid into the thick sauce. Heat gently then stir in the cheese and adjust the seasoning. Serve with creamed potatoes and mixed cooked root vegetables.

**VARIATIONS**
**Tripe au Gratin:** Spoon the tripe mixture into a flameproof dish and top with a little grated cheese and soft breadcrumbs. Place under a preheated grill or in a moderately hot oven until the top is crisp and golden brown.

# WILTSHIRE MEAT CAKES

*Preparation time: 10 minutes*
*Cooking time: 15 minutes*
*Quantity: 4 helpings*

These were a favourite summer dish when home-grown tomatoes were available. Bottled tomatoes were rather too moist.

2 large tomatoes, skinned
    and chopped
8 oz (225 g) minced beef
8 oz (225 g) sausagemeat
½ teaspoon paprika
1 oz (25 g) soft breadcrumbs
1 tablespoon chopped parsley
1 egg
salt and pepper

**For frying:**
1 oz (25 g) dripping or fat

Mix the tomatoes with all the other ingredients. Form into 8 small round fairly flat cakes. Heat the dripping or fat in a large frying pan. Cook the cakes rapidly for 2 minutes on either side then lower the heat and cook steadily for 11 minutes. Serve with creamed potatoes and a green vegetable or cold with a salad.

**Let's** use some of our points to solve the pudding problem. For some men and most children it's the "afters" that make the meal.

## GINGER RHUBARB CRISP

*Preparation time: 20 minutes*
*Cooking time: 30 minutes*
*Quantity: 4 helpings*

1 lb (450 g) rhubarb,
 trimmed weight
2 oz (50 g) cooking
 dates, chopped
2 oz (50 g) sugar,
 preferably Demerara
2 tablespoons water

**For the topping:**
2 oz (50 g) margarine
1 oz (25 g) sugar,
 preferably granulated
1 tablespoon golden syrup
1–2 teaspoons ground ginger,
 or to taste
4 oz (115 g) rolled oats

Cut the rhubarb into 1½ inch (3.75 cm) lengths and put into a pie dish with the dates, sugar and water.

For the topping, melt the margarine with the sugar and syrup in a saucepan. Stir in the ginger and rolled oats. Mix thoroughly then spoon over the rhubarb; spread flat with a damp (not wet) knife. Make sure all the fruit is covered.

Bake in a preheated oven set to 180°C (350°F), Gas Mark 4 for 30 minutes.

### VARIATIONS

Use cooking apples instead of rhubarb. In this case, precook the apples for 10 minutes before adding the topping.

Other fruits can be used when in season. Soft fruits do not need precooking before adding the topping.

## NORFOLK PUDDING

*Preparation time: 15 minutes*
*Cooking time: 40 minutes*
*Quantity: 4–6 helpings*

**For the batter:**
4 oz (115 g) plain flour
pinch salt
1 level tablespoon dried egg
 powder with 2 tablespoons
 water or 1 fresh egg
½ pint (scant 300 ml) milk
 or milk and water

**For the fruit base:**
½ oz (15 g) fat
1 lb (450 g) cooking apples
2 tablespoons dried fruit,
 if available
2 oz (50 g) sugar

**For the topping:**
little sugar

For the batter, sift the flour with the salt and dried egg powder then add the rest of the liquid and beat until a smooth batter. If using a fresh egg, add it to the sifted flour and salt.

Preheat the oven to 220°C (425°F), Gas Mark 7. Put the fat into a large pie dish or casserole and heat for a few minutes in the oven. Peel, core and thinly slice the apples, add to the hot fat with the dried fruit and sugar. Mix well, cover the dish and return to the oven for 5 minutes. Uncover the dish, pour the batter over the fruit and bake for 25–30 minutes, or until well-risen and brown. Top with sugar and serve at once.

## GYPSY TART

*Preparation time: 25 minutes*
*Cooking time: 35–40 minutes*
*Quantity: 4–6 helpings*

There are several different recipes for this tart. This is the one made when rationing was still in force in 1945. Evaporated milk was highly prized. It was obtainable on the points system (the system under which rationing was controlled; everyone had an allowance of 16 points a month).

**For the shortcrust pastry:**
6 oz (175 g) plain flour
pinch salt
3 oz (85 g) fat
water, to bind

**For the filling:**
1 oz (25 g) butter or margarine
2 oz (50 g) sugar,
 preferably Demerara
1 level tablespoon golden syrup
1 egg
¼ pint (150 ml) evaporated milk

For the pastry, sift the flour and salt into a bowl, rub in the fat and add sufficient water to make a dough with a firm rolling consistency. Roll out and use to line an 8 inch (20 cm) flan tin or ring on an upturned baking tray.

Preheat the oven to 200°C (400°F), Gas Mark 6 and bake the pastry blind (See Apricot and Lemon Flan, page 47) for 15 minutes. Take the pastry shell out of the oven and lower the oven temperature to 160°C (325°F), Gas Mark 3.

While the pastry is cooking, prepare the filling. Cream the butter or margarine with the sugar and syrup. Beat the egg and add to the creamed mixture then slowly stir in the evaporated milk. Spoon into the partially baked pastry case, return to the oven and bake for a further 20–25 minutes, or until the filling is firm. Serve cold.

# ★1946★

**D**URING THIS YEAR **rationing became more stringent again. Even children were affected when the sweet ration, normally 12 oz (350 g) a month, was halved. There were cuts in the meagre allowances of some other foods and in July bread was put on ration. This caused a great uproar, for at no time during the war had this happened.**

There were queues at bakers' shops and one heard more about the British Housewives League. This was formed by angry women who felt that the Government was not doing enough to improve the quantity and variety of foods available. Other women's organizations joined in the protests and so did building, foundry and farm workers. Their protests arose from the fact that the miners' meat ration was increased but not those of other people doing heavy work.

Fuel supplies were bad and fuel cuts were quite normal. This made cooking meals even more challenging.

In spite of all the problems, the food manufacturer, Bird's Eye, produced a frozen food that would be popular for many decades to come. I was asked to present their frozen Fish Fingers to the media at a hotel in London. The company also planted their first peas in 1946, though it would be several years before they were ready to be frozen and sold to the public.

An important radio programme was launched in October 1946. This was *Woman's Hour* which was, interestingly enough, at first compèred by a man.

An even more exciting event was the restart of BBC Television. There had been experimental transmissions before the war but now the BBC were launching their programmes for the future. The hours of viewing were severely limited.

The very few members of the public who were fortunate enough to view television were fascinated to see ballet and plays and some cooking. The cookery programmes were given by Philip Harben.

The good food news was that small supplies of imported fruits were coming into the country. Bananas were among the first of these. Adults, who remembered this fruit with delight, promised their children a great treat when they tasted their first banana. Not all children were enthusiastic, particularly if they tried to eat the fruit with the skin on, as happened from time to time. Dried bananas also began to make an appearance about this time. Clementines were imported for the first time. Whale meat, a food Britain was to hear more about in the coming year or so, was served at a special luncheon in London. Poultry, which had been almost unobtainable for town-dwellers during the war years, became more available but the price was increased to an unbelievably high 5s 4d (over 25 p) per 1 lb (450 g).

Many of the chickens available were elderly boiling fowls, who had given good service in laying eggs, and now that time had ended they were killed and sold as boiling fowls. These needed prolonged cooking to make them tender. The good thing was their bodies contained a good deal of natural fat. This meant that if the birds were simmered (not boiled as the name suggests) you obtained good tasting tender chicken, plus excellent stock with a thin layer of precious fat on top which could be used in cooking.

## SAUSAGE SAVOURY BALLS

*Preparation time: 15 minutes*
*Cooking time: 15 minutes*
*Quantity: 8 balls*

These make a good cold dish to take on a picnic, or they can be served hot with mixed vegetables.

1 oz (25 g) cooking fat
1 medium onion, finely chopped
1 small dessert apple, peeled, cored and grated
12 oz (350 g) sausagemeat
2 oz (50 g) soft breadcrumbs

**For the coating:**
little milk or beaten egg
1–1½ oz (25–40 g) crisp breadcrumbs

**For frying:**
1–2 oz (25–50 g) dripping

Melt the fat in a pan, add the onion and cook for 5 minutes, taking care it does not brown. Blend with all the other ingredients and form into 8 balls. Coat the balls with milk or egg then roll them in crisp breadcrumbs.

Melt the dripping for frying in the pan until hot and fry the sausage balls quickly until brown on all sides. Lower the heat and cook for a further 10 minutes.

### VARIATION
If bread is scarce, omit the crumbs in the mixture and use the same weight of mashed potato. Simply coat the balls in seasoned flour instead of the crisp breadcrumbs. In this case, the milk or egg is not necessary.

## BEEF AND PRUNE HOTPOT

*Preparation time: 25 minutes, plus soaking time for prunes*
*Cooking time: 2 hours*
*Quantity: 4 helpings*

As fuel cuts were usual during 1946, dishes like this would be cooked whenever fuel was available and reheated as required. I remember being asked to warn people on *Woman's Hour* that meat dishes like this must be thoroughly reheated before serving. Onions were not plentiful during the winter months and leeks were often substituted, although the severe frosts at the end of 1946 made even these difficult to buy.

4 oz (115 g) prunes
water
little Marmite or ½ stock cube
8–12 oz (225–350 g) stewing beef
1¼–1½ lb (550–675 g) potatoes, thinly sliced
2 onions or 3 leeks, thinly sliced
salt and pepper
1 oz (25 g) margarine

Put the prunes into a container, cover with plenty of water and leave to soak for at least 12 hours. Strain the prunes but save ¼ pint (150 ml) of the water, adding a very little Marmite or the stock cube to it to give more flavour. Cut the beef into thin strips.

Arrange a layer of potatoes and onions or leeks in a casserole; season lightly. Add the meat and prunes, then the rest of the onions or leeks with more seasoning. End with a neat covering of potatoes. Pour the prune liquid over the ingredients. Top with small dabs of margarine. Do not cover the casserole at this stage, as the lid could stick to the margarine.

Put the casserole into a preheated oven set to 160°C (325°F), Gas Mark 3 and heat for 15 minutes, then put on the lid and cook for a further 1½ hours. Remove the lid for the final 15 minutes so the potatoes brown slightly.

## PLUM DUMPLINGS

*Preparation time: 25 minutes*
*Cooking time: 25 minutes*
*Quantity: 4 helpings*

These satisfying dumplings were really very delicious. The plums should be just ripe, but firm enough to split. The plums should not be too large for the amount of pastry given.

8 plums
4 teaspoons plum jam
water (see method)

**For the dumplings:**
8 oz (225 g) self-raising flour or plain flour with 2 teaspoons baking powder
pinch salt
2 oz (50 g) shredded suet or margarine
1 oz (25 g) sugar
water, to bind

**For the coating:**
little sugar

Halve the plums, carefully remove the stones then sandwich the halves together with the jam. Bring about 2 pints (1.2 litres) of water to the boil in a large saucepan.

For the dumplings, sift the flour, or flour and baking powder, and the salt into a bowl, add the suet or rub in the margarine. Stir in the sugar and then gradually add sufficient water to make a mixture with a soft rolling consistency. Roll out to about ¼ inch (6 mm) thick then cut into 8 portions. Moisten the edges of each portion of dough with water and wrap around the plums; seal the joins firmly.

Drop the dumplings into the boiling water, allowing the water to boil briskly for at least 8 minutes so the pastry rises, then lower the heat to a steady simmer for about 17 minutes. When cooked, remove the dumplings from the water with a perforated spoon or fish slice. Dust with sugar and serve hot.

## CARROT AND POTATO CHOWDER

*Preparation time: 25 minutes*
*Cooking time: 25–30 minutes*
*Quantity: 4 helpings*

Many people had learned quite a lot of American recipes from meeting service men and women from the USA. Chowder, a very thick and satisfying American soup, was ideal for the extreme cold of the winter of 1946.

1 lb (450 g) potatoes
12 oz (350 g) carrots
2 large onions
2 bacon rashers
   (optional)
1 oz (25 g) cooking fat
   or margarine
¾ pint (450 ml) water
salt and pepper
1–2 teaspoons mustard
   powder
½ pint (300 ml) milk
2 tablespoons chopped
   parsley or watercress
   leaves

Peel the vegetables then cut the potatoes and carrots into neat dice about ⅓ inch (8 mm) in size; do not make them smaller, as they would break in cooking. The onions can be finely chopped. Remove the rinds from the bacon and dice the rashers.

Melt the fat or margarine and the bacon rinds, add the onions and cook gently for 5 minutes. Remove the bacon rinds and add the diced bacon; cook for a few more minutes then pour in the water. Bring to the boil, add a little seasoning and the carrots. Cook for 5 minutes then put in the potatoes. Continue cooking slowly for 15 minutes, watching the vegetables to ensure they do not break. Blend the mustard powder with the milk, add to the soup and heat through.

Top with the parsley or watercress just before serving.

### VARIATION
Use a mixture of vegetables instead of just the carrots, onions and potatoes.

## WOMAN'S HOUR

The start of *Woman's Hour* roused enormous interest and the programme had very high listening figures. I was asked to take part in the programme on its second day and not only gave a recipe for a seasonal stew but also had to answer questions on the air about sponges and baked custards from cooks who were listening to the programme: surprisingly, these were male cooks from the Royal Navy! Even at the beginning of its life *Woman's Hour* appealed to men as well as women.

'WOMAN'S HOUR'

Alan Ivimey introduces Marion Cutler 'Answering Your Questions — Pensions'; Marguerite Patten with today's recipe; 'Housewives' Choice' of gramophone records; and the current serial story, Stanley Weyman's 'Under the Red Robe'.

At 2 p.m.

'WOMAN'S HOUR'

AT 2 p.m.

*A daily programme of music, advice, and entertainment for the home*

Today, Alan Ivimey introduces Mary Manton on 'Mother's Midday Meal'; Kay Beattie on 'Putting Your Best Face Forward'; 'Housewives' Choice' of gramophone records; and the current serial story, Stanley Weyman's 'Under the Red Robe'

'WOMAN'S HOUR'

Alan Ivimey introduces a doctor on 'Your Health Problems'; Elizabeth Crocker with today's recipe; 'Housewives' Choice' of gramophone records: and the current serial story, Stanley Weyman's 'Under the Red Robe.' The Rt. Hon. Margaret Bondfield, J.P., LL.D., Deborah Kerr, film actress, and Mrs. Elsie May Crump, housewife of Chorlton-cum-Hardy, give their reactions to yesterday's programmes

'WOMAN'S HOUR'

Alan Ivimey introduces Elizabeth Dennis on 'Your Winter Clothes'; Godfrey Winn on 'What is a Happy Woman?'; 'Housewives' Choice' of gramophone records; and the current serial story, Stanley Weyman's 'Under the Red Robe'

AT 2.0 p.m.

## 'Television is Here Again

Tomorrow afternoon the BBC Television Service resumes its daily transmission from the Alexandra Palace after an interval of more than six years. Before the war the Alexandra Palace station led the world in television, and, on the eve of the reopening, this programme explains how a television service is run, recalls what pre-war television was like in Britain, and outlines what viewers will see in the coming months. Written by Robert Barr. Produced by John Glyn-Jones. Tonight at 9.30

*G. M. GARRO-JONES, M.P., Chairman of the Television Advisory Committee, who broadcasts at 9.15*

## SAVOURY BREAST OF MUTTON

*Preparation time: 25 minutes*
*Cooking time: 1¾–2 hours*
*Quantity: 4 helpings*

Mutton was still available in 1946. Today, one could substitute 2 smaller breasts of lamb in this recipe and shorten the cooking time to 1¼–1½ hours. Any fat left after cooking the meat would be carefully saved.

1 large breast of mutton

**For the stuffing:**
1 large cooking apple, peeled, cored and finely diced
1 medium leek, thinly sliced
8 oz (225 g) sausagemeat
2 tablespoons chopped parsley
1 teaspoon chopped mint
½ teaspoon chopped thyme
salt and pepper

Cut away the bones from the meat (use them to make a good stock).

Blend all the ingredients for the stuffing together. Spread over the breast and roll up firmly. Tie with string. Put into a preheated oven set to 160°C (325°F), Gas Mark 3 and cook until tender. Serve with jacket potatoes and green vegetables.

**WHY JAM IN CANS?**
There is a shortage of jam jars. To keep supplies going a lot of jam is being put in cans. When you open the can there is no need to turn the jam out — it will keep just as well in the can.

## DAILY SERIAL

*Dick Barton begins his career as a special agent this evening at 6.45. You can follow his adventures at the same time every day from—*

**MONDAY TO FRIDAY**

## CHESTNUT CREAMS

*Preparation time: 25 minutes*
*Cooking time: 30 minutes*
*Quantity: 4–6 helpings*

My memory of hot chestnuts goes back to 1946–1947 when we had a terribly cold winter that lasted for many weeks. A man had a barrow with a stove on from which he sold roasted chestnuts just outside Harrods, where I was working. I used to buy a bag of these several times a week. They warmed my hands as I sat in the train and ate them. Chestnuts were on sale that winter and this dessert was a great favourite in my home.

1 lb (450 g) chestnuts
1 teaspoon vanilla essence
3 tablespoons apricot jam
2 tablespoons water
1 oz (25 g) sugar
7½ fl oz (250 ml) unsweetened evaporated milk (whipped as page 59)

Wash the chestnuts then slit the skins on the rounded side in the shape of a cross. Put into boiling water, boil steadily for 10 minutes then remove from the water and take off the outer shells and inner brown skins while still warm. Put the chestnuts into enough boiling water to cover, add the vanilla essence and simmer for 10–15 minutes, or until soft. Sieve or mash most of the nuts, saving 2 or 3 for decoration.

Heat the jam with the water and sugar, add the chestnut purée and blend well. Leave until quite cold. Fold into the whipped evaporated milk and spoon into glasses. Top with halved nuts.

**A MODERN TOUCH**
Use unsweetened canned chestnut purée and whipped cream.

*"Don't talk to me about Food . . .*

## HOME-MADE BREAD

*Preparation time: 30 minutes, plus time for proving*
*Cooking time: 40 minutes*
*Quantity: 2 loaves*

When bread became rationed, many people who had never attempted to make bread before, bought yeast and started to bake. Fresh yeast was difficult to obtain but tins of dried yeast were available. The method used here is for fresh or dried yeast; see the 'modern touch' at the end of the recipe for a note about using quick-acting yeast.

1½ lb (675 g) plain flour
½ teaspoon salt
¾ pint (450 ml) water
½ oz (15 g) fresh yeast or
  2 teaspoons dried yeast
  with 1 teaspoon sugar

Sift the flour and salt into a mixing bowl. Heat the water until just warm.

If using fresh yeast, cream it then add the water and leave until the surface is frothy. If using dried yeast, add it with the sugar to the water, top with a sprinkling of the flour and leave until frothy. This takes 12–15 minutes.

Make a well in the centre of the flour, pour in the yeast liquid and mix well. Turn out on to a floured board and knead. Use the heel of your hand (base of the palm) with a pulling and stretching movement. You can tell if the dough is sufficiently kneaded by firmly pressing it with a finger. If the impression comes out then the dough is ready for the next stage. If it stays in then continue to knead and test again.

When sufficiently kneaded, shape the dough into a ball and return to the bowl. Cover with a cloth and leave in a warm place to prove (rise) until double the original size. In an airing cupboard it will take about 1 hour; if left at room temperature, it will take about 2 hours.

Turn the dough on to a floured surface and knead again (this process is known as 'knocking back').

Form the dough into 2 round loaves and place on a baking tray to prove again until almost twice the original size. Cover it very lightly with a cloth. This stage will take about 45–60 minutes at room temperature.

Meanwhile, preheat the oven to 220°C (425°F), Gas Mark 7. Bake the bread for 35–40 minutes. To test if the loaves are baked, remove them from the tray and tap the base. They should sound hollow.

### VARIATIONS

If you want to use only 1 lb (450 g) flour, use ½ pint (300 ml) water but the same amount of yeast. Reduce the salt slightly.

If you use 3 lb (1.35 kg) flour, use double the amount of fresh or dried yeast.

Rub about 1 oz (25 g) cooking fat or lard or margarine into the flour and salt. This gives a more moist bread.

### A MODERN TOUCH

Use strong instead of plain flour. This was not on sale in 1946.

Use the modern quick-acting yeast which can be mixed with the flour. Follow the packet instructions.

## MORE KINDS OF BREAD

Having made ordinary bread, you can vary it in many ways. When more ingredients became available, rather more elaborate breads were made. The following recipes are based on the Home-made Bread, left:

**Cheese Bread:** Add 2 oz (50 g) finely grated cheese to the flour. Flavour the flour with a good shake of pepper and a pinch of mustard powder as well as the salt.

**Fruit Bread:** Add 2–3 oz (50–85 g) dried fruit to the flour. ½–1 teaspoon allspice can be sifted with the flour.

**Herb Bread:** Add 2 tablespoons chopped parsley and 1 tablespoon chopped chives to the flour.

**Malt Bread:** Add 2 tablespoons malt extract to the other ingredients. This bread is better mixed with milk, or milk and water, rather than all water. If using liquid malt (rather like a thick syrup), you will need slightly less liquid than given in the recipe. If using powdered malt or Ovaltine (a good source of malt), use the same amount of liquid as in the basic recipe.

**Rolls:** Make the bread dough; when it has been proved, divide it into about 18 portions and form into rounds or the desired shapes. Put on baking trays and allow to prove again for about 25 minutes. Bake in a preheated oven set to 230°C (450°F), Gas Mark 8 for 12–15 minutes.

## BAKING POWDER ROLLS

*Preparation time: 5 minutes*
*Cooking time: 12–15 minutes*
*Quantity: 8–10 rolls*

These were often made during the time of bread rationing. The basic recipe here can be varied by adding chopped parsley, or other herbs, for a savoury roll or a tablespoon of sugar to make a sweet roll.

8 oz (225 g) self-raising flour
   or plain flour with 2 teaspoons
   baking powder
good pinch salt
½–1 oz (15–25 g) margarine
   milk, or milk and water, to mix

Preheat the oven to 220°C (425°F), Gas Mark 7. Sift the flour, or flour and baking powder, and the salt into a bowl. Rub in the margarine and blend with the milk, or milk and water, to a soft dough. Take off small pieces and form into rolls or finger shapes. Place on an ungreased baking tray and cook for 12–15 minutes. Eat when fresh.

☆ ☆ ☆ ☆ ☆ ☆ ☆ ☆ ☆ ☆ ☆ ☆ ☆ ☆ ☆ ☆ ☆ ☆ ☆ ☆ ☆ ☆ ☆ ☆ ☆

## SWISS BUNS

People who had never used yeast before became very enthusiastic about their home baking. They realised that if they had hungry children yeast buns could be made with little or no fat. These buns are based on the Home-made Bread dough (see page 28).

To make 7 or 8 Swiss Buns, take off about a quarter of the yeast dough after it has proved. Form into finger shapes 4 inches (10 cm) long and put on to baking trays, leaving room for the buns to spread slightly as well as rise. Prove for about 25 minutes, or until well risen, then bake in a an preheated oven set to 230°C (450°F), Gas Mark 8 for 12 minutes. Allow to cool then cover with a thin layer of icing made by mixing sifted icing sugar with a little water. Eat the buns while they are fresh.

Make the Swiss Buns more interesting by kneading grated lemon or orange zest into the dough and mixing the icing sugar with the fruit juice or sifting some cocoa powder with the icing sugar.

☆ ☆ ☆ ☆ ☆ ☆ ☆ ☆ ☆ ☆ ☆ ☆ ☆ ☆ ☆ ☆ ☆ ☆ ☆ ☆ ☆ ☆ ☆ ☆ ☆

# RING DOUGHNUTS

No-one had sufficient fat to cook proper round doughnuts. These doughnuts, based on the Home-made Bread (see page 28) are fairly flat, so they can be fried in the minimum of cooking fat. To make ring doughnuts, allow the bread dough to prove, then take off the amount required. Roll out on a lightly floured board and cut into rings with two different-sized cutters. Place on a baking tray and allow to prove for about 25 minutes, or until well risen.

Heat 1–2 oz (25–50g) fat in a frying pan and put in the doughnuts. Fry quickly on either side until golden in colour then reduce the heat and cook steadily for about 5 minutes. Lift out and drain on crumpled tissue paper, if you have it (use kitchen paper today), then roll in a little sugar.

## MALT AND FRUIT BREAD

*Preparation time: 15 minutes*
*Cooking time: 1 hour*
*Quantity: 1 loaf*

In 1946, many parents gave their children extract of malt for health reasons; it also made an excellent flavouring for a baking powder bread. The recipe can be varied by using powdered malt or Ovaltine (see Variation, right).

2 level tablespoons malt extract
2 level tablespoons golden syrup
2–4 oz (50–115 g) dried fruit
5 tablespoons milk or milk and water
8 oz (225 g) self raising flour or plain flour with 2 teaspoons baking powder
½ level teaspoon bicarbonate of soda
pinch salt
1 egg

Grease and flour a 1½ lb (675 g) loaf tin. Preheat the oven to 180°C (350°F), Gas Mark 4. Put the malt, syrup and milk, or milk and water, into a saucepan and heat gently until melted. Add the fruit to the hot mixture and leave until cold.

Sift the flour, or flour and baking powder, with the bicarbonate of soda and salt. Add the malt mixture then the egg. Beat well and spoon into the prepared tin. Bake for 50–60 minutes or until firm to the touch. Cool in the tin for 5 minutes then turn out.

### VARIATION

Use powdered malt or Ovaltine and mix this with the flour. Melt the syrup with ¼ pint (150 ml) milk as in the recipe above, then add the fruit. Allow to cool then continue as the recipe.

## HALFPAY PUDDING

This pudding is a traditional English recipe, adapted to the lack of fat in 1946. When bread rationing began in July it would not have been made. The high percentage of breadcrumbs makes it a very light pudding.

*Preparation time: 15 minutes*
*Cooking time: 1½ hours*
*Quantity: 4 helpings*

2 oz (50g) self-raising flour with ½ teaspoon baking powder or plain flour with 1 teaspoon baking powder
4 oz (115 g) soft breadcrumbs
pinch salt
2 oz (50 g) shredded suet
1–2 oz (25–50g) sultanas
1–2 oz (25–50g) currants
2 tablespoons golden syrup
little milk

**For the sauce:**
3 tablespoons golden syrup

Sift the flour and baking powder into a bowl, add the rest of the ingredients, using enough milk to make a mixture with a sticky consistency.

Put the golden syrup for the sauce into a greased 1½ pint (900 ml) basin and add the pudding mixture. Cover tightly and steam over boiling water for 40 minutes, then lower the heat to simmering for a further 45 minutes. Serve hot.

### VARIATION

If suet is not available, use melted margarine instead.

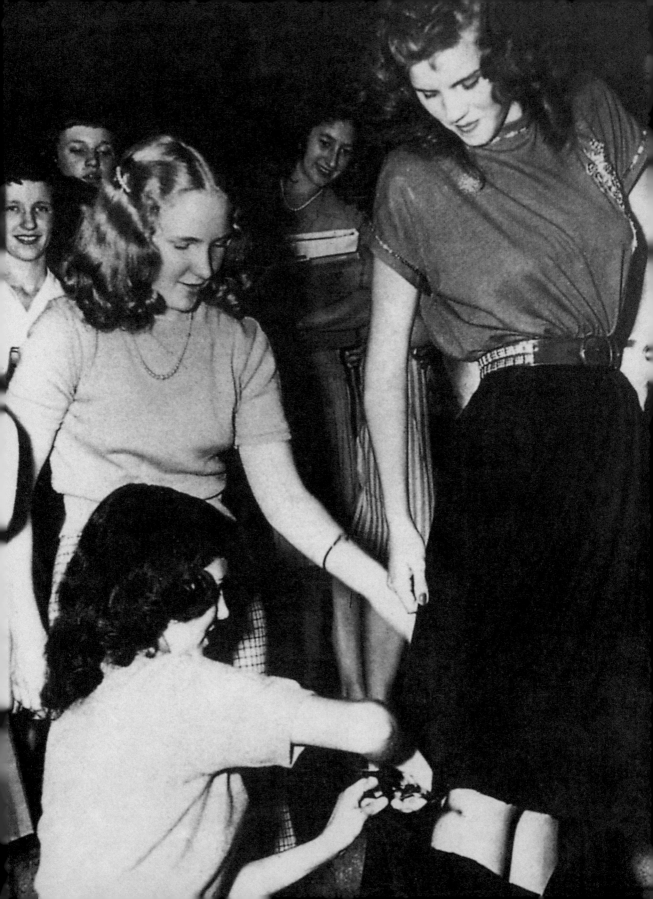

# ★1947★

THIS YEAR IS memorable because of the exceptionally long and cold winter. It started in 1946 and continued throughout the spring of 1947. Frozen pipes were a feature in many houses, for few had central heating or good protection against frost. Transport was bad due to the weather.

Bread rationing continued during this year until July but, apart from rationing, supplies of food and coal were difficult because of transport problems.

The Government was anxious to increase our exports, most of which had been lost during the war years, so women were being persuaded to work in factories and elsewhere.

Lord Woolton was honoured at the Mansion House for his work at the Ministry of Food during the war years and praised for the effectiveness of the Ministry's Food Facts which gave information and recipes to inspire cooks.

The showing of Christian Dior's New Look fashions in the spring created a great deal of excitement for women. At last we were seeing glamorous and flattering styles, so different from the Utility clothes of recent years.

The engagement of Princess Elizabeth to Prince Philip Mountbatten and their wedding celebrations later in the year were inspirng and joyous events. The splendour of the pageantry and ceremonial of the wedding day was like a breath of new life in the midst of the somewhat dreary and uninspired existence of these early post-war years. The Government announced that extra clothing coupons would be allocated for the wedding dress but that Princess Elizabeth would not have a trousseau due to the clothing restrictions.

Some gadgets for the home began to appear on the market but not as many as people wanted. Refrigerators were being made but many went for export. Icing pipes and syringes became very popular, although we really had no extra sugar for piped icing, and cream was still unavailable. Mock cream or butter icing (generally made with margarine) were used to decorate cakes. Some nuts came on the market in time for Christmas. Whale meat, which was not on ration, became more readily available and the Ministry of Food gave suggestions and recipes for using it: I have included two recipes using whale meat in this chapter.

In November, the first women's television magazine programme was started by the BBC. I was the television cook on this programme and for many years to come. My first recipe before the cameras was 8-Minute Doughnuts, the recipe for which I have included here. Philip Harben had preceded me as a television chef and from time to time both of us appeared on the same programme.

In May, there were reports that the Ministry of Food was thinking of getting supplies of horsemeat to augment the meat ration. Most people viewed this with horror and fortunately nothing came of the idea.

A little extra meat, sugar and sweets were made available for Christmas 1947. The extra rations were very welcome, for this had been a difficult year with bad weather lasting to the spring and shortages of many foods.

For some families this was the first Christmas when everyone was together. In 1946 many men and women were still serving abroad in the armed forces.

# WHALE MEAT

Over the years I have been asked repeatedly to describe whale meat. Nowadays, we would be horrified at the thought of using these magnificent and protected mammals for food, but in 1946 we were anxious to have more generous helpings of meat so the Government were ready to persuade us to avail ourselves of this unrationed 'bonus', which became better known in 1947. Whale meat looked like a cross between liver and beef, with a firm texture. Because the raw meat had a strong and very unpleasant smell of fish and stale oil, I loathed handling whale meat to create recipes or to use in my demonstrations to the public. When cooked, the smell was not apparent.

The Ministry of Food's *Food and Nutrition* booklet for September 1947 included advice on preparing and cooking whale meat: 'Tests were made in our Experimental Kitchens using the best cuts of whale meat, which was bought in its frozen state, thawed out slowly and treated as ordinary beef steak. It was found that although the raw meat looked somewhat unattractive and is not very satisfactory grilled or cooked as a joint, most people cannot distinguish it from beef steak when it is finely cut before cooking or mixed with strong flavours.'

## HAMBURGERS

*Preparation time: 15 minutes*
*Cooking time: 15 or 30 minutes*
*(see method)*
*Quantity: 4 helpings*

I demonstrated this recipe at Harrods, which shows that the liking for hamburgers in Britain goes a long way back.

1 large potato, grated
1 medium onion, finely chopped
12 oz (350 g) minced whale
 meat or beef
1 teaspoon Worcestershire sauce
½–1 tablespoon chopped parsley
salt and pepper

**For the coating:**
crisp breadcrumbs (optional)

Mix all the ingredients together, form into round cakes. These can be rolled in crisp breadcrumbs, although this is not essential.

Either grill for 15 minutes or bake on a greased baking tray for 30 minutes in a preheated oven set to 190°C (375°F), Gas Mark 5.

When fat is available, the Hamburgers can be fried.

## HUNGARIAN GOULASH

*Preparation time: 20 minutes*
*Cooking time: 2 hours*
*Quantity: 4 helpings*

This recipe comes from the Ministry of Food's *Food and Nutrition* booklet for September 1947, in which they gave advice on using whale meat.

2 lb (900 g) onions, sliced *
1¹/₂–2 oz (40–50g) dripping
  or cooking fat
4 level teaspoons paprika
2–3 teaspoons salt **
¹/₄ level teaspoon pepper
1 lb (450 g) whale meat, cut
  into 1 inch (2.5 cm) cubes

* The high proportion of onions .is because at this time of the year British onions were plentiful.

** Ministry recipes tend to be generous with salt. No liquid is given in the ingredients but it was assumed one would cover the food with water or beef stock.

Fry the onions in the melted dripping or fat in a saucepan until pale golden brown, taking care not to let them burn. Add the seasonings and stir well. Place the meat in the pan with the other ingredients and the liquid. Cover the pan and simmer for 2 hours.

### VARIATIONS

Use stewing beef or boned neck of mutton or lamb instead of whale meat or mix two meats together in true Hungarian style, i.e. whale meat and pork, or beef and pork, or lamb and beef.

JOAN MARTIN MAY

*Recipes by the Ministry of Food.*
*Gardening Instructions by the Ministry of Agriculture.*

## FOOD FACTS

*WHAT'S LEFT IN THE LARDER?*

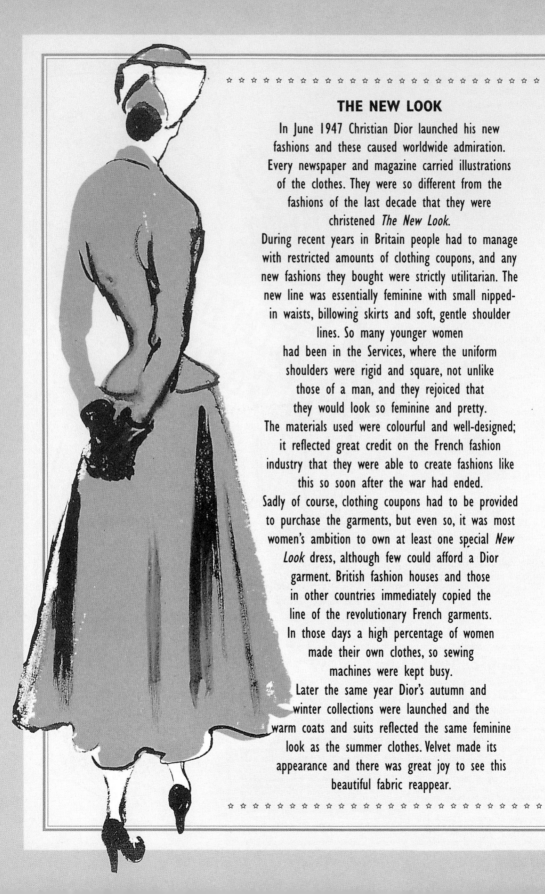

## THE NEW LOOK

In June 1947 Christian Dior launched his new fashions and these caused worldwide admiration. Every newspaper and magazine carried illustrations of the clothes. They were so different from the fashions of the last decade that they were christened *The New Look.*

During recent years in Britain people had to manage with restricted amounts of clothing coupons, and any new fashions they bought were strictly utilitarian. The new line was essentially feminine with small nipped-in waists, billowing skirts and soft, gentle shoulder lines. So many younger women had been in the Services, where the uniform shoulders were rigid and square, not unlike those of a man, and they rejoiced that they would look so feminine and pretty.

The materials used were colourful and well-designed; it reflected great credit on the French fashion industry that they were able to create fashions like this so soon after the war had ended.

Sadly of course, clothing coupons had to be provided to purchase the garments, but even so, it was most women's ambition to own at least one special *New Look* dress, although few could afford a Dior garment. British fashion houses and those in other countries immediately copied the line of the revolutionary French garments. In those days a high percentage of women made their own clothes, so sewing machines were kept busy.

Later the same year Dior's autumn and winter collections were launched and the warm coats and suits reflected the same feminine look as the summer clothes. Velvet made its appearance and there was great joy to see this beautiful fabric reappear.

## HERRING AND EGG PIE

*Preparation time: 20 minutes*
*Cooking time: 40 minutes*
*Quantity: 4 helpings*

Fresh herrings were in good supply during the early part of 1947 – provided the bad weather allowed transport to distribute them. There had been disputes during the autumn of 1946, with many fishermen dissatisfied with the prices offered them by the Fishing Industry Board. Herrings were dumped back in the sea, an action which shocked the public, for wasting any food was considered a crime.

4 large fresh herrings
2–3 fresh tomatoes, sliced, or bottled tomatoes
2 tablespoons chopped parsley
2 tablespoons grated onion or finely chopped leek
2 eggs, hard-boiled (see Chicken Roll, page 39, for advice on hard-boiling reconstituted dried egg)
salt and pepper

**For the topping:**
1 lb (450 g) cooked potatoes
1 oz (25 g) margarine
2 tablespoons milk
2 oz (50 g) cheese, grated

Cut the flesh from the herrings into 1 inch (2.5 cm) dice. The roes should be finely chopped. Put in a pie dish with the sliced fresh tomatoes or well-drained bottled tomatoes, the parsley, and onion or leek; slice the eggs and add them, with a little seasoning.

For the topping, mash the potatoes with the margarine, milk, half the cheese and seasoning to taste. Spoon over the herring mixture. Top with the last of the cheese.

Bake in a preheated oven set to 190°C (375°F), Gas Mark 5 for 30 minutes. Serve hot.

**How to bone a herring before cooking**

1. Cut off head and remove the guts, retaining the roe. Then cut along the belly with a sharp knife or scissors.

2. Open fish gently, carefully loosening the small bones on each side of the backbone.

3. Starting at the head end, prise up backbone with thumb and forefinger and pull steadily away from the flesh.

## DUTCH MEAT PUDDING

*Preparation time: 15 minutes*
*Cooking time: 1 hour*
*Quantity: 4 helpings*

This was a way of using left-over cooked potatoes. The wartime spirit of 'waste not' still applied long after rationing ended.

4 oz (115 g) soft breadcrumbs
3 tablespoons milk
1 large onion, finely chopped or grated
2 large tomatoes, skinned and chopped
8 oz (225 g) cooked potatoes, mashed
8 oz (225 g) minced raw beef
1 egg
2 tablespoons finely chopped parsley
2 teaspoons Worcestershire sauce
salt and pepper

Put the breadcrumbs into a basin with the milk, leave soaking for 15 minutes then mix in all the other ingredients. Spoon into a 2 pint (1.2 litre) greased basin. Cover tightly and steam for 1 hour. Turn out and serve with sliced cooked beetroot.

**VARIATION**

This is a good way to use up cooked meat. Follow the recipe above but steam for only 40 minutes and add rather more onion, if possible.

## 8-MINUTE DOUGHNUTS

The reason I chose this recipe for my very first appearance
on television was because I was told that only a boiling ring
would be available. This meant I had to cook something in a
frying pan or saucepan. I had found this particular recipe popular
in demonstrations so repeated it before the cameras. The
'doughnuts' were fairly flat, rather like a fritter, for there was
insufficient fat to fry a thicker mixture. They have a pleasant taste
and were very popular with children. When these were made
originally I used more baking powder than in the recipe on the
right, even with self-raising flour, for the flour of 1947 was still
very heavy. During recent years paper for draining fried foods had
been unobtainable; now it was beginning to appear.

## 8-MINUTE DOUGHNUTS

*Preparation time: 4 minutes*
*Cooking time: 8 minutes*
*Quantity: 8 cakes*

8 oz (225 g) self-raising flour or
   plain flour with 2 teaspoons
   baking powder
2 tablespoons sugar
pinch salt
2 eggs
¼ pint (150 ml) milk

**For frying:**
2 oz (50 g) cooking fat

**For the coating:**
little sugar

Mix all the ingredients together to form a thick batter. Heat the fat and fry spoonfuls of the mixture for 8 minutes. Cook fairly quickly until golden brown on all sides then lower the heat to cook the mixture through to the centre.

Remove from the pan, drain on crumpled tissue paper (use kitchen paper today) then roll in sugar.

### VARIATIONS

Add 2 tablespoons sultanas to the mixture.

**Apple Doughnuts:** Add 1 peeled and grated cooking apple to the mixture and use 2 tablespoons less milk.

## SUMMER MEAT MOULD

*Preparation time: 20 minutes*
*Cooking time: 2 minutes*
*Quantity: 4–6 helpings*

After the terrible winter, the summer of 1947 seemed particularly good and cold dishes were required. This was a favourite recipe. A mixture of left-over cooked meats, beef plus ham or chicken and ham were favourites. Hand-operated mincing machines were a favourite kitchen appliance. Leaf gelatine had been used in homes, as well as in catering establishments, before the war but powdered gelatine, used in this recipe, had begun to appear.

½ pint (300 ml) tomato juice
2 teaspoons gelatine
12 oz (350 g) cooked meat,
   minced

## CHICKEN ROLL

*Preparation time: 30 minutes*
*Cooking time: 2 hours*
*Quantity: 8 helpings*

This is a splendid dish if entertaining a large number of people. If fresh eggs are available they should be used, though people did hard-boil reconstituted dried eggs. They were carefully mixed (1 level tablespoon dried egg powder to 2 tablespoons water), spooned into sturdy egg cups, covered and steamed until firm. Although these did not look like 'proper' hard-boiled eggs they tasted quite good for yolks and whites were combined in the egg powder.

1 small chicken
4 oz (115 g) soft breadcrumbs
2 tablespoons chopped
   parsley
2 tablespoons chopped
   chives or spring onions
1 teaspoon chopped thyme
   or ½ teaspoon dried thyme
2 eggs
4 tablespoons chicken stock
   (see method)
4 tablespoons evaporated
   milk or top of the milk

**For the filling:**
3 eggs, hard-boiled

**For the coating:**
crisp breadcrumbs (or see
   variation, right)

Cut all the flesh from the chicken and put the bones, with oddments of skin and giblets not required for this recipe, into a saucepan. Cover with water and simmer gently for 45 minutes. Strain the liquid. Some is used in the variation, Chaudfroid of Chicken, below; the rest can be used in a soup.

Mince the chicken flesh, including the cooked or uncooked liver from the giblets, if liked. Blend the chicken with all the other ingredients to make a soft mixture. Press out to a large oblong shape on a floured board. Place the hard-boiled eggs in the centre then form the chicken mixture around these to make a well-shaped roll. Wrap the roll in well-greased greaseproof paper or a floured cloth.

Put the roll into a steamer and cook for 1¼ hours. Carefully remove the paper or cloth and coat in crisp breadcrumbs. Serve hot or cold.

### VARIATION

**Chaudfroid of Chicken:** Allow the chicken roll to become quite cold. Dissolve 1 level teaspoon gelatine in ¼ pint (150 ml) chicken stock. When cold, but not set, blend with ¼ pint (150 ml) mayonnaise or salad dressing. Leave until fairly firm then spread over the uncoated chicken roll with a warmed palette knife. Garnish with tiny pieces of radish and tomato. Serve with various salads.

5 tablespoons finely chopped
   spring onions
2 tablespoons grated cucumber
1 tablespoon chopped parsley
1 tablespoon chopped chives
1 teaspoon chopped fresh thyme
   or ½ teaspoon dried thyme
salt and pepper
few drops Worcestershire sauce

Pour 3 tablespoons of the tomato juice into a basin, sprinkle the gelatine on top and allow to stand for 3 minutes, then place over a pan of hot water until dissolved. Heat the rest of the tomato juice, add the dissolved gelatine, then stir the meat into the hot mixture – this softens and moistens it. Leave until cold then add the remaining ingredients.

Spoon into a mould and allow to set. Turn out and serve with a potato salad and a mixed salad.

## WAYS TO SERVE DRIED BANANAS

**Bananas in Salads:** Slice and soak the dried bananas in a little vinegar or water to soften slightly (although some people may prefer their firm chewy texture). Add to a green salad. Dried bananas are an excellent addition to a fresh fruit salad.

**Banana Fritters:** Halve the dried bananas, soak for a short time in water then drain well. Make up 1 quantity of 8-Minute Doughnut batter (see page 39), but add 2 tablespoons of milk, or the banana soaking liquid. Coat the bananas in the batter and fry in 2 oz (50 g) cooking fat. Heat the fat and fry the fritters for 8 minutes. cook fairly quickly until golden brown on all sides, then lower the heat to cook through to the centres. Remove from the pan and drain on crumpled tissue paper (use kitchen paper today).

---

### FOOD FACTS

# filling THE PLATE

**T**HE CHILDREN at home, expectant appetites and the unexpected guest are all part of the housewife's "holiday" programme. Here are some handy fill-the-plate recipes which will help you. Cut them out and keep them by you.

**APPLE CHARLIE**

*Ingredients:* 6 oz. breadcrumbs, 1½ lb. apples, 1½ level tablespoons jam.

*(For 4)* **Method:** Grease a 1½ pint basin and press heaped spoonfuls of the breadcrumbs round the sides and on the bottom to form a lining. Peel, core and slice the apples, place in a pan with no liquid and cook gently until pulped. Beat in the jam, turn the mixture into the lined basin and cover with a layer of crumbs. Cover with a piece of greased paper and steam for ½ an hour. Turn out like a steamed pudding.

**MEAT HASH**

*Ingredients:* 6 oz. macaroni or 6 oz. pearl barley, 1 oz. dripping or cooking fat, 3 *(For 4)* level tablespoons flour, ½ pint vegetable stock or water, gravy browning, salt and pepper to taste. 6 oz. cooked meat, chopped, 1 lb. mixed vegetables, diced and cooked.

**Method:** Cook the macaroni or barley in boiling salted water. Make a brown sauce, with the fat, flour and stock or water, add a few drops of gravy browning and season well. Add the meat and vegetables and heat through. When macaroni or barley is tender, drain well, replace on a hot dish. Pile hash in centre and serve very hot.

**BAKED CARROT and ONION PIE**

*Ingredients:* 1½ lb. carrots, 6 oz. turnip, 8 oz. onion or leek, 4½ level table- *(For 4)* spoons flour, ¾ pint milk and vegetable stock, 1 level teaspoon salt, pinch of pepper, pinch of nutmeg, 2 oz. grated cheese, 2 slices bread (cut 1 inch thick from a large loaf) diced, 2 tablespoons melted margarine or dripping.

**Method:** Prepare and slice carrots, turnip, onion or leek. Boil in a little salted water until tender. Strain vegetables, keeping the liquid for the sauce, and place in a greased pie-dish. Blend the flour with a little of the cold milk, bring the rest of the liquid to the boil and pour on to the blended flour. Return to saucepan, stir until it boils and boil gently for 5 minutes. Add the seasonings and cheese and pour the sauce over the vegetables in the pie-dish; cover with the diced bread and sprinkle over the melted margarine or dripping. Bake in a hot oven for 15-20 minutes until brown on top:

*Fish Fact:* Fish landings vary with sea weather: that is why your fishmonger sometimes has plenty, sometimes only a little. But over the whole year fish landings have been 20% more than before the war. Fish is a fine protein food. Some fish, like herrings, are rich in fat as well. Where there's fish there's a good meal!

**THE MINISTRY OF FOOD, LONDON, S.W.I.**     **FOOD FACTS No. 390**

---

## ORANGE AND LEMON SPONGE

*Preparation time: 25 minutes*
*Cooking time: 20 minutes*
*Quantity: 1 cake*

There were now some oranges and lemons available and they would give flavour to this cake, which would be made for a special occasion. Nothing would be wasted at this time. Citrus fruit rind was used a great deal to make marmalade, with apples providing the pulp, and to flavour cakes like this one. Reconstituted dried eggs would still be used by most people. It would have been necessary to explain to people who had not used citrus fruit in cooking for years that 'zest' was the top part of the rind, without bitter pith.

- 4 oz (ll5 g) margarine
- 4 oz (ll5 g) caster sugar
- 1 teaspoon finely grated lemon zest
- 1 teaspoon finely grated orange zest
- 3 eggs
- 6 oz (175 g) self-raising flour or plain flour with 1½ teaspoons baking powder
- ½ tablespoon lemon juice
- 1½ tablespoons orange juice

**For the filling and decoration:**
- 4 oz (ll5 g) margarine
- 8 oz (225 g) icing sugar, sifted
- 1 tablespoon orange juice squeeze lemon juice

Preheat the oven to 180°C (350°F), Gas Mark 4. Grease and flour two 7–8 inch (18–20 cm) sandwich tins.

Cream the margarine and sugar with the fruit zest until soft and light.

Beat the eggs well and add gradually to the creamed mixture. If the mixture shows signs of curdling, then fold in some of the flour. Sift the flour, or flour and baking powder, and fold into the creamed mixture with the fruit juice. Divide the mixture between the tins and bake in the oven until firm to the touch. Turn out on to a wire cooling tray.

For the filling and decoration, cream the margarine and icing sugar together and gradually beat in the fruit juice. Use a little of the mixture to sandwich the cakes together and the remainder to spread or pipe over the top of the cake.

## BANANA AND RHUBARB COMPOTE

*Preparation time: 10 minutes*
*Cooking time: 15–20 minutes*
*Quantity: 4–6 helpings*

Dried bananas became quite popular, as they were very sweet and could be eaten without cooking; children really liked them. They had a somewhat sticky consistency. In this recipe, they help to sweeten rhubarb. The rhubarb would be the garden variety, not forced rhubarb. If using the latter, reduce the amount of water slightly.

4 dried bananas, thickly sliced
7½ fl oz (225 ml) water
1–2 tablespoons honey,
    golden syrup or sugar
1 lb (450 g) rhubarb (trimmed
    weight), neatly diced

Soak the bananas in the water for 30 minutes then simmer for 5 minutes. Add the sweetening, stir until dissolved then add the rhubarb. Cover the pan and simmer gently until just tender.

---

---

## APPLE CROQUETTES

*Preparation time: 15 minutes*
*Cooking time: 10 minutes*
*Quantity 4 helpings*

It is advisable to use the flesh from baked apples for these croquettes, since no extra water is added to the fruit. If you do stew the apples in a little water, then drain away any extra liquid.

2 large baked apples
2 tablespoons fine soft
    breadcrumbs
1 tablespoon milk or cream
pinch mixed spice
2 oz (50 g) sugar

### For the coating:

1 tablespoon flour
1 reconstituted dried egg
    (see page 10) or fresh egg
1½–2 oz (40–50 g) crisp
    breadcrumbs

### For frying:

2 oz (50 g) butter or margarine

Remove the skins of the apples and mash the pulp in a bowl. Add the rest of the ingredients. Chill until cold. Form into 8 croquette shapes. Coat in the flour, then dip in the beaten egg and roll in the crisp breadcrumbs.

Melt the butter or margarine in a frying pan and fry the croquettes until golden brown, turning them several times during the cooking process. Serve the apple croquettes with cream or the top of the milk.

### VARIATIONS

**Apple and Lemon Croquettes:** Omit the mixed spice and milk or cream. Add the finely grated zest of a lemon. and 1 tablespoon of lemon juice. Serve with a little hot lemon curd.

Orange zest and juice can be used instead of lemon. Serve with hot orange marmalade.

THE IMPORTANT THING IN THE OLYMPIC GAMES IS NOT WINNING BUT TAKING PART. THE ESSENTIAL THING IN LIFE IS NOT CONQUERING BUT FIGHTING WELL.

BARON de COUBERTIN

# ★ 1948 ★

**B**Y THIS YEAR the British public were feeling more and more frustrated about the lack of food and household goods. There were many reports and rumours of people 'black-marketing', i.e. obtaining far more food than their legal rations. The Government exhorted everyone to accept the situation and not grumble.

One group of foods, preserves, was taken off the ration this year. The usual ration had been 1 lb (450 g) per person per 2 months, so it was a pleasure to know that now one could spread marmalade thickly on the breakfast toast. Preserves were also used to eke out the sugar in cooking, as you will notice in several recipes in this chapter.

The RAF were joining with American forces to drop food and fuel over Berlin to beat the Russian blockade of the city.

In the summer of 1948 there was a serious dock strike at Southampton, one of our major ports. Over 200 ships were held up, many of them carrying food from abroad. The fresh meat ration was cut to 6d (just over 2 p) and troops had to be brought in to try to save food supplies.

The 14th Olympic Games, the first to be held since 1936, were held in Britain, at the Wembley Stadium, in London. They were accounted a great success, although often christened the Austerity Olympics because of the stringent rationing and lack of special projects in this country. Germany, Japan and the Soviet Union did not participate.

Cooks sought to present food in a more elaborate and attractive manner, and wanted to entertain their friends. Cocktail parties became the vogue, for they were more practical than trying to eke out the rations to prepare dinner parties. I have included some of the cocktail party savouries of the time in this chapter.

A new fish, that received a great deal of publicity, was canned snoek. This came from South Africa, and the Ministry of Food was very anxious to promote it as a replacement for canned salmon. In spite of all the official praise, the British people hated snoek and within a relatively short time it disappeared from the shops.

The quality of fresh eggs was very poor, with eggs being stale and often bad. The Ministry now decreed that any eggs bought on ration that were bad must be replaced.

Once again, the Ministry of Food published a specially economical Christmas Cake with Mock Marzipan, and you will find recipes for both at the end of this chapter. Although more nuts were coming into Britain, including ground almonds, they were still relatively scarce and expensive.

Because we had been without nuts of any kind during the war years these were regarded as a special treat by the general public and a very necessary food by vegetarians.

We had been used to buying inexpensive monkey nuts (peanuts in their shells) before the war but now shelled peanuts were more generally available. These were also known as ground nuts.

In November 1948 the nation had a reason to rejoice. A son, Charles, was born to Princess Elizabeth and Prince Philip. The picture on page 51 shows the happy new parents at the christening of their young baby.

★ ★ ★ ★ ★ ★ ★ ★ ★ ★ ★ ★ ★ ★ ★ ★ ★ ★ ★ ★ ★ ★ ★ ★ ★ ★ ★ ★

## COCKTAIL SNACKS

These are some of the cocktail savouries that could be made in 1948. Although many basic foods were still scarce, cocktail 'nibbles' like olives and anchovy fillets were becoming available.

### Cheese Whirls

Make the biscuit dough as for Cheese Butterflies (right). Roll out to a ¼ inch (6 mm) thick oblong. Spread with Marmite. Roll firmly, like a Swiss roll, then cut into slices. Place on baking trays and brush with milk. Bake as for Cheese Butterflies.

★ ★ ★ ★ ★ ★ ★ ★ ★ ★ ★ ★ ★ ★ ★ ★ ★ ★ ★ ★ ★ ★ ★ ★ ★ ★ ★ ★

**Curried New Potatoes:** Use bite-sized potatoes. Scrub well and cook in their skins.

For 24 potatoes use 1 small onion, which should be very finely chopped or grated. Fry the onion in 1–2 oz (25–50 g) hot margarine. Add 1 teaspoon curry powder, a few drops of Worcestershire sauce and 2 table-spoons water. Add the well-drained cooked potatoes and turn around in the hot curry mixture until coated. Serve on cocktail sticks.

**Cheese Potatoes:** Cook new potatoes. When cold, cut into halves. If possible, take your cheese ration in cream cheese. Blend this with finely chopped chives and a few chopped nuts. Spread over the cut side of the potatoes.

**Princess Mushrooms:** Cook very small mushrooms then remove and set aside their stalks. Fill the mushroom caps with cream cheese or grated cheese mixed with a little margarine or mayonnaise. Garnish with the cooked stalks.

**Seafood Bites:** Top rounds of toast with peeled prawns, cooked mussels or tiny pieces of crabmeat. Garnish with a little mayonnaise and watercress leaves.

**Stuffed Eggs:** There were occasions when one could buy gulls' eggs and these were small enough to make good cocktail snacks. Cook the eggs for about 5 minutes until hard-boiled. Carefully shell and halve. Remove the yolks and blend with a little anchovy essence, mashed sardines or chopped prawns. Return the filling to the white cases and place on small rounds of toast, spread with fish paste.

## CHEESE BUTTERFLIES

*Preparation time: 15 minutes*
*Cooking time: 12–15 minutes*
*Quantity: 15 canapés*

Use these economical cheese biscuits within a day or so of baking. Store in an airtight tin before filling with the cream cheese. The biscuits are a good way to use up the ends of cheese that may have gone hard and can be grated very finely.

6 oz (175 g) plain flour
salt and pepper
½ teaspoon mustard powder
2 oz (50 g) cooking fat
   or margarine
2 oz (50 g) Cheddar
   cheese, grated
1 egg

### For the filling:
1 oz (25 g) margarine
1 level tablespoon dried
   milk powder
2 tablespoons finely
   grated cheese
pinch mustard powder
few drops vinegar
little milk

Preheat the oven to 180°C (350°F), Gas Mark 4. Grease flat baking trays.

Sift the flour with the seasonings, rub in the fat or margarine and add the cheese. Mix well then gradually add enough beaten egg to make a dough with a firm rolling consistency.

Roll out thinly and cut into approximately 30 small rounds. Cut half the rounds down the centre to form the wings. Place on greased, flat baking trays and bake until pale golden in colour and firm to the touch. Allow to cool on the trays.

Cream the margarine with the milk powder, cheese, mustard and vinegar. Gradually add a little milk to give a firm spreading consistency. Spread or pipe a line of filling on the biscuit rounds then place the 'wings' in position.

### A MODERN TOUCH
Increase the amount of fat and cheese in the biscuits to 3 oz (85 g). Omit the milk powder in the filling and double the amount of cheese.

## DO YOU KNOW what traffic is?

TRAFFIC is everyone on the roads, streets, and pavements. Whether walking, riding or driving, we are all part of it. Any one of us can cause an accident — or help to prevent one.

If everything went at one mile an hour, there might be no accidents. But, for all our sakes, traffic must *move* — as swiftly as is safe. Road Navigation (based on the Highway Code) is the art of getting about easily, swiftly and *safely* — and helping others to do the same. It's largely a matter of considering others *on* the road, as most of us do *off* the road. It will pay us all to become skilful Road Navigators.

GET HOME SAFE AND SOUND

*Issued by the Ministry of Transport*

## AVOCADO CANAPÉS

*Preparation time: 5 minutes*
*No cooking*
*Quantity: 12–16 canapés*

Avocados began to appear in large towns and good greengrocers. They were called avocado pears at first, which gave people the idea that they were just like an ordinary pear. When first sampled, they were disliked by many people, unprepared for the new taste. As people became accustomed to the taste, avocados became more and more popular.

1 large or 2 smaller ripe
   avocados
1 tablespoon lemon juice
salt and pepper
3 teaspoons finely chopped
   or grated onion
2 teaspoons olive oil or
   melted margarine
12–16 small savoury biscuits or
   rounds of bread and butter
12–16 small peeled prawns
   or shrimps

Halve and peel the avocado(s), remove the stone(s) and mash the pulp with the lemon juice and seasoning. Add the onion with the oil or margarine and spoon on to the biscuits or bread. Top with the prawns or shrimps.

### VARIATION
The avocado mixture makes an excellent sandwich filling or a topping for grilled or baked white fish.

# SNOEK

As a Ministry leaflet explained, 'Already we have seen people pulling wry faces at the mention of snoek; many of them who have never tasted it have assured us it is too salty; others regard it as 'ersatz' (this word, meaning a poor imitation, had become much used during the war). Why has the Ministry of Food imported this fish? The answer is that its purchase is part of our policy of replacing foods previously imported from dollar sources by foods produced within the sterling area. 'The price is reasonable: 1s 4½d (7.5 p) for ½ lb (225 g). This compares with 2s 4½d (12.5 p) for ½ lb (225 g) red salmon and 1s 6d (8 p) for Group 3 (pink) salmon. The point value is, at the moment, very low: 1 point for the ½ lb (225 g) as compared with red salmon 14 points and Group 3 (pink) 6 points.'

**RECIPE of the WEEK**

## SNOEK AND TOMATO DISH

*Preparation time: 10 minutes*
*Cooking time: 6 minutes*
*Quantity: 4 helpings*

Snoek is a cousin to mackerel, sword-fish and tuna. It is found in the seas round southern Africa. In Australia, the fish is known as barracuda and in Chile as sierra.

1 oz (25 g) dripping or
  cooking fat
8 oz (225 g) spring onions,
  chopped
1 lb (450 g) tomatoes,
  skinned and sliced
1 x 8 oz (225 g) can
  snoek, flaked
1 teaspoon sugar
salt and pepper

Melt the fat, put in the onions and cook until golden brown; add the tomatoes and cook gently until tender. Add the snoek, sugar and seasoning and cook gently until thoroughly hot. Serve with potatoes and a green vegetable.

### A MODERN TOUCH

Use canned tuna or salmon for this dish.

"Steady, now, mother. If it springs at you I'll slosh it with this axe."

## COFFEE CREAMS

*Preparation time: 15 minutes*
*Cooking time: 10 minutes*
*Quantity: 4 helpings*

By 1948 it had become easier to buy better quality instant and ground coffee, so coffee-lovers enjoyed a better beverage. We tended to use coffee flavouring a great deal in desserts and cakes, for it was such a pleasure to have this.

1 oz (25 g) cornflour
¼ pint (150 ml) milk
½ pint (300 ml) moderately
  strong coffee
2 oz (50 g) sugar, preferably
  soft brown
7½ fl oz (250 ml) unsweetened
  evaporated milk, whipped
  (see Economical Ice Creams,
  page 59)

**To decorate:**

whipped evaporated milk or
  Mock Cream (see page 71)
little grated chocolate

Blend the cornflour with the cold milk. Bring the coffee to the boil, pour over the cornflour and mix well. Return to the saucepan with the sugar and stir over a low heat until thickened. Cover with a damp piece of greaseproof paper to prevent a skin forming and leave until cool, then fold in the whipped evaporated milk. Spoon into glasses and leave until quite cold.

To decorate, top with more evaporated milk or Mock Cream and grated chocolate.

## MOIST ORANGE CAKE

*Preparation time: 15 minutes*
*Cooking time: 50 minutes*
*Quantity: 1 cake*

Preserves help to save sugar in baking but do measure them carefully, for too generous an amount would make the cake heavy.

6 oz (175 g) self-raising flour or plain flour with 1½ teaspoons baking powder
½ level teaspoon bicarbonate of soda
2 oz (50 g) margarine or cooking fat
4 level tablespoons orange marmalade
1 teaspoon finely grated orange zest or few drops orange essence
2 oz (50 g) sugar
6 tablespoons orange juice or milk
2 eggs

Preheat the oven to 160°C (325°F), Gas Mark 3. Line an oblong tin measuring 7 x 4 inches (18 x 10 cm) and at least 2 inches (5 cm) deep with greased grease-proof paper.

Sift the flour, or flour and baking powder, with the bicarbonate of soda into a mixing bowl. Put the margarine or cooking fat, marmalade, orange zest or essence and the sugar into a saucepan. Stir over a low heat until melted. Add to the flour. Heat the orange juice or milk in the saucepan in which the ingredients were melted, stirring well so nothing is wasted. Add to the flour and beat vigorously. Lastly, add the eggs and beat again.

Spoon the mixture into the prepared tin and bake for 50 minutes, or until the cake is firm to the touch. Leave to cool in the tin for 30 minutes then turn out.

## APRICOT AND LEMON FLAN

*Preparation time: 25 minutes*
*Cooking time: 30 minutes*
*Quantity: 4–6 helpings*

Jam tarts were made with a somewhat sparse amount of apricot jam during rationing but this recipe, with its generous amount of jam, became possible when preserves came off ration in 1948.

New cooks may not have baked pastry cases 'blind', the term for baking an empty pastry case. Simply put greased greaseproof paper (greased side downwards) into the pastry shape, top with crusts of bread (these can be used afterwards for rusks) or pieces of macaroni. This method keeps the pastry base flat during cooking.

Shortcrust pastry made with 6 oz (175 g) flour etc. (see Gypsy Tart, page 21)

**For the filling:**
1 oz (25 g) margarine
1 teaspoon finely grated lemon zest
5 tablespoons apricot jam
1 oz (25 g) fine soft breadcrumbs
1 egg
1 tablespoon lemon juice

Preheat the oven to 190°C (375°F), Gas Mark 5. Make the pastry, roll out and use to line a 7–8 inch (18–20 cm) flan dish or tin or a flan ring placed on an upturned baking tray.

Bake the pastry case blind for 10 minutes only, removing it from the oven and reducing the oven temperature to 180°C (350°F), Gas Mark 4.

Meanwhile, cream the margarine for the filling and add the rest of the ingredients. Spoon the mixture into the partially cooked pastry case, return to the oven and bake for a further 20 minutes. Serve hot or cold.

## DOCK STRIKE

As explained on page 43, there was a dock strike in the summer of 1948 and as all foodstuffs were so valuable the Forces had to be called in to help distribute these. Servicemen also came to the rescue in January of the previous year. This was due to the stoppage by road haulage workers. Although the dockers did not come out on strike they gave support to the strikers by blacking any goods that were due to be carried by road. This dispute, like the later one in 1948, affected supplies of fresh meat badly and many homes had to depend upon the old standby — corned beef — when they could not purchase fresh meat. Favourite recipes using this canned beef were brought into use, see below.

Another serious dock strike occured in October 1954, when it was estimated that 51,000 workers were affected. By this time of course supplies of food were more plentiful but it was reported that the strike cut Britain's sea trade by half.

### USE CORNED BEEF

**To make fritters:** coat sliced beef with egg and crumbs and fry until crisp.

**To grill:** slice and brush with a little melted fat; grill for a few minutes.

**To roast:** do not slice the beef, brush the outside with a little melted fat, coat in chopped herbs and roast until piping hot. Serve with roast onions and roast potatoes.

**Cheese Toasts:** mash the corned beef, flavour with a little Worcestershire sauce and a skinned chopped tomato. Place on hot toast, top with grated cheese and put under the grill until the cheese melts.

Use diced corned beef in a Shepherd's Pie: in a casserole with finely chopped vegetables: as a sandwich filling.

*What on earth can I pack for his lunch tomorrow?*

## MOCK MARZIPAN

*Preparation time: 10 minutes*
*No cooking*
*Quantity: enough to cover top of*
*7 inch (18 cm) cake*

2 oz (50 g) margarine
2 oz (50 g) caster or icing
    sugar, sifted
1–2 teaspoons almond essence
8 oz (225 g) plain cake crumbs

Cream the margarine and sugar with the essence. Add the crumbs and knead the mixture. Roll out.

## MINISTRY OF FOOD CHRISTMAS CAKE

This was the recommended recipe from the Ministry of Food both in 1947 and again in 1948. The ingredients make a very acceptable fruit cake.

*Preparation time: 20 minutes*
*Cooking time: 2½ hours*
*Quantity: 1 cake*

4 oz (115 g) margarine
3 oz (85 g) sugar, preferably
    soft brown
2 reconstituted dried eggs
    (see page 10) or fresh eggs
3 level tablespoons warmed
    golden syrup or treacle *
8 oz (225 g) plain flour
pinch salt
½ level teaspoon bicarbonate
    of soda **
1 level teaspoon ground
    cinnamon

1 level teaspoon mixed spice
1 lb (450 g) mixed dried fruit
3 tablespoons cold well-strained
    tea

* Warm the syrup or treacle then measure it.
** Do not exceed this amount.

Line a 7 inch (18 cm) cake tin with greased greaseproof paper. Preheat the oven to 150°C (300°F), Gas Mark 2.

Cream the margarine and sugar. Gradually add the beaten eggs then the syrup or treacle. Sift all the dry ingredients together then add to the creamed mixture with the fruit and tea. Spoon into the cake tin and make a hollow in the centre so the cake will stay flat on top. Bake for 2½ hours or until firm to the touch and the sides have slightly shrunk away from the tin. Cool in the tin.

When cold remove from the tin; store in an airtight container.

# ★ 1949 ★

**A**LTHOUGH THERE WAS to be no further permanent de-rationing of major foodstuffs for several years, on the whole the food situation was less grim than in the past. Many more unrationed foods were becoming plentiful. There were reasonable supplies of imported fruits and vegetables as well as seasonal home-grown varieties. Chickens and other poultry, rabbits and pigeons were to be found in the shops and the variety of fish was greater and the quality better. There were some complaints that expensive restaurants and hotels were 'snapping up' unrationed food.

There was a temporary drop in the rations of sugar in the summer of 1949, due to a dollar shortage and, for the same reason, the sweet ration was drastically reduced to 4 oz (115 g) from the usual 12 oz (350 g) per month. Britain had to devalue the pound by 30 per cent.

A Ministry of Food report in this year noted that there were hopes that Australia would build up its meat supplies, so that it would supplant the Argentine as our main supplier of imported meat.

The Ministry of Food booklets continued to stress the importance of a nutritional diet.

A survey done in this year stressed the growth of eating out in Britain. For many people, the habit had begun in the war years when they ate at British Restaurants, which had served simple and inexpensive meals.

Clothes rationing, which was introduced in 1941, ended in July but Utility clothes, made to fairly strict guidelines, were still to be available in the shops and these would be cheaper than more elaborate garments.

There was great enthusiasm for the new Pressure Saucepans. Pressure cookers had been made in the past but they had been large and heavy. The modern pans were the size of a large saucepan and very easy to use. The pans were quite revolutionary, for they cooked food within minutes, rather than the hours needed for dishes like stews. The flavour and nutrients of the food were retained and, because of the short cooking period, an appreciable amount of fuel was saved.

Throughout the war years, when people bottled fruit, they had asked me about bottling vegetables. This was not possible in an oven or ordinary sterilizer, for the temperature was not sufficiently high to destroy harmful bacteria that could cause botulism. A pressure cooker, which reached higher temperatures, made vegetable bottling practical and safe.

The demand for refrigerators had been steadily growing, for people had realized their advantages in storing food at safe temperatures, as well as allowing one to make delectable cold dishes, including ices and sorbets. Before the war, it was recorded that only 250,000 homes in Britain had a refrigerator; gradually throughout the 1950s that number rose until by 1961 twenty-three per cent of all homes had one.

Britain had to wait for home freezers to come on the market. The small freezing compartment in the refrigerators of this era were only sufficiently deep to contain freezing trays for making ice or shallow containers so people used these for freezing ice cream or sorbets. The temperature in the freezing compartment was too high to contemplate freezing other foods.

# PRESSURE COOKERS

The new small pressure cookers (known as pressure pans) caused a sensation. The idea of being able to cook a stew within minutes, rather than hours, was much appreciated. There were still severe fuel cuts and we were urged to save fuel which, of course, was possible with the shorter pressure cooking times. Some people found the initial sound of the pans as they came to pressure a little alarming, so I had to reassure both the press and the public that they were safe and that the results of cooking all kinds of food were very satisfactory.

I wrote the first pressure cooking book for Harrods. The recipes from it I have included here typify the foods we cooked at that time.

**Pressure cooking tip**
When using a recipe that is made with self-raising flour, or uses baking powder, the mixture must be steamed, without pressure, for the first part of the cooking period so that the mixture rises.

**Adapting pressure cooker times:**
If you do not possess a pressure cooker the recipes that follow can be cooked by the usual means; here are timings:

**Dried Pea Soup:** 1¾–2 hours cooking. Use double the amount of water.
**Cod and Tomato Savoury:** 25 minutes in a steamer.
**Beef Stew:** 2–2½ hours simmering. Use double the amount of water.
**Steak and Kidney Pudding:** 3 hours steaming.
**Brigade Pudding:** 2 hours steaming.
**Brown Betty Pudding:** 1¾ hours steaming.

## DRIED PEA SOUP

*Preparation time: overnight soaking*
*Cooking time: 20 minutes*
*pressure cooking*
*Quantity: 4–6 helpings*

Dried peas had been available throughout the years of rationing and were an item on the points system. The problem about them was that they needed prolonged cooking after soaking. The pressure cooker meant they could be cooked in a relatively short time.

The very new liquidizers (blenders) that became available meant you could use one instead of rubbing ingredients through a sieve in the traditional manner – another excellent time saver.

8 oz (225 g) dried peas
2 onions
2 carrots
1 small turnip, optional
1 pint (600 ml) water
1 teaspoon sugar
1 sprig mint or pinch dried mint
salt and pepper

Cover the peas with cold water and soak overnight.

Peel and chop the onion, carrot and turnip neatly if you do not want to sieve or liquidize the soup. If you intend to serve it as a smooth soup, then chop the vegetables quite coarsely.

Drain the peas and put into the pressure cooker, do not use the trivet (rack). Add the other ingredients. Fix the lid and bring up to pressure. Maintain for 20 minutes. Allow the pressure to drop to room temperature.

Sieve or liquidize the ingredients then return to the pressure cooker, without the lid, to heat.

### VARIATIONS

Add a little top of the milk before serving the soup.

**Butter Bean Soup:** Use butter beans instead of dried peas with the same vegetables plus 1 or 2 tomatoes, if available. Substitute a sprig of parsley for the mint and allow 30 minutes pressure cooking time.

Both the Dried Pea Soup and the Butter Bean Soup can be soaked, drained and then cooked in an ordinary saucepan for 1¾–2 hours. Use 2 pints (1.2 litres) of water for cooking and cover the pan tightly.

## BEEF STEW

*Preparation time: 15 minutes*
*Cooking time: 5 minutes, then*
*15 minutes pressure cooking*
*Quantity: 4 helpings*

1 lb (450 g) stewing steak
salt and pepper
2 medium onions
4 medium carrots
1 medium turnip
1 oz (25 g) dripping or fat
¾ pint (450 ml) water
little gravy flavouring or
    yeast extract
1 oz (25 g) flour
1 tablespoon chopped parsley

Cut the steak into neat 1 inch (2.5 cm) cubes and season lightly. Peel and dice the vegetables. Heat the dripping or fat in the bottom of the pressure cooker then add the steak and cook quickly for 5 minutes. Turn the meat during this time so it browns on all sides.

Add ½ pint (300 ml) of the water with any flavouring required plus the vegetables. Fix the lid and bring to pressure. Maintain this for 15 minutes. Cool rapidly under cold water then remove the lid. Blend the flour with the rest of the water, add to the pan and stir over a moderate heat until the liquid thickens. Taste, adjust the seasoning and add the parsley.

## COD AND TOMATO SAVOURY

This dish was a good one to demonstrate that ovenproof glassware was safe in the high heat of a pressure cooker.

*Preparation time: 5 minutes*
*Cooking time: 4 minutes*
*pressure cooking*
*Quantity: 4 helpings*

1 onion, grated
8 oz (225 g) tomatoes, sliced
2 tablespoons chopped parsley
2 tablespoons breadcrumbs
salt and pepper
12 oz (350 g) cod or other white
  fish, without bones or skin

Grease an ovenproof dish that will fit inside the pressure cooker.

Mix the onion, tomatoes, parsley and breadcrumbs. Season the mixture. Spoon half into the bottom of the dish, add the fish, then add the rest of the tomato mixture.

Put the trivet into the pressure-cooker, add ½ pint (300 ml) water. Stand the dish on the trivet. Fix the lid and bring to pressure. Maintain this for 4 minutes then allow it to drop to room temperature.

## STEAK AND KIDNEY PUDDING

*Preparation time: 30 minutes*
*Cooking time: 30 minutes steaming plus 55 minutes pressure cooking*
*Quantity: 4–6 helpings*

**For the suet crust pastry:**
8 oz (225 g) flour etc.
  (see Brigade Pudding,
  page 57)

**For the filling:**
1 lb (450 g) stewing steak
4–6 oz (115–175 g) ox or lambs'
  kidneys, skinned
1 tablespoon flour
salt and pepper
little stock or water

Prepare the suet crust pastry and line the basin (see Brigade Pudding, page 57). Dice the meats for the filling.

Blend the flour with the seasoning, roll the meat in this mixture then put into the pastry-lined basin. Add enough stock or water to come half-way up the meat. Roll out the remaining pastry for the lid, place in position then cover the pudding.

Pour 2 pints (1.2 litres) boiling water into the pressure cooker. Stand the pudding on the trivet. Fix the lid and steam the pudding for 30 minutes. Bring up to pressure and cook for 55 minutes. Allow the pressure to drop to room temperature then serve.

**VARIATIONS:**
Steam the pudding for about 3 hours.

**Rabbit or Chicken Pudding:** Use diced rabbit or chicken and sliced onions instead of the meat. If the rabbit or chicken is young the pressure cooking time can be reduced to 35 minutes. For older flesh follow the cooking time above.

**A MODERN TOUCH**
Use the weight that gives LOW pressure and allow 1 hour pressure cooking time. If cooking young rabbit or chicken, allow 40 minutes.

## BROWN BETTY PUDDING

*Preparation time: 20 minutes*
*Cooking time: 30 minutes*
*pressure cooking*
*Quantity: 4–6 helpings*

This pudding is excellent when prepared in a pressure cooker.

1½ oz (40 g) margarine
4 oz (115 g) soft brown breadcrumbs
1 lb (450 g) cooking apples, weight when peeled and cored
2 oz (50 g) sugar
2 oz (50 g) sultanas or other dried fruit
½–1 teaspoon mixed spice
2 level tablespoons golden syrup
1 tablespoon water

Use just under half the margarine to grease a 1½–2 pint (900 ml–1.2 litre) basin then coat with a scant 1 oz (25 g) of the crumbs. Peel, core and slice the apples, mix with the sugar, dried fruit and spice.

Fill the basin with alternate layers of crumbs and apple mixture, beginning and ending with crumbs. Mix the syrup with the water, pour over the pudding then top with the rest of the margarine, cut in small pieces.

Cover the pudding with a plate or greaseproof paper. Fill the cooker with 2 pints (1.2 litres) boiling water. Stand the pudding on the trivet. Fix the lid and bring up to pressure. Maintain this for 30 minutes. Allow the pressure to drop to room temperature. Serve the pudding with custard.

## BRIGADE PUDDING

*Preparation time: 30 minutes*
*Cooking time: 30 minutes steaming plus 25 minutes pressure cooking*
*Quantity: 4–6 helpings*

One of the advantages for cooks at this time was that more suet could now be obtained, either from the butcher or as shredded suet in packets. Suet was a favourite form of fat for sweet and savoury puddings. It had been extremely difficult to obtain in the wartime years.

**For the suet crust pastry:**
8 oz (225 g) self-raising flour or plain flour with 2 teaspoons baking powder
½ teaspoon salt, or to taste
2–4 oz (50–115 g) shredded suet
water, to bind

**For the filling:**
1 lb (450 g) cooking apples
2 oz (50 g) soft breadcrumbs
2 oz (50 g) currants
1 tablespoon marmalade
3 tablespoons golden syrup

For the pastry, sift the flour, or flour and baking powder, with the salt. Add the suet and enough water to make a soft rolling consistency. Roll the pastry out thinly and use about three-quarters to line a lightly greased 1½–2 pint (900 ml–1.2 litre) basin.

For the filling, peel, core and thinly slice the apples, mix with the other ingredients and spoon into the pastry-lined basin. Roll out the remaining pastry to form a lid. Seal the edges firmly and cover. Pour 2 pints (1.2 litres) boiling water into the pressure cooker. Stand the basin on the trivet. Fix the lid but DO NOT add the weight. Steam steadily for 30 minutes. Bring to pressure and cook for 25 minutes. Allow the pressure to drop to room temperature then serve the pudding hot with custard.

### VARIATIONS
Steam the pudding for 2 hours over steadily boiling water.
**Apple Pudding:** Use 1½ lb (675 g) sliced apples with a little sugar and 2 tablespoons water as the filling.

Other fruits can be used as a filling, i.e. rhubarb and soft fruits. Instead of using suet rub 2–4 oz (50–115 g) margarine or cooking fat into the flour.

### A MODERN TOUCH
Use the weight that gives LOW pressure and allow 30 minutes cooking time.

## IRISH SODA BREAD

*Preparation time: 10 minutes*
*Cooking time: 30 minutes*
*Quantity: 1 loaf*

Although bread rationing had long been over, many people were still keen on baking bread. They had tried to make good soda bread during 1946 and 1947, when bread was rationed, and had been very disappointed. The flour of those days was very heavy. By 1949 flour was improving and it was possible to get a good result.

The variation using potatoes (right) gives another excellent and light bread.

1 lb (450 g) plain flour
½ teaspoon salt
½ level teaspoon bicarbonate of soda
1 level teaspoon cream of tartar
½ pint (300 ml) milk or milk and water

Preheat the oven to 220°C (425°F), Gas Mark 7. Sift the dry ingredients and bind to a soft but not over-sticky dough with the liquid. Form into a large round about 1 inch (2.5 cm) thick. Put on to a baking tray. Mark into sections (known as farls). Bake for 30 minutes.

NOTE: if you can obtain buttermilk, use only ½ teaspoon cream of tartar.

### VARIATIONS
**Potato Soda Bread:** Use only 8 oz (225 g) flour with the same amounts of salt, bicarbonate of soda and cream of tartar. Add 8 oz (225 g) sieved cooked potato then bind with the milk. You will need approximately 7½ fl oz (225 ml). Continue as for the main recipe.
**Oatmeal Soda Bread:** Use 12 oz (350 g) flour and 4 oz (115 g) rolled oats. Other ingredients are as the basic recipe.

## RICH VANILLA ICE CREAM

*Preparation time: 20 minutes*
*Cooking time: 15 minutes*
*Freezing time: 1–1½ hours*
*Quantity: 4–6 helpings*

This recipe has a combination of the 'cream' made with butter or margarine and milk and whipped evaporated milk. This gave the nearest approach possible in 1949 to real cream ices.

In that era most advice stated that the refrigerator should be set to the coldest position 30 minutes before placing the mixture in the freezing compartment and that it should stay in this position during freezing. After the mixture was frozen, the indicator should be returned to the normal position. This advice is no longer considered essential, although the quicker ices are frozen, the better the result.

**For the 'cream':**
2 oz (50 g) unsalted butter
¼ pint (150 ml) fresh milk

**For the ice cream:**
cream' made with the above
    ingredients
1 x 14 oz (400 g) can evaporated
    milk, whipped (see right)
1 teaspoon vanilla essence
2 oz (50 g) icing or caster sugar

To make the cream, heat the butter and milk until just warm then allow to cool. To prevent the butter and milk separating as they cool, tip the mixture from the pan into a bowl and back again several times. When cold, pump vigorously through the cream-maker then chill.

Fold the cream into the whipped evaporated milk with the vanilla essence and sugar. Icing sugar should be sifted before using. Pour into the freezing trays of the refrigerator or a suitable container. Freeze until firm. This recipe does not need whipping during freezing.

### VARIATIONS

**Without the 'Cream':** Use just the whipped evaporated milk, add vanilla essence and the sugar, which could be reduced to 1½ oz (40 g). This mixture could be used as a basis for the following three ice creams instead of the Rich Vanilla Ice Cream.

**Brown Bread Ice Cream:** Fold 2–3 oz (50–85 g) fine soft or crisp

☆ ☆ ☆ ☆ ☆ ☆ ☆ ☆ ☆ ☆ ☆ ☆ ☆ ☆ ☆ ☆ ☆ ☆ ☆ ☆ ☆ ☆ ☆ ☆ ☆ ☆ ☆ ☆ ☆

## ECONOMICAL ICE CREAMS

As cream was still unobtainable, all ice creams had to be based on substitutes, particularly evaporated milk, which was obtainable on the points system. 'Cream' made with a cream-making machine was rather too solid for a good texture, but you could mix some of this with evaporated milk, as in Rich Vanilla Ice Cream, left. In order to get a smooth mixture one needed a fairly high percentage of fat, so canned evaporated milk had to be used undiluted. The best result was obtained by whipping the evaporated milk, which made it a better colour and texture. Whipping evaporated milk is quite a long process. First, put the unopened can into a saucepan of water, making sure the can is completely immersed. Allow the water to boil for 15 minutes. Check from time to time that there is sufficient water, adding more boiling water, if necessary. Remove the can from the water and chill for some hours. Open the can, pour the milk into a large bowl and whisk until light and fluffy.
An even better texture is given by carefully opening the can after 15 minutes' boiling, pouring the hot milk into a container then adding 1 teaspoon gelatine, dissolved in 2 tablespoons water. Chill well for some hours then whip.
The recipes on this page are based upon 1 x 14 oz (400 g) can of evaporated milk, whipped with, or without, the gelatine.

☆ ☆ ☆ ☆ ☆ ☆ ☆ ☆ ☆ ☆ ☆ ☆ ☆ ☆ ☆ ☆ ☆ ☆ ☆ ☆ ☆ ☆ ☆ ☆ ☆ ☆ ☆ ☆ ☆

brown breadcrumbs into the mixture. Use brown sugar, if possible, instead of white. The vanilla essence could be omitted and 1–2 tablespoons rum added.

**Custard Ice Cream:** Follow the recipe above and combine it with ½ pint (300 ml) thick custard, made with custard powder or 2 reconstituted dried eggs (see page 10) or fresh eggs, ½ pint (300 ml) fresh milk and 1 oz (25 g) sugar. This is a children's favourite. Because of the higher liquid content, it is improved by beating briskly halfway through freezing.

**Fruit Ice Cream:** Add 7 fl oz (225 ml) unsweetened smooth fruit purée to the whipped evaporated milk with 2½ oz (65 g) sugar or 10 fl oz (300 ml) to the Rich Vanilla Ice Cream with 3 oz (85 g) sugar.

**Fudge Ice Cream:** Omit additional sugar in this recipe. Melt 3–4 oz (85–115 g) fudge in a basin over hot water. Allow to cool then blend with the other ingredients. Vanilla essence can be added but is not essential.

### A MODERN TOUCH
Use whipped whipping cream or double cream instead of the evaporated milk and cream.

# SORBETS AND WATER ICES

The ices of 1949 were very simple compared with the more sophisticated recipes of the future. In large houses sorbets had been made in the years before the war as a course in the menu of formal banquets. The mixture would have been aerated by the use of an old-fashioned ice cream maker, where someone had the laborious task of turning the handle. Few people had these in their homes and the modern electric ones were many years ahead. The sorbets of 1949 were made lighter by the use of gelatine and egg whites. Fresh eggs were still on ration but people living in the country and those who kept chickens were able to use them. There were no fears in 1949 about using uncooked eggs.

## Fruit Sorbets

Make 1 pint (600 ml) smooth fruit purée, either by liquidizing fresh or cooked fruit or rubbing it through a sieve to get rid of all pips and skin.

Sprinkle 2 level teaspoons gelatine on to 4 tablespoons water, stand for 3 minutes then dissolve over a pan of hot water.

Heat ¼ pint (150 ml) water with 2 oz (50 g) sugar until the sugar has dissolved. Add 2 tablespoons lemon juice, then mix in the dissolved gelatine. Add to the fruit purée and freeze until mushy.

Whisk 2 egg whites until stiff then fold into the fruit mixture and continue freezing.

## Water Ices

Use the recipe on the left, but omit the gelatine and egg whites. Freeze until firm. Always remove from the freezing compartment of the refrigerator about 15 minutes before serving.

## Sundaes

Restaurants began to serve sundaes as desserts and people at home decided to copy them. As fresh cream was still unobtainable, most people omitted a cream topping, although Mock Cream (see page 71) could be used.

## Peach Melba

Spoon ice cream into sundae glasses. Top with halved, skinned fresh or well-drained canned peach halves. Top with Melba Sauce.

For Melba Sauce, put 8 oz (225 g) fresh raspberries into a saucepan. Blend 1 level teaspoon arrowroot or cornflour with 3 tablespoons water and add to the pan with 3 tablespoons redcurrant jelly. Stir over a low heat until the mixture has thickened and become clear. Sieve or put into a liquidizer (blender). Processing in a liquidizer does not get rid of all the pips.

When fresh raspberries are unavailable use canned and 3 tablespoons liquid from the can to blend with the arrowroot or cornflour.

## Coupe Jacques

Spoon ice cream into sundae glasses, top with a fresh or well-drained canned fruit salad and Melba Sauce (Peach Melba, above).

## Poires Belle Hélène

Spoon ice cream into sundae glasses, top with peeled fresh or well-drained pear halves and Chocolate Sauce.

For Chocolate Sauce, put 2 oz (50 g) butter or margarine into a saucepan with 2 oz (50 g) caster sugar, 2 level tablespoons golden syrup, 4 tablespoons water and 2 oz (50 g) cocoa powder or chocolate powder for a milder taste.

Stir over the heat until the ingredients have melted. If serving cold, add an extra tablespoon water.

---

## JAM SAUCES

Preserves were taken off the ration at the end of 1948, so by 1949 people were buying generous amounts to make sauces to serve with steamed puddings. The recipes below give 4 good helpings.

### Jam Sauce

Put 6–8 tablespoons jam into a saucepan. Blend 1 level teaspoon arrowroot or cornflour with ¼ pint (150 ml) cold water, add to the pan and stir over a moderate heat until the mixture boils and becomes clear. To give more flavour to the sauce add 1 tablespoon lemon juice.

### Redcurrant Sauce

This is a lovely clear sauce, without thickening, which is ideal for spooning over puddings and ice cream.

Put 8 tablespoons redcurrant jelly and 3 tablespoons water into a saucepan. Stir over a low heat until the jelly has dissolved. Use hot.

If using the sauce cold, increase the amount of water to 5 tablespoons so the sauce does not become too thick.

# ★1950★

THE NEW HOUSE OF COMMONS was opened by King George VI in October. The old building had been severely damaged in an air raid in 1941.

Newspapers reported a French plan for a European Federation. The idea was originally to control coal and steel production in France and Germany. The organization would be open to other European states, including Russia, and further projects were envisaged.

British troops left Hong Kong in the summer to aid the Americans fighting in South Korea. Throughout the subsequent months there were worrying reports of severe action.

Information about the increases in teachers' salaries showed there was still a large differential between the amounts paid to men and women in this profession.

A supermarket where the customers walked around and selected their own goods was a big contrast to shopping locally. Most people deposited their ration coupons with their grocer and butcher. This meant it was difficult to buy rationed foods, such as fats, sugar, tea and meat at other shops. There were however, more unrationed foods available.

Sainsbury's opened their first self-service store in Croydon. The first credit cards were launched by Diner's Club.

The BBC transmitted a television picture to France in August. This was the first time such an event had happened. The sale of television sets increased by 250 per cent during the year and this was reflected in the heavy postbag I received from viewers about all kinds of cookery matters. Some people wanted recipes from abroad, an interest reflected in articles published during the year in the Ministry of Food's *Food and Nutrition*. Information was given about the way people lived in various parts of the world, including such far-away places as Papua. An article on Indonesia went into some detail about the value of soya beans and soya milk.

Such articles did not detract from the Ministry's prime objective, which was to stress the importance of good nutrition. In order to make sure young people were eating wisely, the Ministry launched a film entitled *Feeding the under 20s*. The Ministry of Food's excellent *A.B.C. of Preserving* was published this year. It was sold at 6d (2½ p) by Her Majesty's Stationery Office.

British cooks had never used much oil in cooking, but in the June issue of *Food and Nutrition* there was a lengthy article about different kinds of oil – a portent, perhaps, for the years to come.

Ice cream was becoming Britain's favourite dessert and between-meal snack, though people did not have to make their own, unless they wished to. In 1939, annual ice cream sales in Britain were estimated to amount to £6,000,000. In 1940 the manufacture of ice cream had ceased, although a little was produced in the later years of the war to boost morale. By 1950, sales of ice cream had reached £14,000,000.

The commercial ice cream of this era was not of good quality, due to the shortage of basic ingredients. The public complained that it seemed 'full of air'. This was possibly true for the product was aerated to a great degree during manufacture.

⋆ ⋆ ⋆ ⋆ ⋆ ⋆ ⋆ ⋆ ⋆ ⋆ ⋆ ⋆ ⋆ ⋆ ⋆ ⋆ ⋆ ⋆ ⋆ ⋆ ⋆ ⋆ ⋆ ⋆ ⋆ ⋆ ⋆ ⋆ ⋆

# USING A LIQUIDIZER

By 1950, the number of people who had bought
liquidizers (blenders) had risen enormously,
so I was asked to give a number of
demonstrations on using them.
Liquidizers made simple work of producing
smooth purées of vegetables, fruit and other
ingredients. One lesson we had to stress in
demonstrations was that the goblet should
not be too full, for the mixture rises quite
dramatically, and the lid should be firmly placed,
or even held, in position when switching on.
In spite of this, people reported being showered
with soup or other liquid mixtures
because they failed to do this.
The liquidizer could only deal with small
amounts of solid foods at one time.
Food processors were unknown in 1950.

⋆ ⋆ ⋆ ⋆ ⋆ ⋆ ⋆ ⋆ ⋆ ⋆ ⋆ ⋆ ⋆ ⋆ ⋆ ⋆ ⋆ ⋆ ⋆ ⋆ ⋆ ⋆ ⋆ ⋆ ⋆ ⋆ ⋆ ⋆ ⋆

## HAM AND TOMATO PÂTÉ

Skin, deseed and chop 3 medium
tomatoes. Dice 5 oz (150 g) lean ham.
Put half the ingredients with a little
made mustard and a shake of pepper
into the liquidizer goblet, place the lid
in position, switch on and process
until smooth. Carefully remove the
purée and repeat with the remaining
ingredients.

### VARIATIONS

Add 1 or 2 spring onions or pickled
cocktail onions.
    Use cooked chicken or 3 hard-
boiled eggs instead of ham; season
well.
    Use lightly cooked liver instead
of ham, season well and add a pinch
of sugar.
    Use smoked or cooked fresh
cod's roe instead of ham with seasoning and a squeeze of lemon juice.

## RABBIT PÂTÉ

*Preparation time: 30 minutes*
*Cooking time: 1½ hours*
*Quantity: 6 helpings*

Rabbits, which had been a valuable
part of family fare in the country during the war years, began to appear in
towns to be cooked in various ways.
This recipe adds a touch of luxury to
meals as a first course, or it makes an
excellent main dish with salad.

1 medium rabbit
3 bacon rashers
good pinch ground cinnamon
2 reconstituted dried eggs
    (see page 10) or fresh eggs
salt and pepper
1 tablespoon chopped mixed
    herbs or 1 teaspoon mixed
    dried herbs
2 tablespoons port wine

Take the liver, heart and kidney from
the rabbit. Put these, with the derinded bacon, through a mincer. Mix with
the cinnamon, one of the eggs and a
little seasoning.
    Cut all the flesh from the bones of
the rabbit, and put through a mincer.

Add the herbs, the second egg and
port wine, season well. Spoon half the
minced bacon mixture into the base of
a small casserole, add the rabbit flesh
then cover with the remainder of the
minced bacon mixture. Press down
firmly with the back of a wooden
spoon. Cover tightly. Stand in a roasting tin half-filled with water (this

stops the pâté drying in cooking).
    Cook in a preheated oven set
to 160°C (325°F), Gas Mark 3 for
1½ hours.
    When cooked, carefully remove
the casserole lid, put a plate with a
light weight on it on top of the pâté.
Leave the pâté until cold, then turn
out of the dish.

## SPEEDY TOMATO SOUP

*Preparation time: 10 minutes*
*Cooking time: 5 minutes*
*Quantity: 4–6 helpings*

The liquidizer did not remove all the skins and pips from tomatoes but most people did not mind that. If one wanted the soup to be absolutely clear, the ingredients needed to be sieved after liquidizing or cooking, or the tomatoes concassed (the skins and seeds removed) before liquidizing. The flavour of this soup is delicious, as the cooking time is so short. It is also good served as a chilled soup without any cooking.

At first we were inclined to use ordinary British (strongly flavoured) onions, instead of the milder spring onions or shallots but if liquidized before cooking they retained a rather biting taste.

> 1 lb (450 g) tomatoes, chopped
> 1 small bunch spring onions or
>    2 shallots, chopped
> ½ small dessert apple, peeled
>    and chopped
> ¾ pint (450 ml) water or
>    chicken stock
> salt and pepper
> 1 teaspoon sugar
> 1 small sprig parsley
> few thyme leaves or pinch dried
>    thyme (optional)

There are too many ingredients in this recipe to liquidize all at once so put half the ingredients into the liquidizer goblet, place the lid in position then switch on. Tip the liquidized ingredients into a saucepan and repeat the liquidizing process with the remaining ingredients.

Cook the soup for 5 minutes only and serve.

### MODERN TOUCHES

A tablespoonful of tomato purée intensifies the flavour. A few basil leaves, a herb little known in the 1950s, can be used instead of the thyme. Milder red or sweet onions are excellent in this soup.

## LIQUIDIZERS AND OTHER APPLIANCES

In 1950 I gave a number of demonstrations using liquidizers and electric mixers due to the rise in their demand. It was not necessary to have special recipes for a mixer but what was essential was to use the machine correctly for each cooking purpose. I have included several of the recipes I used at these demonstrations in this chapter. There was not room to have a range of appliances in use in the Food Advice Bureau in the Harrods Food Hall. For many years this had been the Ministry of Food Bureau but towards the end of the 1940s its name was changed to Harrods Food Advice Bureau.

With the assistance of other home economists, I gave demonstrations each morning and afternoon to give the public the best help with their cookery problems and to suggest new and exciting dishes that could be made on the still meagre rations, plus the welcome unrationed foods arriving in Britain. At the beginning of 1950 I was asked to be responsible for a second bureau as well Harrods Home Service. This enabled me, with my assistants, to gave demonstrations of liquidizers, mixers, pressure cookers and other appliances, including exciting new washing machines, ironers and refrigerators.

## GRILLED PIGEONS

During this year the producer of the well-known and popular radio series *The Archers* came to Alexandra Palace, the home of BBC Television at that time, to ask me to demonstrate recipes using pigeons. The birds were causing much damage to crops at a time when it was essential that farmers produced as much wheat and corn as possible. Pigeons for grilling must be very young, often they are known as squabs. Allow 1 pigeon for each person. Wash and dry the birds and split lengthways. Season, then brush the birds with a generous amount of melted fat.

Preheat the grill and place the birds with the skin side uppermost on the grill pan. Cook for 5 minutes. Turn over and brush the under side with more fat. Continue cooking for a further 5 minutes. Turn the birds once more and cook until tender. To give more flavour to the flesh a few chopped herbs, such as parsley, thyme or rosemary, can be mixed with the melted fat. Serve the pigeons with redcurrant or apple jelly.

## PIGEON RAGOÛT

*Preparation time: 25 minutes*
*Cooking time: 1¹/₂ hours*
*Quantity: 4 helpings*

This is an excellent dish to make in summertime when tomatoes and cherries are in season.

    1 oz (25 g) flour
    salt and pepper
    2 large or 4 small pigeons, halved
    2 oz (50 g) dripping or cooking fat
    4 small onions or bunch spring onions, sliced
    4 small tomatoes, sliced
    ³/₄ pint (450 ml) brown stock
    4–5 oz (115–150g) ripe cherries

Blend the flour with a generous amount of seasoning and coat the pigeons. Heat the dripping or fat in a pan, add the pigeons and cook gently for 10 minutes, turning over once or twice. Lift out of the pan and place in a casserole.

Add the onions and tomatoes to the pan and cook for 3 minutes then spoon over the pigeons. Pour the stock into the pan, stir well to absorb the meat juices and then pour into the casserole. Cover tightly.

Preheat the oven to 160°C (325°F), Gas Mark 3 and cook the casserole for 45 minutes. Add the cherries (which can be stoned first) and continue cooking for a further 30 minutes.

**VARIATION**
Use a little less stock and add a few tablespoons of port wine to the other ingredients in the casserole.

Jelly tablets and crystals were now easily obtainable. For many people these were simpler to use than gelatine. The recipe on the right turns an ordinary lemon jelly into a delicious sweet.

## APRICOT AND LEMON JELLY

Make ¹/₂ pint (300 ml) smooth apricot purée by processing in the liquidizer cooked or canned apricots with a little of the syrup from cooking or canning. Make a jelly with ¹/₂ pint (300 ml) water, as instructed on the packet. Add the apricot purée. Pour into a mould and leave until firm. Turn out and decorate with Mock Cream (see page 71) and blanched almonds.

## VARIATIONS

Use canned pineapple or peaches instead of apricots. Fresh pineapple should never be added to any form of gelatine for it prevents the jelly from setting. The only solution is to cook the pineapple first.

Use a purée of uncooked raspberries with a raspberry jelly. A liquidizer does not get rid of all the pips so the purée needs to be rubbed through a sieve.

# RETURN OF DRIED FRUITS

Although limited supplies of dried fruit were available on the points system throughout the years of rationing, it was a joy to have a really wide choice of the fruits free from restrictions. They enabled us to make some interesting dishes.

## ORIENTAL FINGERS

*Preparation time: 25 minutes*
*Cooking time: 25–30 minutes*
*Quantity: 6–8 helpings*

**For the filling:**
2 oz (50 g) glacé cherries
2 oz (50 g) blanched almonds
 or other nuts
2 oz (50 g) dates, weight
 without stones
1 oz (50 g) sultanas
1 oz (25 g) butter or margarine
1 oz (25 g) caster or light
 brown sugar

**For the sweet shortcrust pastry:**
8 oz (225 g) plain flour
4 oz (ll5 g) butter or margarine
2 oz (50 g) caster sugar
little milk to bind

**For the topping:**
little icing sugar

Chop the cherries, nuts and dates for the filling into small pieces. Put into a saucepan with the rest of the filling ingredients and stir over a low heat until the fat and sugar have melted. Leave the mixture until cold.

Preheat the oven to 190°C (375°F), Gas Mark 5.

Sift the flour into a mixing bowl or the bowl of an electric mixer, add the butter or margarine and rub in by hand, or switch on the mixer, until the consistency of fine breadcrumbs. Do not over-handle. Add the sugar and gather the dough together. Gradually add sufficient milk to make a dough with a firm rolling consistency.

Divide the mixture into two equal portions and roll both out to oblongs about ¼ inch (6 mm) thick. Place one on an ungreased baking tray. Cover with the filling and then with the second sheet of pastry. Seal the edges lightly. Bake for 20–30 minutes until pale golden in colour and firm. Cool on the tray. When cold, cut into squares or fingers. Dust with sifted icing sugar.

## DATE AND WALNUT BARS

*Preparation time: 25 minutes*
*Cooking time: 25–30 minutes*
*Quantity: 12 cakes*

Various kinds of fresh nuts came back into the shops fairly soon after the war and dried nuts, used in this recipe, arrived at about the same time. In those days ready-cut candied (often called crystallized) peel was not available; you had to remove large lumps of sugar and chop the peel. Sugar was still regarded as a precious commodity so the pieces removed would be used to sweeten fruit.

4 oz (ll5 g) cooking dates
2 oz (50 g) walnuts
2 oz (50 g) glacé cherries
2 oz (50 g) mixed candied peel
4 oz (ll5 g) self-raising flour or
 plain flour with 1 teaspoon
 baking powder
2 oz (50 g) margarine
2 oz (50 g) sugar, preferably
 light brown
1 egg

Grease and flour an 8 inch (20 cm) square tin. Preheat the oven to 190°C (375°F), Gas Mark 5. Chop the dates, walnuts, cherries and peel.

Sift the flour, or flour and baking powder, into a bowl. Rub in the margarine, add the sugar then the rest of the ingredients. Spoon into the tin. Bake for 15 minutes or until brown, then reduce the oven temperature to 180°C (350°F), Gas Mark 4 and cook for a further 10–15 minutes, or until firm. Cut into portions while still warm, then remove from the tin.

The reason I'm glad
And my smile's so bright
You see on my tray
The food is just right

MINDER STOKEN
KORTER KOKEN
DAN BEHOUDT GE
GEUR EN SMAAK

EET IEDERE DAG GROENTE

A Good Breakfast

## CONGRESS TARTS

*Preparation time: 25 minutes*
*Cooking time: 20 minutes*
*Quantity: 9–12 tartlets*

When ground almonds came back on the market I had many enquiries about how to make real marzipan or almond paste and requests for recipes such as this one. I had demonstrated Mock Congress Tarts many times in the war years using semolina or fine breadcrumbs, with almond essence and lemon squash to give a semblance of the correct flavours.

**For the shortcrust or sweet shortcrust pastry:**
6 oz (175 g) flour, etc.
  (see Gypsy Tart, page 21, or
  Oriental Fingers, page 67)

**For the filling:**
little jam
2 oz (50 g) butter or margarine
2 oz (50 g) caster sugar
½-1 teaspoon finely grated
  lemon zest
1 egg
1 tablespoon lemon juice
2 oz (50 g) ground almonds

**To decorate:**
9–12 blanched almonds

Make the pastry as on pages 21 or 67. Preheat the oven to 190–200°C (375–400°F), Gas Mark 5–6. Use the higher setting for shallow tartlets and the lower one for deeper tarts.

Roll out the pastry and line 9–12 patty tins. Put a teaspoon of jam into each pastry case.

Cream the butter or margarine with the sugar and lemon zest. Beat the egg with the lemon juice and add to the creamed mixture together with the ground almonds. Spoon over the jam, top with an almond and bake for 15–20 minutes.

### VARIATION

Omit the almonds when baking the tarts. Top with Lemon Icing (see Lemon Sponge, page 86) and the almonds.

## BABAS AU RHUM

*Preparation time: 25 minutes plus time for proving*
*Cooking time: 10–15 minutes*
*Quantity: 8–10 cakes or 12–14 smaller ones*

Cooking with yeast had become so popular with my audiences at Harrods that every Friday afternoon I gave a baking demonstration and included some kind of yeast recipe. These light yeast cakes were a great favourite. Rum was easily obtainable by 1950.

½ oz (15 g) fresh yeast or ¼ oz (7 g) dried yeast, (see comments on yeast,
  Home-made Bread, page 28)
¼ pint (150 ml) milk or milk and water
2 oz (50 g) caster sugar
8 oz (225 g) plain flour
pinch salt
2 eggs
½ teaspoon vanilla essence
2 oz (50 g) butter or margarine, softened

**For the syrup:**
4 tablespoons water
4 tablespoons sugar or honey
squeeze lemon juice
3–5 tablespoons rum

**To decorate:**
Mock Cream (see page 71)
glacé cherries

Cream the fresh yeast in a basin. Warm the milk, or milk and water, add to the yeast and blend well. If using dried yeast add this to the warm milk with a teaspoon of the sugar. Sprinkle a little flour on top of the liquid. Leave until bubbles form.

Sift the flour with the salt into a mixing bowl, then add the rest of the sugar. Make a well in the centre and add the yeast liquid. Beat the eggs with the vanilla essence, add to the dough and mix very well. The mixture is too soft for kneading but it should be beaten well with a wooden spoon or the dough hook of an electric mixer, using a slow speed. Stop when the mixture looks smooth.

Place the softened butter or margarine over the dough, do not mix it in at this stage. Cover and leave in a warm place to prove for about 35 minutes or at room temperature for about 45–50 minutes. The dough should become almost double its original size.

Blend in the softened butter or margarine and beat again with a spoon or the dough hook. Grease 8–10 individual flan tins; if these are not available, use 12–14 castle pudding tins. Half fill with the dough and allow to prove for 15–20 minutes. Preheat the oven to 220°C (425°F), Gas Mark 7. Bake the larger cakes for about 15 minutes and the smaller ones for 10 minutes, or until just firm. Turn out on to a dish.

For the syrup, heat the water with the sugar or honey and lemon juice, add the rum. Prick the hot cakes with a fine skewer and spoon the hot syrup over them. When cold, decorate with Mock Cream and glacé cherries.

### VARIATIONS

**Savarin:** Put the dough into a well-greased 8 inch (20 cm) ovenproof ring mould. Prove then bake for 20–25 minutes. If necessary, reduce the oven temperature to 190°C (375°F), Gas Mark 5 after 10–15 minutes. Soak with the syrup as before. This cake is delicious filled with fresh fruit salad and served as a dessert.

2–3 tablespoons of currants could be added to the dough in both recipes.

In 1950 the Communists from North Korea invaded independent South Korea. The
invasion took place without any prior warning. The United States of America
offered military aid to South Korea and the United Nations backed
any opposition to the Communists.
A number of British naval ships were already in the area and these were
placed under the command of the American General Douglas MacArthur.
The first British troops arrived in South Korea at the end of August.
They consisted of men from Scottish and Middlesex regiments.
Later in 1950 the Chinese entered the war on the side
of the North Koreans.

## MOCK CREAM

People had become used to making mock cream in various ways. Since few homes possessed a cream-making machine, this recipe had become the favourite way of producing an acceptable substitute for real cream. Blend I level tablespoon cornflour with ¼ pint (150 ml) milk. Tip into a saucepan and stir carefully over a low heat until the mixture becomes very thick. Pour into a basin, cover to prevent a skin forming, and leave until cold.

Cream 1 oz (25 g) butter or margarine (it is worthwhile using butter if you can spare it) with ½–1 oz (15–25 g) caster or sifted icing sugar. Very gradually beat teaspoons of the cornflour mixture into the creamed fat and sugar. An electric mixer does this very efficiently but whether mixing by hand or by machine, the secret is to incorporate the cornflour mixture slowly and beat hard.

For a less thick cream use 7½ fl oz (225 ml) milk.

To make a thick cream, follow the method given but use 4 oz (115 g) butter to the 7½ fl oz (225 ml) milk.

There is a recipe for making a pouring cream with a machine on page 59 (Rich Vanilla Ice Cream).

### Egg Nog

This was a favourite drink when liquidizers were first introduced. Manufacturer's would demonstrate the machine using the egg in its shell. I doubt whether many people did the same thing in their own home. This was a recipe where reconstituted dried egg did not give a particularly good flavour, it had to be a fresh egg.

Put a fresh egg with 1–2 teaspoons sugar and ½ pint (300 ml) milk into the goblet. Add 2–3 tablespoons brandy or whisky. Cover and switch on. Serve cold or heat for just I minute, taking care the mixture does not boil.

### FRUIT MILK SHAKE

Put a spoonful of crushed ice or ice cream into the liquidizer goblet. Add a small or ½ large sliced banana or a few strawberries or other fruit and a good ½ tumbler of milk. Cover and switch on until smooth and frothy.

NOTE: It is essential that the ice is crushed, as otherwise it would damage the blades of the liquidizer. Put the ice cubes on to a clean teacloth, cover with the cloth and crush with a rolling pin.

# ★ 1951 ★

IN MAY THE Festival of Britain was opened by the King and Queen. It was created on 27 acres of bomb-damaged land on the south side of the Thames. The idea was to combine fun and fantasy in the Pleasure Gardens of Battersea Park; the objective of the Government-sponsored Festival was to show the world that, in spite of the present austerity, Britain was looking forward to a much brighter future. To make certain that all the refreshments sold at the Festival were as good as possible, a committee of people in the food world were asked to visit the Festival regularly and check on the food and drink. I was a member of the committee.

The King also opened Festival Hall.

The election held in this year brought the Conservatives back into power, with Winston Churchill as Prime Minister once again.

The survey of the time spent in the home by most housewives established that, on average, they worked 75 hours a week, with overtime on Saturdays and Sundays. This did not take into account that a number of women were also doing part or full-time work outside the home.

Tuppence (2d) was taken off the meat ration at the beginning of the year. This meant that the average weekly ration was now about 4 oz (115 g), the lowest it had been. Butchers estimated that, with rising prices, it would take the meat coupons from 3 ration books to buy 1 lb (450 g) meat a week.

One good thing was that chickens, rabbits and pigeons were more readily available. Rice was also available again, after some years of shortages.

Some interesting fruits and vegetables, such as avocados, red and green peppers and aubergines, were becoming more generally known. I tried to take a rather unusual fruit or vegetable to each television programme and explain just how to serve it.

The number of refrigerators on sale in Britain was increasing and various firms were advertising their models quite extensively. Cream was still unobtainable, so I made various ice creams in one of my television programmes using the recipes for Economical Ice Creams in the 1949 chapter (see page 59).

The range of subjects that readers of magazines and viewers of television wanted to have discussed was very varied. Young men and women, many of whom had gone straight from school into the forces, had not had a chance to learn to cook basic meals in their own homes. Now, they wanted to learn basic principles and know how to choose food, such as vegetables and fish, wisely. While the allowance of meat was so low there was little point in dealing with a selection of cuts of meat; that had to wait until after the summer of 1954.

Older people thought nostalgically of our traditional recipes from before the war and wanted these shown on television. None of these requests was easy to fulfil, due to the strict rationing still in force.

Television in these days was such a personal medium. People wrote copious letters to all who appeared before the cameras. The viewers felt they knew you well and could write and comment on the programme and also on the dress you wore and the way you had your hair.

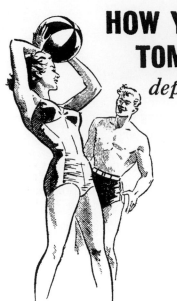

# HOW YOU FEEL TOMORROW

## *depends a lot on*
# TODAY...

### FISH PILAFF

*Preparation time: 20 minutes*
*Cooking time: 30 minutes*
*Quantity: 4 helpings*

This mixture of rice, fish and other ingredients makes a very satisfying and easily prepared meal.

1 lb (450 g) white fish, skinned
2 oz (50 g) margarine
2 medium onions, chopped
1 garlic clove, crushed (optional)
6 oz (175 g) long-grain rice
1 pint (600 ml) water
salt and pepper

2 medium tomatoes, skinned
    and chopped
2 oz (50 g) raisins

Cut the fish into 1 inch (2.5 cm) dice, removing any bones. Heat half the margarine in a large saucepan, add the fish and cook carefully for 5 minutes until slightly brown and nearly tender. Remove from the pan with a fish slice and place on a plate.

Heat the remaining margarine in the same pan, add the onions and garlic, if using, and cook for 5 minutes. Put in the rice and stir until it is well blended with the onions. Add the water, bring to the boil, season well, then lower the heat. Cover the pan and cook for 10 minutes. Stir well, then put in the tomatoes and raisins. Cook for a further 5 minutes, stir once more, then add the fish. Continue cooking until the rice is tender, the fish is very hot and any excess liquid has evaporated. The dish should be moist but not too wet. Serve with mixed vegetables.

### CHICKEN BROTH

*Preparation time: 20 minutes*
*Cooking time: 1½ hours*
*Quantity: 4 helpings*

bones from a chicken
3 onions
3 carrots
2 celery sticks
salt and pepper
1¼ pints (750 ml) chicken
    stock (see method)
1½ oz (40 g) long-grain rice
few canned or cooked peas
    or beans, if available
½ pint (300 ml) milk

**To garnish:**
diced toast
chopped parsley

Break the bones of the chicken with a small weight. This makes it easier to extract the flavour. Put the bones into a saucepan. Peel and roughly chop 1 onion, 1 carrot and the celery. Add to the bones with 2½ pints (1.5 litres) water and a little seasoning. Cover the pan and simmer for 1 hour.

Peel the remaining onions and carrots and cut into ½ inch (1.25 cm) dice. Strain the stock and measure out 1¼ pints (750 ml). Pour into a saucepan, bring to the boil, then add the rice and the diced vegetables. Cook steadily for 30 minutes, then add the peas and the milk. Simmer for another 5 minutes, then garnish and serve.

### VARIATIONS
Make the stock in a pressure cooker. Allow only 30 minutes cooking time and use 1½ pints (900 ml) water: this is sufficient because the liquid does not evaporate as much in a pressure cooker as it does in a saucepan.

Save a little cooked chicken breast from the carcass and dice this neatly. Add to the soup with the milk.

### RED AND GREEN
### PEPPER SALAD

*Preparation time: 15 minutes*
*No cooking*
*Quantity: 4 helpings*

2 green peppers
1 red pepper
4 oz (115 g) Cheddar cheese,
    grated
2 tablespoons finely diced
    gherkins
2 large tomatoes, skinned and
    finely chopped
3 tablespoons mayonnaise
salt and pepper
lettuce

Cut a slice from the stalk end of the peppers and deseed them. Chop the slices and all the red pepper very finely. Mix with the cheese, gherkins, chopped tomatoes and mayonnaise. Spoon the mixture into the green peppers and chill for a time. Cut into slices and arrange on a bed of lettuce.

## SAVOURY CHEESE PIE

*Preparation time: 30 minutes*
*Cooking time: 40 minutes*
*Quantity: 4 helpings*

The small amount of meat available during 1951 meant that cheese was often used to make a main dish, such as in this pie, which is not unlike a filled quiche.

**For the savoury pastry:**
6 oz (175 g) plain flour
salt and pepper
½ teaspoon mustard powder
3 oz (85 g) margarine or
    cooking fat
1 oz (25 g) cheese, finely grated
1 tablespoon chopped parsley
water, to bind

**For the filling:**
1 oz (25 g) margarine
2 medium onions, chopped
2 medium cooked potatoes,
    diced
2 tomatoes, thinly sliced
2 eggs
¼ pint (150 ml) milk
1 tablespoon chopped parsley
2 oz (50 g) cheese, grated

To make the pastry, sift the flour with the seasonings, rub in the magarine or fat, add the cheese and parsley and enough water to make a pastry with a firm rolling consistency.

Wrap the pastry and chill briefly in the refrigerator then roll out and use to line an 8 inch (20 cm) shallow flan tin or dish. Preheat the oven to 190°C (375°F), Gas Mark 5 and heat a baking tray at the same time. Stand the baking tin or dish on the hot baking tray and cook the pastry case 'blind' for only 15 minutes (see page 47). Remove the pastry shell from the oven and lower the oven temperature to 160°C (325°F), Gas Mark 3.

While the pastry is cooking, make the filling. Heat the margarine, add the onions and cook gently for 8 minutes. Mix with the diced potatoes and put into the partially cooked pastry shell. Top with the sliced tomatoes. Beat the eggs, add the milk and the rest of the ingredients. Season to taste and pour over the potato mixture. Return the pie to the oven and bake for approximately 25 minutes, or until the filling is set. Serve hot or cold.

## MOUSSAKA

*Preparation time: 35 minutes*
*Cooking time: 1 hour 20 minutes*
*Quantity: 4 helpings*

2 medium aubergines,
    thinly sliced
salt and pepper
4 medium potatoes,
    thickly sliced
1½ oz (40 g) margarine or
    cooking fat
3 medium onions,
    thinly sliced
4 medium tomatoes,
    thickly sliced
8 oz (225 g) lamb, mutton
    or beef, minced

**For the sauce:**
1 oz (25 g) margarine
1 oz (25 g) flour
12 fl oz (350 ml) milk
1 egg
2–3 oz (50–85 g) cheese,
    grated
pinch grated or ground
    nutmeg

**To garnish:**
chopped parsley

Sprinkle the aubergine slices with a little salt, leave for about 20 minutes then drain and rinse in cold water. Dry well. This draws out the slightly bitter taste from the skins. Put the aubergine and potato slices into a steamer over a pan of boiling water. Cover and steam for about 10 minutes or until just soft but not mushy.

Heat the margarine or cooking fat, add the onions and cook slowly for 5 minutes. Add the tomatoes and the meat, mix well and cook gently for another 10 minutes, stirring all the time.

For the sauce, heat the margarine, add the flour and then most of the milk. Stir over a moderate heat until the sauce thickens. Remove from the heat. Beat the egg with the remaining milk and whisk it into the hot sauce, together with half the cheese, seasoning and nutmeg.

Arrange layers of the onion and meat mixture and the aubergines and potatoes in a casserole. Spread a little sauce over each layer. End with a potato and aubergine layer and the last of the sauce then top with the remaining cheese. Bake for 1 hour in a preheated oven set to 160°C (325°F), Gas Mark 3. Top with parsley and serve hot.

**A MODERN TOUCH**
There is no need to salt the aubergines today.

## AVOCADO AND ORANGE COCKTAIL

*Preparation time: 10 minutes*
*No cooking*
*Quantity: 4 helpings*

Avocados were becoming better known. The partnership of avocados and oranges makes a perfect start to a meal.

**For the dressing:**
3 tablespoons olive oil
1 tablespoon lemon juice
   or white wine vinegar
salt and pepper
2 oranges
2 ripe avocados
lettuce heart

Mix together the oil, lemon juice or vinegar and seasoning. Cut away the peel and pith from the oranges then, working over a basin so no juice is wasted, cut out the orange segments. Remove any pips or skin. Add a little of the orange juice to the dressing. Any juice left can be put into a fruit salad. Halve, stone and skin the avocados and cut the flesh into neat dice. Put into the dressing with the orange segments.

Shred the lettuce finely, put into individual glasses then top with the avocado mixture and dressing. Chill well for a short time before serving.

**VARIATION**
Use grapefruit segments instead of orange or use a combination of orange and grapefruit.

## LEMON FLUMMERY

*Preparation time: 15 minutes*
*Cooking time: 10 minutes*
*Quantity: 4 helpings*

I had made this recipe during the war years, using the very oddly flavoured lemon squash then available: what a joy to be able to use real lemons.

½ teaspoon finely grated
   lemon zest
3 tablespoons lemon juice
cold water (see method)
2 oz (50 g) sugar
½ oz (15 g) gelatine
   (see note right)
2 reconstituted dried eggs
   (see page 10) or fresh eggs

Put the lemon zest, lemon juice and nearly all the water into a saucepan, add the sugar and heat gently for a few minutes to soften the zest and dissolve the sugar. Pour the remaining cold water into a basin, add the gelatine, allow to stand for 3 minutes then place over a saucepan of very hot water until dissolved. Stir into the lemon mixture and mix well. Take the pan off the heat and whisk in the well-beaten eggs.

Return the pan to the heat and simmer gently, whisking all the time, for 4–5 minutes. Pour the mixture into a rinsed mould and leave until firm then turn out.
NOTE: With modern gelatine, use 1 sachet, i.e. 0.4 oz (11 g).

## FRUITY RICE

*Preparation time: 15 minutes*
*Cooking time: 2 hours*
*Quantity: 4 helpings*

Rice was little used in Britain except for puddings or to accompany a curry, so the lack of rice in previous years had not been a great problem. Now rice had returned, people could make good puddings, although one or two people did try making a pilaff with long-grain rice.

2 oz (50 g) short-grain rice
1 pint (600 ml) milk
1 teaspoon finely grated
   lemon zest
2 teaspoons finely grated
   orange zest
2 oz (50 g) sugar, or to taste
3 tablespoons raisins
3 tablespoons sultanas

**For the topping:**
2 oranges
1 oz (25 g) sugar

Preheat the oven to 150°C (300°F), Gas Mark 2. Put all the ingredients for the pudding (but not the topping) into a 2 pint (1.2 litre) pie dish and bake for 1¾ hours.

Meanwhile, prepare the topping. Cut away the peel from the oranges then cut the fruit into thin rings, removing any pips. Take the pudding from the oven and arrange the orange rings over it. Sprinkle with sugar then return to the oven for 15 minutes. Serve hot.

The travelling salesman from Walls Ice Cream had been a feature on the roads before the war and it was a welcome sight to see him back again. There were also some women doing the same job.
The roads at that time were relatively quiet compared to modern day traffic, so that riding a bicycle and stopping frequently to sell ice cream was not the danger it would be today.

# THE FESTIVAL OF BRITAIN

The Festival was opened by the King and Queen on 4 May 1951. This was 100 years after the Victorian Great Exhibition. A team of distinguished experts, led by Hugh Casson, the famous architect, created this Festival on what had previously been wasteland near Waterloo.
To quote the words used at the time:

'The whole of this large expanse was planned to create a feeling of fun, fantasy and colour'.

The scene on the left shows the Festival in full swing. The Festival was sponsored by the Labour Government. One of the ministers, Herbert Morrison, described its purpose as 'the people giving themselves a pat on the back'. Certainly the public flocked to the Festival where they could enjoy the various sights, the funfair and the pleasure gardens. In addition to the Festival of Britain the new Festival Hall was opened. This provided a first class concert hall with modern amenities.

## GINGER BUNS

*Preparation time:*
*5 minutes*
*Cooking time:*
*2–15 minutes*
*Quantity: 12 cakes*

1 oz (25 g) crystallized ginger
6 oz (175 g) self-raising flour or plain flour with 1½ teaspoons baking powder
1 oz (25 g) cornflour
1 teaspoon ground ginger, or to taste
pinch mixed spice
4 oz (115 g) margarine
4 oz (115 g) soft brown sugar
2 teaspoons golden syrup
1 egg
milk, to mix

Preheat the oven to 200°C (400°F), Gas Mark 6. Grease and flour 12 patty tins or place paper cases in the tins. Finely chop the crystallized ginger.

Sift the flour with the baking powder and spices. Cream the margarine, sugar and syrup until soft. Beat the egg, add to the mixture, then fold in the flour and enough milk to make a firm dropping consistency. Lastly add the crystallized ginger. Spoon the mixture into the tins or paper cases and bake until firm.

### VARIATION
When cold, the cakes can be coated with a thin layer of ginger-flavoured icing (see Ginger Icing, page 86), and a thin slice of crystallized ginger.

## ECONOMICAL BOURBON BISCUITS

*Preparation time: 15 minutes*
*Cooking time: 10–12 minutes*
*Quantity: 15 complete biscuits*

3 oz (85 g) margarine
2 oz (50 g) caster sugar
2 level tablespoons
    golden syrup
few drops vanilla essence
6 oz (175 g) plain flour
1 oz (25 g) rice flour or
    fine semolina
1 oz (25 g) cocoa powder
few drops of milk,
    if necessary (see method)

### For Chocolate Butter Icing:

1½ oz (40 g) butter
    or margarine
2 teaspoons cocoa powder
2oz (50 g) icing sugar

Preheat the oven to 160°C (325°F), Gas Mark 3. Lightly grease two baking trays.

Cream the margarine, sugar, golden syrup and vanilla essence until soft and light. Sift the flour with the rice flour or semolina and cocoa powder into the creamed ingredients and knead very thoroughly. Try to avoid using any milk if possible, but the dough should be a firm rolling consistency.

Flour a pastry board very sparingly – you do not want a floury outside to these biscuits. Roll out the dough until it is just over ⅛ inch (3 mm) thick and cut into fingers about 1 inch (2.5 cm) wide and the required length.

Place the fingers on the baking tray and prick lightly at regular intervals. Bake for 10–12 minutes, or until just firm. Leave on the trays until cold.

Cream the butter or margarine for the icing, sift the icing sugar and cocoa into it and mix well. Sandwich the biscuits together with a little of the icing.

### VARIATIONS

The Chocolate Biscuit recipe on page 99 makes a richer biscuit.

### Chocolate Butter Icing 2:

Supplies of icing sugar were still uncertain so you could make the filling without it by creaming together 1½ oz (40 g) butter or margarine, 1 level tablespoon golden syrup and 1½ oz (40 g) sifted chocolate or cocoa powder.

In this case chocolate powder (if available) makes a less strongly flavoured filling.

## REAL MARZIPAN

Mix together 4 oz (115 g) ground almonds with 2 oz (50 g) caster sugar, 2 oz (50 g) sifted icing sugar and a few drops of almond essence. Bind with the yolk of an egg.

## MARZIPAN BUNS

These would be a good cake for a children's party. They are based on the recipe for Home-made Bread (see page 28). Use the same ingredients as for Home-made Bread After the dough has proved in bulk, take off about half to make a loaf then use the remainder for these buns.

Make 12–15 round balls with the dough. Make a deep indentation in each of the balls with your finger and put a little marzipan inside (see above). Gently roll the dough again until the marzipan is completely enclosed.

Place the buns on a baking tray and allow to prove until almost double in size. Preheat the oven to 220°C (425°F), Gas Mark 7. Bake the buns for 12–15 minutes.

While the buns are still hot, brush them with a glaze made by dissolving 2 tablespoons sugar in 2 tablespoons hot water.

## CONTINENTAL FRUIT BREAD

*Preparation time: 30 minutes,*
*plus time for proving*
*Cooking time: 35–40 minutes*
*Quantity: 2 loaves*

This is a delicious bread to eat with butter when fresh. Slices can be toasted when the bread gets stale.

Use the ingredients for Home-made Bread (see page 28), but use ¾ oz (20 g) fresh yeast or 3 teaspoons dried yeast and decrease the water by 4 tablespoons

**Additional ingredients:**
2 oz (50 g) margarine or
   cooking fat
2 oz (50 g) sugar
1 teaspoon grated lemon zest
3 oz (85 g) sultanas
2 eggs

**For the topping:**
little milk
1 oz (25 g) chopped almonds

Sift the flour and salt for the bread into a mixing bowl. Rub in the margarine or cooking fat then add the sugar, lemon zest and sultanas. Cream fresh yeast or dissolve dried yeast (see Home-made Bread, page 28), add the warm water and beaten eggs then continue as in the method for Home-made Bread, allowing the dough to prove in bulk.

When it has proved, divide into four portions. Form two of these portions into oval shapes about 8 inch (20 cm) long and 4 inches (10 cm) wide. Cut each of the other two portions into three strips and plait them loosely. Place over the oval shapes. Brush with milk and sprinkle with almonds.

Allow to prove until nearly double in size. Bake the bread in a preheated ovenset to 200°C (400°F), Gas Mark 6 for 35–40 minutes.

# ★1952★

IN JANUARY NEWSPAPERS **and television carried pictures of the King and Queen saying farewell to Princess Elizabeth and Prince Philip at the start of their journey to Australia. They were going to stay in Kenya for a safari holiday en route.**

One week later the nation learned that George VI had died peacefully in his sleep. There was genuine grief throughout Britain and the Commonwealth, for the shy quiet man, who had never expected to be king, had earned everyone's respect and affection. It was a sad return to this country for his young daughter, who was now Queen Elizabeth II.

In November the Queen opened her first Parliament. By then, there was much talk about the new Elizabethan age and just what Britain would achieve under this Queen Elizabeth in the years to come.

In February tea came off ration and there was much rejoicing. We had always been a tea-drinking nation and the small amount allowed meant one never seemed to have sufficient to enjoy odd cups of tea. Over the years since 1940, when rationing began, people had developed ways to eke out the tea. If any tea was left in the teapot it was strained into a vacuum flask to be heated later. Many people used the tea leaves twice, the second brew was weak, but it still gave a warming drink.

Television had made people more aware of all sorts of sporting events, including tennis at Wimbledon. A competitor who endeared herself to the public was the American Maureen Connolly, known as Little Mo. She won the women's singles at her first attempt at the age of17.

Little Mo went on to win the Wimbledon championship for a further two years.

The Duchess of Kent was a great supporter of Wimbledon and the Kent family still is.

Appliances that had been on sale for several years and had grown rapidly in popularity were electric mixers and liquidizers (often known as blenders). The mixer took away the hard work of creaming and other tasks and cooks were grateful for this. Some people were not entirely satisfied with the results of cake-making with an electric mixer and I had many letters from ladies who had made wonderful sponges and light cakes, indeed in some instances winning prizes before the war. Now, having saved their rations to repeat their success, they were disappointed at the results when using a mixer. I had to demonstrate that one must take time and learn how to reconcile the cookery techniques of hand-mixing to the use of an efficient electric appliance.

Liquidizers were a joy and in many cases the sieve, which was time-consuming and quite hard work to use and clean, was now superfluous. The liquidizer would give smooth purées of vegetables or fruits within seconds, so that soup-making and many desserts were now possible for busy people.

For several television programmes during the year I demonstrated invalid cookery. It was a fact that during the war years people had rarely complained about illnesses unless they were very serious. Now, people were very concerned with gastric problems and diets. Some of the recipes I gave on television are in this chapter.

By 1952, Bird's Eye had started quick-freezing peas at Lowestoft in Suffolk.

## GINGER NUTS

*Preparation time: 15 minutes*
*Cooking time: 15 minutes*
*Quantity: 15–18 biscuits*

The baking instructions for these biscuits may seem rather unusual but they give the best result. If the baked biscuits are not quite as crisp as you would wish, return them to the oven at the lower heat for a few more minutes.

2 oz (50 g) margarine or
    cooking fat
2 level tablespoons golden syrup
1 oz (25 g) light brown sugar
4 oz (115 g) plain flour
1 level teaspoon bicarbonate
    of soda
1/2–1 teaspoon each of mixed
    spice, ground cinnamon
    and ground ginger

Preheat the oven to 200°C (400°F), Gas Mark 6. Grease two baking trays very well.

Melt the margarine or cooking fat with the syrup in a saucepan. Remove from the heat, and add the sugar. Sift the flour very thoroughly with the bicarbonate of soda and spices, add to the melted ingredients and mix well. If the mixture is a little sticky, allow it to stand in a cool place for at least 15 minutes. Roll into 15–18 small balls and place these on the trays, allowing space for them to spread.

Bake for 5 minutes, then immediately lower the oven temperature to 180°C (350°F), Gas Mark 4 and bake for a further 10 minutes. It helps the temperature in an electric oven to drop if the door is opened slightly until the setting is reached. Cool the biscuits on the trays. When cold, store in an airtight tin away from other biscuits.

### VARIATION
**Chocolate Nuts:** For this variation on the Ginger Nuts above, sift 3 oz (85 g) plain flour with 1 oz (25 g) cocoa powder and 1 level teaspoon bicarbonate of soda. Melt the fat and syrup as for Ginger Nuts, add the sugar and 1/4 teaspoon vanilla essence. Add the dry ingredients, knead well then roll into balls. Bake as for Ginger Nuts. One of the three spices could be used in these biscuits, if liked.

☆ ☆ ☆ ☆ ☆ ☆ ☆ ☆ ☆ ☆ ☆ ☆ ☆ ☆ ☆ ☆ ☆ ☆ ☆ ☆ ☆ ☆ ☆ ☆ ☆ ☆ ☆

## COME TO TEA

People in Britain were tending to entertain quite a lot, in spite of the continued rationing of many foods. When the tea ration was abolished, I had a great many requests for more cake and biscuit recipes for special tea parties.

The cake and biscuit recipes most in demand were those that used fairly low quantities of fat and sugar. The Chocolate Gâteau recipe, below, is typical of the kind of special cake parents or grandparents made for their family or friends for a special occasion. They would have to use part of their precious sweet ration in the form of plain chocolate in order to produce it.

☆ ☆ ☆ ☆ ☆ ☆ ☆ ☆ ☆ ☆ ☆ ☆ ☆ ☆ ☆ ☆ ☆ ☆ ☆ ☆ ☆ ☆ ☆ ☆ ☆ ☆ ☆

## CHOCOLATE GÂTEAU

*Preparation time: 20 minutes*
*Cooking time: 1 hour*
*Quantity: 1 cake*

3 oz (85 g) plain chocolate
3 oz (85 g) butter or
    margarine
2 large eggs
3 oz (85 g) caster sugar
4 oz (115 g) self-raising
    flour or plain flour with
    1 teaspoon baking powder

**For the decoration:**
Rich Chocolate Butter Icing
    (see page 98)
chocolate vermicelli

Preheat the oven to 160°C (325°F), Gas Mark 3. Line a 7 inch (18 cm) cake tin with greased greaseproof paper.

Break the chocolate into small pieces, put in a heatproof bowl and melt over a pan of hot water. Cool slightly. Melt the butter or margarine in another bowl. Separate the eggs, add the yolks with the sugar to the chocolate and whisk until thick and creamy. Sift the flour, or flour and baking powder, into the other ingredients then add the melted butter or margarine. Fold the ingredients gently together.

Whisk the egg whites until they stand in soft peaks. Take a tablespoon of the whites and beat briskly into the chocolate mixture then gently fold in the remainder. Spoon into the cake tin and bake for about 1 hour or until firm to a gentle touch. Cool in the tin for 5 minutes then turn out on to a wire rack to cool.

When cold, top with the butter icing and a dusting of the chocolate vermicelli.

### VARIATION
Make three times the amount of the Rich Chocolate Butter Icing. Split the cake through the centre and fill with some of the icing. Cover the sides and top of the cake with the remainder of the icing, then coat with chocolate vermicelli.

# LEMON SPONGE

*Preparation time: 20 minutes*
*Cooking time: 30 minutes*
*Quantity: 1 sponge cake*

It may be surprising to anyone who has not used dried eggs to learn they make very good sponges and that the reconstituted eggs whisk up well with the sugar. The sponge is lighter if you can spare an extra 1 oz (25 g) sugar.

This is one of the recipes where cooks were inclined to use the electric whisk for the whole process of making the sponge. While the machine is ideal for whisking the eggs and sugar, it is essential to fold in the flour by hand. If you whisk in the flour with an electric beater you destroy the light texture.

3 oz (85 g) flour
  (see method)
3 reconstituted dried eggs
  (see page 10) or
  fresh eggs
3 oz (85 g) caster sugar
½–1 teaspoon finely grated
  lemon zest
1 tablespoon lemon juice

**For the filling (optional):**
lemon curd or lemon
  marmalade

**For Lemon Icing:**
6 oz (175 g) icing sugar,
  sifted
little lemon juice

Sift the flour on to a plate and leave at room temperature for at least 30 minutes. This lightens the flour. This sponge can be made with plain flour, without any raising agent, for the lightness incorporated into the eggs and sugar makes the sponge rise. It may be wiser if you have not made this very light sponge before to use self-raising flour or plain flour sifted with ¾ level teaspoon baking powder.

Preheat the oven to 180°C (350°F), Gas Mark 4. Line a 7–7½ inch (18–19 cm) cake tin with greased greaseproof paper or grease and flour it well. Put the reconstituted dried eggs or fresh eggs with the sugar and lemon zest into a bowl. Using a hand or electric whisk, whisk until the mixture is like a thick cream; you should see the trail of the whisk in the mixture. Sift the flour into a bowl. Using a large metal spoon or spatula, not the electric whisk, gently fold the flour, then the lemon juice, into the mixture.

Pour or spoon the mixture into the tin and bake until firm to a gentle touch. Allow to cool in the tin for about 5 minutes then turn out on to a wire rack to cool.

If you would like a filling, split the cake horizontally and spread with the lemon curd or marmalade.

For the Lemon Icing, blend the icing sugar with enough lemon juice to give a firm spreading consistency. Put on to the top of the sponge and spread with a warm knife.

## VARIATION

Divide the mixture between two 7–7½ inch (18–19 cm) sandwich tins and bake for 12–15 minutes.
**Ginger Icing:** This icing (referred to in Ginger Buns on page 79) is made as the Lemon Icing for Lemon Sponge, above. Blend ¼–½ level teaspoon ground ginger with the icing sugar, or omit the ground ginger and mix the icing sugar with syrup from preserved ginger.

# ATHOLL CAKES

*Preparation time: 20 minutes*
*Cooking time: 12–15 minutes*
*Quantity: 9–12 cakes*

3 oz (85 g) butter or margarine
3 oz (85 g) caster sugar
1½ teaspoons finely grated
  lemon zest
3 oz (85 g) plain flour with
  1 teaspoon baking powder
1 oz (25 g) rice flour or cornflour
1 egg
1½ tablespoons lemon juice
2 tablespoons finely chopped
  candied lemon peel

Grease and flour 9–12 patty tins or put paper cases in the tins. Preheat the oven to 190°C (375°F), Gas Mark 5. Cream the butter or margarine with the sugar and lemon zest. Sift the flour with the baking powder and rice flour or cornflour.

Beat the egg, add to the creamed ingredients with the flour mixture, lemon juice and peel. Spoon into the tins or paper cases and bake the cakes until firm.

# AUSTRALIAN CAKES

*Preparation time: 10 minutes*
*Cooking time: 12 minutes*
*Quantity: 12 cakes*

4 oz (115 g) self-raising flour
  with 1 teaspoon baking
  powder or plain flour with
  2 teaspoons baking powder
4 oz (115 g) cornflakes
3 oz (85 g) butter or margarine
4 oz (115 g) sugar
1 egg
milk, to mix

**For the decoration:**
6 glacé cherries

Preheat the oven to 200°C (400°F), Gas Mark 6. Grease and flour 2 baking trays. Sift the flour and baking powder; lightly crush the cornflakes. Rub the fat into the flour, add the sugar, cornflakes, beaten egg and enough milk to make a sticky consistency.

Put spoonfuls of the mixture on the trays, allowing space for the mixture to spread out. Top each cake with a halved cherry and bake until firm.

## BEEF TEA

*Preparation time: 10 minutes*
*Cooking time: 2 hours*
*Quantity: 1 helping, about ¹/₂ pint (300 ml)*

The instruction about using this flavoursome clear soup quickly was very necessary at the time the recipe was written, for the majority of homes still did not contain a refrigerator and freezers were unknown.

8 oz (225 g) lean stewing beef
¹/₂ pint (300 ml) water
pinch salt

Cut the meat into neat dice. Put into a strong jug or the top of a double saucepan. Add the water and salt. Cover the container and stand over a pan of simmering water. Allow the water to simmer steadily for 2 hours then strain the beef tea through muslin.

Leave the beef tea until quite cold then skim any fat from the surface. Heat, adjust the seasoning and serve with crisp toast.

Do not make large quantities of beef tea, for it should not be kept longer than a day.

## HADDOCK QUENELLES

*Preparation time: 15 minutes*
*Cooking time: 10 minutes*
*Quantity: 4 helpings*

People often forget how difficult it was to get good fish during the war years, so many fishermen were at sea in the Royal Navy or the Merchant Navy. The variety of fish was limited and often it was far from fresh when it arrived on the fishmonger's slab. Now numerous pre-war varieties were becoming available again and cooks were returning to some of the well-remembered classic recipes. This fish dish would be ideal for all the family, as well as for an invalid.

10 oz (300 g) haddock fillet, weight when skinned and boned
2 oz (50 g) butter or margarine
2 egg yolks or 1 reconstituted dried egg (see page 10)
4 tablespoons soft breadcrumbs
salt and pepper
1 pint (600 ml) milk

Rub the blade of a sharp knife over the raw fish to get fine flakes. Put these into a basin and pound well to give a smooth texture. Melt the butter or margarine and add to the fish with all the rest of the ingredients, except the milk. Form into 8 finger shapes.

Pour the milk into a large frying pan, add a little seasoning and bring to the boil, then lower the heat so the milk is just simmering.

Poach the quenelles in the milk for 10 minutes. Turn them around several times so they cook evenly. Lift the fish on to a heated dish, and keep warm while making a sauce with the milk.

### VARIATIONS
Use whiting instead of haddock. Finely chopped parsley or a little dried parsley can be added to the fish.
**Chicken Quenelles:** Substitute minced raw chicken breast for the fish. Poach for 15 minutes.

## CHICKEN TERRAPIN

*Preparation time: 10 minutes*
*Cooking time: 12 minutes*
*Quantity: 1 helping*

1 egg
½ oz (15 g) butter
  or margarine
2 teaspoons flour
4 tablespoons milk
salt and pepper
1 oz (25 g) cooked rice
2 oz (50 g) cooked chicken
  breast
few drops lemon juice

**To garnish:**
toast triangles

Hard-boil the egg, and cool it quickly in cold water. Shell and chop the egg. Heat the butter or margarine, stir in the flour and the milk and continue stirring to make a thick sauce. Add the chopped egg and the rest of the ingredients and heat thoroughly. Form into a neat round on a heated plate and garnish with triangles of crisp toast.

## BACON AND CHICKEN TOAST

*Preparation time:10 minutes*
*Cooking time: 8 minutes*
*Quantity: 1 helping*

1 lean bacon rasher, derinded
1 oz (25 g) butter or margarine
1 egg
3 tablespoons finely diced
  cooked chicken
salt and pepper
1 slice bread

Cut the bacon rasher into small pieces. Cook in a pan until crisp. Meanwhile, place half the butter or margarine in a basin. Stand over a pan of boiling water. Add the beaten egg, chicken and seasoning and stir until the egg is just set. Toast the bread, spread with the remaining butter or margarine. Top with the bacon, then the egg and chicken mixture.

## PLAICE AND TOMATO FILLETS

*Preparation time:*
*10 minutes*
*Cooking time: 10 minutes*
*Quantity: 1–2 helpings*

1 medium tomato,
  skinned and halved
2 small plaice fillets,
  skinned
1 oz (25 g) butter
  or margarine
salt and pepper
2 tablespoons milk

Place half a tomato on each fish fillet, roll round the tomato and put on to a plate. Top with the butter or margarine, add a little seasoning and the milk. Cover with a second plate and place over boiling water. Steam the fish for 10 minutes.

The small amount of liquid makes an unthickened sauce.

**VARIATION**
Use tomato juice instead of milk.

## SAVOURY EGG

*Preparation time: 5 minutes*
*Cooking time: 5 minutes*
*Quantity: 1 helping*

1 oz (25 g) butter or margarine
2 tablespoons milk
1 teaspoon Worcestershire sauce
1 teaspoon finely chopped
    parsley
1 teaspoon finely chopped
    spring onion
salt and pepper
1 egg
1 slice bread

Put half the butter or margarine with the milk, sauce, parsley, onion and a very little seasoning into a small pan. Bring just to boiling point.

Break the egg into a cup and carefully slide into the hot liquid. Poach gently, spooning the savoury liquid over the egg until the white is just set.

Toast the bread, spread with the remaining butter or margarine and top with the egg. Serve at once.

---

## LEMON BARLEY WATER

*Preparation time: 10 minutes*
*Cooking time: 3 minutes*
*Quantity: nearly 1³/₄ pints (1 litre)*

As both lemons and pearl barley were now obtainable, this refreshing drink formed part of one invalid menu I demonstrated on television.

3 oz (85 g) pearl barley
2 lemons
1½ pints (900 ml) water
2 oz (50 g) sugar, or to taste

Put the pearl barley into a saucepan and cover with cold water. Bring to the boil and allow to boil for 3 minutes. Strain the barley and discard the water. This blanching process whitens the barley and gives it a better texture and taste. Tip the barley into a large jug.

Pare the zest from the lemons and put into a saucepan with the 1½ pints (900 ml) water. Bring the water to the boil and pour over the barley. Add the sugar. Leave until cold, then strain and add the lemon juice.

---

---

## EGG IN POTATO CREAM

*Preparation time: 10 minutes*
*Cooking time: 10–15 minutes*
*Quantity: 1 helping*

Cream was not available for several years after the war ended so we still had to be content with the top of the milk. In spite of this, we tended to use the term 'cream' in many recipes.

4 oz (115 g) cooked potatoes
1 oz (25 g) butter or margarine
1 tablespoon cream (from top
    of the milk)
2 tablespoons grated cheese
salt and pepper
1 egg

If the potatoes are leftover, heat them gently in a saucepan, mash well then add half the butter or margarine, the cream, half the grated cheese and a little seasoning. Form into a ring shape on an ovenproof plate. Break the egg into the centre of the ring and top this with the last of the cheese and fat. Preheat the oven to 200°C (400°F), Gas Mark 6 and bake for 10–15 minutes. Serve at once.

## Whatever the pleasure
## Player's complete it

*Player's* *Please*

PLAYER'S NAVY CUT CIGARETTES & TOBACCO     [NCC 784K]

*It's worth going .*

*out of your . . .*

*way to get . .*

*SILMOS LOLLIES!*

## MILK JELLY

When jelly tablets became more plentiful and of a better quality many recipes were devised using them. I remember demonstrating how to make individual portions of a milk jelly — ideal for an invalid — as part of a television programme on dishes for the invalid. I presented a tray showing several dishes suitable for someone not well in front of the cameras, quite ignoring the heat of the studio, which was much hotter then than in modern times. While I spoke about the dishes there was a sudden gurgle and the milk jelly collapsed into a pool of liquid — so much for an attractive invalid tray!

To make a milk jelly that does not curdle, simply dissolve the jelly tablet in ¼ pint (150 ml) very hot water. Allow to cool, but not set, then make up to 1 pint (568 ml — not 600 ml, in this case) with cold milk. Pour into a large mould or several small moulds and leave until set.

THIS WAS A year of great celebrations in honour of the Coronation of Queen Elizabeth II on 2 June. This Coronation was unique in that people throughout Britain, and in other countries too, who owned television sets could watch the solemn and moving ceremony and share the excitement of the cheering crowds who lined the route to Westminster Abbey. Open house was offered to many neighbours and friends so they could share in the rejoicing on this splendid occasion, with all the best of British pageantry.

Queen Elizabeth and Prince Philip came out on to the balcony of Buckingham Palace six times during the evening to acknowledge the cheers of the crowd. There was a firework display on the Victoria Embankment of the Thames in London.

A British expedition had been attempting to climb to the top of Mount Everest. On 1 June, to add to the feeling of national pride, it was announced that the summit had been reached by the New Zealander, Edmund Hillary, with Sherpa Tenzing Norgay. British heads were certainly held high during June of 1953.

Earlier in the year there had been bad news. In February, the east coast of England had been devasted by floods, caused by hurricane winds and exceptionally high tides. Sea defences collapsed from Lincolnshire to Kent. Early reports were that over 280 people had lost their lives, many people were missing and thousands were made homeless. There were dramatic rescues of people trapped on the roofs of their houses. The total damage was estimated at hundreds of millions of pounds.

Queen Mary, the widow of George V and grandmother of the present Queen, died in her sleep in March, aged 86. This dignified lady had not changed her style of dress for 50 years. She wore long dresses and coats and elaborate toques and carried a gold-topped cane.

In spite of the peace talks signed in 1952, fighting had continued in South Korea. In July, it was announced that at last the guns would fall silent. About two million men and women been killed in this war.

In December, smog (fog) masks were made available on the National Health Service for the sum of one shilling (5 p). These were to counteract the effect of the bad fogs (known as pea-soupers) in industrial areas of Britain.

In March, eggs came off ration. This was most welcome, for people had missed eggs almost more than other foods. Dried eggs had been a valuable stop-gap, although there were two different opinions about them. Some people loved them, others were ultra-critical of their flavour. With greater supplies, the freshness of eggs improved a great deal.

In April, real cream became available once more. This was never rationed for it was illegal for dairy farmers to produce cream for sale. It is strange to think that many younger teenagers had never tasted cream. Reaction about cream was mixed; older people greeted it with enthusiasm, younger people with some reservations, since many found it rich and greasy and declared they preferred evaporated milk.

In September, sugar was taken off ration. This was a good season to have more supplies of sugar, for bottling fruit in syrup, rather than water, and making plum and other jams.

## CORONATION DAY

2 June 1953 was celebrated throughout Britain and the Commonwealth for television helped people everywhere feel they were very much part of the event. There was this feeling that we were entering into a new and exciting second Elizabethan era and that the young queen headed a nation that might well reflect the glories of her illustrious predecessor.

At this time, only a minority of homes had television so most people who owned a set kept 'open house' so they shared the excitement with friends and neighbours. Party food was the order of the day and the recipes in this section were typical of those made for the celebrations. Fortunately, this year saw the end of some rationing so catering was easier and more enjoyable. The meal at lunchtime was generally in the form of a buffet.

## SALMON DIP

Dips were relatively new at this time. This was a good dish to serve with drinks on Coronation Day. The French term 'crudités', meaning raw vegetables, was gradually becoming known. This dip is sufficient for 6.

Flake 8 oz (225 g) well-drained cooked or canned salmon (weight without skin and bones) and mix with 1 tablespoon lemon juice, 5 tablespoons mayonnaise, 2 tablespoons double cream, 1 tablespoon tomato ketchup, 3 tablespoons finely grated cucumber (without skin) and 2 teaspoons chopped parsley or fennel leaves with seasoning to taste.

Put into a small bowl on a large platter and surround with narrow strips of raw carrots, red and green peppers, radishes and crisp small biscuits to dip into the creamy mixture.

## CORONATION CHICKEN

*Preparation time: 25 minutes*
*Cooking time: 1¼ hours*
*Quantity: 6–8 helpings*

This recipe has been known since the Coronation as the dish of the day. There have been several versions, but basically it is a mixture of cold chicken, fruit and a mild curry-flavoured dressing. Curry paste was less well-known than curry powder in 1953; it is better for cold dishes but curry powder could be substituted. Real cream was available by the time of the Coronation. The chicken can be roasted but it is much more moist if steamed or, better still, simmered in water with an onion, several carrots and herbs.

**For cooking the chicken:**
1 chicken, about 4 lb (1.8 kg) when trussed
1 onion, sliced

2–3 carrots, sliced
small sprig parsley
small sprig tarragon
salt and pepper

**For the salad:**
10–12 oz (300–350 g) can halved apricots
7½ fl oz (225 ml) mayonnaise
2 teaspoons curry paste, or to taste
4 tablespoons single cream
2 tablespoons fruit syrup
3 oz (85 g) blanched flaked almonds
mixed salad ingredients (see method)

Put the chicken into a large saucepan with the other ingredients for cooking. Cover and sim-

mer gently until just tender. When cold, skin the chicken, take the meat off the bones and cut it into bite-sized pieces.

Drain the apricots and cut into thin slices, saving 2 tablespoons of the syrup (the rest can be used in a fruit salad). Mix the mayonnaise with the curry paste, cream and fruit syrup. Add the chicken, apricots and half the nuts. Pile neatly on to a dish; top with the remaining nuts. Serve in a border of finely shredded lettuce, thin slices of tomato and cucumber.

**VARIATIONS**
Add chopped spring onions to give a more savoury taste.
Use fresh or canned pineapple instead of apricots.

## HUZARENSIA

*Preparation: 25 minutes*
*No cooking*
*Quantity: 4 helpings*

This Hussar's Salad, with its beef meat content, became a great favourite.

6 oz (175 g) cooked tender beef, neatly diced
1 lb (450 g) cooked new potatoes, neatly diced
2 small cooked beetroot, peeled and diced
1 large cooking apple, peeled and diced
2–3 tablespoons small cocktail pickled onions
2–3 tablespoons diced pickled gherkins

**For the dressing:**
1–2 teaspoons French mustard
3 tablespoons mayonnaise
1 teaspoon vinegar from pickles

**To garnish:**
mixed salad

Mix all the ingredients together then blend with the dressing and arrange in the centre of the mixed salad.

## LINZERTORTE

*Preparation time: 30 minutes*
*Cooking time: 30–35 minutes*
*Quantity: 6–8 helpings*

This Austrian spiced tart could only be made when ground almonds became available.

**For the pastry:**
6 oz (175 g) butter or margarine
2 oz (50 g) caster sugar
1 teaspoon finely grated lemon zest
1 egg
8 oz (225 g) plain flour
½ teaspoon ground cinnamon
2 oz (50 g) ground almonds

**For the topping:**
1 lb (450 g) fresh raspberries
sugar to taste
2 tablespoons redcurrant jelly
1 tablespoon water
little icing sugar

For the pastry, cream the butter or margarine and sugar with the lemon zest. Add the beaten egg, then then fold in the flour, cinnamon and almonds. Turn out on to a lightly floured board and knead until smooth. Wrap and chill for at least 30 minutes.

Roll out two-thirds of the dough into a round to fit inside an 8 inch (20 cm) fluted flan ring placed on an upturned baking tray (this makes it easy to slide off when cooked). Roll out the remaining pastry into narrow strips ¼ inch (6 mm) thick and 8½ inches (21 cm) long. Put the raspberries over the base, dust with a little sugar then cover with a lattice of the strips. Moisten the ends and seal well.

Preheat the oven to 180°C (350°F), Gas Mark 4 and bake for 30–35 minutes or until firm. Allow the tart to become cold.

Melt the jelly with the water then brush over the fruit. Dust with sifted icing sugar.

SURELY LARD IS FINE FOR PASTRY!

...AND SO IS MARGE!

but...Spry makes Pastry Lighter

## CHICKEN AND MUSHROOM SALAD

*Preparation time: 15 minutes*
*Cooking time: 3–4 minutes*
*for the mushrooms*
*Quantity: 4 helpings*

8 oz (225 g) cooked chicken, diced
4 oz (115 g) celery heart, diced
2 tablespoons sliced or chopped olives
little mayonnaise
lettuce
watercress
1 oz (25 g) butter or margarine
4 oz (115 g) button mushrooms

Mix the chicken, celery and olives with mayonnaise. Spoon on to a bed of lettuce and watercress.

Melt the butter or margarine and lightly fry the button mushrooms. Spoon on to the salad immediately before serving.

## END OF SWEET RATIONING

February 1953 saw the end of sweet rationing — a joy for
the children and for many adults, too. I was 'deluged' with requests
for real chocolate icings to put on cakes — often bought from the
baker — and for chocolate cakes and desserts.

### RICH CHOCOLATE BUTTER ICING

Melt 2 oz (50 g) plain or milk chocolate in a heatproof bowl over hot water. Cool slightly. Add 1 oz (25 g) butter and beat well then sift in 2 oz (50 g) icing sugar and 2 or 3 drops vanilla essence.

**GROWING UP
ON THE COCOA HABIT**

## CHOCOLATE BISCUITS

*Preparation time: 15 minutes*
*Cooking time: 15 minutes*
*Quantity: 24–30 biscuits*

4 oz (115 g) margarine
4 oz (115 g) caster sugar
few drops vanilla essence
2 oz (50 g) plain flour
1 oz (25 g) rice flour or
  cornflour
2 oz (50 g) chocolate powder

**For the Chocolate Icing:**
3 oz (85 g) plain or milk
  chocolate
½ oz (15 g) butter

Preheat the oven to 160°C (325°F), Gas Mark 3. Lightly grease two baking trays.

Cream the margarine, sugar and vanilla until light. Sift the flour with the rice flour or cornflour and chocolate powder. Add to the creamed ingredients and knead well. If the mixture seems a little sticky, wrap and chill for a time.

Roll out the dough to ¼ inch (6 mm) thick and cut into rounds or fancy shapes. Put on to the prepared trays and prick lightly. Bake for 15 minutes, or until firm. Cool on the trays.

Break the chocolate for the Chocolate Icing into small pieces and put into a heatproof bowl with the butter. Melt over a pan of hot water – do not leave too long or the chocolate will lose its gloss. Cool slightly, then spread over the biscuits with a flat-bladed knife.

## UNCOOKED CHOCOLATE CAKE

*Preparation time: 20 minutes*
*No cooking*
*Quantity: 1 cake*

8 oz (225 g) plain sweet or
  digestive biscuits
3 oz (85 g) plain chocolate
3 oz (85 g) butter or margarine
1 oz (25 g) caster sugar
few drops vanilla essence
1 level tablespoon golden syrup

**For the topping:**
2 oz (50 g) butter or margarine
few drops vanilla essence
4 oz (115 g) icing sugar
approximately 2 teaspoons
  milk
1–2 oz (25–50 g) chocolate drops

Crush the biscuits into fine crumbs. Break the chocolate into small pieces, put in a heatproof bowl and melt over hot water. Cool slightly. Add the butter or margarine with the sugar, vanilla and syrup to the chocolate and beat until soft and creamy. Add the crumbs and mix well.

Place a 7–8 inch (18–20 cm) flan ring on a serving plate and fill with the crumb mixture. Press down very firmly and chill overnight or for several hours. Remove the flan ring.

Cream the butter or margarine for the topping with the vanilla, sift in the icing sugar and mix well. Gradually beat in enough milk to give a fairly firm spreading consistency. Coat the top of the cake then decorate with the chocolate drops.

---

## CHOCOLATE FLOATING ISLANDS

*Preparation time: 20 minutes*
*Cooking time: 20 minutes*
*Quantity: 4 helpings*

As well as being able to use chocolate in cooking, there were more fresh eggs available and one could make meringues and meringue toppings for desserts.

In this version of the classic dish, the egg whites are poached in water so they remain white. The custard mixture, made with chocolate and egg yolks, is partially thickened with a little cornflour, which helps to prevent the egg mixture curdling.

3 oz (85 g) plain chocolate
1 pint (600 ml) milk
1 teaspoon cornflour
3 large eggs
4 oz (115 g) caster sugar
½ teaspoon vanilla essence

**For the decoration:**
1 oz (25 g) plain
  chocolate

Break the chocolate into pieces. Pour ¾ pint (450 ml) of the milk into a saucepan, add the chocolate and heat until it has melted. Blend the cornflour with the remaining cold milk. Separate the eggs, add the yolks and half the sugar to the cornflour mixture and beat well. Pour into the chocolate-flavoured milk.

Either leave the mixture in the saucepan or transfer it to a basin placed over a pan of hot water. Cook slowly, whisking most of the time, until the custard thickens sufficiently to coat the back of a wooden spoon. Pour into a serving dish, cover and leave until cold.

Meanwhile, whisk the egg whites until very stiff. Gradually beat in the remaining sugar. Pour about 1 pint (600 ml) water into a frying pan, and add the vanilla essence. Bring just to boiling point then lower the heat so the water simmers steadily. Drop spoonfuls of the meringue on to the water. Poach for 2 minutes then carefully turn over and poach on the second side. Lift on to a sieve placed over a plate and leave until cold. Spoon on to the chocolate mixture.

Grate the chocolate for the decoration over the meringues. Serve very cold.

## LEMON MERINGUE PIE

*Preparation time: 30 minutes*
*Cooking time: 50 minutes*
*Quantity: 4–6 helpings*

I can still remember my feeling of pleasure when I was able to demonstrate a real Lemon Meringue Pie on BBC Television.

**For the short or sweet shortcrust pastry:**
6 oz (175 g) flour etc. (see Gypsy Tart, page 21, or Oriental Fingers, page 67)

**For the filling:**
2 small or 1 large lemon(s)
1 oz (25 g) cornflour or custard powder, whichever is available
approx. ½ pint (300 ml) water (see method)
2 oz (50 g) caster sugar
2 egg yolks
½–1 oz (15–25 g) butter or margarine

**For the meringue:**
2 egg whites
2–4 oz (50–115 g) caster sugar (see method)

Make the pastry as on page 21 or 67. Preheat the oven to 200°C (400°F), Gas Mark 6 if using shortcrust pastry, but only to 190°C (375°F), Gas Mark 5 if using sweet shortcrust pastry. Roll out the pastry and use to line a 7–8 inch (18–20 cm) flan tin or ring on an upturned baking tray. Bake blind (see page 47) for 15 minutes or until the pastry is firm but still pale in colour. Remove the pastry shell from the oven and reduce the oven temperature to 150°C (300°F), Gas Mark 2.

While the pastry is cooking prepare the filling. Grate the lemon(s) finely to give 1–1½ teaspoons lemon zest. Use just the coloured part of the rind so there is no bitter pith. Halve the lemon(s) and squeeze out the juice. You need 3 tablespoons, or 4 tablespoons if you like a very sharp flavour.

Blend the cornflour or custard powder with the cold water. Use the full quantity with 3 tablespoons lemon juice but remove 1 tablespoon water if using the larger amount of fruit juice. Pour into a saucepan, add the lemon zest and juice. Stir over a low heat until the mixture has thickened well. Remove from the heat. Whisk the egg yolks and stir into the lemon mixture with the butter or margarine. Spoon into the partially cooked pastry case, return to the oven and bake for 10 minutes.

For the meringue, whisk the egg whites until stiff and gradually fold in the amount of sugar required. If serving the pie hot, you can use the smaller amount. Spoon over the lemon filling and bake for 25 minutes.

## CHEESE AND HADDOCK SOUFFLÉ

As the war had put an end to formal long menus in the majority of homes, soufflés had come to be regarded more as light main dishes or an hors d'oeuvre for a three-course meal rather than as a savoury at the end of a meal.

This dish became quite famous when reports circulated that it was a favourite with the Duke and Duchess of Windsor.

*Preparation time: 15 minutes*
*Cooking time: 15 or 25–30 minutes (see method)*
*Quantity: 4–6 helpings, as hors d'oeuvre*

1 oz (25 g) butter or margarine
1 oz (25 g) flour
¼ pint (150 ml) milk
3 tablespoons single cream or top of the milk
½ teaspoon finely grated lemon zest
1 teaspoon lemon juice
3 eggs
2 oz (50 g) Parmesan cheese, grated
3 oz (85 g) smoked haddock, finely flaked
salt and pepper
1 egg white

Preheat the oven to 190°C (375°F), Gas Mark 5. Grease one 6 inch (15 cm) soufflé dish or 4–6 individual soufflé dishes.

Heat the butter or margarine in a large saucepan, stir in the flour then add the milk and cream. Bring to the boil and stir briskly as it becomes a thick sauce. Remove from the heat and stir in the lemon zest and juice.

Separate the eggs and beat the yolks into the sauce, then the cheese and haddock. Do not reheat. Taste the mixture and season.

Whisk the 4 egg whites until quite stiff, then gently fold them into the other ingredients. Spoon into the dish or dishes. Bake the small soufflés for approximately 15 minutes or the large one for 25–30 minutes. The soufflé is nicer if well risen and golden brown but still slightly soft in the centre. Serve at once.

**VARIATION**
Use finely grated mature Cheddar cheese instead of Parmesan.

## EGGS OFF RATION

Although most people had become very accustomed to
using dried eggs in all kinds of recipes from omelettes to
batters and cakes, it was a great joy to have shell eggs
off ration. Immediately, I was asked about making
meringues and meringue toppings for desserts, such as the
popular Lemon Meringue Pie, which I have included here.
Although dried eggs made an acceptable soufflé, the result
with fresh eggs, where the yolks and whites could be
separated, was infinitely better.

IN FEBRUARY OF this year Queen Elizabeth with Prince Philip arrived in Australia for their tour. This was the first time a reigning monarch had visited the country. *Gothic*, the ship in which they arrived, was greeted by about 500 craft and crowds of cheering people. Their children, Prince Charles and Princess Anne, stayed in Britain, in the charge of their grandmother, Queen Elizabeth the Queen Mother.

The scope of television was clearly illustrated in June when Pope Pius XII appeared on British television screens simultaneously with his appearance on the screens of seven other European nations.

I was the subject of an interesting incident this year. One afternoon I had been demonstating how to make bread on BBC Television. When I arrived home I was asked to telephone the BBC, who told me with great excitement that they had received a call from America during the course of the transmission saying 'they could see a dame making a pud'. The reception was entirely due to freak weather conditions, not to satellites, so I was the first person ever to be received on American television direct from Britain.

One piece of news that was received very seriously by many people was that the plague myxomatosis was affecting rabbits even more seriously than it had done in 1953. In some places, Kent in particular, the rabbit population was almost entirely wiped out. For the past years rabbits had helped to eke out the meat ration.

For several years, there had been much talk about runners achieving a four-minute mile.

This was the year it happened! Roger Bannister, a medical student, achieved the distance in 3 minutes 59.4 seconds.

In June of this year Winston Churchill and the American President Eisenhower signed the Potomac Agreement in Washington. The President was famous for his leadership during the war. The Agreement emphasised the comradeship of the two countries and their pursuit of world peace and justice.

In May all fats, such as butter, margarine and cooking fat, came off ration. This gave rise to advertising campaigns on the rival merits of individual fats for various cooking purposes.

In June meat was finally removed from rationing. This was the last of all rationed foods to be derestricted. Throughout the years from 1940 lack of meat had caused great problems to the population. We were a nation of meat-eaters who longed for juicy steaks and roasts. At last these would be coming. The major meat market at Smithfield, London, normally opened for business in the morning at 6 a.m. In celebration of meat being freed from rationing it opened six hours early, at midnight, so supplies could be sent out early to butchers in anticipation of a great rush of customers.

Ration books were no longer necessary and many people burned theirs or ripped them up in anticipation of easier times ahead.

Nutritionists of the future would say we were a healthier nation during the long years of rationing. The British people were not thinking of that in 1954. They were just so thankful that they could shop at leisure, avoid queues for various foods and buy the ingredients that they and their families liked best.

## FATS OFF RATIONING

The derationing of all fats made a great difference to the kind of cooking done. I was deluged with requests to demonstrate flaky and puff pastry. Often I had a frantic telephone call at Harrods from someone making puff pastry to say 'it has become sticky (or greasy); what do I do?'

It was quite difficult to make people, who had never made these richer pastries before the war, to realise you had to be patient and allow the pastry to rest in a cool place — obviously, the refrigerator (if you had one) — between foldings and rollings.

Frying became a popular form of cooking, for fat was not regarded as the health hazard it is today. When discussing food values in 1954, it was accepted that fats created warmth in the body and were an excellent source of energy.

## MAKING CHIPS

The only way most people could produce fried potatoes before the ending of fat rationing was by shallow frying in the little amount of fat they had saved or to use the oven method, which was not real frying but a very acceptable substitute. You greased and heated a flat baking tray, laid potato slices (chips were the wrong shape for this method) in a single layer on the hot tray, brushed them with a few drops of melted fat and cooked them at a high temperature. In 1954, electric deep-fat fryers were not used and oil was used only rarely for cooking, so frying chips would be done in an ordinary pan with a frying basket (if you had one), with lard or cooking fat as the frying medium.

**To make the chips:** Peel potatoes, cut into finger shapes, and keep in cold water until required then dry very well before cooking.

**To cook the chips:** Put lard or cooking fat (or oil if you prefer) into the pan, which must never be more than half full. Heat to 170°C (340°F). To test without a thermometer, drop a cube of day-old bread into the hot fat. It should turn golden coloured in one minute. If it changes colour in a shorter time than this, then the fat is too hot and must be allowed to cool slightly.

Put in the potatoes (if you have a large number, fry them in batches) and cook steadily for 6–7 minutes, or until tender but still pale. Remove on to a dish.

Just before serving, reheat the fat or oil until it reaches 190°C (375°F) – a cube of day-old bread should turn golden within 30 seconds. Fry the potatoes for a second time until they are crisp and golden brown.

Turn out the potatoes on to absorbent paper to drain then serve. The potatoes can be sprinkled with a little salt before serving. Garnish with parsley.

# LOBSTER CUTLETS

*Preparation time: 20 minutes*
*Cooking time: 8 minutes, plus 25 minutes for the sauce etc.*
*Quantity: 4 helpings*

**For the cutlets:**
1 medium-sized cooked
  lobster
1 oz (25 g) butter or
  margarine
1 oz (25 g) flour
¼ pint (150 ml) milk
½ teaspoon finely grated
  lemon zest
1 tablespoon finely grated
  onion
1 egg
salt and pepper
4 oz (115 g) soft fine
  breadcrumbs
2 teaspoons chopped parsley

**For coating and frying:**
1 tablespoon flour
1 egg
2 oz (50 g) fine crisp
  breadcrumbs
2 oz (50 g) fat

**For the sauce:**
2 oz (50 g) butter or
  margarine
2 oz (50 g) mushrooms,
  finely chopped
1 tablespoon finely chopped
  onion
1 oz (25 g) flour
¼ pint (150 ml) lobster stock
  (see method)
¼ pint (150 ml) milk
3 tablespoons cream or
  top of the milk
few drops Worcestershire
  sauce

Remove the shell from the lobster and place the shell in a pan with water to cover. Put a lid on the pan and simmer for 8 minutes, then strain. This gives stock with the flavour required for the sauce. Remove the intestinal vein from the lobster and finely dice the flesh.

Melt the butter or margarine for the cutlets, stir in the flour and then the milk, lemon zest and onion. Stir briskly as the sauce comes to the boil and becomes very thick. Add the lobster and the rest of the ingredients for the cutlets. Mix well then chill for a time. Form into 4 large or 8 small cutlet shapes.

Coat in the flour, then in the beaten egg and crumbs. Heat the fat and fry the cutlets until crisp and brown on both sides.

Melt the butter or margarine for the sauce, add the mushrooms and onion, cook gently for 5 minutes then blend in the flour, the lobster stock and milk. Stir briskly as the sauce comes to the boil and thickens, add the cream, Worcestershire sauce and seasoning.

Serve the lobster cutlets with the sauce, garnishing the dish with the very small lobster claws, if liked.

# PUFF PASTRY

When fat came off the ration it gave people a wonderful opportunity to make richer cakes and pastries. I demonstrated making flaky and puff pastry with great regularity at Harrods Food Advice Bureau.

8 oz (225 g) plain flour
pinch salt
squeeze lemon juice
water, to bind
8 oz (225 g) butter

Sift the flour and salt into a mixing bowl. Add the lemon juice and enough cold water to make a pliable dough.

**Stage 1.** Roll out to a neat oblong (see sketch on page 106) and place the butter in the centre.
**Stage 2.** Fold the corners A and B over the pastry, hinging at C and D, to cover the butter. Bring down the top third of the dough, E to C and F to D.
**Stage 3.** Turn the dough at right angles so you have the open end towards you.
**Stage 4.** Depress the dough at intervals (known as ribbing the pastry).
**Stage 5.** Roll out the dough to an oblong. Fold as Stage 2 then repeat Stages 3 and 4. Continue like this, giving 7 rollings and 7 foldings in all.

## A MODERN TOUCH
Strong (bread-making) flour is excellent for this pastry and for Flaky Pastry.

## FLAKY PASTRY

8 oz (225 g) plain flour
pinch salt
6 oz (175 g) butter, or half
    butter or best margarine
    and half lard
squeeze lemon juice
water to bind

Sift the flour and salt into a mixing bowl. Divide the fat into three portions and cut into small dice. Rub one third of the fat into the flour, then add the lemon juice and sufficient water to give a pliable dough.

**Stage 1.** Roll out the dough to an oblong shape.

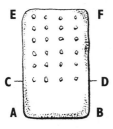

**Stage 2.** Dot the second third of the fat over the top two-thirds of the dough, as shown in the sketch.

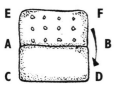

**Stage 3.** Fold the corners A and B over the pastry, hinging at C and D, to cover the fat. Bring down the top third of the dough, E to C and F to D.

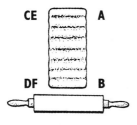

**Stage 4.** Turn the dough at right angles so you have the open end towards you. Continue rolling and folding so you do 3 rollings and foldings.

## VOL-AU-VENTS

These light pastry cases became the most popular pastry dish when people were able to make puff pastry. The days of frozen puff pastry were some little way ahead. Savoury vol-au-vents would be filled with diced fish or meat in a creamy sauce; sweet cases were filled with jam and whipped cream.

Make the Puff Pastry (see page 105) and ensure it is well-chilled before trying to cut out the shapes.

Roll out the dough to ½–¾ inch (1.5–2 cm) thick. Cut into rounds – the size depends upon how large you want the vol-au-vents to be; for medium-sized cases, use a cutter of about 2½ inches (6.5 cm) in diameter.

Take a 1½ inch (3.5 cm) cutter and press into the pastry, going approximately half way through the dough. Place on a lightly dampened baking tray. Chill well before baking.

If making the cases for a savoury dish, brush the rims with beaten egg yolk. For a sweet dish, brush with lightly whisked egg white and dust with a very little sugar.

### TO BAKE VOL-AU-VENTS

Preheat the oven to 230°C (450°F), Gas Mark 8. Bake the cases for 10 minutes at this temperature or until they have risen well, then reduce the oven temperature to 180°C (350°F), Gas Mark 4 and continue cooking for a further 5 minutes or until firm.

Carefully remove the centre rounds with a knife, and set them aside to be the lids of the cases after they are filled. If there is any slightly uncooked pastry in the centre, return the cases to the oven and cook for a further few minutes.

If serving hot, fill the hot pastry with the hot filling.

If serving cold, make sure both pastry and filling are cold before putting them together.

## SAUSAGE ROLLS

*Preparation time: 30 minutes*
*Cooking time: 20–25 minutes*
*Quantity: 12 rolls*

Butchers were able to make far better sausages, so the combination of these plus home-made pastry ensured a good result.

Flaky Pastry, made with 6 oz
    (175 g) flour etc. (see left)
8 oz (225 g) sausagemeat

**To glaze:**
1 egg

Preheat the oven to 220°C (425°F), Gas Mark 7. Roll out the pastry until very thin and cut into two long strips, each measuring approximately 5 inches (13 cm) wide. Moisten the edges with water.

Make the sausagemeat into similar lengths and place on the dough. Fold the pastry to enclose the sausagemeat. Press the edges together and flake them by cutting the edges horizontally with a sharp knife to give several layers.

Cut each strip into about 6 portions. Place on a baking tray. Make 2 or 3 slits on top of each roll and brush with the beaten egg. Cook until golden brown and firm. If necessary, lower the oven heat slightly towards the end of the cooking time so that the pastry does not over-brown.

### COMMONWEALTH TOUR

In February 1952 Princess ELizabeth and her husband, Prince Philip,
left Britain for a special tour. The Princess was deputising for her
father, who was too unwell to travel.

Within a few days the couple had to return from their first stop in
Africa as King George VI had died very suddenly.

With the Coronation celebrations in Britain in 1953 it was not until
the early days of 1954 that the tour could be rearranged. As one
might expect, all the various nations wanted to welcome their new
ruler. Queen Elizabeth and her husband visited many of the countries
that formed part of the Commonwealth and in each of these they
were received with great enthusiasm.

As the picture above shows there were many ceremonial occasions
but there was also time to meet people in the various countries and
enjoy the different scenery and cultures, plus the warmer weather,
which made a contrast to the winter chill of Britain.

## MEAT OFF RATION

When meat came off ration in June 1954 this had a special significance. It meant the end of the rationing of all foods, which had begun in 1940. Ration Books could now be discarded.

Most people had longed for juicy steaks and joints when the supply of meat was so scarce, so to celebrate the end of meat rationing it was certain that cooks would celebrate by buying these. Two of the meat recipes of the time I give here are for ways of serving steak — these were well-known at the time, and now could form part of family fare. There is also a recipe from Czechoslovakia, which symbolizes the increasing interest in dishes from abroad.

## STEAK DIANE

*Preparation time: 10 minutes*
*Cooking time: 4 minutes*
*Quantity: 4 helpings*

2–3 oz (50–85 g) butter
1 onion or shallot, finely chopped
4 very thin slices sirloin or rump steak
1–2 teaspoons Worcestershire sauce, or to taste
few drops brandy (optional)
1 tablespoon chopped parsley

Heat the butter in a large frying pan, add the onion and cook gently for 2 minutes. Add the steaks and cook for 1 minute on either side. Lift out of the pan on to a hot dish. Add the sauce and brandy. Ignite, if wished, add the parsley, then spoon over the steaks.

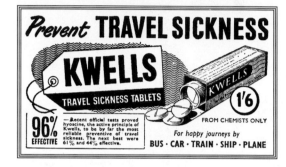

## STEAK AU POIVRE

*Preparation time: 10 minutes*
*Cooking time: 5 minutes, or to taste*
*Quantity: 4 helpings*

1 oz (25 g) peppercorns
3 oz (85 g) butter
4 fillet or rump steaks
3 tablespoons brandy
   (see method)
4 tablespoons beef stock
   (see method)

Lightly crush the peppercorns, press into both sides of the steaks and leave for 20 minutes so the meat absorbs the flavour of the peppercorns. Heat the butter in a large frying pan and cook the steaks to personal taste.

Lift on to a heated dish. Pour the brandy or stock, or use half brandy and half stock, into the pan. Ignite, if wished, then pour over the steaks. Serve with fried potatoes and other vegetables.

## ZNOJEMSKY GULAS

*Preparation time: 25 minutes*
*Cooking time: 45 minutes*
*Quantity: 4 helpings*

This Czech version of Gulasch was given me by a refugee. It is quickly cooked for tender cuts of steak, not stewing beef, are used.

1 lb (450 g) rump or
   sirloin steak
1 oz (25 g) flour
salt and pepper
pinch cayenne pepper
3 oz (85 g) butter or
   margarine
3 medium onions, finely
   chopped
1 tablespoon paprika,
   or to taste
1 pint (600 ml) beef stock
2 tablespoons tomato purée
2 medium potatoes, cut into
   small dice

Cut the meat into 1 inch (2.5 cm) dice. Blend the flour with the seasonings and coat the meat.

Melt the butter or margarine in a large pan, add the meat and fry steadily for 5 minutes. Remove the meat from the pan, then add the onions and cook for 5 minutes. Stir in the paprika, then gradually add the stock. Bring to the boil, add the tomato purée then the potatoes. Cover the pan and simmer for 20 minutes or until the potatoes are softened. Sieve or liquidize the mixture to give a smooth thickened sauce. Return to the pan and add the beef. Cook for 10–15 minutes or to personal taste.

Serve the Gulas with pickled cucumbers or gherkins.

# ACKNOWLEDGEMENTS

I should like to express my gratitude to the many people who passed on their carefully preserved mementos of the days leading up to the VE and VJ Days in 1945 and especially to the following people and organizations.

My friends who were in the Ministry of Food Advice Division and who lent me leaflets and pictures: Mary Bass, Gwen Conacher, Joan Peters, and also Georgie Pender for her help in providing information about the Tube Refreshment Service.

Margaret Coombes, Jane Hutchinson, Edna Taylor and McDougalls, who lent me cherished cookery books.

The Ministry of Agriculture, Fisheries and Food (MAFF) for the wartime food information leaflets and the records they sent me about food rationing.

The Department of Education for a wartime leaflet, and recipes on canteen meals for school children.

The Savoy Group of Hotels and the Dorchester Hotel for their menus.

The Unilever archive for food leaflets and recipes.

The Press Departments of Buckingham Palace, The Guildhall and 10 Downing Street, who searched through their records to see what events took place in 1945.

The WRVS and especially their archivist, Mrs Megan Keable, for the loan of material from their archive, including wartime recipe booklets and a 'History of the WRVS'.

The various embassies and government offices I contacted to learn about Victory Day memories in other countries.

My sister Elizabeth Brown-Moen for the picture and information about Norwegian celebrations.

Angela Holdsworth and the BBC for their help in providing some of the recipes in the chapter 'After the War' which they found while researching the major BBC television series *After The War Was Over*.

Dr Louise Davies, PhD., F.I.H.Ec. who kindly loaned her copies of *Food and Nutrition*. Dr Davies created and subsequently edited for the Ministry of Food booklets which were sent to educational establishments and home economists. Thanks also go to Birds Eye Wall's, Kenwood and Woman's Weekly.

Marguerite Patten

## Picture Credits